# THE POEMS OF
# ST. PAULINUS OF NOLA

# Ancient Christian Writers

## THE WORKS OF THE FATHERS IN TRANSLATION

EDITED BY

JOHANNES QUASTEN      WALTER J. BURGHARDT

THOMAS COMERFORD LAWLER

No. 40

# THE POEMS OF
# ST. PAULINUS OF NOLA

TRANSLATED AND ANNOTATED

BY

## P. G. WALSH

*Department of Humanity*
*University of Glasgow*

## NEWMAN PRESS

New York, N.Y./Ramsey, N.J.

Library of Congress
Catalog Card Number: 74-77484

ISBN: 8091-0197-1

PUBLISHED BY PAULIST PRESS
*Editorial Office:* 1865 Broadway, New York, N.Y. 10023
*Business Office:* 545 Island Road, Ramsey, N.J. 07446

PRINTED AND BOUND IN THE UNITED STATES OF AMERICA

# CONTENTS

# THE POEMS OF
# ST. PAULINUS OF NOLA

# INTRODUCTION

Pontius Meropius Paulinus, whose prose letters have been translated in two earlier volumes of this series,[1] was one of that small group of committed Christian intellectuals who in the late fourth and early fifth centuries changed the face of Europe by turning away from the secular pursuits of imperial administration and literary study to embrace the service of Christ.[2] Though of lesser intellectual stature than Ambrose, Jerome, and Augustine, he is to be accorded a significant importance in that period of Christian humanism, above all for his role in inspiring so many acquaintances in his native Aquitania to follow his example.[3]

The nature of the Christian commitment to which he inspired so many others both during and after his lifetime was explored not only in his prose letters but also in his poetry; in fact his later fame as Christian apologist has derived more from his poems than from his prose writings, and a considerable body of his verses has survived. The standard edition[4] ascribes thirty-three poems to him; four other compositions previously credited to him are rightly relegated to an appendix as spurious.[5] Of the thirty-three presented in the text, Poem 4 may belong to another versifier in the ambit of Ausonius,[6] Poem 5 is certainly by Ausonius, Poem 32 is clearly not by Paulinus, and Poem 33 is of doubtful provenance.[7] On the other hand, we must include in the corpus of our poet a short composition preserved in an inscription, a translation of which has been appended at the end of our collection.[8]

Of the thirty poems to be confidently ascribed to Paulinus, the first three date from the period during which he resided comfortably on his Aquitanian farm near Bordeaux. Having in all probability held the suffect consulship in 378, the year before Ausonius, and later the governorship of Campania in 380/81, he returned from this high career-post to Bordeaux in 381–3.[9] By late 383[10] he had married Therasia in Spain, and had settled to the leisurely existence of an Aquitanian land-magnate. These first three poems may have been composed before his departure to Italy in 378, or equally well between 383 and 389, the year of his final departure from Aquitania to Spain. However slight, they provide the sole testimony from Paulinus' own pen of his life in the secular world, for no prose letters have survived to document the period before 389.

The next four poems which can definitely be ascribed to Paulinus, Nos. 6–9, are scriptural meditations. Though they cannot be securely dated, it may be inferred from their character and content that they belong to the early period of Paulinus' conversion to deeper Christian commitment in 389 or thereabouts.[11] The following two poems, Nos. 10 and 11, which form part of the famous correspondence with Ausonius, were written during Paulinus' long sojourn in Spain between 389 and 395. So too was Poem 12, the first of the *Natalicia*, or birthday poems, which he henceforward composed each January in honour of his patron St. Felix; this first of them was written in January 395, just before Paulinus quitted Spain to found his monastic community at Nola.

The remainder of the extant poems were all written at

Nola during the fifteen years after his arrival there. We know from external evidence that he lived on in his monastery in Campania until 431, and a prose letter from his pen written about 425 has survived.[12] But none of the extant poems was written after 409. This may be attributable to the rupture of communications between Italy and Gaul caused by the barbarian invasions. Paulinus composed his poetry largely for the benefit of friends and acquaintances in Gaul, and the difficulties in maintaining regular contacts may have discouraged him from regular composition. Nola itself was overrun after the fall of Rome, and Paulinus became a prisoner of the invaders.[13] But it is idle to speculate on the reasons for the absence of poetry dateable to the last twenty years of his life; poems may have been composed and lost, though the evidence of the *Natalicia* does suggest that Paulinus was having increasing difficulty in finding apposite themes in later years.

## NATURE AND PURPOSE OF THE POEMS

If we except the first three poems, which are juvenile works composed in the secular world, we may visualize the whole corpus of Paulinus' poetry as having been written with a single unifying purpose. That purpose was to encourage Christians, and especially literate Christians like himself, to persevere in a life of Christian commitment, and to demonstrate to nominal Christians and to benevolent non-Christians the nature of that commitment. This purpose Paulinus attached to his poetry goes far to explain the enormous paradox which confronts the student who compares the texture of his prose letters with that of his poems.

In the prose letters, Paulinus shows himself making a conscious effort to renounce the formative influences of the great classical authors. He seems to fear a reproach similar to that heard by Jerome in his celebrated dream, *Ciceronianus es, non Christianus*, for he apologises whenever he finds himself quoting a Terentian tag or using a Virgilian phrase.[14] The texture of the prose letters is shot through with biblical Latin; they are frequently a virtual mosaic of scriptural phrases.[15] But in the poems he is demonstrably the literary disciple of Virgil, Horace, and Ovid.[16] It has been assumed that the sole reason for his composing according to such classical canons was his inability to shake off the formative influences of his education at Bordeaux; on this judgment he is envisaged as a lacklustre imitator, a traditionalist whose verses strike a staler note than the exciting new medium of the Ambrosian hymn.[17] But such a criticism must be modified if it is acknowledged that Paulinus writes primarily for the edification and instruction of men who scrutinise Christian claims through classical spectacles. "It should be kept in mind that Paulinus is writing out of his education for a reader of identical background";[18] this judgment on the poems addressed to Ausonius may be extended to the corpus as a whole. The form in fact subserves the purpose.

With this controlling purpose of fortifying or instructing literate Christians, the traditionalist poet embarked on a bold range of poetic compositions, many of them recognisable as adaptations for Christian purposes of classical genres. The largest group in the Paulinus corpus is the series of fourteen *Natalicia* addressed to St. Felix; they represent a Christian exploitation of the *genethliakon,* or classical birthday poem in which a person is felicitated on the anniversary of his birth. But the day being celebrated by Paulinus is the day of Felix's death, for on that day he was born into heaven, into a glorious eternity with Christ. Secondly, we may consider together Paulinus' experimentation with a Christian *epithalamion*, or marriage song, a Christian *epikedeion*, or mourning song, and a Christian *propemptikon*, or poem of farewell to a departing friend; these three poems attempt to build a new Christian dimension on occasions recognised as milestones in the progress of secular life.

Thirdly, there is a group of poems in which Paulinus versifies scriptural themes, three of them being developed versions of individual Psalms and the fourth a Christian panegyric of John the Baptist. We may visualise these as the poet's attempt to present the message of the Scriptures in a form more familiar and therefore more acceptable to literate Christians and non-Christians with literary pretensions. Further, this tradition of versifying the Scriptures, in which Paulinus is only one practitioner of many,[19] sets before the Christian community a new set of exemplars and ideals to replace the heroic figures and the theological attitudes manifested in the pre-Christian literature of Rome. Fourthly, there is a group of four letters written in verse,[20] though these are not homogeneous in their nature. Two of them form part of the celebrated correspondence with Ausonius, and in them Paulinus strives to explain to his former confidant the nature of his Christian commitment. The others belong to the genre known as the *protreptikon*, a poem of advice and instruction; in the first Paulinus recommends to his friend Jovius scriptural themes in preference to subjects derived from the Graeco-Roman cultural tradition, and in the second he advises Cytherius, a magnate in the secular world of Aquitania, on the nature of his son's education for the monastic life. Finally, there are a few epigrams which originally adorned the walls of Paulinus' churches at Nola, and which have been discovered in excavation at Cimitile. These five groups of poems we may now consider separately in further detail.

## THE NATALICIA[21]

Of the birthday poems composed by Paulinus in succeeding years for the feast of St. Felix on January 14, thirteen have survived in full, and we have fragments of a fourteenth.[22] These fourteen poems can be dated and their themes schematized as follows:

| Poem No. (Hartel) | Natalicium No. | Date | Length (lines) | Theme |
|---|---|---|---|---|
| 12 | 1 | 395 | 39 | Prayer for safe passage to Nola |
| 13 | 2 | 396 | 36 | Joy at being at Nola |
| 14 | 3 | 397 | 135 | Description of the feastday |
| 15 | 4 | 398 | 361 | Biography of Felix, part 1 |
| 16 | 5 | 399 | 299 | Biography of Felix, part 2 |
| 18 | 6 | 400 | 468 | *Nachleben* of Felix; miracle 1 |
| 23 | 7 | 401 | 335 | *Nachleben* of Felix; miracle 2 |
| 26 | 8 | 402 | 429 | *Nachleben* of Felix; further miracles |
| 27 | 9 | 403 | 647 | Visit of Nicetas; buildings at Nola |

As a genre, the *Natalicia* are a Christian development of the ancient *genethliakon*. In such poems as Propertius 3.10 and Tibullus 2.2, the poet describes the festive dress of the person whose anniversary is being celebrated, the offering of incense to the gods, and the festive gathering that ensues. These motifs, with introductory emphasis on the birthday as a day of good omen, form the staple of the Roman *genethliakon*.[23] Already in pagan literature one may note the tendency to celebrate not only the day of birth but also the anniversary of a death,[24] and this becomes the obvious precedent for the Christian *natalicium* to follow, for that day marks the entry into eternal life.

The sequence of Paulinus' *Natalicia* begins in January 395, when Paulinus and his wife Therasia are on the point of leaving Spain for Nola after Paulinus has been ordained priest by popular clamour.[25] Paulinus' devotion to St. Felix had been awakened during the period of his governorship of Campania in 380–81, when Nola formed part of his province, and this clearly played an important part in his decision to espouse monastic life. There is every indication that initially he planned the length and sequence of the topics systematically. After the first poem expresses Paulinus' aspiration to be soon at Nola, the second in the series, composed in 396, offers a brief thanksgiving for his physical reunion with the saint's mortal remains. After these two brief poems in prayer-form,[26] the third poem, which he devotes to a description of the feast at Nola, is considerably longer. Then *Natalicia* 4 and 5, a versified life of St. Felix in two parts perhaps inspired by the publication of the *Life of Martin* by Sulpicius Severus, are organized as compositions of approximately equal length. The following three poems, composed in 401–3, take as their themes the manifestations of the power which the dead Felix exercises through Christ at Nola. But from the ninth poem in the series onwards, Paulinus gives the impression of searching for *ad hoc* topics. The ninth neatly combines the two themes of the visit of Bishop Nicetas to Nola and the completion of renovations and new buildings; Paulinus escorts his guest around the site of Cimitile to point out the recent improvements he has made. But the tenth includes a good deal of repetition of the content of the ninth, which suggests that the poet is having difficulty in finding new topics. Finally, the themes of the last three extant *Natalicia* are all recent episodes at or near the shrine of Felix, so that the yearly poem by this stage has become a chronicle of the more remarkable manifestations of the saint's powers during the previous twelve months.

St. Felix himself, the central figure of the *Natalicia*,[27] became widely known to contemporary and later Christians through these poems of Paulinus.[28] From Poems 15 and 16, the fourth and fifth *Natalicia*, we can derive a circumstantial account of his life. It should be emphasised that these two poems, together with incidental references in other poems of Paulinus, constitute the sole documentation, and from them all other accounts stem. Unfortunately Paulinus, so characteristically uninterested in the

precise historical aspects of his subject,[29] neglects to provide firm chronological indications of the period in which
Felix lived, or any information about the kind of source
material available to him. I incline to the view that he had
before him a short popular life of the saint on a scale comparable to St. Jerome's *Vita Pauli;* hence the notably detailed information about his provenance, his family, his
boyhood, his early ecclesiastical career, his rescue of Maximus, and his sustained heroism during persecution. This
basic information was artistically augmented by Paulinus
or by his source, as in the account of the suffering Felix
endured in prison, which seems to owe something to the
experiences of Victricius, and in the depiction of his escape, where the deliverance of St. Peter by an angel provided the inspiration.[30] Hence though scholars point to
such expressions as *perhibent* and *ut ferunt* to support the
thesis that Paulinus relied solely on oral testimony, the
bones of a written biography seem to me firmly discernible
beneath the flesh of Paulinus' account. One need hardly
add that when a historian like Livy is reporting the views
of written authorities, he frequently introduces them with
such phrases as *ut ferunt, traditur memoriae,* and the like,
so that these are in no sense a warrant for the assumption
that Paulinus is versifying mere folk traditions.

The references in the poems to the remoteness of the
age in which Felix lived, and to the obsolete condition in
which Paulinus found his tomb, must form the bases for
conjecture on the era in which the saint lived. Lebrun[31]
drew attention to these to refute the suggestion that Felix
suffered under the persecutions of Diocletian in the major
ordeals suffered by Christians in 303 and subsequently;
Paulinus indicates that he is describing the lapse of a much

longer period than a mere seventy or eighty years.[32] It is much more probable that the persecutions in which Felix was a victim were those of the mid-third century. The conditions described by Paulinus would accord with the persecution inaugurated by the emperor Decius in 250, during which Pope Fabian and thousands of others were executed, and which ceased upon that emperor's death in 251; equally they accord with the persecution of Valerian, whose rescript of 258 ordered the execution of bishops, priests, and deacons, and claimed Pope Sixtus II and Cyprian amongst its victims.[33] It is in fact perfectly possible that Felix endured both these waves of persecution. Poem 15 may refer to the events of 250–51, Poem 16.38 ff. to the abatement of the attacks in 251 (*pax visa reverti*), the ensuing description of the resumption of Felix's trials to the persecution by the emperor Valerian in 258, and finally the promised restoration of Felix's possessions (Poem 16.258 f.) to Gallienus' restitution of ecclesiastical property which took place in 261.[34]

Besides being the major source for the life of Felix, the *Natalicia* are a mine of information on numerous other topics of which the prose letters leave us ignorant. The general historian of the period will probably consider as most important the fragment of autobiography.[35] Paulinus briefly outlines his journey from Aquitania to Italy, his immediate visit to the shrine of Felix, his governorship of Campania[36] (during which he built a paved road to Cimitile and erected a hospice there for the impoverished), then his return journey to Bordeaux, his marriage in Spain and subsequent life in Aquitania, the mysterious death of his brother, and finally his decision to abandon the secular world for the monastic life.

But the most detailed information contained in the *Natalicia* relates to the conditions of life in the monastery at Nola. Paulinus describes the buildings in great detail, not merely the structures[37] but also wall paintings[38] and furniture, which included an ornamental cross of unusual design.[39] There is an interesting account of difficulties with the water supply, and the way in which they were resolved.[40] One of the poems carries a long section on members of the monastic community and the liturgy which they sang;[41] there is also information about visitors, notably Nicetas, who is also mentioned in Paulinus' letters.[42] The poems are much more explicit than are the letters in describing the difficulties and attitudes of Paulinus and his community under the stress of the barbarian invasions.[43]

Great emphasis is laid on the collection of relics housed at Nola,[44] and on their efficacy in miraculous occurrences. It is important to set these miracle narratives within the proper psychological framework; only if we understand the chain of theological cause and effect accepted by Paulinus can we achieve a sympathetic attitude towards the claims he makes for Felix's powers. Men like Felix are in life the authentic descendants of the apostles, and the same grace which had inspired the first Christian saints is infused in them, so that Christ performs similar miracles through them.[45] Even after they have died, their bones are the receptacles of latent power through which Christ works to effect events which transcend the natural plane. The miracles claimed range from such impressive cures as the instantaneous healing of a punctured eyeball to such trivial stories of animal fidelity as that of the fat porker and that of the reluctant heifer, both recounted in Poem 20.[46] All these events, however remarkable or however

trivial, Paulinus envisages as the working of Christ's providence within the divine creation, with the practical purpose of demonstrating to men the truth of the Christian
claims.

Finally we must consider the audience to whom Paulinus addressed his *Natalicia*. Initially they were addressed
to the ear of the saint alone; the first, written in Spain, and
the next three, composed at Nola, contain no hint of a
wider audience beyond his immediate entourage. But his
composition of a verse life of Felix in two yearly install-
ments brings a change of practice. He first recites the
annual poem to a listening audience at Nola;[47] but he has
few illusions about the qualities of appreciation inherent
in a large proportion of his audience. The unlettered
rustics he describes whiling away vigils with joking and
heavy drinking, or trooping openmouthed around his
churches at Cimitile,[48] are hardly the most suitable recip-
ients for a recitation of Virgilian hexameters, however
homely the content may on occasion be. So when we find
evidence that the *Natalicia* were sent on to friends in Gaul,
it may be inferred that they were written with such cul-
tured readers prominently in mind.[49] It is a misreading of
Paulinus' entire psychology to assume that because so
many of the topics in the later *Natalicia* are concerned
with the care of Felix for the local inhabitants, he is adapting the content to a rustic audience.[50] No scholar would
think of passing such a judgment on Ovid's story of
Philemon and Baucis, and it is helpful to envisage the
homely anecdotes in Paulinus' poems as a Christian development of the technique of story-telling practised in the
*Metamorphoses*. But Paulinus insists that by contrast with
the fiction of Roman mythology, the stories which he tells

are the truth; however foolish they appear to the wise of this world, the stories of the faith of Campanian rustics and of Christ's response to that faith are expressions of a conviction of that divine dispensation which is to be preached to the whole world.

## The Genre Poems

In the three genre poems composed to commemorate respectively a marriage, a death, and a departure, it is especially clear how Paulinus is attempting to build a Christian superstructure on the classical foundation, with the implicit purpose of contrasting the differing ethos of the two cultures in their attitudes towards significant occasions in the course of human life.

Poem 25 is an *epithalamion,* a marriage song celebrating the nuptials of Julian of Eclanum and his bride Titia.[51] We know from the evidence of St. John Chrysostom how Christian weddings at this date were frequently celebrated in as licentious a fashion as pagan weddings conducted in the traditional Roman way;[52] and the poet Claudian, a contemporary of Paulinus, has left us two marriage songs for Christian weddings[53] which are both as pagan in tone as the *epithalamia* of Catullus and Statius. In these poetic treatments of the pagan wedding,[54] a general pattern is noted by the rhetoricians. After an introduction set in the framework of pagan theology, the second section discusses the blessings of marriage, the third is a laudation of the couple being married, and the final passage invites the deities to lend their presence and bless the marriage. It is instructive to observe how Paulinus in his exordium addresses Christ and witheringly dismisses Juno, Cupid, and

Venus as symbols of sexual lust. He next condemns the appurtenances of the pagan marriage—the procession and the dancing, the gifts, the costly garments and the jewelry —and outlines the nature of Christian adornments, which are the virtues, and of the Christian procession, which comprises a chorus led by bishop Aemilius singing holy songs. And in the final verses, where the pagan scheme contained an expression of hope that children might be born of the marriage, Paulinus emphasises the nobility of a life of continence, and expresses the hope that if there are children they will consecrate their virginity to Christ.[55]

With Poem 31 Paulinus introduces us to a Christianised *epikedeion*, or poem of lamentation, which thus becomes a Christian *consolatio*.[56] Here the implicit contrast which he seeks to develop is between the dull hopelessness of the pagan uncertainty about life after death and the Christian doctrine of eternal blessedness for those who believe. This is why a large section of the poem is theological explication, which some have criticised as striking an inapposite note in a work which purports to offer personal consolation.[57] But as always we are to take into account Paulinus' wider didactic aim; with this central treatment of the doctrine of Christ's Resurrection, he is expounding the fundamental plank of the Christian virtue of hope. The child who is commemorated, Celsus, and his parents Pneumatius and Fidelis are by no means out of the poet's mind, but they are in the front row, so to say, of a larger congregation of Christians with ears to hear. And as is always the case with good sermons, Paulinus is preaching hope to himself also; this dead child Celsus bore the same name as his own son, who likewise died young,[58] and his own consolation is to rivet his mind on the certainty of a future life.

Hence after the exordium, which after the tradition of the genre records the detail of Celsus' character, age, manner of death and burial, Paulinus diverges totally from the conventional Roman dirge.[59] His message is that since Christ redeemed us for life in heaven, we must train our hope on resurrection. Believing with the converted Thomas in Christ's Resurrection, we can then believe in our own; just as God can renew life in the dead elements of nature each year, so He has the power to renew our life after the Judgment. So we should weep not for death in this life but for the sins which may consign us to eternal death. Our obligation in this life is above all to deny ourselves and to care for the poor; as so often in the prose letters, Paulinus here introduces the parable of Dives and Lazarus, and also that anointing of Christ's feet by Mary Magdalen which we can imitate by caring for the poor. Finally comes an apostrophe to Celsus, dead yet eternally living, begging him to intercede with God for his familiars on earth; on this last note Paulinus consummates the contrast between the Christian certainty in the life to come and the pessimism inherent in Roman notions of death and the hereafter.

Paulinus exploits the classical tradition of the *propemptikon*, the poem of farewell to a departing friend, when he composes a valedictory to Nicetas, the missionary bishop of Dacia famed as the probable author of the *Te Deum*.[60] In the basic scheme of the Latin *propemptikon*,[61] the poet first seeks to persuade his friend to stay, then curses sailing, then prays to the gods for the protection of the traveller, and finally expresses a desire that he may one day return, with an imaginative account of that happy reunion.[62] When we compare Paulinus' poem with this conventional scheme, we at once notice in the exordium a Christian

change of direction; though Nicetas will be absent in the
flesh, his spiritual presence will abide at Nola. There follows a detailed account of Nicetas' route on his return to
Dacia; this is not a regular feature of earlier *propemptika*,
but the poem of Statius incorporates such geographical
detail and Paulinus is following his example. Thirdly, the
section on the sea journey is also transformed; where the
classical poets express fear for friends exposed to the
caprices of the ocean, Paulinus records a serene trust in
the providential ordering of the weather, and where Statius
invokes the Nereids, Paulinus stresses that Nicetas is under
divine protection as he journeys like Jacob over the floods.
Finally, where the classical poets enthuse over the prospects of physical reunion, our poet stresses that as Christians Nicetas and he will be reunited in heaven.[63]

It will thus be clear that Paulinus is deliberately turning
these classical-genre poems to preach various facets of his
Christian message. The marriage song has become an
exhortation to continence, the consolation has become the
expression of Christian hope, and the valedictory has
become the medium for the pivotal notion in Paulinus of
the *caritas Christiana*—that no distance, no time can truly
separate those who are joined together as limbs of the body
of which Christ is the Head.[64]

## THE SCRIPTURAL POEMS

Poems 6–9 comprise a group of compositions in which
the poet can be seen at work versifying the Scriptures and
developing the implications of their content for literate
readers. He was far from being a pioneer in this work. Even
if Commodian is disregarded as being of disputed date and

provenance,[65] there was the influential precedent of Juvencus, who about the year 330 had conflated the four Gospels to produce a life of Christ in his *Libri Evangeliorum
IV*.[66] There is also the poetic adaptation and development
of Scripture for liturgical purposes in the singing of hymns
and Psalms. Paulinus had immediately before him the
example of Ambrose at Milan, where the Psalms were
adapted for antiphonic singing, and where some hymns
paraphrase passages from the Old Testament to develop
the themes in a Christian direction.[67] Paulinus was already
practised in the techniques of versifying continuous prose
from his secular studies; Poem 3 shows him at work on the
versification of the *De regibus,* a prose treatise of Suetonius.[68]

Poem 6, the *Laus sancti Iohannis,* is in essence the
versification of Luke 1. Its title and its scope in the single
surviving manuscript justify the label of panegyric, but it
is possible that the complete work has not survived, and
that Paulinus wrote a *vita* with the additional versification
of Matthew 14 and Acts 19.[69] For though there is a long
previous history of the prose panegyric,[70] the panegyric
in verse was a new form in the West in Paulinus' day, not
only in Christian writing but also in the secular literature;
Claudian is the first to use it for such secular purposes in
the 390s.[71] If, as is usually suggested, these scriptural compositions were already in existence before Claudian wrote
his panegyrics, Paulinus must have been deliberately writing in the Christian tradition with Juvencus' work as the
model.[72] One notes how the epic flavour (Gabriel as God's
messenger like Virgil's Mercury,[73] the speeches recalling
the Virgilian techniques) would assist the reader who was

familiar with the *Aeneid* to absorb more sympathetically the scriptural message.

The other three scriptural poems are versification of Psalms 1, 2, and 136. It is possible that these represent a mere fraction of Paulinus' scriptural paraphrases, others having been lost. One should pay close attention to the use of different metres in these poems. I have suggested elsewhere[74] that the use of the iambic senarius in Poem 7, as against the employment of the dactylic hexameter in Poems 8 and 9, has the purpose of evoking in the classical reader's mind the exordium of the second epode of Horace:

> *Beatus ille qui procul negotiis. . . .*

That poem of Horace is a glorification of the joys of rustic retirement, an expression of revulsion from the debased *mores* of contemporary life at Rome.[75] Now the message of Psalm 1 also preaches precisely the desirability of retirement, but retirement from the life of sin to ponder night and day on God's law and to cultivate purity of mind. When Paulinus begins his paraphrase of that Psalm with the line

> *Beatus ille qui procul vitam suam. . . ,*

he is inviting his classically oriented readers to recall the Horatian epode, and thus to contrast the purpose of Christian retirement with that of the pagan. That Christian purpose is the preparation for the future life, and Paulinus inserts into the framework of the Psalm a lengthy section on the Judgment, which so often throws its shadows across his writing.[76]

Just as Paulinus' elaboration of Psalm 1 contains this

instruction for literary contemporaries on the superiority of Christian retirement over pagan, so his versification of Psalm 2 represents an exhortation to the governing class to heed the warnings of Scripture and to turn to the service of God. It is tempting to set this composition in the context of the religious controversies preoccupying the Roman establishment in the 380s. In opposition to the attempts of Gratian and Theodosius I to establish a Christian state and to outlaw paganism, the largely non-Christian Senate had vainly tried to restore the Altar of Victory in 384. It is to this kind of defiance that the message of Psalm 2 ("You who wield the reins of state, pay heed with humble hearts") has a striking and contemporary relevance. Poem 8 shows Paulinus making a careful choice of a Psalm which if heeded will convert Rome from the status of Babylon to that of Sion.

Psalm 136, "By the waters of Babylon. . . ," was chosen by Paulinus for paraphrase in Poem 9 because once again this Old Testament theme seemed to have a pressing relevance to the age. The Jews, the chosen people of old, had been the victims of persecution by Babylon. Now in the Christian imagery, pagan Rome is called the daughter of Babylon, and as such is contrasted by Christian apologists with the new Jerusalem, the *civitas Dei*. The Psalm predicts vengeance on Babylon for the overthrow of Jerusalem with this striking imagery: "Blessed will be he who takes your little ones and dashes them against the rock." Paulinus is able to exploit this imagery to interpret the meaning of the Psalm as the future triumph of the new Jerusalem over the Babylon that is Rome, for the rock on which Babylon's children will be dashed is the Rock founded by Christ.

It would, therefore, be profoundly wrong to interpret these scriptural paraphrases as merely private devotional exercises. The versification of all three Psalms represents much more. They have a contemporary relevance as shots in the ideological battle which Paulinus wages on the secular Roman world. It thus becomes clear why these particular Psalms were chosen by Paulinus. This does not preclude the possibility that others with similarly relevant themes may have been versified by Paulinus, but these three must have struck him as of particular significance for his day.

## The Letters

### (a) The Correspondence with Ausonius

Poems 10 and 11, which are addressed to Paulinus' friend and mentor Ausonius, are undoubtedly the best known and the most discussed by scholars. Seven letters from Ausonius to Paulinus have survived;[77] of these seven, the first four[78] were written whilst Paulinus was a near neighbour in the secular life of Aquitania. The chronological sequence of the other three letters of Ausonius and of the two of Paulinus is probably as follows:[79]

late
389—Paulinus retires with Therasia from Aquitania to Spain
390—Ausonius sends a letter which does not arrive
391—Ausonius sends *Ep.* 28
392—Ausonius sends another letter which was received by Paulinus but is now lost
393—Ausonius sends *Ep.* 29

393—Paulinus, Poem 10, acknowledges receipt of the
    three letters of Ausonius of 391–93
394—Ausonius, *Ep.* 27, answers Poem 10
394—Paulinus, Poem 11, replies to *Ep.* 27

This correspondence has achieved deserved fame because it embodies the clearest confrontation between
Ausonius' nominal Christianity (now widespread in Aquitania as a result of imperial support from Gratian and
Theodosius) and the deeper sense of total commitment to
Christ which motivates Paulinus. The contrast is all the
more telling, and the division more poignant, because the
two men had been such intimate friends. The five surviving letters of the years 391–94 document this dichot-
omy. Paulinus describes as best he can his conversion to a
life of full Christian commitment; Ausonius shows that
he totally fails to comprehend his friend's motive for forsaking the secular world of Bordeaux—thus showing that
at this date the monastic ideal had been little diffused
amongst Christians at large.

It should be stressed that Ausonius emerges from his
poetry as a convinced Christian believer whose poems
reflect a knowledge of basic theology and more than a
passing acquaintance with Scripture. To suggest that his
religious convictions reflect nothing more than "a cold and
perfunctory homage to Christ"[80] is somewhat unjust. It
is true that he writes as a Roman through and through, as
one who almost certainly acquired his Christianity as a
result of his connexions with the imperial court.[81] But he
has embraced it dutifully, and in one poem he explicitly
rejects the traditional offerings of incense and honey-cakes
to the Penates, proclaiming his allegiance to the God of

orthodox Christianity and showing himself untainted by the Modalist heresy.[82] Then in the following poem he sets down the prayer he prays, a meditation of belief in Father and Son richly adorned with scriptural allusions and echoes of the Nicene Creed.[83] Yet in a revealing final section of that poem, we find him praying to the Christian God for precisely what the intelligent Roman pagan sought from his deities,[84] so that in both worship and moral aspiration he devotes precisely the same niche to religious activity as a contemporary like Symmachus devoted to his relations with the Roman gods. There is on the one hand the direct substitution of the Trinity for the Penates, and on the other the aspirations for pious living which are no deeper than those of a Horace or a Juvenal. It is amusing to note how in a subsequent poem in the book called *The Daily Round*, Ausonius declares that he has devoted enough time to prayer, and turns to the traditional activities of the leisured gentleman.[85] It is in this sense that we may term him a Christian Roman rather than a Roman Christian; the bulk of his poetry proclaims his allegiance to and his pride in his descent from classical Rome.

This secular atmosphere emanating from Ausonius was part of the air which Paulinus had earlier breathed, though there was another more deeply spiritual Bordeaux in which he was also rooted.[86] The confrontation with Ausonius reveals how totally he has rejected that secular world of his earlier experience, and repeatedly in the prose letters he proclaims himself emancipated not only from its distinctions and wealth but also from its philosophy and literature. Letter 1, written early in 395, documents with precision this frame of mind in which he rejects all the secular values for which an Ausonius stands:

Even though a man be a brother and friend and closer to you than your right hand and dearer than life itself, if he is a stranger and an enemy in Christ *let him be to thee as the heathen and the publican.* . . . We must not fear the displeasure of such men; indeed we should desire it, for from their taunts and curses is born the abundant reward which God has promised in heaven. . . . Let them enjoy their pleasures, high offices, and wealth, if indeed these are theirs. For they prefer to have these on earth, where our life ends, than in heaven, where it abides.[87]

Though this letter is addressed to Sulpicius Severus with reference to his circle in Aquitania, the echoes of the controversy between Paulinus and Ausonius seem pronounced.

Poem 10, replying in 393 to the three letters of Ausonius which have arrived simultaneously, lays great emphasis on Paulinus' rejection of the pagan Muses, for "the fictions of literature" cannot harmonise with the study of God's law. Paulinus is anxious to remain Ausonius' devoted son, but not at the price of returning to the old manner of life. He explains that he is the instrument of God's transforming hand, that his conversion rejects all interest in this transient world so as to concentrate on the perennial truth. As always, the shadow of the Judgment lies over his thoughts: "This is the cause of my fear and toil, that the last day may not overtake me asleep in the pitch darkness of barren activity. . . . This is why I have decided by my proposed course to forestall disaster. . . ."[88]

Poem 11, composed in the following year, is concentrated on the theme of Paulinus' piety towards his former mentor, and says little of the rejection of Ausonius' way of life. Paulinus is here attempting to deepen Ausonius' appreciation of the nature of Christian friendship. In a moving passage, which is perhaps the best-known extract from his poetry,[89] he demonstrates how the *amicitia* demanded by Ausonius, that intimacy in social and literary diversions so esteemed by the pagan Romans, is transcended by the new *amicitia* which only Christians can share. Such friendship survives not merely separation in space on this earth but even the separation of time, because even death "will not loose me from your love, for the mind survives the limbs which fall away, and . . . it lives and it remembers forever." There can be no clearer example of the way Paulinus seizes on a concept familiar to an educated Roman, and demonstrates the enhanced value which it gains when baptised by the Christian faith.

### (b) The Protreptika

The other verse letters in the corpus, Poems 22, 24, and 32, can be grouped under this heading,[90] but since Poem 32 is demonstrably not by Paulinus it can be ignored here.[91] Poem 22 is addressed to Jovius, an Aquitanian kinsman of Paulinus who was also the recipient of Letter 16.[92] We cannot be certain whether Jovius had taken the first faltering steps towards Christianity. His position is different from Ausonius', for whereas Ausonius publicly proclaims his adherence to the doctrines of the Creed, Jovius' thinking and writing were exclusively concerned with the theories of the provenance and destiny of man as set out by the great philosophers and poets of Greece and Rome.[93] He had presumably refused to take the easy path of conformism because he had serious intellectual doubts about the dogmas of the Christian faith.

As in Letter 16, Paulinus appears to be shaping the idiom of his advice to accommodate the cultural susceptibilities of Jovius. In urging him to turn from composing on Greek epic themes to take up the matter of the Christian revelation, he designedly uses a celebrated Virgilian phrase, *maior rerum tibi nascitur ordo.*[94] As in Letter 16, he devotes a long section to criticism of the pagan philosophers and poets before outlining the radical alternative proposed by Christian beliefs. In urging him to devote his talents to proclaiming the mighty works of God, he uses the classical epithet *Tonans,*[95] the Thunderer, of the Christian deity; it is significant that nowhere else in his poetry does he so use this conventional title of Jupiter.

Like Jovius, Cytherius, the recipient of Poem 24, is also an upper-class Aquitanian, "splendid in the vaunted possessions of worldly position, literature, and family,"[96] but unlike Jovius a committed Christian who is entrusting his son to the monastic school of Sulpicius Severus at Primuliacum.[97] Poem 24 is at first sight a *protreptikon* only in its second part. The letter as a whole purports to be an answering greeting in response to a letter for Paulinus which Cytherius had entrusted to a messenger Martinianus. The first part of Paulinus' poem is a dramatic account of the shipwreck of Martinianus off southern Gaul, in which the captain and other unbelievers died while the few Christians and those who attached themselves to them escaped. The poet sees this as God's warning of what will ensue at the Judgment when the sheep are separated from the goats. This first section of the poem finally describes how

Martinianus reached Marseilles in the ship's boat, found another vessel to take him to Ostia, and from there travelled overland to convey to Paulinus the substance of Cytherius' lost letter, together with his own traveller's tale.

The second part of the poem describes how Cytherius has offered his son to God as a second Isaac. Paulinus instructs the parents on the implications of this decision by use of Old Testament typology, with extended portrayal of the boy as a second Samson and a second Joseph. Then there is a final exhortation to the parents themselves; it is a reminder of the need for men to lighten themselves of the luggage of this world before approaching the seat of judgment.

Naturally enough, this poem has been criticised as lacking an integral unity. "C'est donc une oeuvre assez disparate . . . toute la première partie est une sorte de hors d'oeuvre."[98] But this is to ignore a subtly unifying thread running through the whole poem. Martinianus' deliverance from shipwreck is a parable of the separation of believers from unbelievers at the Judgment. Just as Martinianus escaped physical death because he wore the mark of the Christian, so the son of Cytherius will guarantee himself a similar escape from the shipwreck of the world by embracing monastic life. And the final words, the exhortation to Cytherius and his wife to divest themselves of the goods of this world, are a continuation of the theme; in this way they will ensure that they, too, will be survivors from the wreck to win the safe harbour of heaven.

## THE EPIGRAMS

In Letter 32 to Sulpicius Severus, Paulinus enclosed some verses which were to be inscribed in Severus' church at Primuliacum, and others which he had inscribed in his own churches at Nola and Fundi;[99] presumably he thought that these might find a use also in Aquitania. "Poem 30" comprises two such inscriptions discovered by excavation on the site of Cimitile.[100] They both commemorate the renovation of the buildings which was described in Letter 32 and in Poems 27 and 28. The inscription translated at the end of our collection comes from a tomb at Cimitile.

This tradition of Christian epigrams began with epitaphs incised on the graves of Christians. Damasus, in his tenure of the papacy between 366 and 384, was an influential figure in the literary development of the genre, for he composed such epigrams for wider devotional purposes.[101] Ambrose wrote similar verses for his churches in Milan.[102] It is probable that Paulinus knew of the pioneering work of both these predecessors. He visited Rome regularly each year for the feast of Saints Peter and Paul, and must have observed Damasus' inscriptions in St. Peter's.[103] Ambrose is claimed as a friend, and it is probable that Paulinus had visited him in Milan in 381–3, on his return to Bordeaux from Campania; in any case he corresponded regularly with him, and received relics from him for his churches.[104]

## THE SPURIOUS POEMS

Hartel prints in an appendix[105] the text of four further poems, none of which is to be attributed to Paulinus.

The first of these, containing 122 lines, is attributed to Prosper of Aquitaine in the two surviving manuscripts. Rosweyde suggested Paulinus as the author, but Lebrun rightly rejected this ascription.[106] The poem is an exhortation to the poet's wife to join him in a life of dedication to God. It is written at a time of widespread devastation and violence,[107] so it must be dated to 407 or later. The poet makes it clear that he has not yet set out on his *peregrinatio pro Christo*.[108] Since Therasia travelled with Paulinus to Nola in 395, the internal evidence of the poem is sufficient to reject the ascription to Paulinus.

The second poem no longer survives in manuscript.[109] Lebrun notes[110] that it appears to be a paraphrase of St. Bernard's *Laudes de nomine Iesu*, yet wonders if the transmission has not come in the reverse direction. Green[111] rejects the ascription to Paulinus on the grounds of lines 51 ff. (*salve, o Apollo vere, Paean inclite . . .*), remarking that Paulinus is one of the few Christian poets who would not have made this equation. This learned Ovidian section (lines 51–59), together with the use of certain words not found in Paulinus but popular in Bernard's time,[112] makes me reasonably certain that this is a twelfth-century composition by a writer who knows and imitates Paulinus.

The third poem has survived in one manuscript of the fifteenth century,[113] the scribe of which attributes this and the following poem to Paulinus. But even a cursory glance at the prosody reveals the poem to be Merovingian or later. *Homo* is scanned with first syllable long, and likewise *penetrat;* the second syllables of *dies, extra,* and *intra* are scanned short; the first syllable of *conscientia* is scanned short, as is also the second syllable of *tua* in the ablative. One need not mention the lengthening of short syllables in arsis in the hexameter and at the diaeresis in the pentameter to find it incredible that Cardinal Mai should ever have ascribed this poem to Paulinus, the most scrupulously correct of versifiers.[114]

The fourth and last of these spurious poems likewise survives in one manuscript only. The content reveals that the attribution to Paulinus was wholly incorrect. In a plea to "the highest king" for help, the poet reveals that his brother is captive in a foreign land, and that his sister-in-law is supporting her four children by begging. The poet's sister has been a nun from her earliest years. This content, so alien to Paulinus' situation, suggests a later date. So, too, does the prosody.[115]

*     *     *

The translation here presented follows the text of Hartel[116] except at points designated in the notes. Hartel is a learned, industrious, and intelligent editor, but too often he departs ill-advisedly from perfectly defensible manuscript readings into emendation. In many passages I have preferred the traditional readings.

Though these poems have not been translated as a whole into any language, a number of them have been separately rendered by various hands. I have consulted the version of H. G. Evelyn White for Poems 1–5, 10, and 11;[117] that of A. Pastorino for 10 and 11;[118] that of McHugh for 12–15;[119] that of R. Kalkman for 16 and 18; [120] that of Fantazzi for 17 and 31;[121] that of A. Kern for 19;[122] that of J. Bouma for 25;[123] and that of R. C. Goldschmidt for Poem 27.345–647 and Poem 28.[124] Various anthologies and studies have afforded subsidiary help with shorter extracts.[125] The translation of Poems 10, 11, 13, 16–18, 22, 25, 26, and 31 by S. Constanza[126] came to my notice after my translation was completed.

\* \* \*

I should like to record my gratitude to Rev. Professor Thomas Halton of the Catholic University of America for assistance in obtaining on loan the dissertations from his university listed above. I should also like to thank the editors of *Ancient Christian Writers* for their encouragement in this undertaking at the time when longanimity was required. Finally, I should like to thank Mrs. Ruth Pepper for her competent typing of the script, as well as for helpful emendation of inconsistencies in presentation.

# POEM 1[1]

## *To Gestidius*[2]

Paulinus greets the lord Gestidius, rightly worthy of reverence.

It is of course insulting to proffer a rustic gift from the land to the father of a household who has shoals of luscious seafood. But to give me a pretext for a word in your friendly ear, and to let me seem to be attaching some mark of respect to these informal words, I have sent a handful of figpeckers from the miserable few which the slave-boys yield up in the evening. My embarrassment at their small number induced me to append further words in slight verses, as if to increase the number by my chattering. Since both birds and words are blameworthy, you must pardon both in your kind and friendly way, and so ensure that the meagre gift is not uncivil, nor the chattering loathsome.

Take,[3] then, these birds, which sought nourishment in the bush-strewn country. The crafty fowler lurked under cover of fern. Deceiving and beguiling the birds with mimic whistling, he caught the gullible flock on limed twigs. Then he brought back his tiny booty at considerable pains, and laid out his catch along his shelves. The top row glistens with fat birds, which gradually thin out on the lowest plank; and so that the scragginess may be less oppressive, the beauty of the plump ones delights the eye, which lights first on the fat birds.

# POEM 2[1]

Give no thought to the rich gifts you send to me, so that the affectionate present of a poor friend may be pleasing to you. For what appropriate return could I make for those fish which the neighbouring shore with its teeming waters supplies for you, and which are so choice in handsome appearance? Whereas I can scarcely find an odd mussel spawned in the dark seaweed in some deep hole among the rocky shallows. To offer you a share of these resources, I have sent over to you sixteen shellfish still smelling of the nectar of the sea, their sweet inwards bulging with twin-coloured meat. I beg you to accept them gladly and not to disdain them as cheap. Their size is small, but the love with which I apportioned them is great.

## POEM 3[1]

Europe and Asia, two of earth's greatest limbs (Sallust[2] with some hesitation makes Africa an appendage of Europe, though it can be called a third part of the whole) have been ruled by many whom story expunges, their barbarian names not having consigned them to the language of Rome. There is Illibanus and Numidian Avelis; Vonones the Parthian and Caranus who gave his name to the kings of Pella; Nechepsos, who taught empty mysteries to magicians, and one who ruled anonymously, and then Sesostris. . . .[3]

The reckless one who gave his name to the Sea of Icarus, and he who took a prudent course over the sea to the Chalcidian citadel. . . .[4]

# POEM 4[1]

## A prayer

Almighty Father of creation whose power is supreme,[2] hear me if my prayer is righteous. Let no day of mine be sad, nor any night disturb my tranquil sleep.[3] May other men's possessions have no attraction for me; rather, may mine be of service to those who beg them. May none entertain desires to injure me; or if such desires exist, may they not harm me. May no chance arise of malevolence to others; instead, may I obtain the prospect of calm benevolence.[4] May my mind be happy with what it has, and not surrender to base gain; may it prevail over the enticements of the body in virtuous approval of a chaste bed. May my harmful tongue, so popular with malicious ears and ever guilty of the spread of poison, loathe foul jokes and disgusting words. May I be prostrated by no man's death, nor gain by any man's demise. May I never envy anyone, nor ever lie. May my household attend me in gladness, and my well-fed native-slave,[5] both as trusty comrade and shining attendant, joke before a feast not bought,[6] together with my diligent spouse and offspring from that dear spouse.[7] These are the blessings God bestows on chaste manners; this way of life is its own guarantee of eternal life for the age to come.

## POEM 5

### *A prayer*[1]

Almighty God, You are known to me only through the mind's obeisance. The wicked do not know You, but You are known by every devout person. You have no beginning and no end. You are older than any age which has been or will be. Your shape and limit no man can grasp, nor any tongue utter. Only One is permitted to behold You, be present to listen to Your bidding, and sit at His Father's right hand; He is the Creator of the world, the Source of all creation, the Word of God, the Word Who is God,[2] pre-existing before the world He was to make, begotten before time was, brought forth before the sun and ruddy morning star brightened the sky. Without Him nothing was made, and through Him all things were made.[3] His throne is in heaven;[4] below Him as He sits lie earth, sea, and the impenetrable confusion of shadowy night. He is unsleeping, He is the Mover of all things, lending life to the sluggish; He is God, sprung from a Father unbegotten. Affronted by the deceit of an arrogant race, He summoned the Gentiles to His kingdom,[5] so that He could be worshipped by the superior stock of His adopted line.[6] Our ancestors were permitted to behold Him, and by seeing the Godhead they were privileged to have seen the Father also.[7] He bore our infection, and by enduring the mockery of grim death taught us the path that leads back to eternal life. He taught us that not only the soul returns, but with body entire we enter the realms of heaven, leaving empty the secret vault of the tomb covered by the empty soil.

27. Son of the highest Father, You bring salvation to our age. To You Your Sire has entrusted all the Father's powers, holding back nothing grudgingly and abounding in gifts. Open a way to my prayers, and bear this entreaty to Your Father's ears.

31. Father, grant me a purpose unflinching in the face of all sins. Divert from me the serpent's wickedness, the poison that will harm. Let it be enough that the snake destroyed Eve of old, and deceived Adam, too.[8] Let us, their later descendants, the generation foretold by truthful prophets, escape the snares which the death-bearing serpent weaves.

37. Open a path to bear me aloft, so that I may leave behind the bonds of my sick body. There the milky way of bright heaven overtops the wandering clouds of the wind-swept moon. By that path the holy leaders retired, and there of old Elias was snatched up uncorrupted, advancing beyond the lower air in his four-horse chariot.[9] There, too, Enoch went prematurely in the solid flesh.[10]

43. Father, grant me the breath of eternal light for which I long, since I do not swear by stone deities,[11] but look to the one altar of tremendous sacrifice, and bring to it the unblemished offering of my life;[12] and since I acknowledge You as the Father of the sole-begotten Lord and God, and intermingling with both the Spirit Who flitted over the waves of the sea.[13]

49. Sire, give me pardon and heal my tortured heart, as I refrain from seeking You with the inwards or the outpoured blood of cattle, nor do I hazard Your will from their obscure entrails; and though exposed to error, I re-

frain from sin, and desire rather than presume to be approved as good and chaste. Account worthy my repentant soul as I loathe my mortal body and feel silent sorrow, as deep fear tortures my thoughts and my wounded mind foresees the ultimate pains of hell and experiences its own punishment.[14]

58. Father, grant that these prayers be approved at my supplication. Let me fear and desire nothing,[15] and consider enough to be enough. Let me desire nothing base, nor be the cause of shame to myself. Let me inflict on no man what I would not at that time wish inflicted on me.[16] May I not be damaged by any real sin, nor be besmirched by suspicion, for there seems little distinction made between a true culprit and one suspected. May no chance occur of power to do ill, and the peaceful opportunity of kindly dispositions be at hand.[17] Let my food and dress be modest. May I be cherished by friends, and always remain a father without damaging that title.[18] May I feel no pain in mind or body. May all my limbs perform their functions peacefully,[19] and no experience of being crippled lament the loss of any faculty.

71. May I enjoy peace and live untroubled, counting as nothing the marvellous things of earth. When the last hour of my day comes, may I be conscious of a life well spent, and neither fear nor desire death.[20] When Your kindness makes me appear cleansed of secret wickedness, let me despise all things, and let my only pleasure be to hope for Your judgment. As long as that judgment postpones its due time and that day delays its dawning, drive afar the savage snake who lies in ambush with his alluring falsehoods.

79. O Son, in the presence of Your eternal Father

propitiate Him and present these prayers, devoted but fearful through melancholy guilt. You are Saviour, God and Lord, Mind, Glory, Word, Son, true God of true God, Light of Light,[21] abiding with the eternal Father, reigning for all ages. The harmonious songs of tuneful David sing your praise, and make the air resound with voices that will echo "Amen."

# POEM 6[1]

## *In praise of St. John*[2]

Highest Father of creation, eternal Power of heaven, and You, too, O Christ, our Salvation and Glory of the saints, and You, O Spirit joined equally to Father and Son,[3] you govern men's minds and tongues and lend them the strength which faith alone has deserved. You have full power to infuse intelligence into the stupid and voice into the dumb. So grant that John may be drawn from the Gospel-source and cascade into my verses whose waters are dry. He is indeed as great a man as could be bestowed on the world by Him who ordered the birth of such a man by an unprecedented miracle; but it is licit to devote my slight abilities to great themes, and the realm of heaven does not disdain mean praise. Moreover, praise of the deserving merit of the blessed is itself a part of their deserts.

14. This is no new or original song I shall sing. The prophets proclaimed it all before,[4] and holy men[5] have consecrated in prose the promise of his birth, his life, and his death—if death it was which merited heaven by its blood. I have merely committed myself to unfolding the words in tuneful rhythms, and to give relaxation to the minds of readers by my verses. It was thus (for one can compare great with small, the ancient with the recent, the perfect with the boorish, the eternal with the transient) that David, a name worthy of veneration, adapted to his lyre all that earlier men had said under God's inspiration,

39

and sang harmonious songs to his heavenly lyre. For me, too, it is right to be mindful of God, and for my heart, though buried in numerous sins, to admit sensations of heaven.

27. Zachary, of old a priest of Syrian race, tended with due care the temple entrusted to him. His life was worthy of giving service to God because of his devotion and faith, earnestness and modesty; and his fostering wife Elizabeth was sprung from the ancient stock of holy men, and equal in virtues to her great husband.[6] But she was without child, a state which matrons of old designated as shameful,[7] and in sadness she lived out a barren old age, and her sum of years ruled out all hope of offspring. It chanced that the whole people was making solemn sacrifice to God, and the devoted priest had kindled the sacred fires, adorning the innermost altar with divine flames.[8] See, a messenger from heaven stood by the sacred altar; striking in dress and venerable in countenance, he proved by looks and garb that he was sent from heaven. Then he relaxed his holy breast by uttering these words:

43.[9] "O priest, beloved by the Lord of heaven, hear the commands of the eternal God. His care of devoted people is never-ending; continually guarding the chaste heart, He knows how to bestow the love earned by holy men. First, He does not wish your family to die out, or its seed to perish here, so He has made fruitful the womb of your spouse, who in her declining years was beginning to fade.[10] Yet why do you doubt that God can do all things? You, too, have the limited thoughts of mortals. But you will believe, and He will prove it. There will be born a boy, one worthy of so great a Guarantor, a boy

blessed for eternity. At once from his earliest years he will
be greater than you, and in his invincible breast will have
sacred power, the gift of his Creator rather than of his
father.

56. "But the first name which you are to bestow on
your son does not lie within your control and competence.
Assuredly God Himself who bids him be born, bids also
that he be John.[11] This shall be his titular name. He shall
be an offspring boundless in merit, such merit as none
could divine before his birth, save He who shall bestow
and grant you joys through so great a son. Nor shall He
grant these joys to you alone, for fame is insignificant if
enclosed within a single house. The whole world, extending from the rising of the sun to the bounded twilight of
its waning, will take joy with you in your child. And not
surprisingly, for he shall be void of all foul vices, living
a heavenly life without stain of sin, keeping his heart sober
from the wine which induces madness, avoiding all cups
of the drink that inclines us to evil. Whereas he shall
promise salvation to those members of the human race who
even after sinning will be reborn by means of holy water,
he will have no sin in himself of which to be cleansed.

73. "Let me speak no more to you in diverse riddles.
As a learned priest you cannot be ignorant of the deserving
merit of Elias.[12] For him the law of hateful death was
relaxed, and he spends his unending life in his own body.
A flaming chariot, whirled by the swift exertion of fiery
horses, transported him aloft to heaven. Your son will be
his equal in the crown of his deserts, and will have as
much glory and power. So do not hesitate through doubting belief to give thanks worthy of so great a gift, so that

the anger of your kind God may not be roused to pronounce a deserved punishment following upon this reward."

84. With these words, the winged angel glided up into the breezes, and lent fragrance to the air from afar with his holy scent. The priest stood rooted there, his fearful mind in turmoil. His hesitating heart pondered the promise; he doubted whether he had deserved a kindness so great that the highest God had taken the trouble to send a messenger from the heights of heaven to announce such clear instructions from his Lord to the servant. He feared that he was beguiled; he thought it was a dream. He assessed his own character less generously than was just, proclaiming that he did not deserve such treatment. So faith itself made him unfaithful, and in his unwillingness to believe himself worthy, he deserved punishment for his scepticism.

96. At once the tongue in his doubting mouth was tied. It forgot its own movement, and as it tried to utter wordsounds it stuck in sluggish idleness. As he sought to tell the strange event to his people, his attempt was vain, and his mouth was fast closed and dumb.[13] He retired in sadness, pondered his grief within his mind, and begged pardon for his fault from the depth of his heart. How great is the loving-kindness of God, and how open to entreaty His divine power! Repentance was sufficient. Time's due process of fulfillment rolled on, and, strange to say, Elizabeth's belly distended and swelled, her holy womb bearing a sacred weight. At the full time the gift of a child came forth.

108. After the holy Gabriel had served as the messenger to Zachary, he made a second journey with much loftier

purpose, to Mary who was betrothed to a husband but chosen rather by God,[14] since to bear the Salvation of the world this chaste maiden preserved her virginity untouched. When his person, distinguished with heavenly beauty, stood before her eyes, she dropped her chaste gaze, and her ruddy cheeks coloured as the blood welled up. He said: "Girl more blessed than all maidens past, present, and future, in the whole world traversed by the orb of the sun, you have been chosen by the great God to be called the mother of Him whose Father is God Himself. Come, then, and in your blessedness conceive this Burden, for you are unstained by a husband and unprofaned by any intercourse, but pregnant by the word of God. Let your womb provide a body for Him who made heaven and earth, sea and stars, who always was, is now, and ever shall be in all time the Lord of the world and the Creator of light. He Himself, the Light of heaven, will put on mortal limbs by your aid, and appear before the eyes and assemblies of men. Raise your spirits untroubled to the reward of such great glory. God will give you strength and faith, for He has decided to be your Son, though the Son of the Lord, and He rules and guides all things by His nod."[15] With these words at once he left her gaze and the earth and made for the upper air he knows so well with easy motion. The commands of God were fulfilled. The girl immediately believed, and her ready faith added to the merit of her former life. The seed lay hidden with its causes unrevealed, and fashioned a body which was God's. The holy Burden grew, and her devoted womb cherished the heavenly Lord.

139. Meanwhile her Child, though not yet born, impelled holy Mary in her pregnant state to journey forth

and visit Elizabeth again, who though now of an age to
command respect was carrying and was soon to bear the
boy beloved of the Lord.[16] The mother hearkened to her
son, for the strength of her faith was strong, and she went
where she was bid. John stirred his mother's womb, and
filled her heart with divine inspiration. The prophet
was as yet unborn and enclosed in the womb, but already
he saw things past and things to come as a prophet does.
When Elizabeth at a distance saw Mary gleaming with
fiery light, she bestirred herself from afar and advanced
to meet her with rapid steps. Stretching out adoring hands
she said "Hail, mother of the Lord, hail, devoted maiden.
Though you have not shared a marriage-bed and know
no intercourse with a husband, you will bring forth God.
So important was it for you to be chaste, that you might
win the title and reward of a virgin bride. Why has the
glory of this service fallen to me, when I am undeserving
and unworthy of so great a gift? Why has the glory of
heaven descended into our hearth and cheap abode, introducing into our dark recesses so powerful a Light? Yet
may He show Himself gentle and mild to those who worship Him, and after His birth may He afford the favour
which He showed before." With these words[17] she clasped
Mary in her arms and joined in her embrace, and in
reverence to God implanted kisses on that devoted womb.

163. Come now, Judaea, guilt-stained with the blood
of your King, even if you put no trust in the words of
your forebears, if you believe that the prophets and Moses
himself were deceivers, if the unloving harshness of your
perverse race thinks David deceives us, then believe those
yet unborn. John tells us through the holy mouth of his
mother what he beholds when enclosed in his mother's

womb. Who, pray, instructed John about the One enclosed in the chaste womb of the virgin, about the great
birth awaiting the new age? But hidden things are revealed
to saints when they are invisible to the unholy.

173. But my course has transgressed its bounds and
makes for the broad plains. It forgets me and presumes to
advance too far. I hope that one day I may have the ability
and consolidated strength to drive a powerful four-horse
team over that area as well. But now let us resume the
path begun. Let a man's writings tell of mortal things, and
the divine Scriptures tell of the Lord.

179. Now the time prescribed by nature was fulfilled,
and the famed boy was brought forth from the womb at
the due time. The promises of God when disbelieved
brought great punishment, but certain faith fulfilled them,
and the infant child proved them. Their relatives in the
locality assembled according to custom, to decide on names
derived from those of aged parents, and to attach them
to the child once merits had been compared. But the
mother, made aware through her son of the heavenly
command, said that the decision was not in the hands of
relatives.[18] So it was decided to consult the father who had
long been silent, his voice impaired. The only means by
which he could make a sign which the tongue could not
reveal was by written symbols. He was consulted, picked
up a tablet, and wrote John.[19] All showed surprise, recalling that no earlier members of the family of his parents
had this appointed name. How efficacious was this faith,
however late! Because his right hand signalled what his
mind had believed, the punishment of the sin was absolved.
The bolts of his shuttered tongue were loosened and un-
barred; the old man now answered with his voice, and

revealed to his relatives the commands of God long hidden, and in approving what had been done he guaranteed what was to come. Who could doubt that the boy would be as promised, since Zachary saw that by the Lord's command the law of nature could be relaxed and the child brought forth by a birth so extraordinary? The punishment or pardon of the father set before the eyes of all an example of disbelief which all would make famous, and fear and hope simultaneously besieged their minds.[20]

205. Meanwhile John's cradle-days glided by, and the appearance of his divine power was manifest in them. From him there was no sound of appealing chuckling; meaningless noises gave place. That gravity which is preferred to mental levity fashioned his still childish mouth with the character it was to bear. So as soon as the boy implanted his first steps with balanced tread and words marked his utterance with definite meaning, he regularly listened to the words of his holy father, or learned the outstanding deeds of men of old, or the laws which God Himself had established through the agency of Moses and which the slab of ancient rock preserves. These and the other teachings he contemplated and discussed to strengthen his young mind, for we must not believe that he to whom God had granted knowledge of the future was ignorant of the past.

219. But once strength of manhood entered his limbs (his mind, already filled with God, had outstripped the lingering years), he decided that he must there and then learn what people cannot teach—how to avoid the infection of the food and drink which are together deleterious to a holy life. So he left the house of his holy father,

though it was without stain, and he eschewed the crowds and harmful gatherings of men. He made his way to a trackless area of deserted country, so that there his mind unstained could look only on itself, and freed from occupations could devote itself to the holy commands.[21] His garment was fastened with the bristles of the humped camel, so that he could harden his tender limbs against soft living and ward off heavy sleep by pricking his body; a cheap belt bound it to his braced loins.[22] Ready food was afforded by wild honey,[23] fruit, and grass growing in uncultivated rock-country, and falling waters lightened his parched thirst.

236. What place was there here for vices? What entry could debased desire find in this region to the recesses of his consecrated mind? In what could he sin, since he desired nothing? How could a man who requires nothing retire into the secret haunts of wicked thoughts? He lived as mankind first lived; when the world was new the Creator had invested it with this way of life for the ages to come, until the evil persuasion of pleasure infiltrated itself, and brought with it soft living and the love of possession.[24] This was the cause of hatred, disputes, deceit, envy and anger, slaughter, warfare, bloodshed, conflicts, battles and deaths. This was the source of the affront to God which savage hell will expiate. But why do I censure overmuch these universal faults and remain unmindful of myself, for whom it is appropriate not to brood over sins committed but to hope for pardon? Rather, I shall do better to admire that model invincible and inimitable by any of the earliest age, who by his toil transcended human achievements. He was a man half-god, for free of all stain,

once he had tortured his body with such savage punishment, he laid down what our fitting reward was to be, even though we had sinned.

255. Now after he had spent a long time strengthening his peerless mind in such pursuits and decided that he had found the necessary objects of his search, a voice coming forth from heaven addressed him: "Beloved prophet, you have devoted sufficient time now to your own improvement. It is now time for the gifts which you know are yours to be of service to others, and to save what is now lost. So advance to the holy waters of the limpid Jordan. There you must cleanse any man who repents and makes confession of the deeds of his former life, and at last ponders in thought the better life. Any man who with the mind of faith believes that you expunge his sins with holy water will be reborn, and then his ensuing days should be such as to prove that those who are cleansed have condemned their earlier life."

268. John at once obeyed the words he heard with obedient mind, and went down to the banks of the river prescribed. In words compelling reverence, he preached there the commands of God and infused in the hearts of believers the new salvation. With the liquid he poured on them he washed away those believers' sins, loosed men's fears, remitted the punishment due, and quenched the fire with the waters. He urged them to forget their sins, and he made their bodies new for their new life.

276. Father, everlasting Creator of men and things, at how many stages does Your Love spare us! What father ever steeled himself to pardon so often a sinning son? You give Your people the intelligence to recognise good or evil. Not content with that, You bind us with the fetters of the

law we must keep, and You lay down punishments for the wicked and rewards for the just. Even he who rejects these can return whenever he likes, for pardon is within reach, and the holy bath is manifestly available to renew life, to blot out former deeds, and to make men new. What further do we seek? Yet there is still further pardon if anyone falls headlong with body defiled, and profanes this gift as well; even if his sin has developed much too far, he can abandon it and return. Once he has condemned himself, he merits pardon. If he repents, the guilt has no effect.

291. How true Your word is that the weight is light and the yoke fastened to us is sweet,[25] when an individual is pardoned so many times! Yet we go on sinning, and there is no end to the wickedness of the human race. None the less, Your glory increases, for the greater the guilt of the accused, the greater the fame of the One who spares. So every mind and every tongue should offer and sing thanks to You to the fullest of their human powers; and if they cannot find favour, they should strive to become somehow pleasing. Should we raise our sails, kindly Father, a boundless ocean opens for Your praises, but my mind trembles in envisaging the great burden, and in full knowledge consults its own strength, and leaves such themes to be proclaimed by those more worthy.

303. Let us return to our theme. It was your task, holy John, to renew the purity of minds by washing men's bodies. It was not the first utterance of the Lord when he advised you by speaking aloud through the clouds;[26] many generations earlier God spoke through the mouth of His holy prophet Isaias, the greatest of that ancient era. "My Son," He said, "I shall send a servant before Your face,

who will cleanse the paved and thorny ways, and reduce the lofty mountains for Your steps, and raise the level of the lowly valleys; he will make the crooked straight and smooth out the rough, soften the hard, and constrain the whole world to become level."[27] Is it not you, pray, kindly John, who comes as the gift of the highest Father, you who were promised with Christ? And does not He who sent His Son put to our credit you who were foretold by the prophets and now share in the glory of the ranks of angels? God's clemency first emerged through you; the power of granting pardon was first entrusted to you. When numerous miracles bestowed on His new people sought their realisation in you, Christ said of you: "It has been granted to behold a prophet such as no previous ages ever saw. I say (and I alone know the past and the future) that of all mortals brought forth by woman in days gone and in days to come after the regular fashion of mankind, there will be none who can rank himself before John."[28]

328. This is what Christ says of you, and he sees all the secret thoughts of the human heart, and all the courses of the ages in sequence, just as we see what lies before our eyes. . . .[29]

# POEM 7[1]

Blessed is the man who isolates his way of life far from the company of irreligious men, no longer dwelling in the path of sinners or sitting in the seat of corruption, but who concentrates his whole heart on God's law, pondering night and day His commands for life's conduct, and ennobling his mind with habits of purity. He will be like a river-tree which feeds on the nourishing moisture of the bank; soon to yield his fruit in fullness at the due time, green with the foliage that never withers, he will endure as living wood with undying leaves.[2]

13. Such glory as this will not attend the godless. The anger of God will sweep them from His face as the wind whirls off dusty ashes. Accordingly, the hordes of men scattered throughout the world will be divided in such a way that the godless who have denied God the worship which is His due will not rise again for judgment, but will be punished. Blatant guilt needs no investigation to uncover it, because those who do not bear the sign of salvation on their heads will flaunt before them the mark of impending death.[3]

24. But the great crowd of sinners not hostile to God will rise again not to glory but to be submitted to scrutiny. The man who is to reveal[4] and render an account of his actions, and be approved or condemned according to his differing deeds, cannot sit with the saints.

30. Those who are ignorant of the law will fall, scat-

tered in disorder; he who fell while living under the law will be judged by the law.[5] Fire will be the judge, and will rush through every deed. Every act that the flame does not consume but approves will be allotted eternal reward.[6] He who has done deeds which must be burnt will suffer injury, but will safely escape the flames; yet wretched because of the marks on his charred body, he will preserve his life without glory. He was conquered by the flesh, but not perverted in mind; therefore, in spite of his denying to the law the allegiance which was its due, by his frequent involvement in many sins, he will never be exiled from the shores of salvation, for he preserves the eternal glory of the faith.[7]

44. So as long as all of us in this world maintain life's course and our days continue, we must keep our feet firmly on the right path, and not be seduced on to the slippery and broad highway.[8] It is better to struggle on the narrow path and to enter by strenuous exertion.[9] God gladly acknowledges the way of good men, but the path of the godless will be destroyed and levelled.[10]

# POEM 8[1]

Why have the nations growled their dissent and the peoples devised vain plots? Princes have taken their stand with kings against the Lord and His anointed One, frantically growling: "Let us burst our bonds, let us dislodge their yoke from us." But He who sits with eternal dominion over the whole heaven will laugh at them, will speak to them in His just wrath, will threaten them with words inspiring terror, and will confound those wicked men: "I have been appointed King by Him, with power matching His; I proclaim the Lord's command on holy Sion. The Lord said to me: 'You are my Son. Today I have begotten You. Ask, and you will be my Heir, with dominion over the nations. Your right of possession will be proclaimed over all lands. You have a rod of iron, for with powerful dominion You govern arrogant peoples throughout the world. You shatter their hearts as though they were vessels of baked clay, to change them for the better.'"

16. Now then, all you kings and princes who rule and judge the subservient hearts of men and wield the reins of state, pay heed with humble hearts. Serve the Lord in trembling, and temper the joy of your faith with fear. Let the alliance of these opposites bring together different emotions in one heart, so that fear may not oppress your minds, or joy undo them, through the absence of gladness or of the fear of terrifying death. Proclaim justice and

learn upright manners; stand in fear of God's justice and rejoice in His kindness, that He may never show anger against the world which merits it, and that you may not justly perish through forsaking the path of justice. Henceforth make haste to quit the path of wickedness. Soon the great wrath of mighty God will be kindled, so that God with His judgment may disquiet the whole world, and separate the chaff for the fire and the wheat for salvation.[2] Then all who maintain in Him the hope of faith will be blessed.[3]

# POEM 9[1]

We sat as prisoners, a band of Jews, by the alien waters of grim Babylon. We wept in misery as we recalled with mindful hearts our native Sion. On that bank, planted with pliant willows and affording friendly shade to visiting throngs, we sighed over that exile which we deservedly incurred from God's just anger. There, within the walls of that Assyrian city, in lugubrious silence we thrust from our minds the thought of glad songs, and hung our lyres on the willow branches. Oppressive anger caused our grim sorrow, for the wicked foe who had dragged us from home bade us sing for his pleasure the hymns we used to re-echo in the holy temple.

14. Shall we then sing God's praises, songs appropriate to virgin bands, in the midst of barbaric rites, polluted tombs, and altars kindled with funeral fires? Shall we sing them in our distress for men who take joy in our grief, and convert a holy liturgy to wicked wantonness by singing sacramental hymns for the diversion of the enemy? How shall we bear to sing sacred hymns in our present wretchedness? Or how can Babylon reasonably demand the hymns of Sion? This foreign land does not obtain as its deserts the song of the Lord, for the holy words flee from unworthy ears.

24. But if as master you put harsher pressure on your captives, if your desire to know the holy songs of Sion is so strong, if you proceed to force me to recount to you the

hymns of Sion which are God's and not yours, hear the promise of the avenging God to His captured city. Do not expect to rejoice for long in this your triumph, in which, foe of God, you bid us reveal to you our sacred song. Hear the Lord's hymn, Sion's song. "If, Jerusalem my love, I forget you, my city, may my right hand be ever forgetful of myself; may my tongue cleave with thirst to my mouth if I do not embrace you with abiding love, and if in the first period of my joy, on the threshold of the kingdom promised to me forever, I do not remember to prefer you before all lands."

39. Be mindful on that day of the sons of Edom,[2] and change their role with ours, so that they may in disarray witness the day on which your people will dwell in Jerusalem's ancient city. That nation turns its back on you, and now threatens Jerusalem with cruel destruction, saying: "Level that hated city to the ground, lay it bare by force until nothing stands, and the walls are reduced to nothing."

46. Unhappy daughter of wretched Babylon, happy will be who for our sakes requites you for what you have done to us! Equally happy will he be who seizes your little cherished ones and dashes them against the unyielding rock.[3] If you desire to live happily on after the elimination of Babylon's stock, destroy by the power of faith the sins which flourish within you, before the flames wax strong. Christ the Rock is now at hand; with strong arms dash upon Him the serpent's brood. For Babylon means "confusion,"[4] and her daughter is the flesh, the mother of sins, that horde which blights salvation and introduces evil seeds into the body's fibre. You must conquer these if you wish to prevail over death. If

such foes enclosed within your bones are allowed to grow
and become strong, you will have a hard struggle to conquer them. Govern these vices while they are small, while
they are infants with limbs yet unformed, while they are
unschooled and creep from the heart's womb through the
breast which they occupy. Unless you take prior action
against them, this progeny of earth will gain strength,
bring your soul in harmony with sins, and so kill it. So do
not hesitate to slay this band. It will be no sin if you
extirpate the race which will harm you, and steep the
avenging Rock in their evil blood. The just man rejoices
if his wicked offspring dies. For by slaughter of this kind
the man of God increases in holiness—that is, by killing the
sins that play tyrant over his body, and by exulting over
the crowd of vices crushed by Christ's power.

# POEM 10[1]

## To Ausonius

This is the fourth summer which has now come round
for hardy reapers, and as many winters have manifested
their rigours with the hoary frost.[2] During all that time
not a consonant had reached me from your lips, not a word
had I seen penned by your hand. So long it was before a
scroll enriched by your words of greeting brought a pro-
fusion of gifts long denied. The varied texture of three
letters,[3] full of life, was contained there, yet the sheets of
verses formed a triple poem. Beneath the bitter sweetness
of your manifold complaints, troubled love merged with
rebuke, but in my eyes your fatherly gentleness remained
more evident than harsh criticism, and in my heart the
words of kindness cancel out the bitter ones. Even so,
those charges must be rebutted in due course, and treated
in the sterner voice of the avenging heroic measure.[4]
Meanwhile, the lighter iambic will briefly take the field
first, to repay my debt of words in a different metre. The
elegiacs now give their greeting, and having performed
this and made a beginning, a first step for others, they say
no more.

19. Why, father, do you bid the deposed Muses return
to my charge? Hearts dedicated to Christ reject the Latin
Muses and exclude Apollo.[5] Of old you and I shared common cause (our zeal was equal if our poetic resources
were not) in summoning deaf Apollo from his cave at
Delphi, invoking the Muses as deities, seeking from groves

or mountain ridges that gift of utterance bestowed by
divine gift. But now another power, a greater God, inspires my mind and demands another way of life.[6] He asks
back from man His own gift, so that we may live for the
Father of life. He bids us not spend our days on the emptiness of leisure and business, or on the fictions of literature,
so that we may obey His laws and behold His light which
is clouded by the clever powers of philosophers, the skill
of rhetoricians, and the inventions of poets. These men
steep our hearts in what is false and empty. They form
only men's tongues, and bring nothing to bestow salvation
or to clothe us in the truth.[7] What good, what truth can
they possess who do not have the Head of all, God who is
the Kindling and the Source of truth and goodness, whom
no man sees except in Christ?

47. He is the Light of truth, the Path of life, the Power
and Mind, Hand and Strength of the Father. He is the Sun
of justice, Source of blessings, Flower of God, God's Son,
Creator of the world, Life of our mortality, and Death to
our death. He is the Master of the virtues. He is God to
us and became Man for us by stripping off His nature and
assuming ours, forging eternal relations between man and
God, while He Himself is both. So when He has flashed
His rays over our hearts, He cleans the enfeebling foulness
from our sluggish bodies and renews the dispositions of
our minds. All that delighted us before He draws away,
and in its stead leaves a pleasure that is chaste. By His
rights as Lord He demands wholly our hearts, tongues,
and heads. He wishes to be the object of our thought and
understanding, our belief and reading, our fear and love.
The empty enthusiasms aroused on the path of our present
existence by our labours in this life are effaced by belief

in a future life with God. That faith does not cast away as sacrilegious or cheap the riches we seem to scorn, but advises us to lend them to Christ our God, and have them stored in heaven. He has promised us more than we give, He has promised to pay back with abundant interest what we now scorn or rather lodge with Him. God will guard that sum without defrauding us, and as Debtor will return it augmented to His creditors. With greater generosity He will with abundant interest restore the money which we spurned.

81. I beg you not to regard me as idle or wayward, not to charge me with want of affection because I devote leisure or attention to Him with dedication, and trust to Him all I have. How can affection be lacking in a Christian? Being a Christian is the reciprocal guarantee of affection, and the mark of impiety is non-subjection to Christ. This is the affection I am learning to possess. How can I refrain from showing it to you, my father, to whom God has willed I should acknowledge every sacred duty and expression of affection? To you I owe my training, my distinction, my literary skills, the glory of my eloquence, my secular career, my reputation; to you I owe my preferment, my sustenance, my education, for you are patron, teacher, and father.[8] Then why do I absent myself from you so long? This is your reproachful question, your angry reaction impelled by fatherly love. This course is expedient or necessary or my whim, and whichever it is, is pardonable. Pardon me out of love if my conduct serves my ends, and rejoice with me if I live the life I want.

103. Your[9] affection is roused to utter complaints worthy of respect, and you rebuke me because I shall have been absent from my native land for a full three years,

wandering through another world, forgetful of that sharing in your life which I earlier maintained. I cherish and
duly revere the feelings of your fatherly heart, the anger
which leaves your affection undiminished, and for which
I should be grateful. But I could wish, father, that your
prayers for my return were addressed to one who could
answer them. I cannot believe that you can obtain my
return by addressing your fruitless aim to a non-deity, by
supplicating the Castalian Muses whose power is spent.
These deities will not help you achieve my return to you
and to my native land. Your call, your request, is addressed to deaf nobodies, the Muses; a light breeze will
bear it away, by windy gusts.[10] It is not sent to God, so
it cleaves to the insubstantial clouds, and does not enter
the starry hall of the King above.

119. If you are keen to have me return, train your eyes
and prayers on Him who with His thunder shakes the fiery
summit of the highest heaven, who flashes forth His triple
flame without the tumult of empty rumbling,[11] who bestows from the sky a sufficiency of sun and rain, who is
wholly present everywhere, over or within all that is, who
governs all things by dispensing Christ into all creation.
Through Christ He possesses and moves men's minds, and
orders our times and our regions. But if His dispositions
are opposed to our prayers, He must be diverted by prayer
to grant our wishes.

128. Why do you accuse me? If the course I take at
God's prompting wins your displeasure, that Prompter
who wills to fashion or convert my thinking should be
accused first, if that were lawful. For I shall freely admit,
if you are thinking of the old me whom you knew, that
I am now no longer the man I was when I was not con-

sidered wayward. (Yet I *was* wayward, my eyes enveloped in falsehood's darkness, wise in what God brands as fool-ishness,[12] living on death's sustenance.) So your obligation to pardon me is greater because the uncharacteristic nature of my action lends you readier awareness that the highest Father performs this change in me. I do not think that by saying this I shall be considered to have admitted the reprehensible sin of a debased mind, though willingly pro-claiming that I have amended my former life through a purpose not my own. I admit that my attitude has changed. My mind is not my own—or rather, it was not mine before, but now it is mine through God's agency. If He saw anything in deed or thought of mine worthy of His tasks, the thanks go first to you and the glory is owed to you, for the object of Christ's love was brought to birth by your injunctions. So you should be glad rather than querulous because I, that Paulinus of yours, reared by your intellectual and moral training (whose father you admit yourself to be even now when you consider me wayward), have so changed my scheme of life that I have deserved to belong to Christ whilst remaining the son of Ausonius. Christ will ascribe to your glory the prizes He gains, and will bestow on you the first fruit from your tree.[13]

154. Accordingly I beg you, think better of me, and do not destroy that highest of rewards by cursing the blessings which have sprung from your fount. My mind is not deranged, my way of life does not shun men's com-pany like the rider of Pegasus who you write lived in a Lycian cave.[14] Yet many do dwell in trackless regions through divine prompting—for example, famous philoso-phers of old, seeking to exploit their learning and inspira-

tion. Similarly now there are some who have as celibates adopted Christ and follow this form of life. It is not through lack of mental resource or barbaric habits that they choose to live in uninhabited places. They turn towards the stars on high and look to God. They concentrate on the vision of God and the depths of truth. Freed from empty occupations, they love the leisure prescribed by Christ and their own love of salvation, and they loathe the din of public affairs, the bustle of business, and all the activity that is hostile to God's gifts. In hope and faith they follow God, for there is the guarantee of a reward which the Creator will certainly bestow on those who do not despair, provided their present world and its empty possessions are not their master and their glowing minds reject things visible to win what is invisible, attaining the secret realms of heaven.

174. For it is the transient that is exposed to our gaze, and the eternal is denied to it. It is in hope that we pursue our mental vision, rejecting the various aspects and appearances of the material world, and the possessions which sorely agitate our bodily eyes; yet those on whom the light of truth and goodness has dawned seem to have the notion fixed firmly in their minds of the eternity of the age to come, and the emptiness of the present world.

181. I myself, however, do not share their glory, so why talk of me in the same breath? I have the same faith in the object of my prayer, but even now I dwell in pleasant surroundings, lodging on the pleasant shore of a luxuriant coast. So why this downright hostility to the region?[15] If only it were a justified jealousy which began to gnaw at me, the taunts sustained in Christ's name would be agreeable to me. A mind strengthened by divine power

experiences no sensitive shame, and the fame which I spurn in this world is restored to me at Christ's adjudication.

189. So, revered father, do not reproach me for turning waywardly to these pursuits, and do not make my wife or mental aberration grounds for slander. Mine is not the disturbed mind of a Bellerophon,[16] and my wife is no Tanaquil but a Lucretia.[17] I do not regard it as forgetfulness of my native heaven when my eyes are trained upward on the highest Father, for he who worships the one Father is truly mindful of heaven.[18] So reassure yourself, father, that I am not forgetful of heaven, I am not out of my mind, and I dwell in the haunts of men whose very pursuits attest their saintly character, for an irreligious race could not have knowledge of the highest God. True, there are many regions and groups of inhabitants which show no devotion to or awareness of religious law,[19] but what area is without rustic ritual, and how does the foreign wickedness inherent in them harm me? Why do you cast up at me the desolate glades of Vasconia[20] and the snowy reception afforded by the Pyrenees, as though my life were restricted to the threshold of Spain, and as though I had no city or country residence whatsoever in the region where wealthy Spain lies open to the world, watching suns set day after day? And even supposing that I chanced to have lived on brigand-infested hills, you cannot believe that I am congealed in some barbaric abode, transformed into one of those peasants whose primitive hospitality I shared. Evil does not enter a chaste mind, and a shower of dirt does not stick to smooth bristles. So also in the forest of Vasconia, whoever lives a life of integrity and justice untainted by sin[21] catches no infection of evil manners from an unpolished host.

215. Why should I incur accusation on this charge when I dwell and have dwelt in various regions close to proud cities and renowned for the fertile crops of their inhabitants? And even if my life were in the region of Vasconia, why should its uncivilised inhabitants not rather become moulded to my manners, and abandon their primitive religion to change to ours? You assume that my Spanish dwellings are in ruined cities, you traverse in your verses abandoned towns, you convert into objects of reproach the hilltown Calagurris, and Birbilis[22] perched on precipitous crags, and the hill down which Hilerda[23] slopes, as though I were dwelling in them as an exile from home and city, far from the abodes and roads of men. But surely you do not think that they are the wealth of Spain? Are you unaware of the Spanish world, the region in which heavy Atlas is rooted beneath the weight of heaven, the mountain which is the most southerly point and boundary of that land, and which isolates the lofty peak of Calpe[24] flanked by twin seas? Are Birbilis, Calagurris, and Hilerda the only noteworthy spots in a Spain which boasts its Caesarea Augusta, its attractive Barcinus, its Tarraco[25] looking down on the sea from its impressive heights? Why should I recount the cities which excel in their soil and their urban buldings, in the region where fertile Spain runs down to two seas, swelling the Atlantic with the river Baetis[26] and the Tyrrhenian sea[27] with the Ebro, and spanning the broad plains which divide the separate seas to set the boundaries of her region at the edge of the world?

239. Celebrated lord, if you were minded to write of the region where you live, would you be inclined to pass over elegant Burdigala and prefer to describe the grimy Boii?[28] When you lavish your leisure on the hot springs

of Maroialum,[29] and present yourself with a life amid shady glades, dwelling in abodes with fertile soil, do you thereby live in murky huts, in cabins of thatched straw, in a wasteland worthy of the skin-clad Bigerri?[30] Can you, the influential consul, spurn the proud city of Rome yet refrain from scorning the sand-dwelling Vasatae?[31] Shall I complain bitterly that because your countryside is green and fertile in the fields of Poiteau, the consular regalia of Ausonius has retired to Ravaunum,[32] and the consul's robe is befouled in some ancient shrine there? (In fact, it lies in the venerable city of Latin Quirinus,[33] amongst palm-embroidered, imperial robes of equal eminence, distinguished and gleaming from afar with unfrayed gold, and preserving the fresh distinction of your perennial merit.) Or when you dally beneath the roof of your Lucanian farm,[34] dwelling in lofty halls that vie with the houses of Romulus, will it be claimed that you are dwelling in the hamlet of Condate[35] because the place which gives its name to the district provides the pretext?

260. Many topics can be apposite for joking, and even badinage which misrepresents the truth is permissible. But to force one's soft tongue against an aching tooth, to insert a sting in jocose flattery, to sour bittersweet quips with the vinegar of sharp-toothed satire[36]—this is often appropriate to poets, but never to fathers. Loyalty and paternal love demand that reports contrived and inserted into chaste ears by malevolent gossip should not be permitted to get a firm hold in the heart of a father concerned for his son's welfare. Even the stupid talk of the malicious mob does not invariably regard it as a sin to alter one's previous habits or way of life, and indeed a change for the better wins praise. When you hear that I am different, you should

inquire about my aim and form of service. If I have
changed from uprightness to crookedness, from piety to
ungodliness, from thrift to extravagance, from decency
to foulness, and if my life is idle, sluggish, and withdrawn,
you must show compassion to a friend who has become
corrupted. Anger in that case can rightly rouse a fond
father to recall his fallen friend to decent ways, and by
stern admonition he can restore a more satisfactory situation.

278. Likewise, if you chance to hear that I have chosen
the vocation of dedicating my heart to holy God, that I
follow Christ's revered service with attentive belief, and
that I am convinced by God's prompting that an eternal
reward is in prospect which man purchases by sustaining
losses in this world, I cannot think that this is so repugnant
to a conscientious father that he considers it mental aberration to live for Christ in the way that Christ laid down.
This "aberration" is what I want, and I do not regret it.
I do not mind being stupid in the eyes of those who follow
a different course, provided that my decision is wise in the
eyes of the eternal King. A man's existence is short, his
body feeble, his days transient, and without Christ he is
dust and shadow.[37] The praise and condemnation he expresses have no more validity than he who expresses them.
He dies, and his error accompanies him; the decree dies
and passes away with the judge who pronounced it.

294. If we do not take fearful care to live in accord
with Christ the Lord's command in our allotted span on
earth, too late once we cast off our mortal bodies will be
our plaint that we feared the unsubstantial reproaches of
men's tongues, but did not stand in awe of the grave anger
of God's judgment. I myself believe that Christ sits on His

throne on the right of His eternal Father, that He is established as King over all, and that He will come with the lapse of time to judge all nations on the balance of the scales, bestowing rewards appropriate to different deeds. Believing this, I struggle fearfully and with urgent zeal, hoping I may be spared and not be annihilated in death before I loose myself from sin.

304. My believing heart with inner apprehension tremblingly awaits His coming. My soul is preoccupied with this, and anxious for what is to come, fearing that it may be shackled with enfeebling care for the body and weighed down with material possessions; fearing that if the ravaging trumpet sounds from the opened heavens, it may not be able to rise on light wings into the breezes to meet the King. It longs to fly to heaven amidst thousands of honoured saints, who will with easy effort raise their feet weightlessly through the void, unencumbered by bonds of earth, to the stars aloft.[38] They will journey on fleecy clouds,[39] passing among the stars to worship the heavenly King amid the upper air, to unite their glorious columns with the Christ they adore.

316. This is the cause of my fear and toil, that the last day may not overtake me asleep in the pitch darkness of barren activity, prolonging my wasted days in empty occupations. What shall I do if Christ in flashing revelation from His heavenly citadel appears before me while I nod over languishing prayers? What if I am blinded by the sudden rays of the Lord's coming from the opened heavens and, stupefied by the shaft of light, I make for the grim refuge of the sightless darkness?

324. This is why I have decided by my proposed course to forestall disaster, so that doubt in the truth or love of

this life (with the pleasure of possessions and the toil of responsibilities) should not confront me with such a death. I am resolved to end my worldly cares while life remains, to entrust my possessions to God against the age to come,[40] and to await harsh death with untroubled heart. If you approve this, take pleasure in the rich hopes of your friend. If you disapprove, leave me to win approval from Christ alone.

# POEM 11[1]

## *To Ausonius*

You mention that my tongue continues and persists in speechlessness while you are never silent. You rebuke my decision to live idle in hiding. You add the additional charge of neglect of friendship. You charge me with fear of my wife. You hurl remorseless verses at my person. I beg you, refrain from wounding your friend; do not seek to mingle bitterness with the words of a father—absinth, so to say, with honey. It was and it remains my abiding care to observe every duty towards you and to show you faithful affection. At any rate, I have never besmirched the deference which is your due by the slightest blemish. I have always been apprehensive of offending you even with a look, of wounding you with an unguarded reaction. When facing you with deference, I ordered my features more carefully and let my eyes gladden my face, so that no mistaken suspicion should cause a cloud to descend on my revered father, even if it was confined within the silence of your heart. My household has followed this example in honouring you now as previously, and the harmony in our affection for you is as great as the concurrence of our minds in the worship of Christ.

20. Tell me the nature of the rancour that has clouded your heart against your own. What is the gossip that rumour has so readily dinned into your ears, expelling

your judgment and afflicting unaccustomed blows on a
loyalty long-standing and of proved affection, so that
with its evil prompting it wounded a father so well-
disposed to his children? My heart feels a sincerity un-
feigned; my love is innocent of neglect of my father,
rejects every undeserved charge, and is unwilling to be
reproved by untrue accusations, because it is genuinely
without stain. But being as sensitive to affronts as it is
free from guilt, it is hurt more seriously by an unjust
wound.

30. You complain that I have shaken off the yoke[2]
which joined me to you in literary pursuits. But I maintain
that I never shouldered it, for equals undertake a yoke. No
man joins a strong partner with a weak, and it is no harmonious pair if those forced together are unevenly balanced. If you join a calf to a bull, or a horse to a wild ass,
if you compare coots with swans or the nightingale with
the magpie,[3] if you equate hazel shrubs with chestnut
trees, or the wayfaring tree with the cypress,[4] then you
can compare me with you. Tully and Maro[5] could hardly
be equal yoke-fellows with you. If love is the yoke we
share, this is the only yoke which I dare boast of sharing
with you, for in love the modest can vie with the great,
and share its reins. Sweet friendship brings equality
through my eternal compact with you, and through our
equal observance of perennial love towards each other.
No malicious gossip looses this yoke from our necks; no
lengthy absence from my native soil has destroyed or will
destroy it. Though I be separated from you by a whole
world or a whole lifetime, I shall never be divorced from
you in mind. Life itself will quit my body before your
features vanish from my heart.

49. Throughout the entire span granted and allotted to humankind, for so long as I am contained by this confining body, I may be separated from you by the length of a world, but you will not be far from my face[6] or removed from my eyes. I shall hold you fast within me. I shall see you with my heart's eye and embrace you with loving mind. You will be before me everywhere. When I am freed from the prison of my body and fly forth from the earth, whatever the heavenly region where our common Father sets me,[7] even there I shall have you in mind. The death which looses me from my body will not loose me from your love, for the mind survives the limbs which fall away, and lives on because its birth is divine. So it must keep its feelings and affections as it keeps its life, and it admits forgetfulness no more than death. It lives and it remembers forever.[8]

# POEM 12[1]

Glorious confessor, happy in your deserts as in your name,[2] your mind so powerful in its holiness dwells in the highest heaven, but your power is felt equally throughout the earth. With unfettered voice you proclaimed Christ the Lord, and by scorning harsh punishments you deserved to escape them. Upon the command willingly to release your limbs and render to Christ in manifold torture the soul that you had vowed to Him, you left your empty members to the savage lictors and advanced to the glory of heaven, a martyr who shed no blood.[3]

10. Father and Lord, permit your servants, however unworthy, finally to celebrate this day in the abode for which we long, in that hall in which you take rest, till our frail bodies draw this life to a close. Allow us to pay our devoted vows in person, to take joy amidst the rejoicing crowds. I pray that the punishment we have borne and which our wickedness deserved—our existence without you all these years, so sadly far from your abode, though we have not been absent in mind[4]—may now be enough. Now you must take thought for our longing, which is wearied by this boundless time. Show mindful pity, however late, towards your servants. Crush the hostile forces that delay us, and open up a way of ready access through the world which divides us by a great expanse of boundless sea. If any envious foe blocks our hastening course to you, remove these hindering impedi-

ments and favour the passage of friends, for you are stronger than our foes. Should we decide on a journey overland, accompany your followers on the safe highway; or if our great confidence in you encourages us to journey across the broad sea, allow us to hasten over gentle waves, and provide following winds as servants to your servants, so that under Christ's guidance we may together reach Campanian shores, and then with eager haste race towards your rooftops, finding a haven of peace at your door.

32. There under your dominion we shall bear the sweet yoke, the burden that is light,[5] the slavery so mild. Your righteousness has no need of wicked servants, but you will bear with and love the persons whom Christ's gift has dedicated to you, however mean they may be. You will allow them to serve at your door, to keep your threshold spotless in the morning, and likewise to mount devoted vigil at night; and when their bodies grow weary, to end a life of merit in this service.[6]

# POEM 13[1]

Felix, happy in your deserts as in your name and in your name as in your deserts, that propitious day comes round on which the highest Christ adopted you and set you as His confessor in His Father's halls. So the time is ripe to pour out our gratitude to you in bounteous prayers.

5. Father and lord, best of patrons to servants however unworthy, at last our prayer is answered to celebrate your birthday within your threshold. The long period of three lustrations[2] has rushed by since on this holy day I last dedicated my prayers and my heart to you in person. You know what toils on land and sea have since then kept me far from your abode in a distant world, because I have always and everywhere had you near me, and have called on you in the grim moments of travel, and in the uncertainties of life.

14. You were also my leader when I embarked on the sea, because apprehension of danger vanished through your love. I never sailed without you, for I felt your protection in Christ the Lord when I overcame rough seas. On land and water my journeying is always made safe through you. Felix, I beg you, address a prayer on behalf of your own to that Embodiment of the calm of eternal love and peace, to Him on whose great name you depend.

20. Now we take delight in pouring out our hearts profusely in joy, for we are here at Nola to see this fond day dawn which we have always kept in other parts of the

75

world, the day which made you revered on earth and transported you to the skies. See, the crowds of many hues bring colour to the roads in their mottled throng, and we eye with astonishment countless cities in a single city.[3]

26. Nola, happy in having your Felix as your protector, you win fame from your saintly citizen, and strength from your heavenly patron. You have won the title of city second to Rome herself, once first only in dominion and conquering arms, but now first in the world through the apostles' tombs.[4] Be good and kindly to your own, and beg the mighty Lord that Christ may be appeased, that through His kindness we may come to rest at your anchorage in the harbour of peace, after enduring the waves of the sea, and being buffeted by the waves of the world. I have carefully hauled up and tied my ship upon this shore, so let the anchor of my ordered life grip fast on you.

# POEM 14[1]

That festive day has come again which is attended by crowds in heaven as on earth. It celebrates Felix's birthday, the day on which he died physically on earth and was born for Christ in heaven above, winning his heavenly crown as a martyr who did not shed his blood.[2] For he died as confessor, though he did not avoid execution by choice, since God accepted his inner faith in place of blood. God looks into the silence of hearts, and equates those ready to suffer with those who have already done so, for He considers this inward test sufficient, and dispenses with physical execution in the case of true devotion. Martyrdom without bloodshed is enough for Him if mind and faith are ready to suffer and are fervent towards God. A will prepared to suffer is sufficient, for it is the best evidence of deserving aspiration.

13. So the day which bestowed so great a gift by setting Felix in the heights of heaven is the day of our yearly ritual. It comes after the solstice, the time when Christ was born in the flesh and transformed the cold winter season with a new sun,[3] when He granted men His birth that brings salvation, and ordered the nights to shorten and the daylight to grow with Himself. The twentieth day that dawns on us after the solstice marks the heavenly glory which Felix merited.

21. So Felix has a status both in title and in strength equal to that of martyrs who shed their blood, when he

thrusts out demons with the power of his authority, and frees bodies that are enchained. These baneful princes admit with lugubrious cry that Felix afflicts them with punishments unseen, and with audible groans they attest their hidden torments. They betray the existence of one concealed from human eyes but evident to men's ears, and they reveal his presence in abundant power, when they are pinned within the bodies they have seized. They cry out that Christ shines out in the person of His saint, and they prove it by trembling with shaking limbs and wagging heads, and by the tortures they endure. But it is not their own bodies that they torture. They give vent to their own pain through the mouths of others begging for pardon. The avenger is hidden, but the punishment visible.

36. Moreover, if a more violent foe binds individuals with more oppressive harm, this day frees them through divine power. At this time one can see scattered around the thresholds prostrate breasts cleansed by this sacred remedy, and men mentally restored giving thanks with their own voices. A crowd of gaping men all atremble surrounds them. Tears mingled with joy well from all men's eyes, and all believe that God is present there. Felix is the glory of Christ who knows no limits.

44. This pleasant day is thronged by huge crowds, all dedicating their vows on the sacred portals. The whole of earth and heaven rejoices. The sky seems to smile and the heavens lie exposed. The breezes with their noiseless breath whisper spring, and a milky mesh encompasses the glad sky. Without limit and without rest the inhabitants of cities gather in thick ranks, hastening from darkness to dawn and wearying of awaiting the day. The tedium of the night is dissipated by eager prayers, and torches with

their flames prevail over the darkness. It is delightful to
see one city thronged with many cities, and such numerous
swarms merged in a single prayer.

55. The Lucanian clans gather,[4] the youth of Apulia,
the Calabrians, and all the peoples of Latium, round whom
both seas resound to left and right.[5] Campania, rejoicing
throughout her sixty cities, takes pleasure in the feast as
being her own.[6] The contingent includes the citizens
which rich Capua contains within her large walls, and
those whom fair Naples or Gaurus feeds, those who cultivate the gladdening Massic vines, and those who drink at
the Ufens and the Sarnus;[7] those who work at the dry soil
of the Tanager, and at the fertile fields of the well-watered
Galaesus;[8] those whom the strong Atina and their mother-
city Aricia send.[9] Rome herself, so powerful through the
sacred tombs of the heavenly princes Peter and Paul, is
delighted that her population shrinks because of the glory
of this day. From the mouth of the Porta Capena[10] she
pours forth thousands, dispatching them in a thick swarm
over the hundred and twenty miles to the walls of friendly
Nola. The Appian way is invisible for long distances
through the thick-massed crowds.

71. No fewer are the city-bands which have set out
from other areas, and take the rough road along the steep
Latin way.[11] There are those nurtured by lofty Praeneste
and fruitful Aquinum, and those whom ancient Ardea
sends from the coast abutting on the city.[12] Some have left
Cales and the twin towns of Teanum, where the sober
Aurunci and the rough Apulians dwell.[13] A crowd hastens
also from Venafrum rich in olives,[14] and the tough Sam-
nites leave their high-perched towns.

79. Their devotion has overcome the hard journey. The

love of Christ conquers all, and fostering faith persuades men cold in heart as in habitation to endure harsh rigours and thereby to abandon hardness of heart. One day summons all, and Nola alone receives them, for though her whole extent teems with her own, she has room for all, so that you might think that the walls were being expanded to take in the countless guests. In this way, Nola, you develop the appearance of Rome, and you have won second rank after Rome, which once had primacy only in dominion and victorious arms, but is now first on earth through the tombs of the apostles.[15]

89. You, too, Nola, have obtained the undying crown of your Felix as a double distinction; he was formerly your priest and is now your martyr forever. So as the mother of our friend in heaven, you rightly attain the skies by two-fold merit. Earlier as priest he tended your fostering shrine with devoted reverence, and instructed and governed you with calm direction. And now also Felix adorns you with undying fame, for now he is held sacred, and in your bosom wins the glory which he deserved, for his holy bones are buried in a fragrant tomb here.

98. Now the golden threshold is adorned with snow-white curtains,[16] and the altars crowned with crowds of lanterns. The fragrant lamps burn with waxed wicks of paper,[17] and are ablaze night and day, so that the night shines with the brightness of day, and the day, too, is bright with heavenly glory, gleaming the more since its light is redoubled by the countless lamps.

104. How lucky we also are, for we are granted the chance of seeing and celebrating this day in your presence, of viewing the rewards of our patron, of giving thanks to Christ for proffering such great gifts to His own, and of rejoicing among the happy throngs. Sound praise to God,

my children;[18] fulfil your devoted vows, and assembled in your holy bands sound forth your festive songs. Strew the earth with blossoms and line the thresholds with garlands. Let winter breathe forth the brightness of spring, and the year be in blossom before its time; let nature yield to the holy day, for you, too, earth, owe garlands to the martyr's tomb. But he is flower-decked with the twin garlands of war and peace, and is enshrined in the holy glory of heaven's threshold.

116. I beg you, pray that this day be for us bright with eternal peace. May we be able to rejoice anew when it comes again, to offer here our yearly vows and songs on your feastday, if Christ is appeased and His will complaisant. Our love, our toil is here. Receive these prayers of your followers and recommend them to God, so that once our diligent care has bestowed on you our service over a long life, you may then finally give the signal and release your children who have pleased you by the devotion of our toil. When the souls of your followers are brought before your face,[19] do not refuse to convey them in your fatherly arms to the presence of the gleaming Lord. Prevail on Him who is devoted in His goodness, yet awesome in His majesty, that He may be softened by your prayers and deserving acts, and remit our debts.[20] Felix, when you, too, the mighty portion of holy men, accompany the Lamb[21] in His kingdom, ask that we may be set among the flock of His sheep, so that the verdict of the supreme Judge may once more bestow us on you in such service. Ask that He may not apportion us to His left side amongst the goats that have not pleased Him, but rather set us on His right in the company of the saints, joining us to the bounteous flock of the lambs that win praise.[22]

# POEM 15[1]

My yearly prayer, the yearly debt owed by my tongue,
comes round once more. This is your birthday, Felix held
by Christ in such glorious fame, a birthday dearer to me
than my own. And though it affords general joy to countless throngs, it has a special meaning for us your followers,
because Christ has allowed us to be yours. He has bestowed our worthless persons on you His dear friend, not
because you deserved servants so tawdry (for God deems
you worthy to walk as His companion in perennial
triumphs), but because our goodly Father decided to enrich us, bereft as we are of justice and unworthy of salvation. Thus we, whose evil wealth lay in our sins, might
change the substance of that wealth for the better, and in
place of all riches and aspirations, instead of distinctions of
rank and prestige, obtain Felix as our wealth and native
land and home. You are for us our father and land, our
home and wealth; your embrace has become our cradle,
and your lap our nest. In it we are kept snug, and grow.
Our bodies assume changed shape, for we cast off our
earthly connexion, wings sprout on us, and we are turned
into birds by the begetting of God's word.[2] We know
that Christ's yoke is light[3] since you lift it for us. In your
person Christ is indulgent to the unworthy, and sweet to
the bitter. So we, too, must count this day, your birthday,
a regular holiday, because you destroy the evil in us, and

we die towards the world that we may be born for Christ,
to win blessings.[4]

26. So bestir and arouse yourself, my soul's strength
that is my lyre, and strain with every fibre. Love must
strike my inner self with silent music, my teeth must be
assailed by the sounding instrument of my heart, and the
lyre that is my throat must resound with the quill that is
my tongue. I shall not summon Castalian Muses, the
ghosts of poets, nor rouse deaf Phoebus from the Aonian
rock.[5] Christ will inspire my song, for it is through Christ's
gift that I, a sinner, dare to tell of His saint and of heavenly
things. For You, Almighty One, it is easy to move my lips
in learned rhythms, for You bid the dumb to speak, the
dry to flow, the hard to be melted. For it was You who
made the ass cry back in speech,[6] and children at the breast
to sing Your praises to perfection.[7] You bade the solid
rock dissolve into a river, and waterless land to flow with
sudden streams,[8] watering the desert to give hope to those
peoples. Into their dry souls flowed Your holy grace; it
was Christ who refreshed them, the Rock flowing with
the living spring.[9] So I, O Christ, who am the least of living men, put reliance on this gift, and in my dryness pray
for running draughts of Your water from that spring.
Grant me speech from Your fount, for without You I
cannot speak Your words. They are Yours because praise
of Your martyr is also praise of You, for in Your omni-
potence You grant men divine strength. In triumphing
over the flesh, You defeat the strong with the weak,[10] and
within our bodies conquer the princes of the air.[11]

50. Draw near, then, so that by Your guidance I can
retrace and tell the history of Your Felix from the beginning.[12] His noble lineage originated in the east. No other

land indeed was more suited to be Felix's native region than that which had begotten the patriarchs and the holy prophets, the sacred vessels of Christ. From there the message of the Gospel poured forth its stream from the tongues of the apostles, and welled forth to the whole world.[13] From there came Felix who was owed to God. He was not yet born, but he came in the person of his father, who set out to Italy so that Felix could be born on our shores and have a citizen's regard for them, and recall no other for whom he had been born save ourselves. It was thus that father Abraham followed the Lord's command, exchanged his native land for foreign soil, and left his sacred seed in the fields of Canaan;[14] and from there the stock of Felix set out to a foreign land, so that a sacramental source dispatched him over to us. Sprung from that root, he was entrusted to us by perfection of faith, so that he might be for us a holy channel of faith.[15] And even now as Felix lies at rest in the flesh reposing here, his spirit is alive in Christ, and the deserving works of his lofty virtue, through the agency of Abraham's seed, transform the hard stones which he raises to life to achieve blessings.

72. So he was born in this city of a Syrian father, and dwelt in his beloved Nola which he accounted his fatherland. He was well endowed with a pleasant home, and though he was not sole heir he was wealthy and prosperous. With his brother Hermias (which was also his father's name) he shared earthly wealth, but Felix alone possessed the property of heaven. A difference of decision separated the twin brothers; the world pulled Hermias away, but Christ took Felix for His own. Hermias preferred the transient, Felix the enduring. Hermias clung to the temporal things, Felix abandoned earth for heaven, and his

inheritance for the kingdom. Hermias was the heir of his own father alone, Felix was coheir with Christ.[16]

84. But who would be surprised at offspring so different from the same blood, if he rereads how amongst the sacred children of our ancient parents Rebecca, so fertile in begetting the stock of two peoples, lamented the strife in her womb and complained to God about the struggles in her swollen belly?[17] Already then the disharmony which now rages within the world's womb was seething in the belly of that holy mother. The Jews followed the prickles of hairy Esau to wickedness, and were condemned to be slaves to a younger people, whereas we whose origin was better follow the smooth-faced Jacob through the gentle ways of peace where the path of light leads.

95. So the blood of the two brothers, sprung from identical blood, was different. Hermias, like the rough Edom,[18] pursued the things of earth, and lay a filthy captive in the empty shadow of the world. He chose the harsh laws of his Idumaean parent,[19] lived by his sword and endured the barren toil of pointless warfare; in this he was subject to Caesar's arms, though in his private life he followed the duties laid down by Christ.[20]

102. But my Felix was born to bear the arms of the eternal King, and changed to the allegiance of father Israel.[21] From boyhood his devoted mind fashioned itself for heavenly things, and determined to serve God. No mean grace attended him. That thirst which his spirit, gasping for the light, experienced in welling heart, was matched by the abundant inflow of gifts which it received from God. In his early years he served as reader, and then assumed the rank to which is attached the task of exor-

cising evil spirits with the voice of faith, and banishing them with holy words.[22] Because he carried out this duty with clearly deserving virtue, he obtained the revered insignia of priest as his right, and adorned this deserved distinction with a spirit worthy of the rank.

114. But to ensure that the priest's fillet[23] should not alone adorn his holy head, a stronger reason emerged for enhancing it with a further crown. The grim madness of impious passions broke out. The holy Church was battered in sacrilegious war,[24] and impiety demanded from the whole people especially those whose piety was more impressive. At that time Maximus was bishop,[25] an old man who governed the town of Nola with the sacred laws and with words of peace. His strength lay in having Felix as priest; he had taken him to his heart as a father takes a son, and he desired Felix to succeed him in the see. But then this sudden storm drove him out, and though his faith did not yield he made for an isolated place. During the increasingly intensive search for the bishop, Felix became the prominent barrier before the swords. He was isolated in this hatred for the faith. It was not his office that made him conspicuous; faith is greater than the office, for the office is merely the occasion for manifesting faith. Faith is attacked when the envious dragon awakens his arms, desiring to destroy that source of our rising and his falling.

132. So when the bishop fled harsh torture, Felix alone was sought out as leader of his people, like the head of a body. All vied to bring him down. They attacked as if they were besieging with a massive engine a lofty citadel in a beleaguered town,[26] so that when the mainstay was overcome the rest of the city might tumble and easily

collapse. Such lunacy was worthy of infidels, believing that the faith which the whole world embraced could be blotted out with an individual. Wretched impiety, blinded by hell's darkness, where do you rush to, and who is the target for your weapons? Do you believe that God depends on one man? Even if you destroy human bodies, do you think that the power and purpose of God can be annihilated with them? His strength flows through the limbs of the universe, and by it you are born and obtain sustenance undeserved. Your victory or defeat hangs on His will. By His strength a single man is stronger than a countless multitude, and armed with unarmed devotion lays prostrate men armed with the steel but unarmed within with Christ. Faith defeats them through awareness of heavenly truth; it measures the future life against immediate death, and it joyfully restores to God the mind which is victorious over the conquered body, and transports it to the delighted stars.

153. So what profit, crazed spirit, do you get from attacking holy Felix with such massive madness? His inner mind remains unconquered, for God is hidden there. It is not earthly man's nature alone which now opposes you. God Himself, the object of your attack, takes up the fight. Christ confronts your poison, ancient snake,[27] in the persons of His servants, and enmeshing you in your own snares He brings you low even as His own are slaughtered, triumphing over death by the appearance of death. But through your demoniac goad men's hearts grew wild in error, and were impelled to burn with thirst for carnage, and to demand the blood of saints as the prize for their crime.

164. So when Nola sustained their sacrilegious fury,

and trembled at the swords directed at her holy inhabitants, the revered Felix was sought throughout the ransacked town. The air he breathed with lofty spirit was already that of heaven, so he did not flee, but with that silent spur sharpened his wits for battle. The shepherd fearlessly preserved his trembling flock, ready after the example of the Lord to lay down his life for the sheep.[28] So he eagerly stood his ground like a wall against the savage foe. His flowering faith lent him fresh strength in his hoary years; concentrating his mind on heaven, mindful of Christ, forgetful of the world, he bore God in his heart and his person was filled with Christ. His body now no longer contained him; he seemed a sanctified, greater being, and his eyes and countenance shone with heavenly glory.

177. At once to his joy he was arrested and dragged away by the savage hands of those crazed men. But as the unjust foe is wont to do when he toils to destroy our souls rather than our bodies, he reserved Felix for the sword but first tried him with terrorising techniques, proceeding towards death by stages of punishment. The first stage of torture was devised from the prison. Iron bonds were clamped on him in a pitch-dark cell. His hands and neck experienced the steel unceasingly, and his feet grew numb as the fetters drew them apart. Broken jars were strewn about so that his bed of excruciating sharpness might dispel sleep.[29]

187. But our confessor did not lack rest, nor was he deprived of light, for Christ now associated with him in everything, and shared the suffering. The heavier his punishment, the more garlands of green he gained as he traversed heaven in journeying mind. Though his body

was chained, his free spirit preceded him in flight to the
inner haunts of Christ, and his soul with confident prayer
pondered on his future rewards. So this happy suffering
oppressed Felix with holy pains, confining him with heavy
bonds in the dark prison, and his patience received from
Christ a reward as great as the punishment which his sub-
missive flesh endured from man.

198. Meanwhile, Maximus was sick in the desolate
mountains, but happy to have escaped the deadly eyes and
hands of the executioners. Yet he suffered martyrdom with
torture that was different but no lighter than if he had
exposed his neck to the sword and his limbs to torture or
fire; a keener anxiety for his flock burned and troubled
him. He was consumed with the fire of cold, and grew
numb with the chilling moisture from heaven. Bereft of
food and shelter, he remained sleepless night and day,
joining the one to the other in concentrated prayer.
Stretched out on the bush-strewn terrain, his limbs were
pricked with thorns, and his mind with anxieties. He
fought both outer and inner war, enduring the thorns of
the countryside in his body and the thorns of depression
in his sad heart. He cloaked hardships with other hardships, lightening his physical tortures with bitter mental
suffering, so that the pain in his mind shut out all feeling
of bodily anguish.

213. Though his soul's powers remained unbroken, and
faith despised bodily weakness, his earthly parts grew sick.
His body was overcome with the wintry weather and
hunger, and worn out by his hard bed, it began to fail and
to abandon his spirit. The cold entered more deeply into
the empty marrow of that tired old man, turned his blood
to ice, and began to drive out his life. Then the devotion

of our highest Father was roused for this great bishop, and He did not permit his body to be destroyed by death unseen. He could have fed him as he fed Elias, by sending birds bearing food through that barren and pathless region, or He could have buried him like Moses in a hidden tomb.[30] But God had granted the gift of being buried in secret ground to one only of His friends, for it was right that so great a distinction should be appropriate only for that body which had shone from the close presence and conversation of God; thus when Moses had performed his duties as man, he could take joy in having God alone as witness of his grave.

230. So the kindly Father looked on His bishop and confessor with smiling eye, and did not allow him to waste further in the silence of the forest. He was preparing to join to that worthy bishop a comrade equally worthy in merit, and so from the whole complement of those in gaol He chose Felix as recipient, through his deserving deeds, of the task of supporting the frame of that holy old man, of reawakening life, of warming his limbs, of bringing him back, and of restoring to the astonished sheep the consolation of their dear shepherd. So an angel came[31] flashing down in the silence of the night, and amidst all that crowd of chained prisoners spoke to Felix alone, since holy devotion had imprisoned him. All the terror of the dark prison vanished. Felix was awakened simultaneously by the voice and by the radiance of that holy agent. Trembling, he took in the message with the ear of faith.

244. To begin with, he was numb with fear, as though he were receiving God's command by an apparition of beguiling sleep. He pleaded the excuse that he could not follow, since his chains prevented him, and besides he was

guarded by the bolts and by the warder of that beleaguered prison. But the heavenly voice rebuked his lingering and bade him throw off his chains and rise. Suddenly his fetters softened and fell away from his hands; without assistance his neck cast off its iron yoke, and his feet popped out of the imprisoning stocks now opened. How wonderful is faith! He emerged fearless outside, the prison being opened —though the bolts remained undamaged—and the guard fast asleep. He stepped through those who barred the path; the angel advanced as Felix's light and way through the friendly silence of the still night.[32]

257. It is surely true that the one Christ is present in each and every saint. Just as the same spirit waxes strong in all who are born in Christ, so the grace in holy men harmoniously corresponds. In this modern event I see the occurrence of old when Peter (supreme amongst the column of the twelve disciples) was bidden to depart, and of his own accord emerged from the parting fetters and the barred prison, along the path where the angel preceded him as guide and so robbed Herod of his booty.[33]

266. In the same way God led my Felix through the twin blackness of prison and night; for others it was dark, but for him made bright. Advancing safely through the midst of the guards and following the angel's footsteps with unwavering tread, he was led by paths unknown to seek out his appointed task. After he had traversed secluded glades and pathless countryside, he discovered the haunt of the weary old man, and to his grief saw that he was breathing with difficulty and that his life was now faint. As soon as he recognised the person of his dear father, he rushed to embrace him and kissed the face he knew so well. He tried by warming him to restore heat

to his cold limbs, and by repeated breaths from his gasping mouth to reinduce sensations of life by warming his body. But the body could not be stirred by shout or blow. It was like a corpse, but slight breathing and a quivering in its inner parts betrayed the last vestiges of life.

282. Felix was troubled at this sight, and felt perplexity in his devoted heart, for he saw the bloodless limbs and the face waxen with hunger, but he had nothing with which to succour his needs. There was no fire or nourishment far or near to restore the wasting man with food or to melt his stiffness with fire. He begged and accosted Christ with prayer after prayer, asking by what resource and means he could fulfill the task enjoined on him. The Almighty immediately produced grapes on the bushes, and ordered them to hang close to his head, so that he could easily pluck from the adjacent branch the food that had grown of its own accord. So Felix gained fresh strength from God's help, and his devoted mind took joy in the gift that was offered. He plucked the cluster with his hand and applied it to the mouth of the dying man. But since the teeth of Maximus were now fast closed, and he refused to taste and eat the sweet food, Felix squeezed out the juicy grapes and allowed the liquid to drip in, parting the dry lips with his finger. So with God's help his laborious efforts and struggling hands gradually loosened that clamped mouth, and made a narrow pathway through the opened lips for the pressed grape to insert its puny drops. Thus the bishop's soul regained sensation, his bones warmth, his eyes light; life returned to him in its fullness, and the tongue which had stuck fast, choked by the dryness of his throat, now uttered its normal speech, once the moisture lubricated a path for his voice.

307. So Maximus was restored to life, and saw close before him the face of his Felix that he knew so well. After returning his embrace, he complained at his late coming. "The Lord had promised me that you would be here long ago, Felix, you who are a part of myself. Felix, my most cherished one, what great delay kept you, and where were you? Though my body was frail and momentarily failed, still I was strong in heart, and I endured in faith. The very place and condition in which you see me drawing the last breaths of this life demonstrate that I did not flee through fear of death, nor put my life before Christ. No love of life induced me to flee, but fear for the frailty of this weak body. But I could have sought residence and lived safely in another city if faith had been cheap in my eyes and this life dear. So I made for the unknown mountains and the naked regions of desolation, and laid my neck in the sweet Lord's lap[34] so that He could witness me dying, or else enable me to obtain food. My confidence was not vain, as you see. The Almighty came and chose you as messenger to me and as bearer of His gifts. My son, carry out the command which enjoined on you this devoted task. Raise me on your shoulders, and bear me back to the fold we share."

329. Tireless Felix took pleasure in the task he had prayed for. He lifted his cherished burden like the light weight prescribed by Christ,[35] and bore it at such swift speed that he seemed to be borne rather than bearer. In truth Christ Himself bore the bearer, and God bestowed wings on feet already swift in their devotion. On that same night Felix unaided both surveyed all these tasks and performed them. Once bidden to break his bonds, he reinvigorated the bishop, brought him back restored, and

set him down safe beneath the roof of his house, which only one old lady tended. This meritorious fact too made Maximus rank high as confessor, that one old woman remained as the sum of his household and the extent of his wealth.[36]

341. Felix knocked on the door and awoke her. She was initially paralysed by the noise, and scarcely recognised the voice she knew. She opened the house and admitted her master, her voice and feet quivering, and fear shaking her aged frame. Felix said to her: "Take this trust for safekeeping, a trust which my associates, the stars of the night, and an angel's hands under Christ's guidance entrust to you through my mediation. In your faithful arms receive this jewel of the Lord, which you must restore to us undamaged when the time comes. The Lord will be your judge, as He now witnesses your taking him."[37]

350. Upon these words Maximus broke in and echoed[38] his Felix. "My son," he said, "you, too, must receive a gift in return. He who bade you attend me when I lay at death's door ordered me to give it to you when I was restored." Then he laid his holy right hand on the head of his beloved Felix, and sought for him all Christ's gifts, just as Isaac the revered patriarch blessed his son with the dew of heaven and the riches of the earth.[39] So Maximus blessed and enriched Felix before Christ with the words of a father and an apostle. He wreathed him with the glory of a garland that does not fade, and enriched him with the perennial wealth which even now we behold.

## POEM 16[1]

Season succeeds season, their span receding and returning. Each day expels its predecessor and itself then flees,
thus turning time's wheel.[2] All things pass away, but
the fame of the saints endures in Christ, who renews all
things but Himself abides.[3] So at last you return and dawn
on me, the day for which I longed the whole year through,
the day which renews the sweet festivities and my vows,
the day which demands of me my yearly gift,[4] when you
bring round the birthday in which thousands take joy,
the peoples of countless cities. On this day a particular joy
comes to me, for on it I must dedicate to my Felix the
approved gift of my serving tongue. To him my person
is surrendered and my mind consecrated in the Lord
Christ, and it is right that I should further hymn the saint
in yearly song, offering him the obeisance of my tongue.
So shall I tell of those deserving deeds, and the reasons for
them, which have gained him the meed of heaven's praise,
and immortality, and the fame of great distinction on
earth.

17. The work which preceded this[5] has already described for you the earlier activities of the martyr—his
provenance, family,[6] education, and finally the rank he
held[7] in the performance of sacred duties, when he preferred to serve the enduring Christ rather than to wander
on his father's paths through the trackless world. For his
father had spent his life serving Caesar before gaining his

95

discharge. I have also already mentioned the pains he endured in his foul prison. He faced these pains confessing his faith, and was ready to endure death, too; but God intervened before the swords, loosed and released him from his harsh chains, and summoned him to other deeds, so that bishop Maximus might earlier return to his holy church. Maximus was sick, gasping out his last in a deserted forest, where he had been driven in flight by the attacks of the enemy. Felix, as he was ordered, raised him on his own shoulders and set him down to rest in Maximus' own poor house.[8] When this service had been repaid by blessed words from that happy old man, he departed with the blessing and for a few days hid in silence beneath the roof of his own abode. Yet his mind was not silent as he importuned the Lord of heaven. He aimed his prayer, and with it reached beyond the stars. On the Lord's door he knocked for his deserving kinsman,[9] begging that peace come forth.

38. Meanwhile, the days flowed by, and peace seemed to return. Felix left his hiding place, put his confidence in the climate of the times which had at last turned fine,[10] and began joyfully to associate again with his brothers, and to entrust himself to the now peaceful city. Christ's sheep gave thanks for having regained their shepherd; Maximus at heaven's command reassured his flock, who were fearful at the recent storm. He guided them with his words and governed their troubled hearts, strengthening them in love of the faith. He taught them that what the world accounts bitter or sweet is of no account. He advised them not to yield to fears, and to expose their persons eagerly to fire or sword; and he added weight to his words through having suffered by his witness what he taught ought to be

suffered. He was a teacher to all both by word and by example.

52. The Evil One did not bear with this for long. His black locks stood on end, and his neck was infused with the poison of madness. He directed his venom into wicked hearts so that Felix's kindness stung their black minds. He pierced them with the goad, and the frenzy of the viper's hatred blazed in their wicked minds. Impious anger first sought a home; an unholy love for sin burned in all. Wickedness thirsted for Felix, but he happened to be away from home, and was safe in the middle of the city surrounded as usual by friends as close as brothers, planting words of devotion in the ears of his believing flock. Those who were searching him out now appeared with swords drawn,[11] when suddenly either the hearts of the foe or the features of Felix were transformed. In their madness they did not recognise the man they knew, and they inquired after Felix. When they beheld Felix, they did not behold him. It was he, yet it was not he. Though close to them, he was far away. To his fellow citizens he was at once a stranger and a familiar; he was Felix to the believers, but some other to the enemy, for faith varied his countenance. He himself recognised the stratagem afforded by Christ's help, and smilingly addressed the inquisitors: "I do not know the Felix you are looking for."

72. Thereupon they continued past him, while Felix left the street, and the Lord mocked at the baying hounds which had been beguiled. They had not gone far, asking everyone where Felix was, when some man jeered at them and turned informer. Unaware of the true reason, he thought they were crazed with madness, since they had not observed Felix before their eyes, though they had

spoken to him face-to-face. Shattered by this unprecedented guile, and more crazed still, they then returned and hastened in pursuit of Felix. They were upon him, but he was warned by the din preceding them through the city, and by the universal shouting of the bewildered crowd. He avoided the impending blows by doubling over his tracks. Taking side roads, he removed himself far from the centre of the town, and gained a place which chanced to offer itself as a refuge in his fear. He was out of the teeming city, yet not far from his foul pursuers. Withdrawn from the gaze of his assailants who were almost before his eyes, he somehow or other avoided their hostile swords. Yet he was bound to be captured, because his refuge had no bolt as barrier to withstand the wicked men he sought to repel. There was no door, and there was free access to a public square from the building, which was precariously supported by a section of tumbledown wall.

95. But God's hand interposed itself between the saint and his enemies, and protected that place with a marvellous rampart. This was no barrier consisting of a heap of stones or iron doors, the means by which we mere men shut off abodes. A grimy wall suddenly took shape from the rubble, and a spider obeyed the command to spin a trembling web. With its quivering threads it blocked that hazardous opening, giving the impression of a dirty, deserted ruin.

103. When this scene confronted the menacing pursuers, they drew back in surprise, stood where they were, and said to one another: "It is surely crazy to try to enter, or to imagine that any man got in where the smallest of insects had placed his seal. Can tiny flies break through a net like this? So can we be so foolish as to imagine that a man got through the barrier without breaking the thin

texture with his large frame? That informer a moment ago was a more appropriate victim for our hands. With his treacherous guile he has craftily directed us to this desolate place. He lied when he said that Felix was hiding in this squalid spot, for he has moved off elsewhere. That informer sought to divert our weapons from Felix's person by such evil guile, for he is a friend of the fugitive. So let us leave this place. If we stay any longer here we will be a laughingstock for the mob. Our mistake will be construed as lunacy for we hastened here to search for a man's lair, where the untrodden earth reveals that no entry is possible over the crumbling wall or through the barrier of the spider's web."

120. At once they hastened fast and furious in different directions. But as the song in Scripture tells, Christ God from the citadel of heaven mocked their mad threats, and enfolded His Felix in His sacred wings.[12] The saint, safe in the arms of the Lord, with his helmet and his shield of faith, triumphantly broke the shining missiles, and as confessor he wielded in his mouth the sword of the Word. His hands were armed with holiness, and teeming with God he covered his chaste breast with the breastplate of notable merit.[13]

129. O wisdom of God, rich in many ways, always routing the strong things of the world through the agency of the weak![14] Cities can scarcely protect their inhabitants with high walls; quite often an enemy crushes those who rely on strong fortifications, and their cities' destruction exposes them to death. But here a mere spider protected the saint from armed men when God defended him. The enemy halted, repulsed by a slender web. The strength of iron yielded to unsubstantial thread. Men's salvation is

useless, and my strength lends me no strength if I lack the strength of God. What good was the boundless vigour of giants? Or the kings of Egypt? Or mighty Jericho?[15] Their own inflated glory was the cause of death for all of them, and God's power broke them not by the strength of heroes but by that of the weak. The famed giant died like a dog, felled by a shepherd-boy's sling. The din of trumpets shook down the famous city. The renowned and haughty king lay dead on the sand of the shore,[16] and the riches of the kingdom were equated with his naked corpse. So wherever Christ is with us, a web is a wall; for the person without Christ, a wall will become a web.

149. When the crowds had dispersed and silence had fallen, and the depth of night afforded the safety of darkness for secret flight, Felix emerged and changed his hiding-place, singing to the Lord: "If I walk in the midst of the shadow of night, I shall not fear evils, for Your right hand is with me. I shall pass through hell without being deprived of light."[17] So under God's guidance he occupied in a deserted area the narrow chamber of a rain-tank sited among tiny dwellings. The old cistern with its high cover was dry. Close by a woman consecrated to God dwelt in an adjoining hut. Though she did not know the confessor was in hiding, she gave food to Felix as though she were Christ's accomplice.

161. This is a wondrous tale I shall tell of the Lord's stratagem in feeding His charge through the ministrations of a woman unaware of him. She became possessed in mind by God's plan, and diligently brought bread or other staple foodstuffs, which she had cooked for herself, to the place where Felix lay under cover but under God's eye. But even when she went there, she did not know he was

within; and when she had left, she did not remember entering. When she had busily brought in the food she had prepared, and even though she served with her own hands the saint she had to feed, she was unaware of her great service, and she could not be aware in her mind of what she did not of her own volition but through Christ's power. She would enter, and leave the food in front of his hiding-place at the mouth of the cistern built there. She believed she had left it at home, and so she invariably went away having remembered to leave the food and then forgetting she had left it.

177. Woman blest by God, like one of the birds which of old fed the prophet who retired from the world,[18] you, too, fed a martyr in his secret abode like the bird that obeyed the Lord. You did not know the saint, but you were aware of the service you gave, and so you will recognise with joy your achievement, and the one you served, when Christ God Himself bestows the crown of righteousness on you on behalf of His confessor. Then before Christ up in the judgment-seat, Felix himself will recount to you the meals you served, which God passed over for the sweet enjoyment of His consecrated martyr. It was the same in olden days, when the prophet passed the food cooked for the reapers to the prophet who hungered among the raging monsters; an angel's hand supported Habacuc through the void.[19] The fierceness of the beasts was no longer fierce, because their prey repressed the savage lions, and holy fasting their greedy jaws.[20]

192. They tell that he lived six whole months continuously concealed in that dark, constricting chamber without intercourse among men. He needed no human help because he was ever rich in Christ's consolation.

Christ is said during that time to have come often, having deemed him worthy of His conversation, to have fed him frequently with His own hand, and to have given him drink from heaven consisting not of rain, which the clouds pour on all indiscriminately, but of dew which grace poured down from the upper air separately on Felix alone. For at that time, as often happens, the scorching summer with its excessive sunshine had dried up even the well which had provided him with limited water in hiding. But so that physical thirst should not afflict him who in his thirst for Christ was enduring this punishment of bodily suffering as well, a cloud descended from the clear sky, and gathered into a wispy ball. Through the narrow opening of the cistern it poured its sweet liquid into the mouth of the thirsting Felix as though it were squeezed by hand; so with the milky juice of the heavenly fleece[21] it refreshed the saint who was to be called to heaven. Why should we wonder that Christ now feeds him, cleansed of earthly stain, when the Holy Spirit fed him when still in the flesh, and his bread was the Word, God Himself, the Bread of the heavenly dwellers on which every angel feeds?

215. This era passed, and peace was restored to sheathe men's swords. God advised Felix to leave his hiding-place. He had for long trained his ears to find peace from the cries of the world, blotting out human affairs from his consciousness. When he emerged afresh to the light of day, amid his now despairing flock, appearing in his native city as though from the dead, many hesitated to acknowledge him, and first enquired: "Can it really be you? Are you the great and blessed Felix returned to us after all this time? Where have you come from? Are you a gift of

heaven? Have you returned to earth from Paradise to re-
visit our homes?" Felix confirmed their belief that he was
with them in the flesh, that his life had been saved by God.
All showed joy, and he was hymned by all the people with
the praises he deserved.

229. Maximus the bishop had now ended his long life,
and the flock needed the guidance of a shepherd. The
name which all the fold bleated[22] was that of Felix, who
was crowned for Christ with the glory of confessor, and
whose tongue and manner of life in harmony with his
teaching guaranteed a teacher who would bring salvation.
But to ensure that here, too, he won the crown of righteousness, he kept his lofty distinction hidden in the silence
of his heart. He did not presume to advance himself, on
the grounds that he was unworthy of the honour, and he
asserted that the office was owed rather to the aged Quintus, because he had first attained that distinguished rank
as priest which they shared. The dividing period was one
of seven days.

240. So Felix continued as priest, serving bishop Quintus as well. He advanced in merit because he did not wish
to advance in position. Quintus listened to him in all matters as though he himself was the junior, and he spoke
with Felix's tongue. Quintus governed his flock in office,
but Felix by his teaching. Abundant grace strengthened
Felix, Christ's saint, in other virtues. The battles he endured in time of peace were no less formidable than those
he had waged as confessor with his powerful arms. In grim
times he had despised health of body, and likewise in time
of untroubled peace he spurned riches and positions.[23] He
did not relax in maintaining his merit, but grew more careful, so that he might protect life's blessings which he had

won after overcoming death's dangers. He feared rocks in calm seas.

254. We have mentioned how he despised death and ambition. Now you must hear of the confessor's additional crown. He conquered greed, for as the wealthy heir to his father's riches he had come into the possession of many estates and houses. As a confessor he had been stripped of property, but with the reinstatement of peace he could have demanded his rightful possessions had he so decreed. But he preferred to heed the words of the teacher Paul: "All things are lawful, but not all things are helpful."[24] He put the useful before the permissible, and was averse to reclaiming his lost farms as though he would catch from them the infection of worldly sickness. There were many who reproached him for this, above all Archelais, a woman of ancient name[25] whose faith was as holy as her name was famed; she was a widow of large wealth who revered holy Felix with faithful devotion, and was in turn dear to him. This lady cultivated him with the reverence he deserved. According to the story, she used the right of friendship to lay claim to his intimate affection, and kept wearying his devoted heart with repeated complaints. Why did he refuse the return of property due and available to him? Once he had got it back with the high return from interest, he could distribute it to the poor.

274. Moreover, she regularly offered numerous gifts from her own property. But Felix was totally satisfied in his devoted mind, and laughed in his tranquil heart at her womanly anxiety. He was well aware of those heavenly possessions which he had as compensation for earthly ones. Fortified by these, he made this reply to the pressures of dear friends: "Are you urging me to go back to earthly

possessions, and to lose immortal ones? It is better to have salvation without wealth than riches without life. If I am rich, I shall be without God, whereas in poverty I shall possess Christ. Christ's grace will enrich those who are poor in wealth."

284. Continuing to live in this spirit, he had a modest three acres, not his own property, but leased by him as a tenant. As the holder of this small garden, he cultivated it himself, without a labourer. Rich in his narrow plot, he bestowed even the produce of this upon the Lord, always sharing his crop of vegetables with the poor, and with the poor his table. For him, possession for a single day fulfilled his aspiration. A single garment covered him, and often he had scarcely one; if he possessed two, he warmed a naked man with the better one. Often he swapped new garments for wretched rags, and some poor soul was transformed, shining in Felix's clothes instead of his own black ones. Felix on the other hand was grimy in the beggar's garb, unkempt in body but groomed within. This was the devoted life he lived for God, and then, advanced in meritorious life as in years, he ended his earthly span in the fullness of days; but the span of his holy life was not ended, but rather transformed.[26]

# POEM 17[1]

Are you departing already, and leaving us in haste? Yet it is only distance that you put between us, for we shall be with you eternally in fusion of minds. Do you leave already at the distant call of the land in which you dwell? Yet you also linger here, holy Nicetas, for though you have set out we keep you in our hearts. As you go, be mindful of us, and though you leave, remain with us in spirit. You are implanted in our hearts, so you in turn must take and bear off with you those whom you cherish within.

13. How happy that land and those peoples whom you will now approach as you leave us! It is Christ that will visit them, journeying on your feet and with your countenance. You will reach the distant Dacians of the north, you will be there for both Epiruses[2] to see you, and you will force your way through Aegean waters to Thessalonica.[3]

21. But now your route will take you first through Apulian regions, an extensive journey over long plains, where fleeces treated with Canusian dye blaze forth their crimson.[4] But when it extends a little farther, I pray that Christ will give you kindly seas, and that a light, cloudless breeze will blow from dry Calabria. Just as the bitter[5] waters grew sweet and lost their harsh juices through the mystery of the cross when the hands of the ancient prophet inserted the wood,[6] so may the weather for you now restrain its fierceness, and the sky disperse its heavi-

ness with light, bright air, gently breathing its clear breath into health-giving breezes. Normally it is oppressive with marshy fumes, and bearing the foul smell of snakes it swells our bodies with its mist-laden wind, and exposes them to diseases. May the Lord who has dominion over creation bid it be dissipated or transformed, and may He now provide for His own bishop kindly and health-bearing breezes.

45. Just as once Egypt declined, and was buried in the darkness of thick night, yet where the race sacred to the living God dwelt there was light for the world[7] (and this is now proved to be symbolic of the entire world, because that devoted part of mankind whose faith is pure gleams before Christ, whilst the rest are buried in the darkness of error), so may the Lord favour all the activities of my Nicetas, to whatever shore he betakes himself driven by the wind, until he reaches his native city joyful in the fulfillment of his desire.

57. Nicetas, happily proceed on your return voyage, for your successful journey is accompanied by Christ, whom your people have long been importuning day and night for your return to them. They are like the land thirsting for rain to refresh the seeds, like young calves seeking their mothers when denied their milk. So though we have not had our fill, we are forced to yield to the just entreaties of your peoples rightly demanding back their father, and our prayer is defeated by theirs. Because our hope of keeping you is now snatched away, our love presses us to promote your plan of action. Though we loathe the roads that bear you off, we love as well as loathe them. We hate them for dragging you away, yet love them for having brought your person from afar for us to see.

Now, united with you in surpassing love, we pray that these roads may extend without hardship for you as the name of the highest Christ precedes you on land and sea. May He convert your entire journey into level plains, bring low the lofty mountains, fill in the hollow valleys, smooth out the rough places, and bridge the chasms.[8] As you ride through Hydruntum and Lupiae,[9] virgin bands of both brothers and sisters will surround you, hymning the Lord with one voice. Who could give me the wings of a dove[10] to take my place speedily among those bands who follow your lead and strike the stars with their hymns of Christ our God? Yet though we are constrained by the sluggish bonds of our feeble bodies, in our minds we fly out behind you, and with you sing hymns to the Lord. Since we are bound inwardly to the thoughts you have, even when you sing and pray, our prayers and voices too issue forth with yours.

101. Then when sea succeeds land, the Adriatic gulf will be obediently smooth, the waves will prostrate themselves and the sails will bulge with a gentle westerly wind. You will glide over a calm sea; your ship will be equipped with the cross as sailyard,[11] the prescription for salvation, and thus you will proceed victorious, safe from waters and southerly winds. The sailors will joyfully sing their usual rowing-songs, but adapt the melodies to make them hymns.[12] With their devoted voices they will draw breezes on to the sea to accompany them. The tongue of Nicetas sounding forth like a trumpet will outsing all of them in hymning Christ, and David the perennial harpist will sing over the whole sea.[13] The whales will tremble as they hear "Amen," and the sea-monsters will joyfully swim from afar with playful motions to the bishop who sings

to the Lord. Lively dolphins will frolic on every side, their mouths open, and, mute beasts though they are, they will express their joy in imitation of human tongues. For what creature shows no wisdom or life for God, by whose word all created things were begotten? So the depths of the sea know the praises of God, and though dumb cry them out. Our witness is the beast of the ancient prophet, which was roused from the deep at the nod of the Lord to receive Jonas plunged into the sea, and then to deliver him up after swallowing him.[14] But now the beast attending on our prophet will merely devour devoted songs with his ears; feeding on songs, it will stuff its unfed belly with them.

136. Wherever you extend your journey, over water, over land, and even among enemies, you will proceed armed with the helmet of salvation, and with Christ as your head.[15] May Raphael be sent to fly near you; as once the angel attended Tobias to the Medes,[16] so may he accompany Nicetas as far as the Dacians. May the Guide who once led the fleeing Jacob to safety from the presence of his arrogant brother, likewise guide Nicetas His servant, for he similarly is a fugitive. What the patriarch did once, Nicetas does continually, fleeing from the world towards the walls of high heaven. The ladder which Jacob saw the angels alternately ascending and descending[17] Nicetas strives to mount as his life overtops the clouds. He hastens by the ladder of the cross to the stars, where God gleams over the earth from His shimmering throne, and witnesses the diverse toils and wars of the mind. And just as Jacob was well called Israel because he saw the highest Creator in the depth of his heart, so you, Nicetas, are well named as conqueror of your body.[18] So my conqueror proves

himself a true Israelite without deceit, for he sees Christ God by the light of stable faith.

169. May our God and our Way ever be our Companion here, and our Guide. May His Word be a light to our paths and a lamp for our feet, so that by this torch of true light[19] we may be led through the blind shallows of the dark world till we can attain the desired harbour of salvation. This is what we are making for through the billowing sea as we float on the tide of wandering purpose, sailing in the frail bark of our earthly bodies. But the tiller of the cross now guides this bark within us, and we hoist devoted sails within our hearts, and Christ makes us exultant with a favouring breeze.[20] So may He likewise attend you now as guide on the path on which you now hasten to return, Nicetas, and set you safely back on your ancestral threshold.

189. But when you have crossed the sea there remain further difficult paths on land to reach those blessed shores over which you have been set as bishop. You will journey through the territory of Philippi in Macedonia and through the city of Tomi; you will be a visitor from Troy to the Scupi who border on your land.[21] With what cries of joy will that land now ring, when you teach those arctic peoples to bend their fierce necks to the gentle Christ! Where the north wind binds the rivers with thick frost in Rhiphaean lands,[22] you thaw minds stiff with ice by your heavenly fire. For the Bessians,[23] whose minds are harder than their lands, who indeed are harder than their own snow, have now become sheep, and you lead them as they flock to the hall of peace. Those necks which they always refused to bow to slavery, since they were always unsubdued in war, they now rejoice to bend in submission

to the yoke of the true Lord. Now the Bessians are richer, and delight in the reward of toil. The gold which they previously sought from the earth with their hands they now gather with their minds from heaven.[24]

217. What a change and happy transformation in the world! Those mountains once trackless and bloodstained now protect brigands turned monks, pupils of peace. The land once drenched in blood is now the land of life; the violence of brigands is turned devotedly towards heaven, and Christ smiles on the plundering which lays hold of heaven's kingdom.[25] Where once existed the rule of beasts, there is now the vigorous life of angels. The just man now lives his hidden life in the caves where the brigand dwelt. That plunderer of old is become the plunder of holy men, and the murderer groans because the losses he inflicted are reversed, for Christ despoils him, and he is rightly stripped of the weapons of sinning. With the fall of Satan the envious Cain perishes in turn, and Abel reborn[26] feeds the lambs redeemed at the cost of flowing blood.

237. Well done, Nicetas, goodly servant[27] of Christ, who permits you to transform stones into stars and to build consecrated temples on rocks that live.[28] You tread trackless glades and deserted ranges in your search for the way. You prevail over the barren woodland of unkempt minds, and you transform it into fertile fields. The whole region of the north calls you father. The Scythians become gentle at your words; at war with each other, they abandon their aggressive spirit under your schooling. The Getae run to you, as do also the Dacians, both those who dwell in the hinterland and the cap-wearers living on the bank of the Danube, rich in numbers of cattle.[29]

253. Your work is the creation of calves from wolves,

and the feeding with hay of lion and ox yoked together, and the opening of dens of vipers to children without harm. For you persuade wild beasts to join with domesticated animals and to abandon their fierce ways when you flood men's wild minds with your civilising discourse. In this mute region of the world, the barbarians through your schooling learn to make Christ's name resound from Roman hearts, and to live in purity and tranquil peace. So the wolf lies tamed in your sheepfold, the calf eats in harmony with the lion, the child plays in those grim caves from which the snake has been driven. You transform talented gold-gatherers into gold, and in your treatment of them you imitate what they do, for from them you dig out living gold, using the Word as spade. By storing up this wealth for the eternal Lord, and by redoubling your consecrated talent with these gains, you will be told: "Enter gladly into the joys of the eternal Lord."[30]

277. I pray that when your kindly home, thronged with its holy crowd of brothers, receives you into its choir, you will out of the love of your dear heart let me join them; for thanks be to God for having bound me to you with the hidden bonds of so deep a love that no power can break this inner link. So I embrace and cling to your dear heart continually with the bond of faith, and wherever you go I shall accompany and attend you in mind. The love of Christ kindly poured down from heaven unites you within to my heart, so that even though your face is far removed from me I am not far from you or deprived of you.[31] No lapse of time, no collapse, no migration to another continent, not even death will tear me from you, for when the body's life dies, the life of love will

live on. For as long as I shall dwell in these heavy limbs, I shall ever revere you with mindful heart.[32]

299. You must pray that I may be with you for all time. Your virtue which has cost so much will deservedly place you high upon a lofty peak, and will set you in the city of the living amongst the great towers there;[33] whereas I, as distant from you in position as in merit, far removed in my lowly station from the advocates on high, will look up to you in the distance as you consort with the throngs of saints. Will someone allow me on that day to stand in the shadow of your side, so that a breeze from your place of rest may cool the fire which oppresses me? I beg you to be especially mindful of me on that day. As you recline in the bosom of your holy father, quench the fire that rages round me with water from your finger.[34]

317. Blessed Nicetas, you must go now, yet as you leave, continue to return to me in spirit. Remain with me even though you have reached your native city. God did not appoint you to be master of a single people, nor citizen of a single land. See, our country adopts you for its own. Make your devotion equal and divide your affections. Remain as a citizen in both countries, granting your love to us and your presence to your compatriots. Perhaps this should be accounted your greater fatherland, for here you live in the dwellings of men's hearts not made with hands,[35] and dwell in the living city of men.

333. You are both the bishop and the deserving guest of the kindly Christ, for in your association with the hearts of Christians you are resident in the Master's shrine. Receive my farewell now. Keep me in mind forever. Continue your goodly course, good man that you are, to the end, and win the crown that is reserved for the just.[36]

# POEM 18[1]

I have imposed on myself by a vow of devotion the custom of celebrating this day every year by putting my eloquence to work. This custom demands that I sing of Felix in verses as a yearly tribute from my lips. I must set my joy to music in the song I have promised, and sing of the great merits of my dear patron, for he sought the heights through the narrows and along the hard path where few can make their way, and so he reached the citadel of heaven.

8. Brethren, I beg you, associate yourselves with my verses, applaud, and pour out your hearts with chaste abandon. Holy joy and pure songs befit men of faith.[2] For what man who loves and fears Christ has the right not to rejoice on this day, and to avoid fulfilling his vow with all resources of brain and tongue and wealth, when even the weather with its festive brightness reflects the joy of Christ's servants in heaven? Observe how the created world's gladness at the glory of today shines forth with holy signs.[3] A joyful whiteness covers everything. The rain falls in dry form from fluffy[4] clouds, and the earth is cloaked with a snowy garment. The earth thus covered with snow (its soil and woods, mountains and hills adorned with it)[5] bears witness to the snow-white distinctions accorded the ancient saint. These signs demonstrate that Felix is enjoying the light and peace of angels, and is

famed in the tranquil abode of the saints, from where
snowy fleeces glide down from the silent sky.

25. Christ, God of Felix, come near. Word-God, grant
me now words. Wisdom, give me clarity of mind. Eloquent ability to sing Your praises lies not within man's
resources, for Your saints are Your glory. I grant that
others may outdo me with the costliness of their service in
the precious gifts they bring, when they provide fine curtains, made of gleaming white linen or of material coloured
with bright shapes, for covering the doorways. Let some
polish their smooth inscriptions on pliant silver, and cover
the holy portals with the metal they affix there. Others
may kindle light with coloured candles, and attach lamps
with many wicks to the vaulted ceilings, so that the hanging torches cast to and fro their flickering flames. Others
still can eagerly pour spikenard on the martyr's burial
place, and then withdraw the healing unguents from the
hallowed tomb.[6] I give place also before many richer in
worthless gold, whose pockets laden with money are
emptied to give the poor their fill, who dispense their rich
store with generous hand, and who are present to offer
their souls in marriage to the Lord with diverse dowries,
one in heart if varying in their wealth.

44. All these wth equal alacrity offer dishes rich in
food, or candles, or curtains, or lamps—gifts generous but
mute; whereas I, stripped of wealth, pay my debt from
my own resources, and offer service with the gift of my
tongue. Though I am a worthless victim, I bestow my own
person on my own behalf. But I shall not fear rejection,
for the offering of a poor man's allegiance is not tawdry
in the eyes of Christ, who was delighted to receive the two
coppers which were the wealth of the holy widow, and

praised them.[7] At that time, too, the wealthy were bringing many gifts to God, and filled the temple treasury with large sums. But Christ observed them, and with His insight into the hearts of those offering gifts, He gave the prize to the widow, for she had contributed to the holy chest the substance of her day's sustenance, the two pennies which were her wealth, with no care for her bodily needs. This was why she deserved before the day of judgment to obtain praise for her deed from the very lips of the Judge who is to come, and to be ranked before those whose gold she had vanquished with her penny. That old woman's gift showed poverty, but her faithful heart generosity.

62. Therefore, kind brethren, whom I for my part esteem and who for your part show indulgence[8] to me, listen to me with kindly mind, lending a willing ear not to the speaker but to my subject. My tale will be worthy both of contempt and of wonder—of contempt for my intelligence, but of wonder because of the merits of blessed Felix, which one cannot tell without praising Christ. For all that we admire in Felix comes from Christ, who is the source of strength for holy men, and of life for those who are buried.

70. In previous works[9] I have sung of his native land, his race, and his deeds, and have recounted his life from the very beginning to the time he brought it to its final close and, leaving his corpse in the earth which he quitted, advanced to take his place in the eternal kingdom which he deserved. But the tombs which conceal the limbs of holy men do not likewise conceal their merits, so the life of the soul which survives the body's death perceives the fruits which the body sought. After the demise of the

body, the soul is not dead, but it observes with joy the good fruit, and with pain the evil fruit; and these it will harvest in the time to come, when it is recalled to its body, and is inseparable from the body it has rejoined in the harbour they share.

82. My subject, then, is lengthy. He who has the theme of Felix's achievements accessible to his pen will find his words extending as long as his life, provided that his fund of eloquence can match the range of Felix's deeds and merits. Ever since this day of his birth first laid Felix to blessed rest, and consigned his flesh to earth but his soul to heaven, almost every day dawns on some work of God's confessor. Christ proves him alive even without his body, to show that there is greater power surviving in dead saints than in wicked men alive. You observe the tomb which conceals our martyr's holy bones, and his speechless corpse preserved by a marble covering. To human eyes, to our bodily sight, there is no living person here. The limbs of the buried man lie hidden, the flesh is at rest in peaceful death, buried and awaiting with no idle hope the renewal of life.[10] Why, then, does such great awe encompass this threshold? And who compels such crowds of people here? What power constrains evil spirits, seizes them against their will, forces them vainly protesting with rebellious cries to the tomb of the martyr, and plants them on this holy threshold, where they are almost immovable?

102. Now at last I look back to that day. How sad it was on the abandoned earth, but how glad in heaven when Christ adopted the soul that was His friend, and drew it forth from that pure mouth![11] He brought adornment to heaven, but did not rob the earth of its pledge of love. The dwellers in heaven enjoy the mind of Felix, while we

benefit from his body. The breath of his powerful soul
was alive in heaven, but on earth his deserving merit still
lived. But it is pleasant to set down here all the glory which
Nola bestowed on his kindly body. The city which was
vowed to him had lost one who was her priest in the
liturgy and her father in years, but she was to have him
as her devoted patron in heaven, so that she could console
her love with hope. Thus she hastened to do homage,
thronged as she was with mingled crowds, pouring out
her faithful folk. Grief and devotion then united in all
their hearts; faith and devotion interjoined rejoiced even
as they grieved. Though she believed that Felix had been
summoned by Christ and exalted beyond the skies, yet
she grieved that she was abandoned by so great a teacher.
They seized the sole consolation of their love remaining
to them in the presence of the saint's corpse and his last
remains, once the funeral bier had been laid on its burial
site; the people were possessed with devotion, and in dense
crowds vied in garlanding the limbs set there. A holy
battle of devotion was fought amongst those who cherished
him. He who got the better of his neighbour struggled
to approach nearer to the remains, and took pleasure in
touching the body with his hand. A single glimpse was not
enough; they delighted in lingering on,[12] and implanting
their eyes, and where possible their kisses, on the laid-out
corpse. The people in harmony sang to Christ deserved
praises, and embarked upon the sacred honour owed to
Felix's coffin.

131. In the open country, well away from the city walls
and houses, the extending plain was benign with luxuriant
growth, and the district was more abundantly fertile, as
if the earth already knew beforehand of the tomb which

would be honoured forever by the worshipping world. It rejoiced that it was being blessed by the saint's body, and it bedecked itself attractively with the garb of spring, and bestrewed itself with scented grass to be worthier of receiving the martyr in burial.[13]

138. Meanwhile Felix was mounting the heights in smooth flight. Removed from his holy body, he was met by a joyful crowd of saints who escorted him through the clouds of heaven. Then bands of angels, their columns representing the seven tiers of heaven,[14] met him as he sped in heavenly triumph to the presence of the King, the person of the highest Father. Then they adorned his saintly head with a snow-white crown, but the Father conferred an additional rose-coloured one, since Christ proclaimed him worthy of it, and added to his snowy garment a gown of purple. The two forms of adornment signalled his deserving deeds. He obtained the crown of shining white because he passed to heaven in peaceful death, but though he died as confessor he equally deserved the purple accorded to a slain martyr. Thus he possesses the reward of one who suffered, because he showed willing virtue, yet he is not deprived of the distinction and adornment accorded to peaceful death, because he did not die in battle.

154. So the appropriate acts were performed, and they enclosed the saint's body in a tomb. But the divinely implanted grace in the saint's limbs could not die and be buried with the flesh. There and then a light shone forth from the bones laid to rest, and from that time to the present day it has never grudged giving the proofs of the saint's efficacious merit with its resources of healing. This light will gleam for all the days the world exists, and will

guard forever the saint's ashes. It is the proof that the dead martyr lives. It brings Christ's blessings to the tomb of Felix, and diffuses to all lands far and wide the wondrous fame of Felix. It lends nobility to the one town which was before all others esteemed worthy of so great a guest; and the grace of Christ through Felix's merit has spread Nola's fame so widely that the city, as you see, is enlarged by new citizens, and also by buildings in this place where initially there was a poor mound. That mound had been raised with difficulty in the harsh days, when religion was a crime and the profane world uttered its threats, by the Lord's people who trembled amidst fire and sword, as that former generation has related to their descendants of a later age. They had enclosed this great light under a tiny roof; a mere corner, sacred though it was, was once the tenant of so great a trust. But it was aware of the hidden light, and like a spring has welled forth with splendid shrines. It remains inset like a jewel amongst the buildings, dividing the large expanse surrounding the sacred sepulchre between five basilicas,[15] the roofs of which can be seen afar off, giving to the eye the appearance of a large city.

181. But these lofty structures, huge though they are, are swamped by the crowds. With the growth of faith Christ's grace overflows, and grants them the living Felix as a healing gift. Felix lives on after his body's span, a saint presiding over his own bones; and those bones of the saint's body are not choked with the dust of death, but endowed with a hidden seed of eternal life, so that from the tomb they breathe out the life-giving fragrance of his triumphant soul, by which efficacious healing is granted to the sick who pray for it.

190. One can divine the abundance of strength and glory which will attend those who rise again, since such grace as this invests men who are buried. What splendid beauty will shine from resurrected bodies, when a light like this gleams in these dark ashes! What benefits will saints' crowns be able to afford us lowliest of creatures, when even their ashes bring boons to living men? It is pleasing frequently to observe the marvellous sight of people greeting Felix in different ways, and demanding their individual favours in prayer. You can also see farmers from the fields not only carrying their children in fatherly arms, but often leading sick cattle after them, boldly entrusting them to the saint as if they could see him; and then in their confidence that a cure has been granted to their prayers, they rejoice in the God they have experienced, and believe their animals now cured. And indeed frequently their beasts are speedily healed on the very threshold, and they lead them back now frisky to their dwellings. But because it would be lengthy and superfluous to recount all these miracles that Felix performs by Christ's power, I shall relate one astonishing deed out of many. There are countless others like it, but you can gauge from this one the others which the same power achieved, though they differ in their circumstances.[16]

210. Show generous hearts, I beg you. The harm I inflict on you is slight in my recounting a great deed in a few inconsiderable verses. Remember the widow whom I mentioned in the first part of my discourse. God judged her by the worth of her heart, not by her gift, and preferred her before those who sent large sums, because she gave her all. So too you must bear with me, for my theme is great though the telling is mean. Indeed, my

words vie with the widow's mite, which though cheap became valuable through her devotion of pure gold.

219. There was a poor plebeian countryman who used to relieve his oppressive poverty by the payment he got from his two yoked oxen. At one time he would hitch them to a cart to carry some load on an agreed journey, and at another he would get a meagre return as payment for their work by hiring them out to others for ploughing. The yoked pair was the poor man's hope in trouble, and the sum of his possessions. His children and his own person were no dearer to him than they; indeed, he reared them as if they were children, and he devoted no less care to giving his oxen their fill than to bringing up his darling sons. In fact, he fed his children more sparingly than the dear cattle. He did not feed his beasts on cheap hay or withered chaff, but on the grain he denied to himself and to his children, and he kept them in a sunny shelter while he himself shivered as well as fasted. His own life was one of poverty, but he had riches in the cattle whose fruitful toil satisfied his needs.

234. These, then, were the cherished consolation of his life. But one night when buried in unusually heavy slumber the wretched man lost them, for they were driven off and stolen by a stealthy robber. When daylight came, he got up to yoke them as usual, but the unhappy man vainly searched for them first in their empty stalls, and then outside in the fields he knew so well. But growing weary with vain wandering to and fro, once he saw no marks which established their tracks and his hopes died in the vain search, he at once abandoned human resource. At God's inspiration he directed the unhappy thoughts of a broken heart towards heaven with abundance of devotion. Then

faith gave him confidence, and he took fresh heart. He
entertained hope that his prayer would be answered, so at
full speed he made for the holy abode of Felix. Weeping
profusely as he set foot in the sacred shrine, he prostrated
himself at the doors, planted kisses on the doorposts,[17] and
watered the entire floor with tears as he lay on the ground
before the holy threshold. From Saint Felix he demanded
the return of his oxen stolen by cunning in the night, as
though the saint were their guardian, and rebuked him,
mingling entreaty with complaints.

254. "Felix, God's holy one, support of those in need,
perpetual source of happiness for the wretched and of
wealth for the poor, God has appointed you as an arbour
for the weary, a relief for the downtrodden, and a cure for
the wounded hearts of those who grieve. This is why
poverty puts trust in your fatherly arms, and leans its
head and reclines on you.[18]

260. "Saint Felix, you have always had pity on my
hardships, but now you have forgotten me. Why, pray,
or for what purpose[19] do you abandon me in my nakedness? I have lost the cherished oxen which were your gift,
which on my knees I would often entrust to you, and
which your nursing preserved and fed for me with unbroken kindness. Your protection kept them safe, and
your generous hand made them fat. But last night deprived me of them, wretch that I am. What can I do now?
What steps can I take, hoodwinked in this way? Whom
can I accuse? Or should I rather complain about you, and
accuse my advocate of forgetting me? It was you who
allowed such heavy sleep to creep over my slumbering
body that I did not hear the burglars breaking my bars.
You did not inspire fear to break their hard hearts, or

shine a light through the darkness on their theft, or give any signal to ensure their detection as they fled. Where now shall I take my hasty, madly scurrying steps? Every course I take lies in blinding darkness. Even my own abode now seems closed to me, for there, deprived of the company of my stolen wards, I have nothing that I wish to have. There is no pleasure which is not pointless, which provides consolation for my eyes and toiling body, which delights me now that I am robbed of the sight and enjoyment of my property. Where should I now look for them in my pitiable state? Where and when will I find the likes of them, or how will I buy such replacements if I find them, when my oxen were the sole wealth of my contented poverty? So give them back to me, for I desire no others.

285. "I shall look for them nowhere else, since they are my due here. This threshold must restore them to me, where I put you under obligation and cling to you in my entreaties. Why or where should I seek out thieves unknown to me? You my debtor are here; I will constrain you, the guardian of the oxen, as one of the thieves. You, saint, are guilty in my eyes, for you are in league with them. I have you fast. You know where they are, for by Christ's light you see and lay hands on all things, even those hidden and far removed, for God, who holds everything, encloses them. So whatever the lair of those robbers in hiding, they are not concealed from you, and cannot escape you, for even one hand can contain them.[20] The one God is everywhere; Christ's right hand favours the godly, but takes vengeance on the wicked.

298. "Therefore, restore to me my oxen. Restore them, and lay hands on the thief. But I do not want the guilty

men. Let them go free. I know your habit well, dear saint. You cannot requite evil deeds; you prefer rather to correct evil men by pardoning them than to destroy them with punishment. Let us accordingly make a compact. Share out between us what is mine and what is yours. Let my interest remain undamaged through your help, and like- wise mercy can claim your share, so that your judgment can balance the scales equally. You can acquit the guilty, but return to me the oxen. There, you have the bargain. You have now no pretext for delaying your servant here. Make haste to deliver me from this great worry. It is my firm resolve not to go anywhere, not to be torn from this portal, until you lend aid. If you do not hurry, I shall renounce life on this threshold. You will not find me here if you bring them back and restore them too late."

313. As he made these entreaties with plaintive voice but with the mind of faith, praying all day without cease, the martyr listened and was pleased with his unflattering suppliant. In company with the Lord he joked and laughed at the rebukes he received. Stirred by the faith of the suppliant rather than by the outspokenness of his resent- ment, he hastened to lend aid. The delay extended for but a few hours further.

319. Meanwhile, daylight flitted by and evening was ushered in. The rustic set no limit to his prayers or tears. Clinging to the door, he made this single affirmation: "I will not be dug out from this house of yours; I will die here unless I get from you here and now a reason for living." Finally, however, total darkness made it essential for the shrine to be securely emptied. But the man had lost all count of time in concentrating on his loss. His face was pressed down on the threshold, and his whole body

prevented the door from being barred. But after several people had vainly assailed his ears with requests, force was applied. A crowd of men finally tore him away resisting, and drove him some distance from the holy shrine.

330. When the curators of the shrine drove him off, he wept all the more bitterly, and sorrowfully made for home. The silence of the night echoed with his crying, and that desolate region resounded all around with his loud laments until he reluctantly reached his house. He entered the pitch-black interior of his silent cottage, and from the very door of his still dwelling saw yet again the stall bare of the oxen; and there was no sound of bells, which had always given their customary jingle when shaken by the oxen's heads, or had rung more gently from the pressure of their moving tongues on the hollow bronze, as the beasts chewed the cud in their mouths. This caused him to renew his grief more bitterly at the reopening of the wound. Though anxiety refused him sleep in his suffering, in his wakeful grief he had the consolation of stretching out his body and lying in the stall where his oxen had been stabled. His limbs felt no pain at being bruised by that hard bed; the hardship gave him pleasure. The filth of the foul stall did not appal him, because it brought the familiar smell of his beloved animals; the stench was no stench to a lover. As his eyes lit on any hoofprints they had made with departing steps, he stroked and fondled the trodden earth with groaning, and rubbed with his whole body the prints of their feet now cold. He directed his mind towards that consecrated church of Felix, though he was physically far away. He called on the name of Felix with tears, and poured out his prayers, not despairing of help.

355. The night had now journeyed over the mid-

heaven, steeping the world in the peace of sleep, and on
earth all things were still. The rustic alone remained awake,
a prey to his hope and anxiety. Suddenly he heard a din
outside his gate, and a banging sounded on the door. In
his fear he thought that thieves were again at his house,
and he cried, beside himself: "Why do you seek in your
cruelty to break down my door? It encloses nothing; you
seek in vain. I have no cattle now, so what else are you
after? Others have forestalled you. Only my life remains
to me, left untouched by your comrades as empty of
booty." These were his words of terror, but the banging
on the door continued unceasingly. As it thundered on,
and none of those who knocked answered him, he made
for the door with hesitant, anxious step. He put a troubled
ear to the door, and peered out of a crack in the split wood,
through which a white beam from heaven pierced the
darkness. He kept staring, unable as yet to believe what
he saw; in the dim gloaming he did not trust his eyes
entirely. Yet as he hesitated, the strange appearance of
those who were knocking began to dispel his anxious fear,
and to promise the hope of a happy ending.

376. Those he saw knocking were not men. But he
dared not believe the truth of what he saw. I shall tell of
a mighty miracle though in God's eyes it is insignificant;
every animal in creation shows His wisdom, with that
intelligence with which the Creator has endowed every
kind of brute beast. There stood his fine pair of oxen;
their intelligence guided by the Godhead, they had travelled in darkness over unknown, trackless country to the
house they knew well. They came without a guide, as of
their own accord, yet not of their own accord, since they
had been delivered from those brigands by the stronger

power of a divine deed; Felix had driven them along, controlling them with hidden reins. When they reached the thatched cottage that they knew, they rejoiced to be back, but in their minds the fear was strong of the violence they had undergone. As if they were apprehensive of a robber behind them breathing down their necks, they pounded the door with their heads in unison, using their horns like hands to rouse their master with the din.

391. In his terror the rustic feared even that scene of security, as though it were the foe milling round his barred door. But once again Wisdom breathed into the brute beasts an understanding of the cause of his delay, the realisation that their master feared to release the bolts. They lowed, so that losing his terrors at the sound he would fearlessly open the door to his charges outside. The rustic on seeing this sudden evidence of God's gift continued to hesitate. Even his joy made him flutter anxiously. He did not dare believe it, yet he feared to doubt. He saw them face-to-face, but thought his eyes were deceiving him. His self-examination made him doubt his possible worthiness of so great a kindness, but when he thought of the source of his hope, he recognised the work of his patron Felix, and dared to believe.

405. Now morning was breaking, and the twilight of dawn turning red. The stars were fading as the flight of the last hour of darkness had begun to undrape objects of uncertain colour in the subdued light, or in the faintly glimmering shadows. Then at last the oxen were revealed to him in the form he knew. As soon as their coarse skin began to manifest itself before his eyes, his joyful certainty increased. Drawing back the bolts, he freed the door, which creaked as its hinges were loosened. As he did this,

the yoked oxen burst in together, anticipating his attempt
to open the door, for once the bolts were released the door
easily gave way. Then they joyfully recognised their delighted lord before them on the threshold. They licked
him as he in turn stroked them, and with their lips they
moistened the hands which patted them, with foam-
specked kisses they stained all his garments. As their master
embraced his dear pair of oxen, they gently nuzzled their
kindly lord and fawningly caressed his breast in turn. The
horns of his beloved cattle did him no injury; he drew their
heads as though they were soft to his proffered breast. To
his hands the tongues which by licking could scrape their
food even from trees did not feel rough.

426. Yet in the course of all this the faithful rustic's
heart was not forgetful, and he recalled his obligation. His
first concern was not to lead the panting oxen to their stall
and refresh them with food after their hardship and hunger, but to take them with him to the place where he had
obtained them as his. So he came, leading the returned oxen.
He did not hide his joy in silent prayer, but in relating his
tale attracted dense crowds to listen, and amid the universal
astonishment entered the shrine. The beasts he had be-
wailed the previous day as lost he now led forward, and
revealed to the crowd the triumph of his holy martyr.
The oxen, only recently the booty of thieves and now the
spoils of Felix, were dragged through the midst of the
mob. As they advanced, the huge gathering made way for
them, hymning Christ's glory shown in these dumb beasts.

440. But the rustic who had prompted this great gift
from the Lord on high stood conspicuous in the midst of
the thousands and again wept, but this time for joy. He
fulfilled the vow he owed to the saint, not with oppressive

coin or insensible gift, but with the spontaneous, living present of tongue and mind. With filial words the poor man bore witness to his abundant love, and as Christ's debtor made sufficient payment with this pledge, for Christ was satisfied with the spotless sacrifice of his praise.[21]

448. "Saint Felix, see how I victoriously lead your captives to you before the eyes of all the people, and again consign them, the defeated, to your protection. Since you deigned to restore them when stolen, preserve them now they have returned. But now, kindly martyr, turn your attention to my person, for you observe that you have a further task, this time for me, as I stand by your threshold with eyes nearly blinded, since they are swimming with abundant tears shed not only for my loss but also in my joy. You have removed the reason for my tears, so now heal the wounds arising from them. You took pity, dear saint, on my lost oxen; likewise take pity on the loss of my eyes. You restored my cattle now back with me, so now restore my sight which they need. What benefit is there in their return if my dimmed eyes convert my presence before them into absence?"

462. The folk who were there smiled at this complaint of his. But the martyr in his distant place cocked his ears and heard these devout words from his tactless suppliant, whose eyes then felt the saint's hand and were healed. The rustic, while the folk hymned their praise to God, returned home, his sight and his oxen restored, and with him went the glad triumph which attended both his prayers.

# POEM 19[1]

Only if the sky can forgo its stars, earth its grass, honey-combs their honey, streams their water, and breasts their milk will our tongues be able to renounce their praise of the saints, in whom God Himself is the strength of life and the fame of death. For Him they decided to barter their lives, and by their deaths to ratify the holy faith of nations and to purchase the kingdom of the saints with that precious blood with which as martyrs they besprinkled the entire world and became the seed from heaven for countless races. From the number of these princes Felix was appointed confessor in this city, and the fame of his name has flashed over the length and breadth of the world. But Nola has housed his buried body, and so takes pride as though he were her own star—for every martyr, wherever the region to which his body is committed, is both a star for that district and a source of healing for its residents.

16. The reason for this is that when the earth was shrouded in its ancient darkness, and men's souls were sick throughout the world, the Creator took pity on them, and apportioned sacred tombs of saints throughout the earth, just as He scattered the stars with their light through the night sky. Though the faith of all martyrs remains one, and the grace they bestow is alike, and their strength identical, we observe that the shape of activity of each of them emerges differently. In one place we remember and venerate their high merit, but their tombs are silent; in

another we marvel at the clamouring messages and signal aid received. I believe that where more evil survives through more obstinate wickedness, the more serious disease demands greater assistance. In other words, where more impenetrable error still interposes a deep darkness of faithlessness, and faith is sick and troubled amongst a faltering people, it is certainly right that brighter lights should be kindled there, that the gloom of the world should be dispersed by divine illumination, that dazed and fearful minds and dulled eyes may be directed to the very rays of divine truth, delivered from foul darkness and smeared with the salve of the healing Christ.[2] This salve is ground on a holy grindstone by the skill of the apostles, to heal men's senses, for those who turn to Christ with eyes now restored and hearts filled with the Gospel-draught find His yoke mild and His burden light.[3] That draught successfully clears the cloud which love for the beguiling world draws across our inner eyes, a love which drives our wandering senses unpiloted round the great void, stupefying with its oppressive darkness those who are deceived by its soft seductions, so that they emasculate their vital strength and pursue futile ostentation along the slippery paths of pleasure.

45. Accordingly, the universal-healing Lord sought to divert these diseases from us, and brought forth among various nations saints who with their health-giving sanctity could heal sick mortals. To ensure that His heavenly power exercised its control more markedly, He bestowed saints on the more prominent cities. Though small towns keep certain martyrs, God sent the outstanding ones to honoured cities, allotting to only a few areas the bodies of those whom when living He sent as teachers through

the whole world. This is why He put Peter and Paul in
Rome, because the capital of the world, lunatic from its
many vices and blind in its darkness, needed the leading
physicians.

57. But since God is stronger at restoring our salvation
than is Satan at continuing to imprison us even now by
deceit, the darkness of the world is thinning out. Holiness
has gained the ascendant in almost every nation, and life
has subdued death. As faith grows strong, error is conquered and melts away; hardly any community is left
abandoned to sin and death. All Rome is called by Christ's
holy name,[4] and she jeers at the falsehoods of Numa or
the oracles of the Sibyl.[5] Rome's devoted throng, in company with its sacred shepherds, answers joyfully "Amen"[6]
in the countless folds of the reigning God. Their pious
shout strikes the sky with praises of the eternal Lord, and
the summit of the Capitol shakes and totters.[7] Dilapidated
images in deserted temples tremble on being struck by the
holy voices and smitten by the name of Christ.[8] The
demons scatter panic-stricken from the abandoned shrines.
The spiteful snake vainly hisses with its bloody mouth, and
with hungry jaws laments the salvation of men and his
own deprivation of the blood of cattle. The plunderer
groans, and vainly hastens round the bloodless altars.[9]

76. We see, then, how God in apportioning kindly
gifts to the rest of the earth has scattered His limbs uni-
versally through the great cities. Thus He gave Andrew
to Patras,[10] and John to Ephesus,[11] so that through them
He could tend Europe and Asia simultaneously, dispelling
the oppressive darkness by these great beams. Parthia embraces Matthew,[12] India Thomas;[13] the Africans obtained
Thaddaeus[14] and the Phrygians Philip:[15] Crete adopted

Titus[16] and Boeotia the physician Luke.[17] On you, Alexandria, Mark was conferred,[18] so that the bull could be
driven out with Jupiter, and so that Egypt would not
stupidly worship cattle under the name of Apis;[19] nor
Crete wickedly venerate a buried citizen under the name
of Jupiter;[20] nor the Phrygians celebrate the feast of Cybele by the castration of the Galli, offering consolation to
their polluted mother by such grisly wounds (thus Mount
Ida could bring forth her foliage on a mountain at last
purified, providing virgin pines from her peaks untroubled);[21] nor Greece superfluously consult further
Delphi now silent, but rather despise and grind underfoot
her own Olympus as she mounts higher to Sion, where
Christ sets high His soft yoke on the lofty summit of that
kindly hill.[22] Diana, too, has fled from Ephesus, for John
has thrust her out; she accompanied her brother, who has
himself been routed by Paul's command given in Christ's
name at the expulsion of the Python.[23]

98. Satan has also fled from Egypt, where he had taken
countless forms and countless names appropriate to different monsters. Thus he fashioned holy Joseph into
Serapis,[24] hiding that revered name beneath a name of
death; yet all the time the statue's shape revealed the faith,
for a bushel overtops its head,[25] the reason being that in
ancient days corn was collected at the inspiration of the
Lord before a famine, and with the grain from Egypt's
fruitful breast Joseph fed countless peoples and filled up
the lean years with years of plenty.[26] But to prevent that
holy man's being venerated with further unholy honour,
God's hidden mind sent goads to prick the hearts of that
devout people. They destroyed and shattered Serapis, and
ended the worship of that wicked spirit. Isis does not

wander through the woods of Pelusium seeking Osiris by
means of shaven prophets who beat their breasts and
mourn another's grief with their own sorrow, and who
then in turn put their wailing to sleep and manifest empty
joy like lunatics, lyingly claiming to have found Osiris
with the same guile with which they made their wandering
search for him when he was not lost.[27]

117. In how sad an abyss of foolishness are sunk those
minds bereft of God's light! I ask you, what can be blinder
than the men who seek someone not lost, find someone
who nowhere continues to exist, and manifest a grief
vicarious rather than personal? Wretched error, elect a
course of action. What is the object of your worship and
your lamentation? The things you seek to combine do not
cohere, for grief does not attend honour, yet you cultivate
sorrows, and you believe you must mourn what you regard
as divine. If they are gods, they are not wretched; or if
they are wretched, they are not gods but human as well
as wretched. So pity them if they have endured the experiences of men, or worship them as happy gods; clearly
it is blind lunacy either to worship wretched creatures or
to lament happy ones.[28]

129. Is Isis, then, divine? Can a woman be divine? If
she is a goddess she has no body, and without a body there
is no sex, nor without sex any childbearing. So how did
she obtain the Osiris whom she seeks?[29] And does she not
know where to look for him though she is a goddess? No,
a mother or a woman can never be divine. For there is
only one God. His power is threefold. There is one God
the Father, and in Him one Son, and from Him and the
Father of the Word one Spirit. These three Persons[30] are
one God forever. The single nature of God is God, con-

sisting of Son, Spirit and Father; but the Son is born of the Father and the Spirit proceeds from the Father. No nature in the created order has anything in common with, or similar to, the divine nature.[31]

141. Carthage waxes strong through the martyr Cyprian.[32] The stream of both his words and his blood have brought fertility to the dry sands of Africa.[33] Not far from Carthage the white heap caused by the gathered martyrs has given eminence to Utica with its huge mass of revered slain. One mound of blessed turf covers many bodies, and raises its top high above the fields, bearing witness to those giants in merit by a mountain of a tomb.[34] From that time onward Africa has long been fertile ground for Christ God, and from this great seed it multiples its abundant harvest, bringing forth teachers outstanding in word and faith.[35]

152. Grace as abundant has shone on the lands of the west. Ambrose is outstanding in Italy,[36] Vincent in Spain.[37] Gaul has adopted Martin,[38] and Aquitania Delphinus.[39] Besides these, there are many seeds scattered abundantly over these regions through the burial of saints in them. They light up the whole world with their heavenly power, and dislodge from that whole world the dragon of ancient times[40] who[41] possessed the race of men under the names of a thousand gods. Those names the serpent took over from dead mortals,[42] and conferred them on himself and his followers, over whom he presides in the art of doing harm, and wields foul dominion in the empty lower air, wandering round as head of the demons, and our foe.[43]

164. So this was how our Nola here, through the love of the pitying Christ, deserved the protection of Felix's tomb, and deserved also his cleansing, for the town was

involved in the sightless destruction of the world and lay
dying in deep[44] darkness, long corrupted by worshippers of
gods of stone. In it Venus with her prostitution and the
crazy Bacchus were deities for the wretched townsfolk,
and lust allied to madness celebrated wicked ceremonies
with foul ritual. What chance of life was there here, where
there was nowhere shame or fear? Who would have
shrunk from sinning in a place where bloodthirsty madness
and impure lust were a part of religious observance? For
the inhabitants, sin was their god, for they had come to
believe that all divinity lay in sin. In the whole crowd of
them the man whose hot passion in the rites of Venus
burned foulest was the holiest worshipper; likewise[45] he
who experienced stronger demoniac possession and more
violent delirium within, who offered crazed sacrifice with
self-wounding and deserved to lose his sanity, would be
accounted full of the god and more blessed than the rest.

183. Such a mentality and such divinities were worthy
of sightless souls. Let Venus and her grove serve as god
for those who reject God's service. Let crazy drunkenness,
unholy love hallow such men. Let them worship castration, and label that wretched shame of grisly error the
mysteries of the Mother.[46] This is a faith worthy of those
who have neither faith nor love of the kindly light of
truth, the laws of chastity, or the great name of Christ;
and so they obtain no reward through Christ's blood for
their unworthy life. Let their god be the belly[47] or the
other joys of the flesh, for God Himself is not their god,
and for them no glory underlies the cross of Christ,[48]
since the power of the cross does not deign to enter such
ignoble souls.

195. Then blessed Felix became physician for the peo-

ple of Nola as the other martyrs became physicians in different parts of the globe. He is here perpetually lending this help, and he will bring salvation through the rights he exercises here not only to Nola's citizens but also to all who supplicate him, provided that holy faith in the cross animates the heart of the suppliant. This is the faith that heals and expiates the race of men; where this medicine is not at hand, there the whole kingdom of evil will linger, and Venus will never cease to reign with her adulteries, and Bacchus with his madness, in the man in whom the chastity of Christ and zeal for the cross are absent. God's fire is present where the violence of the cross tortures guilt-stricken hearts within with the blaze of faith, and brings life to the soul by the destruction of sins of the flesh.

209. Nola had for long been downtrodden by these foes and polluted by these monstrous plagues, and she demanded a powerful remedy. God accordingly matched her danger with His assistance, and the city obtained Felix as physician to overcome each and every bane, however ingrained in the blackened hearts of wretched men, to gain the upper hand over those deepset wounds by the power of his merit, to pierce the skin which had hardened over the putrid sores, to squeeze out through the ruptured surface the matter gathered in the ulcers festering below, so that then scar tissue could draw over a smooth skin and cover the cavity of the wound. So Felix shone in the darkness of Nola like a star proceeding from the mouth of God, bearing on his lips the healing word; just as the Light-bringer, bright with the approaching sun, thrusts up glad radiance at its morning rising, its new appearance outshining the setting stars, and announces the rapid approach of day and the imminent retirement of night. It

is the same with the Gospel, which now shines through the whole world as God draws near to pass imminent judgment on all lands,[49] and Christ everywhere brandishes the banner of His arrival, giving His flashing signals through the agency of His friends.

229. From these friends He chose Felix to shine before him in this region, so that He could dispel our darkness with this star, and rout the ancient demons from Nola also. Then, when such residents as these had been driven from men's hearts, God could enter our chaste minds to dwell there; the roles could be reversed, and after fatherly love had released us, the chains formerly binding us could now pin down the lions and fetter their fierceness as they vainly roared against Christ's sheep.[50] This grace remains with us even now. It releases us from sins at the pressing entreaty of the saints, who take vengeance by enchaining and torturing those foes who used to bind us. Like thieves caught red-handed in the beam of a torch and then imprisoned, these enemies now endure the fiery lashes they have deserved at the hands of the saints; or they are ignominiously thrust into the prison of hell, and trembling confess that the Lord's grim judgment is at hand for them and their followers alone. In other words, all whose wayward will has diverted them into Satan's camp, and who have become allied to him by a life like his, share his punishment in hell as they shared his wickedness on earth.

249. This is the day acceptable to God.[51] The true light of salvation now shines out, and we behold a total transformation in our favour. Deceit has fled, Bel[52] has fallen, error has died. The demons who were worshipped as deities in all the shrines are disarmed and tormented throughout God's temples, and those who presumed to

accept honours appropriate to gods are now beaten and subjected to the law of men.[53] These demons whom we observe in the crowded church of Felix being tormented, crying out, and being pulled along in the bodies they have captured, are kept imprisoned in those very bodies into which they thrust themselves; thus their own decision devised for them human torments. So now they play the part of the guilty, and howl at their punishment, whereas before they had been gods of spurious divinity. Before God was worshipped, they had with their counterfeit godhead devoted to their own service living men who saw no sign from heaven; but now that true faith has been exposed by Christ's light, they cannot withstand even men enclosed in the tomb.[54]

266. The nature of the demons' voices makes it more manifest that they who are tortured before the thresholds or tombs of the saints are the same as those to whom the enslaved human race once sacrificed and insanely offered sacred reverence; for they quite often groan with the same voices, so that one can recognise from the shouting their habitual madness. Usually their mouths appear to hang open quite loosely, they gnash their teeth, foam at the lips, cause their hair to stand on end. Their hands pull at their hair and shake it heavenward; they stand on tiptoe, feet and hair erect. From time to time they remember those ancient rites in which they used to lick the entrails of slain cows, to feed on the sacrificial offering, to lead wanton bands in ivy-clad processions. Even now they attest that theirs was the ritual at which the drunken mob uttered the crazed shout "Euhoe";[55] they gaspingly ape this cry of Bacchus with effeminate voices, and swivel their necks with slow circular movements.

283. However, the lifespan of one mortal man could not suffice to dissolve the pollution which had gathered over a long period; the few years in which Felix lived in the flesh as confessor and priest, his words as teacher, his record as martyr, his deserving deeds and duties as presiding priest[56] were not enough. So the almighty Lord caused Felix's mortal span in the body to continue in a higher way, for He extended the healing activities of our busy martyr so that after burial he would exercise the powers which he had wielded whilst still in the flesh through the strength of Christ. In this way he could after death abide physically in the city he had espoused. Though only the spirit of the martyr laid to rest showed its healing presence (since the physical appearance of their dear patron lay concealed from the longing hearts of his beloved people, withdrawn temporarily from their eyes) his ready healing could always be at hand for the curing of the sick. So undying distinction and fame halo Felix, and his efficacious power flourishes without cease. True, he was buried in a mound long ago, and being mortal lies hidden in the covering earth; yet a living grace quickened by God outlives his limbs, and brings fame to the martyr's bones which exhale divinity. He is buried, but the power of his merit lives on among his folk, so that dense crowds from different regions constantly venerate the tiny tomb of the great confessor.

307. But since God is the Father of all men, He allowed this help to pass from His saints to all lands, so that the blessed martyrs could now provide kindly presents[57] from their tombs, and the buried could tend the living. But the Lord did not content Himself with allowing the martyrs to bring radiance with their names or assistance only to

ther own regions. He multiplied the memorials of the saints from these tombs, and in His pity conferred the same martyrs on many regions. I shall state from the beginning the various occasions from which this blessing has originated in various countries.

317. Since the faith had initially not been spread through the whole world alike, many areas of the earth were without martyrs. This I think is why Christ has both inspired princes (in the first place when Constantine was Caesar)[58] and acquainted His servants with His most generous decision to summon martyrs from their earlier homes and translate them to fresh lodgings on earth. So, for example, we know of the recent action of the holy bishop Ambrose; relying on this gift, he translated and set in a different church saints who were earlier unknown but whom he later identified on the information of Christ,[59] and thus he has confounded the raging queen with the light he has uncovered.[60]

329. When Constantine was founding the city named after himself, and was the first of the Roman kings to proclaim himself a Christian, the godsent idea came to him that since he was then embarking on that splendid enterprise of building a city which would rival Rome, he should likewise emulate Romulus' city with a further endowment —he would eagerly defend his walls with the bodies of apostles.[61] He then removed Andrew from the Greeks and Timothy from Asia;[62] and so Constantinople now stands with twin towers, vying to match the hegemony of great Rome, and more genuinely rivalling the walls of Rome through the eminence that God bestowed on her, for He counterbalanced Peter and Paul with a protection as great,

since Constantinople gained the disciple of Paul and the brother of Peter.

342. In widely separated regions along that road, greatly increased help was afforded by these saints to the tasks of human living, and those regions demonstrate this even today. Wherever the carriage, equal to its holy burden, halted at an established post-station, wherever the holy bodies lodged and the bearers of their consecrated ashes rested, the evidences of miracles cry out in each and very place. God's hand is at work with healing strength along all the roads where the holy bodies imprinted their living traces on that sacred journey.

353. This, then, was the means by which the faithful and zealous escorts of the relics were afforded a chance at the prompting of faith to break off some keepsakes from the holy bones as their deserved reward, so that they could individually bear back home for their personal protection the reward for their service and the payment for their toil. As a result, the sacred ashes have been scattered over different areas like life-giving seeds. Wherever a drop of dew[63] has fallen on men in the shape of a particle of bone,[64] the tiny gift from a consecrated body, holy grace has brought forth fountains in that place, and the drops of ashes have begotten rivers of life.

363. From this source Christ's abundance, so rich in its tiniest forms, has fallen on us also;[65] for we, too, have received, in the form a fragment of dust, the sacred tokens of the apostles' flesh. Saint Felix, lord and father of our lodging, guardian of our soul, protector of our salvation, has accepted these in the neighbouring shrine close by. This church, which is newer than the others,[66] preserves

the great distinction of these tiny ashes, and is itself more securely preserved by its patron guardians.[67] For it would be a sad day if ever those patrons appeared in need of saving, they who regularly preserve and with fatherly love deign to attend the interests of their charges and to maintain[68] the defence of those places dedicated to themselves. There are proofs remarkable for their reliability of this dutiful zeal residing in these holy spirits.

378. From amongst these I shall recount one recent event, however briefly, for it is fitting to reveal in words of thanks the kindnesses of Saint Felix on his very birthday. The tale I shall tell is no foreign or ancient one, for I shall report a work recently performed in our own region at this very place. Perhaps you will readily recall it, for it happened in the full light of day. I imagine there is virtually none of you in this audience[69] to whom the story is unknown, for the report went flying afar to distant regions. Some of you will certainly have been in this city at the time when it chanced that a robber became a prey to unlawful temptations, and laid greedy hands on consecrated gifts. That wicked madman chose from all the ornaments in the revered basilica no other loot but an image of the cross. He did not know that it would lead to his exposure rather than be his spoil, rather like the greedy fish which swallows the hook and is doomed to be caught by the food it has seized.

395. What arrogance, pray, impelled the thief, armed him, blinded him, drove him headlong to such monumental recklessness that he did not take refuge in his guilt with the guards who keep vigil, or even better, at the venerable altar which conceals the sacred ashes and fragrantly breathes forth the power of the holy dust, but instead

carried off the object so preeminent not only in power but also in beauty and worth? As you know, there were many other decorative pieces stored in the place which he could have taken, and thus left the golden cross, for consecrated vessels allotted to the reception of the Sacrament were stored away within. But besides these, within the area of the basilica itself there had been set as usual those notable gifts of varying shape which every day you see laid out there, fastened to the pillars all round in symmetrical order—the chandeliers which bear painted candles on projecting points, so that fragrant light is spread by the wicks inside.[70] Then in the middle of the basilica hang hollow lamps, attached to the high ceiling by brass chains. They look like trees throwing out arms like vine-shoots; at their tips the branches have glass goblets as their fruit, and the light kindled in them is, so to say, their spring blossoms. With the abundant foliage of their flames, they resemble close-packed stars, and stud the heavy darkness with countless flashes. The delicate air they dapple with sprouting firebuds, and as they shake their bright foliage and flash repeatedly, the blackness of the night is dispelled with undying torches. Their ambivalent show presents a mingling of light and shade; they confound the uncertain air with their quivering appearance.

425. The thief, then, could see that these were openly accessible to his hand and safer for him to steal, for it was a lesser sin and a lesser prize to remove a lamp of light silver hanging some distance from the site of the altar. But the wretch had big ideas, and was arrogant even in his thieving. He scorned to steal silverware as a cheap abomination, and stretched out his hand for the gold which he had noted was skillfully adorned with precious stones. He

had a heart puffed up with the large aspiration of becoming rich and developing a passion for both jewels and gold. But the only store he laid up was the wicked weight of monstrous crime; he remained heavy with sin but unburdened with wealth. The sacrilegious thief had his punishment to come, but his booty forsook him. Stripped of his thieving spoils but not of his sin, he lives on beggared of his reward but with abundance of stripes for his thieving. Yet I do not believe that he was allowed to embark on this sin without the great will and intention of Christ. Since he had formed the design of stealing at any rate one of these sacred objects, he was allowed to have designs on the one which would make the heinousness of his sin more flagrant.

445. A few days previously this man had taken refuge in the church, pretending he was evading military service,[71] and he had been hospitably admitted as a guest by the caretakers supervising the holy basilica. For almost a whole month he lay hidden there, and had reconnoitred the sleeping quarters, the hours of sleep, and the routine of those on guard. When he had decided on an hour suitable for the crime he planned, in the silence of the night he seized his unholy chance. The doors were fast shut, but he was inside like one of the guards whose guest he was, so he needed no exertion and made no noise. As soon as the guards off their guard began to snatch their sleep in the silent shadows, and to shroud their conquered cares in forgetfulness, he chose the spot for his evil deed.

457. He knew that there was a mobile platform, normally left there to tend the lamps as usual during the night. It furnished a ladder with handy steps, and it had been left available for him by a negligent guard, just where

the image of the cross stood. It is there now, hanging
perpendicularly from a transverse beam, bearing twin
lampholders on the crosspiece, and with a short chain
hanging from the base to support another. In these three
goblets lamps are placed and lit when a feastday so ordains.
But on this occasion the cross merely hung there on show,
without being employed for light, though a little in front
of the glory of the cross there hung from the same beam[72]
a silver goblet fitted for regular use.

468. The thief at once extinguished this lamp, for its
bright beam was an embarrassment to him. He knew that
this light, too, was often wont to fail when the oil ran
dry, and when the tow was bone-dry it would cause the
light to fade in the course of a long night; and the guard
would not be surprised if the lamp went out and the blackness hid the ceiling, for he would think that the darkness
had been induced not by crime but by its natural course.
So the robber bore off the forbidden booty untroubled,
as though he were a guard and not the thieving brigand
that he was. He did not flee, but stayed there without
panicking. One of the many cells set along each side of
the huge building, which provide separate lodgings for
the buried dead,[73] gave him cover and concealment. In one
of these the thief hid; and when he saw the bolts drawn
back in the early morning, he dashed from the opened
basilica, leaving his hiding-place and bearing his crime
with him. Later, after he had been captured, he said that
he had been making for the city of Romulus,[74] in order to
traffic there in his wicked merchandise.

485. Meanwhile, our caretakers had no inkling of this
event during that night or the whole of the next day. In
the late evening they set the ladder to perform their usual

task. But when the one who was to light the lamp began to mount, he found nothing there. The bare beam remained, stripped of its fine adornment, the familiar cross. The poor white-faced guardians did not dare to report this criminal loss, for they recognised that by rights the guilt attached to them. They rushed out in a panic, flying in pursuit of the runaway thief, but nowhere did they pick up any traces of the escaping man. All took different roads, and they surveyed the harbours at different points on the shore.

496. Eight or ten days slipped by during their fruitless scrutiny, and all had returned, regarding the search now as vain. One of the hunters was a lad returning from some distance, having expended empty effort to no purpose. When he drew near to Nola, he stopped on the road. He called on Felix with loud groans and floods of tears, and in his fidelity of heart boldly proclaimed that he was not returning home without the cross. Then he eagerly re-embarked on the journey he had completed. There and then he was met by a man who knew the thief, not as a thief but as a fellow citizen. This lad of ours accosted the other first, asking where he had journeyed from, and the other told him. He was then asked if he had seen the thief. The other replied that the man was in a district close by. The area he mentioned as near to where they conversed abutted on Mount Vesuvius, five miles from Nola. However, nightfall caused suspension of planning. The two agreed to join forces at daybreak. The informer returned with the dawn and acted as guide for our men. The thief was captured and the booty restored.

515. It chanced that the holy day had dawned which marks the birthday of Saint Priscus, whose day Nola

keeps although he was bishop of another see at Nuceria.[75] The people had at the time thronged the basilica of Saint Felix with their customary devotion. After the liturgy, the bishop[76] was just dismissing the pious crowds. God had foreseen the moment when the people would be emerging, and suddenly the thief was led into the church in chains, his thieving hands tied behind his back, to face the outpouring mob. The people were filled with joy, the thief with apprehension. The whole city gathered in haste to see this remarkable prodigy. The crowd, hysterical with mob-hatred, made to attack him, their mingled joy and anger inducing in them confused emotions.

528. I confess I was afraid that the devil with his customary envy would pollute the procession with bloodshed, and heal the earlier wound with a worse one. The thief was rescued from the crowd, and it chanced that the delinquent when seized was shut in the very cell in which he had hidden after seizing the cross; after the recovery of that cross, he was enclosed there to save his life. So then, after regaining his wits, the guilty man himself began to recount his crime and the remarkable hindrances he experienced. He admitted that during those eight or ten days in which he had planned to go to Rome, he was forced back, his feet shackled in such a way that all the time he tried to go he was impelled backward by an unknown force. So he had returned to the district of Vesuvius, where one might say he had been committed to prison, chained by an angel's hand. But the wretch had believed he was his own master because he seemed free in body, whereas a stronger hand had secured him, not with visible chains, but with bonds unseen.

546. It was the avenging Felix who bound him in such

appropriate confusion, who turned him round on such a giddy course and drove him mad, so that he was always off yet never went, and as soon as he had made his precipitate departure, he turned back. Strange but true, he tried to go while remaining stationary, he tried to stay while setting out. He did not realise that what prevented his flight was the very object motivating his attempt to flee, that he carried his fetters with him, and that his own sin formed bonds that could not be broken. For he had committed his heavy booty to the recesses of his clothing where it lay enclosed. This was what made him eagerly and almost crazily look for a hideout yet continue to roam in the light of day over open country. He thought he was under cover, yet he was conspicuous in a plain bare of cover. His sense of guilt had so blinded his mind that he could neither escape by flight nor obtain cover in his wanderings.

560. Fear on the one hand and astonishment on the other confused his guilty soul with warring sensations. He avoided the roads, but had a sluggish apprehension of entering desolate woodland, for he feared that perhaps the very silence of the forest would cry out his great crime, or he thought that monstrous avenging beasts of menacing shape would confront him. The poor creature likewise avoided the crowded highway, and took to the pathless countryside, where he imagined himself safer among strangers. He pushed down the fear in his heart like the theft beneath his shirt—for he had stowed and hidden away the gold in the folds of his garment, which was hitched up high. He had not dared to entrust the stolen object to the silent earth or to a hollow cave, as brigands

do. He feared betrayal, but was too greedy to deposit his ill-gotten gains.

574. This was why the wicked man had entrusted his spoil merely to his shirt. He had knotted his garment tightly, and let it hang loosely above his uncovered knees. This was the lair for his crime which the robber had arranged on his person. With such fear was he rightly enchained that he trusted none to share his wretched thieving. He alone was polluted with the foul crime; his was the garment whose folds guarded the theft, as his was the hand which had dared that sacrilegious plundering. So he bore his own burden, and the death-dealing weight of his booty oppressed and defiled no other besides himself. No part of him remained untouched by wickedness, for he enclosed the spoils of his sin snatched from the sacred shrine, and enclosed them within his hitched-up clothes, covering the cross with a chain of his own making. For soon he was captured, and exchanged his belt for bonds; and when his garment was untied, and the gold fell from the loosened folds, he was bound with the very strap in which he had been wound. The hands which the rash thief had outstretched for holy gifts he withdrew empty of booty but possessed by bonds, for he was made prisoner with his own knotted belt.

595. But if we seek to scrutinise more thoroughly from every aspect the whole chain of the unfolding order of events, especially where the crime escaped detection and was then revealed and manifest, we shall see that Felix with hidden hand performed the wondrous works of God. So far I have told the details of how the thief sought to flee but did not, how he retraced his steps, and repeatedly

reversed the path he had vainly taken, being debarred from distant places and forced back to that neighbourhood.

604. I shall now relate another deed of Felix performed by Christ's hand to reveal the powers deservedly gained by His dear protegé. This is a remarkable exemplar, a sign equal to that other, revealed by the awestruck prisoner himself when he confessed his bold deed. But first I shall describe the appearance of the cross itself because the story demands it.[77] There are two forms of conventional representation—twin arms on an upright,[78] and the extension of five arms by three crossing pieces.[79] Our cross is fashioned in both these shapes. On the one hand, it forms the appearance of a yardarm or ship's mast, or of the conventional Greek symbol for 300,[80] when it is fashioned with a single upright and a crosspiece joined to the top of it. On the other hand, the cross is also designed with a second shape, and tells of the Lord Christ by a kind of monogram. The symbol used in Latin calculation for 10 is written by the Greeks as the letter chi, and the rho splits it. The top of the rho also forms a sigma, for it curves back on the upright and forms a complete circle. Then the upright when bent makes a Greek iota. The same stroke when drawn back with a short spearpoint makes a tau.[81] In this way the six letters which fashion the name higher than all names[82] are gathered in one symbol,[83] the monogram being fashioned by three strokes. The one symbol renders six letters at once. With its three strokes the one symbol shows that the Lord is both three and one, and God is in Christ whom the harmony of the threefold Mind willed to take a body and be born for us.[84]

632. There is further symbolism in the fact that the twin strokes bend back their summits symmetrically as

though they are separate, and below they rest on similar
supports set apart; yet they are joined fast together with
a central link, as they gaze on identical but separated
extremities. Where they merge at mid-point the upright
inset there rises more proudly like a royal sceptre, signifying that Christ God is King over all. It is His cross He
extends in the four extremities of the wood, and so touches
the world in its division of four regions, so as to draw
the peoples of every land into life.[85] Then because Christ
God by His death on the cross becomes all things to all
men,[86] bringing a beginning of life and an end to ills, an
alpha and an omega encompass the cross. Both letters with
the three strokes achieve their separate shapes in a threefold way, the creation of a single Mind but triple Powers.[87]
Christ is for me both alpha and omega, embracing alike
the summits in the highest region of the sky and the
depths below. He has victoriously captured both hell and
heaven; he broke through the gulfs below and pierced the
open skies, defeating death and as victor restoring salvation. After His victory had joined Him to His Father's
right hand, He set the trophy of His body in its heavenly
abode, and implanted the banner of the cross above all
the stars.

656. This,[88] then, is the workmanship on that representation which the thief, hounded vainly by greedy
furies, had unfastened from its hanging hook and borne
away from the holy basilica with defiled hand. It is
wonderfully arranged to delineate the twofold appearance
of the eternal cross, so that our eyes may find ready faith,
should it be our pleasure to gaze closely at it. For now
that it is restored, it shines in the place where it was earlier

set, and now adorns the front of the altar, which is veiled by a curtain, with this symbol of fatherly love.

665. So this representation manifests in the cross the same shape which denotes a balance poised with equal arms,[89] or a yoke symmetrical on its erected beam; or again, the lofty tree with its arms extending sideways (on which the Lord hung and shed His innocent blood for sinning mankind as the world trembled)[90] is like eyes bridging a face with eyebrows on the forehead. At the very bottom of the cross, which is formed with two bars of heavy weight, is attached a small wreath of highly wrought metal encrusted with various jewels. The Lord's cross shines out here, too, with its perennial representation of the living tree, wreathed, so to say, by a diadem.

677. This was the one part of the whole of his loot which the thief had left undamaged by the iron tool with which he had broken up the rest. When after his capture at that time his unfastened belt released his clothing, and the pieces of booty slipped down to the ground, those who discovered it were confused in mind through twin emotions. They were delighted at the discovery, but grieved that it was broken. In surprise they began to question that thief, so careful and yet so reckless (what was broken revealed his blind folly, what survived revealed his care), and he told a story of his crime and God's power which astonished them.

687. His intention had been to break up the whole object. But he had kept this one part intact, being impelled by the divine force with which the inset cross restrained the thief, reckless though he was, by enfeebling him. He admitted himself both his sinful intention and the cross's power, attesting that whenever his hands took up

a tool to attack the wreath which was attached to the cross by a connecting joint, they fell to his sides as though enervated, the blow was repelled, his arms felt weak and paralysed, his muscles grew slack.

695. Now I indulge in a brief onslaught on the wretched thief. Unhappy man, what boundless madness had so turned your brain that, once checked by the bright light of truth, you did not make haste to anticipate all investigation and rush back to replace the stolen object voluntarily? Did so powerful an impulse overpower your greedy heart with darkness that you dared to store away on your person that part of the cross which you feared to break since God had restrained you so often? Tell me, where did that fear of yours take refuge? And when headlong audacity so wickedly steeled your heart to fearlessness, how did you become once more fearful in your scorn? You vacillated before the image[91] of your crime as you sought to depart, for your heart was split between faith and faithlessness. Did you believe in the strength of the cross and the invulnerability of Christ's sign when you feared to touch it with the iron tool, yet also deny that belief by carrying off the cross, though fearful of what you knew? However, your wickedness did not avail you; and now that you have admitted your foolishness and the manifestation of God, you have made us glory in the great triumph of the cross. So let us cease to assail the thief now captured. Robbed of his theft, he finds his poverty sufficient punishment.

716. Now I direct my words to you, revered cross of God, and shall end with thankful praise of you. Cross, you are God's mighty love, glory of heaven, perennial salvation of men, dread of the wicked, strength of the

righteous, light of the faithful. Cross, you bestowed on the earth the incarnate God to minister to salvation, and bestowed on heaven the divine Man to be its King. Through you truth's Light is revealed, and the darkness of evil has fled. You have destroyed the pagan temples uprooted by believers. You are the binding brooch of peace among men, you have reconciled man with God through the covenant of Christ the Mediator. You have become the ladder for man to mount to heaven. Be for us believers a pillar and an anchor, that our house may safely stand, and our ship be safely steered by reliance on the cross, gaining from the cross both faith[92] and a crown.

# POEM 20[1]

Good masters often minister dutifully to their dear charges. They protect subordinate slaves with fatherly love, and show kindness by nurturing with closer care those who with the eyes of love they see are less resourceful or deficient in strength. If any of these, following the usual habit of human nature, wishes to celebrate some vow but cannot do so because of straitened circumstances, the impoverished slave is lent support by his interested master, so that the wealthy lord contributes the expenses lacked by the poor man for a well-laid table. This is my allotted situation under Felix's patronage—I aim to have nothing available from my own store, so that all I have may be through him.

13. Felix's birthday was now blossoming as it had in previous years, but I had nothing with which to mount the feast which my vow has made annual. The day was drawing near, and I had no resource available of any kind. But suddenly my well-endowed patron bestowed on me two hogs and a calf with which to spread a generous table, and from their flesh the poor were fed. But these beasts also provided me with a theme, for God has recently performed a miracle as a marvellous sign through these animals, and by this lofty means encourages men to pay heed to Christ, and not to put the cravings of the flesh before those of faith. For the chain of events to be recounted will show that the highest God gave a sign for the grievous

reproach of our greed through beasts lacking human reason.

28. Though I use the poet's art, the song I sing will not be invented. I shall tell it with an historian's truthfulness and without the poet's deceit,[2] because a servant of Christ should not utter lies. Such techniques can satisfy non-Christians who cultivate falsehood, but our sole technique is faith, and our art of song is Christ. He has taught us that the wondrous peace of unbalanced harmony was of old achieved in Himself, a harmony He bestowed on one body when He assumed the form of man; for He mingled with it His holy divinity by the inpouring of strength, and so established the two within Him, and fused into one two natures far different from each other. So man was God, and God was made man by God the Father also God. The Son is not the Father's grace but His nature, because He is the sole Heir of the highest Father. He alone possesses as His own that which He affords as a gift to those whose holy faith has granted a heavenly reward. So He is truly our poetic inspiration, the true David who has restored the lyre of this body[3] which had long lain idle, its frame crumbling. The Lord has restored it, adopting it for His use when it was silent and its strings broken by that ancient sin. By joining men to God, He has achieved the reinvigoration of all creation to the beauty of its original shape, so that all things might be new, and the dust removed from them. God our Master Himself sought to renew this lyre, and so He hung His own lyre, nailed to the wood of the tree, and gave it fresh life when the cross destroyed the sinning of the flesh. Thus He ordered mortal man from the different nations into a single lyre, and tuned it for heavenly music, drawing peoples of all

races into a single body. Then He struck the chords
with the plectrum of the Word, and the sound of the
Gospel-instrument filled all creation with praise of God.
Christ's golden tortoise-shell resounds through the whole
world; countless tongues sing a single melody; a new song
rings out for God from matching strings.

62. But I will resume my original theme, for it is the
moment to extend to you the promised feast, to place
before you the meal which must be modestly digested by
your eager ears. What I am about to tell I shall not recall
from ancient days, but I shall recount what was seen here
in Nola a few days ago.[4] A stranger to our abode had come
from the neighbourhood of Abella[5] to discharge a vow he
had undertaken. From there he had brought here a hog
which he had long tended with careful attention and kept
alive so that maturing age and fattening could make it
grow. Then on arrival he cut the throat of the fat beast
he had vowed, as men bound by a promise do. The report
of the fat hog had fired the keen hunger of the poor
throughout the district, and all the old people in hope of
a large portion turned their slavering jaws to the rich fare.
Meanwhile, that indigent benefactor cut the meat and
divided it into unequal portions. He removed the pig's
trunk from the scene, and he cooked only the head and
the inwards from the belly he had slit, and divided only
those parts of the slain pig among the poor, leaving the
whole of the flesh for his own enjoyment. He thought
that thus he had fulfilled his vow, and he joyfully embarked on his journey back, presuming to set the rest of
the pig on the beast behind him. The greedy man mis-
takenly considered that he was bearing home with the
pork the sacred pledge of his vow duly kept, but what he

carried represented the destruction of his life and an obstacle to his journey. In fact there and then he was not
allowed to travel a mile along the road. The day was bright
and the road surface level, so it was not through fear of
the dark or through encountering rough ground that he
fell from his horse. He seemed pinned to the ground; he
made to rise, but could not pull himself up to recover his
strength and stand. He began to cry out that his feet were
held fast, and to demonstrate this by lying with his feet
closed together as though enchained.

93. At this moment another strange event became
linked with the accident. As the unhappy crowd of his
relatives surrounded the man lying enfeebled on his back,
the beast, now burdened only with the pork since it was
rid of its rider and abandoned by its guide, drew up of
its own accord, without anyone pulling its head. It seemed
to know without prompting the reason for its minor
stumble, or to realise that someone was blocking the road
it had begun to take. So it turned direction and fled back
again. With hasty step it raced back to our hospitable
dwellings, outstripping all the people on the spot whose
careful attention to the fallen man detained them. Gingerly
he leaned his weight on their support as though his bones
were broken, and said he could not walk because his knees
had stiffened. With tearful words he confessed that bonds
unseen gripped his feet, and that he had deserved that fall
in the light of day as a punishment. So his trusty followers
bore him back to our holy halls, their arms supporting the
heavy body of the sick man. He begged to be taken back
to the very threshold of Felix the healer, convinced that
he would find there a quick remedy. When to the astonishment of the congregation he was borne into the sacred

basilica flanked by a dense crowd, the people arranged in three groups on long benches[6] were thunderstruck—the old men, the wretched gathering of poor, the grey-haired matrons sitting in friendly lines.

117. Besides these, there were many attracted to the holy shrine from regions far distant, drawn by personal devotion; they too witnessed this holy sign, for this remarkable change of fortune occurred without an interval—in fact on the very same day. The man who had departed from that threshold a little earlier on his own feet was now being borne back within with the aid of others' feet, leaning on them and physically supported. On the other side stood the saddled horse, still laden with the pork, before the door of his host, with none of the man's comrades holding him. There was no one standing by familiar to the horse to see that it was relieved of the weight of its burden and led back into its familiar stable. The horse seemed endowed with human reason, standing as if seeking and imminently awaiting its owners. It stood unmoving on the one fixed spot, pricking its ears and breathing the air from its nostrils, seeking to sniff out the familiar scent of men it knew.

134. The horse's flight and stance there were a source of wonder to the guests. The strange course of events made that beast, well known to those acquainted with it, a doubtful quantity. No witness to the accident was present, for they had all gone into the holy basilica of the martyr, crowding round the man who was supported on their arms. There the sick man was stretched out before the holy threshold, his body prostrate as he clung to and embraced the portals. In suppliant posture he kissed them and washed them with his tears.[7] Acknowledging that he

was the cause of his own grief, he accused himself with complaints like these:

144. "Alas, in my wretchedness I have deserved to suffer this punishment in this very place where any wretched man who comes here gains happiness. But I admit that I have met and am suffering an end just and appropriate to my wilful deserts. So now I suffer the torture meted out as punishment to the guilty. The pain now sears and binds my feet on the very threshold where in my madness I broke my promise by cheating, and converted the gift of my promised offering into the forfeiture of my bodily health. Yet there is, I maintain, a sense in which I can claim a welcome change at this moment from sadness to joy. I now mentally witness a happier future. My ills are extirpated, my punishment has begun to grow sweet, for from it there has now accrued to me this welcome favour of being able so soon in my wretchedness to touch again the revered threshold of Felix. For if that fall of mine had not occurred or had been trivial, allowing me to continue that journey eagerly begun, my successful course would have been all the unhappier because my baneful guilt would have remained, and my rebellious flesh would not have been conscious of the wound driven deep into my bones. The strength of my uninjured body would have hidden the danger which my wicked deed caused me to incur. My purpose would have hardened and bound me fast unresisting, if I had not fallen and been bound fast in punishment.

167. "So, Felix, so powerful a healer in the name of Christ the Lord, I ask that you and the powerful Lord will consider it enough to have devised a punishment for me not in anger but in friendly concern for my health, to

deliver me from the bonds of guilt encompassing my body. Look on this evil servant, this greedy runaway whom you rightly dragged back in the bonds my crime deserved. Here is your unhappy debtor, arrested, confined, and tortured, an exemplar set before all men of the need to fear God. All of you should note with trembling hearts the punishment you see me now wretchedly bearing as a lesson to other men. There are surely others guilty of this sin, but it was thought best to make an example of one, so that my punishment might appear as a prior judgment for those who do not mend their ways.

180. "But now, kindest Felix, I beg you, indulgently spare and give loving support to your wretched servant. Death-pains force me to repeat loud prayers. Hasten to me, lest swift death outpace the tardy healer. Yet I know that the hand that castigates and will spare at your bidding is the Lord's. Only hasten to loosen from my weary, exhausted person the chains which your holy eye sees, and which I feel. You secretly and silently tied the legs of your runaway with a hidden chain. Now that I have returned, loose me by a healing which none can witness."

190. The crowd of religious people, gathered open-mouthed around, watched and heard him shouting this out as he clung to the doorposts of Saint Felix and washed them with tongue and lips. While he still lay there, he was stirred with hope, and he rebuked his retinue for all their slowness and dilatory obedience. He ordered the hog to be brought, and then all the parts of it to be given to the poor. For himself he asked only that life be granted and that his food be the sight of plenty being given to the poor. His comrades quickly vied in carrying out these orders inspired by faith. They went to the familiar lodg-

ing, and there lightened the beast of his burden. The meat was cut into pieces and the fire cooked the portions in the bubbling cauldrons. When cooked, great quantities were borne in on huge platters. The needy, their hunger satisfied, offered words of thanks to God, and their sated bellies asked pardon for the donor. As soon as the vow had been duly completed, the debtor was loosed from the grasp of the inner bonds he had incurred. His feet were healed by the Lord's pity, and like a horse released or a bird breaking a snare he rushed forth, skipping along like a bounding deer.

210. This was a wondrous demonstration of faith offered to men's eyes. The whole district took joy in God's love so readily offered, and in the merits of Felix which had such power that Christ's presence was in him, controlling events in accordance with what men deserved, equally powerful as healer of the man restored to sanity and as avenger against the wicked. You should note the depth of wicked guile that wretched man had practised earlier when he divided the hog between the poor and himself. When he should have discharged his vow in its entirety, he had divided up merely the head and the inwards of the hog, and in his foolishness and wickedness had allotted himself the rest, comprising the whole of the flesh; yet by the very theft which had brought him wretchedness, he later won happiness when God with the lash of His love transformed the sin.

223. This is what God's judgment is like, and this is how God, who is Judge and Father and King, administers His weighty and lofty judgment. He restrains His scrutiny and wields mild justice towards all. His power becomes lighter through the compound of goodness, and He

warns the guilty by pricking them before destroying them
with the thunderbolt. In this way, if the blow of the whip
first applied proves serviceable, the person feels shame for
his sins and regains salvation unharmed. But if a person
warned by the terror of the holy lash decides not to heed
the blow, he will remain unhealed and destined for death,
and will experience God's anger in its fullness. So the man
from Abella was wretched previously, but subsequently
blessed when he was healed in body and mind by a remedy
like this. Because he knew the reason for his punishment,
and acknowledging it repented as he lay there, he discovered within himself the action which would deserve a
cure. Within a short period he experienced the twofold
power and working of God's peace and anger, which by
rightful law await all men—the avenging punishment
rightly awaiting arrogant sinners, and the compassionate
love saving those who confess their sin.

241. So the same man passed in a moment from health
to sickness, and in a moment from captivity to freedom.
His bonds loosened, with springy step and joyful tongue
he journeyed back, skipping along like the man of old who
was lame from the mother's womb till Peter and John
bade him in the Lord's name to rise and jump on feet made
strong.[8] This poor man, too, became worthy of the threshold of the beautiful gate,[9] for God Himself, the God of
Peter and Felix, has now in our presence healed him,
though newly crippled from a fall, with the same strength
of the Word with which of old He had healed the man
crippled from the womb. Through this aid he departed
rejoicing. Whereas before, stricken within the church,
he had uttered doleful prayers, now, restored to health,
he was offering thanks outside:

254. "With what could I repay my patron Felix? What thanks could I worthily render to him for a gift so great, the instantaneous healing of a wound so deep? No fee did I pay the doctor, no loathing for my bed did I endure; my body did not undergo the remedy of scalpel or cautery or sharp-toothed potion made from sundry herbs—a healing harsher than the disease or the wound. This is the fate of those attended by the dubious skill of the human hand, whose soothing touch and doubtful relief always make us fearful.[10] Look at me. A short while ago I was carried to that tomb of Saint Felix and laid on that threshold so cold. On that hard marble I lay, damaged and in pain. My only words were a prayer, my sole medicine was faith. I neither saw nor felt the presence of the doctor. Who was that doctor but Christ Himself, or Felix sent by Christ and powerful by the name and strength of Christ? At that time I felt the presence of neither, but Christ was there with twin functions, to rebuke me speedily for my sin and to heal me in my pain. The Lord appeared to me in balancing if diverse roles, correcting yet sparing. The Healer and Avenger was hidden from my eyes, but the punishment and healing were made plain.

277. "Now my vow has been fully discharged and I shall go home, eternally rejoicing in Felix my healer, eternally safe with Felix my patron. Now I shall fear no encounter with perils on journeys, as in past days. The danger will be gone because the source of danger is removed. A promise unfulfilled had bound me, and now a promise duly discharged has loosed me. I only pray, Felix, that now your love may bind me. Fasten round me a chain so that neither death nor life can loose me from you.

286. "All who witnessed my pain, and beheld in this

mighty miracle the heavenly hand of Christ behind the power of your merit, must recognise how great a blessing my punishment foreshadowed for them, since they can now ensure that their earthly possessions are meagre, and realise that by seeking gains they are winning the loss of salvation. If it was a fault in me to have robbed the poor of nourishment from the cheap flesh of a beast, what is it in the case of those who with empty love embrace riches perversely, who recline over their buried gold where their heart is, and who reveal that this hidden treasure, which they keep far separated from its true employment, is superfluous? What will they do? What will they say to you, Christ, in self-defence when they have plundered the portion of all those poor and set before themselves no salvation out of their abundant wealth?"

301. The first repast is now cleared. Now we shall lay the welcome second course. It is the same meat again, but we shall serve it spiced in a different sauce; for I shall unfold to you a further miracle Felix sportively enacted with a hog, a story of novel strangeness. This event was prior in time to the other, but though it preceded the earlier narrative it has been kept to be sung now. It does not matter at what moment any miracle was performed, for He who performs them will be the same in different years, the Christ who achieves different miracles with created things in all lands for the praise of His saints.

312. Some farmers who belong to the further reaches of our region, dwelling in Apulian territory beyond Beneventum,[11] had selected from a large litter in their bristly herd a piglet still sucking the milky paps with unformed mouth. They tended it and fed it for a long time to fulfil a vow, and when it was ready they began to lead

it to the consecrated church of Saint Felix, so that its massive body when slaughtered could feed many needy people, and the martyr could take joy in the full bellies of his poor. But the pig was weighted down with fat which was too much for the strength of its feet, and it could not bear its weight for long. At the very start of the journey it fell beneath its own bulk, and subsequently could not be raised by voice, hand, or whip. Its owners sadly abandoned it lying there, entrusting it to friends. Their troubled minds were in a dilemma. On the one hand, feelings of religious obligation made them reluctant to call off the journey that had vowed, but on the other hand they were ashamed to go all that way to show respect to Felix's portals without bearing the promised gift. Their vacillating minds reached the decision to choose from the same litter in fulfilment of their vow a number of piglets equivalent to the adult age of the hog, which still remained motionless, overcome by its own weight. Their devoted faith sought to discharge the debt of the vow which bound it, and by this calculation intended to balance one fat hog with several small beasts.

337. Accordingly, they came to this consecrated place, and having fulfilled their vow they returned to their lodging. This was some distance from here, for at that time it chanced that a large attendance of visitors had filled the houses round the martyr's church with the usual large crowd. So they were happy to lodge in a distant cottage in an isolated country place some distance from here, and there they prepared early next day to start on their return journey, as soon as the crimson dawn brought forth the daylight. One of the guests opened the cottage door and went out of the house. He saw standing there on the door-

step that hog he knew, miraculously ready. It seemed to
say that it was there at the dispatch of the Lord, and
seemed to greet him, for it licked the feet of its elated
master, grunted and fawned on him with affectionate
signs, and sniffed and kissed him with raised snout. And
as though it recognised that it embodied the debt owed by
its master's vow, with its throat it confronted and demanded the tardy knife.

353. Who, I ask, guided it along the roads in this unfamiliar region? How did it get the feet to enable it to
run that huge distance? A short time before it had given
up at the very threshold of its journey, weighted down by
the burden of its hanging fat. Clearly no hand or enclosing
arms had carried the massive beast along that lengthy road;
and its own intelligence did not impel it to find its way on
so lengthy a journey through territory unknown, for even
human persons with the full possession of rational minds,
and with the ready guidance through unknown districts
afforded by explaining tongues, get involved in blind
wanderings when abroad unless they have a guide to make
the way clear for them. So who guided the hog on its way,
and who gave it the will to follow its masters, or the
intelligence to make it aware that it had long been groomed
to discharge a vow? How did the beast feel an anxiety not
often affecting even men of faith? It seemed as if the pig
felt blameworthy for its action in having settled back
sluggishly, and then, smitten by a holy fear, was seeking
by its journey to expiate the guilt incurred by having
remained, and thus atoned for its sin of lazy idleness by
obediently accompanying its masters on their journey,
however late.

373. Clearly it was divine power which directed this

remarkable portent, the pig's great enterprise of making the long journey alone, and its great intelligence in passing undeviatingly across territory unknown. How extraordinary, too, as it journeyed here from the region beyond Beneventum, that if it boldly travelled on the public highway it was nowhere seized by crowds encountering it, or if it journeyed through secluded forests it was not speared by a man or devoured by a wild beast! What hand guided or protected it on its solitary way? It must surely be that it escaped men's eyes through concealment in a cloud, or else that it was borne through the air on a wind rather than journeyed on foot,[12] and then, suddenly[13] gliding down on the breeze to the lodging of his master, the four-footed guest halted before that unfamiliar threshold.

388. I shall recount another miracle manifested in almost similar fashion. This concerns a different species, that of cattle. Some men set out to journey here from an abode equally distant.[14] They had vowed the gift of a heifer; and having so designated it from the moment it sucked its dam's milk-giving udders, they had nurtured it for our poor who gather here in large numbers, and who are fed through Felix's kindness by the generous resources of many. So when the heifer now rejoiced in limbs fully formed and was ready to discharge the vow with full-grown body, they drove it on its way from home. It seems to be the custom of those who bring from afar the sacrifices they have vowed to pay to the holy martyrs to yoke them to a cart in which they themselves can ride. So they approached the beast, seeking to fasten it to the yoke. Though it was unaccustomed to such treatment, it was tame and compliant to the men's demands, for its masters had removed it from the herd when small, and

given it shelter and food. Because of this they thought that
its fierceness was contained, and that it would willingly
offer its neck complaisantly to the yoke. They stroked
it encouragingly, and tried to guide it into the narrow
shafts; the heifer thought that the hands it knew well were
playing with it, and at first it acceded and obeyed their
summons.

409. But when it was now adjacent to the yoke, saw
the thongs, and realised that the reins were being fitted
over its neck, it was angry at the deceit, and was suddenly
transformed into a wild beast. It rejected the yoke from
its neck, and the reins from its back. Defeating their hands,
it shook off the reins, and leapt from the crowd of men
controlling it, making for distant, pathless country, fleeing
from its masters and its familiar home. It fled only a short
distance out of their sight, as a wild animal would, and hid
itself, a runaway, in the dark forest. It sought to flee, but
when its masters departed it stayed within reach of them,
but at a distance, conditioning its flight to avoid being
abandoned in the countryside.

420. At last, when it saw the wagon approach drawn
by two yoked oxen, it showed human intelligence, and as
though aware that its life was in debt to a vow, it began to
accompany the men on their departure. But it did not stay
with them long, for it refused to escort the slow wheels.
Speeding past the groaning wheels at what seemed a taunt-
ing gallop, it flew ahead and looked back at the slow-
moving procession, no longer fearing to be joined to the
yoke. It became friend and guide to the wagon it earlier
loathed, all the time till they reached the consecrated
shrine of Felix.

429. There it halted of its own accord, and came close

to its owner when he called. Like one discharging a vow, it showed pleasure in standing on the very spot where as victim it owed its own blood. The heifer which had revolted and refused human bonds was led without a struggle to a peaceful death. Unschooled by the yoke, it offered its neck to the axe. It joyfully poured out its blood to fulfill its masters' vow, and to provide the poor with food from its slaughtered body.

437. Why should all this have happened? Surely, as the Apostle puts it, God has no concern for cattle?[15] No, the Maker who makes all things for us achieves all in all for us. Through ignorant cattle He performs signs which work on our behalf. By clear signals He works on brute minds to strengthen our faith and make us trust in the truth, so that men may be taught to loose their tongues in speech and tell of that Lord whom the dumb beasts proclaim by signs.[16]

## POEM 21[1]

With the welcome change of season, bright peace
ushers in for us the new year with placid light after our
experience of winter, and unfolds this day, stamped with
the honour paid to St. Felix, for a now carefree people.
Exultant Felix urges us to rejoice with minds untroubled,
now that the cloud of grim war has been dispelled; for
Felix, too, as patron of peace, together with his fathers
Paul and Peter and his brothers the holy martyrs, successfully besought the King of kings to extend with His benign power the duration of Rome's kingdom, to repel the
Getae as they now pressed at the very entrance to the
city, and to divert death or captivity against the very men
who were threatening the Roman kingdom with its final
fate.[2]

13. So now that fear is driven out like a spent storm, it
is pleasant to look back at the clouds dispelled[3] and to
compare our present condition with what is past. How
loathsome was the darkness of these past days of last year,
when madness, kindled by the stirring of God's anger,
blazed in the cities of Latium through the unleashing of
the enemy! Now look in turn at the powerful gifts of
Christ the Peace-bringer. The enemy and their unholy
king[4] alike are slaughtered, and the victory of the boy
Augustus has restored peace; though of tender years, his
courage in battle has emerged triumphant through God's

strength, and he has shattered human resource through Christ's victory over an impious tyrant.[5]

25. But why should I now extend my words on this demonstration by the body politic that it is not the particular concern of my Felix? In fact, this cause, the continuance of Roman safety and the existence of the state, has been undertaken by many advocates. Our leaders Peter and Paul have been in evidence, and all the martyrs, too, both the countless number contained within the confines of great Rome and those revered by the Church amongst countless nations in scattered territories within the boundaries of Romulus' empire; all have kept anxious vigil together in concentrated prayer. My Felix was one of these, playing a large part in their prayers, but the collective gift they begged for is to be credited to all of them, not to any as an individual achievement.

37. So I shall retrace my steps. It is enough for me to have spoken a little on a theme irrelevant to Felix's particular merits. Yet I could not pass it silently by, because a part of the credit for this, too, accrued to Felix. Christ God, the Power supreme, the powerful King of kings, yielded to all the saints at once, and Felix mingled with their imploring crowd when Christ graciously hearkened, matching their devotion with His own. So now I shall refrain from attaching the gifts of the many to Felix's own; I shall sing Felix's specific praises, and tell of the deeds he personally performs in his own abode here.

47. Where, then, shall I begin the weaving of my song? Which kindnesses of Felix shall I recount? Shall I tell of the many blessings performed for all in sundry places, or of the gifts confined to the house here, for which I am specifically in his debt? It is these last I shall prefer to

tell, the gifts I well remember being bestowed on me and
my community. In previous poems I have told rather of
the kindnesses he conferred jointly on others and myself;
so I shall now with thankful heart compose this one about
the wealth he has generously bestowed on us alone. I shall
dispense with my usual habit; just as Felix every year
procures for me material things of different kinds, so I
shall change my tunes and vary the metres. I shall proceed
with one connected work, but regulate the rhythm of my
verse to more than one pattern.[6]

60. For in this fertile field of Saint Felix new flowers
have blossomed, two plants of Christ, Turcius of godly
speech[7] and Sverius in the flower of manhood.[8] Likewise,
there are holy matrons and maidens to match them; they
are the peers of Alfia, famed sister of that notable Philemon of old whom Paul's letter designates in its heading.[9]
There is Eunomia, a maiden now pledged to eternal marriage in heaven.[10] She was snatched from her mother's
breast,[11] for Christ found her pleasing, and with the haste
of love dedicated her to Himself, sprinkling her with the
perfume of His name. Accordingly, the tresses of her
soul are steeped in it, and the chaste head of her mind
anointed with it, and so her breath has the holy scent of
her heavenly Bridegroom. She is the sister of Melania,[12]
and in a sense her daughter, for she takes pleasure in stick-
ing close to her, adopting her sister as her teacher. Both
are together equipped with heavenly jewels of the virtues
like bright gems on beautiful breasts. Behind them follows
a large train of noble ladies, a dedicated crowd of virgins
sharing the same colour of the one fleece.[13] Then Christ
takes joy in His beloved lamb when He hears Eunomia,
schooled by the guiding voice of Melania, fashioning her

vessel with the wholesome tunes of the Psalms, because to God's accompaniment the little girl guides with her pure voice the blessed female chorus, the companions of the saints.

84. So as I pondered inwardly these facts, an apposite gratitude prompted me to imitate this garden, decked with different flowers, by a song that sported in manifold metres. For I marvel that Felix's bosom[14] is crowded and blossoming with glories of different kinds, now that many guests have been sent to him by Christ's guidance. They have come in thick crowds to be the dear children of father Felix, so that he rejoices that all the huts throughout his territory have suddenly sprouted lodgings, and that these sober abodes at last resound with chaste hymns, sung for him by harmonious voices. He marvels at these charges that fill his arms, so worthy of his lodgings in their persons and their voices, their souls matched in virtue though they are of different sexes. He is like an old planter who sees the tenants at work in his fields, and gets pleasure from olive-shoots on a fertile hill, new-grown from the divine seed of Christ. I pray, then, that the arena of my song may flourish in its new meadow, and that the rhythm with its differing metres may hasten to give service, singing the praises of the Lord, the Creator of both voice and every kind of art. Elegiacs must soon follow upon interwoven iambics, while the heroic hexameter must be the head and the base for my composition.

105.[15] Once more the day consecrated to the praise of Felix has dawned, to be celebrated with holy joy and sacrificial victims. Realise that my word "praise" means "death," because the death of holy men can rightly be called their praise; for it is a precious repayment to the

Lord God. This is why the prophet says through the word
of God that praise is given at the end of a life well-
proved,[16] and the divine Word teaches from the mouth
of Solomon that no man is to be proclaimed before his
death,[17] though some perform praiseworthy deeds in this
life, and the praise to be sung at death can be foregathered
in no other life than this.

117. But I believe that the whole matter of this life is
fluid, uncertain, and poised on a slippery slope. The wheel
rises and falls,[18] and quickly transforms our days as it
passes along the rugged paths over which the course of
this life must extend. Because of this, Providence our
teacher warns us that no man should praise or trust either
himself or any other before death. Though the upright
man walks the honourable way,[19] he must none the less
continually fear stumbling until his race is run to the post
and he obtains the palm of glory that he seeks.[20]

129. This is why the blessed martyrs whose perfect
virtue has raised them to a heavenly crown gain the
appropriate praise of honour due. We who succeed them
in our confession of Christ's name all hymn them, for by
shedding their blood for the holy faith they sowed the
blessing of an eternal harvest, so that if we walk in the
martyr's steps we can enjoy a reward equal to that of our
progenitors.

138. Because of this, God's faithful people give thankful
honour to Christ and revere with yearly festivities the days
consecrated to saints, whether confessors or martyrs hallowed by suffering. For on those days they ended their
span of mortal life through life-giving death, and passed
from this spotted world to God. Today is such a day, the
day when Saint Felix found peace, the day on which in

time past advanced years brought an end to his physical life. He had already fought a confessor's battles; but though he was initiated into bloodless death (for it was after the fighting, in time of peace, that the victor was taken up at Christ's call, and joyfully left the earth to pass to his heavenly home),[21] he was not robbed of a martyr's crown, because he had mentally fulfilled his desire to suffer.[22] For he many times entered the contest as a strong soldier, and always conquered the enemy to return a confessor. But God was satisfied with his mental acceptance, and preserved him. He did not deny him the martyr's crown, but conferred on him also that of presiding priest,[23] so that though he had gained the palm in bloodless battle, he could possess the reward of one who had fought. Thus crowned with the purple laurel of confessor, crowned with the chaplet of peace in the garb of his liturgical office, Felix could be twice crowned as confessor and priest of God.

165. So this day which we observe with yearly vows is the day not of his suffering but of his burial. On that day the substances of soul and flesh parted from each other. The soul flew to God, the flesh returned to the earth and rested, hidden in the tomb. It is right that this should be the birthday marked out for saints, for on it they discharge the condition of the flesh and are stripped of the bonds of mortality. They are born for God into the heavenly kingdom, and carry with them the happy hope of resurrection. This is the day I have always so venerated that I considered it my birthday in preference to that on which I was vainly born; the day of my birth indeed is more deserving of grief, for when I was born into this world I came forth a sinner from the womb of a sinner, begotten

of black wickedness, so that I was already guilty when
my mother bore me.

183. So accursed be the day on which I was born out
of wickedness into wickedness;[24] and blessed be for me,
too, the birthday on which my patron Felix was born
amongst the dwellers of heaven and arose to assume that
power by which he could cleanse me of my foulness, loose
me from my bonds, and redeem and absolve me from the
grievous death of my birthday.

191. This same day invariably comes round for all men,
when the year has completed its circular motion. But
every year grace brings some fresh and different gifts
which Christ presents to His comrade so that Felix can
give them to me. So the day is for me transformed, different from the day that comes to all, and it brings various
blessings to inspire my songs.

198. Let us accordingly see what fresh thing it has
brought me this year which can invigorate me to fresh
song. I shall not travel far or adduce things long past in
time or distant in space. These gifts are here, are grasped
close to me. You all behold[25] the gifts presented this year
to us and enclosed in Felix's bosom alone—Christ's slaves
who were earlier nobles in the world but are now destined
dwellers of heaven. Christ Himself, who had made them
rich, has impoverished them in this world so that He may
transport them, now dislodged from the citadel of earthly
distinction, to His kingdom. There is Apronianus, the
glory of the family of Turcius, a boy in years but old towards the motions of the flesh, a nobleman of ancient
stock of Roman citizenry, but more famous in his title as
Christian. The fame of his ancient and of his recent birth
is intermingled; he is a longstanding member of Rome's

senate, but new to Christ's.[26] Pinian his comrade stands close to him, bearing a like yoke, younger in years but matching him in faith. He, too, is a boy distinguished by ancient family, sprung from the first consul of the capital city.[27] That famed Valerius, the first in that line of consuls to hold his name in the Latin calendar, and whom Rome joined to Brutus after the expulsion of the kings,[28] is the most distant ancestor in the remote past of the family of this Valerius, now Christ's consul.

225. What a happy line of descent! Though that Valerius died in pagan error, I pray that he may not bring down this blessed offspring of his stock to his submerged presence in the black pit of hell. Yet as we gaze with the eyes of faith on the past and present history of the human condition, we marvel at the achievements of that lofty founder, and we gaze in awe at the holy sons of such ungodly forbears, designedly derived from that ancient era by a descent of mystical[29] succession. In the darkness of those unholy minds we see that seeds of light gleamed forth from men embedded in the very era of that ancient darkness; though they were pagans, their minds and wills were tested by nature's law.

239. So now from time to time the genius of those ancient ancestors finds echoes in some of their descendants. Thus the famous forbear of the Pinian now mine was chosen as the chief agent of the liberation of his fellow citizens from the harshness of kingship, and so he foreshadowed the birth of this descendant, who in the spirit of his forbear attacked pride from loftier motives and dislodged slavery from his own person. Conquering his own body, he expelled the devil's dominion from his limbs, and now in peace of spirit the chaste freedom of his faithful

soul wears away the yoke of sin. By such action this boy in campaigning as Christ's consul reproduces the quality of his ancestor, for he consults the interest of those to be freed, and on God's behalf dispenses by his action the holy gift of redemption.

255. Hitherto he has rivalled his ancient forbear in delivering from slavery those of his house, as old Valerius delivered his fellow citizens. But what his ancestor achieved in one tiny city whilst Rome was still in infancy, Pinian now does in many cities established in different parts of the world, showing kindness in various places to his own and to outsiders alike.[30] Through the wealth of his holiness he has removed the yoke of slavery from the necks of numerous children released from brazen bonds in the darkness of their prison by this loan of gold.

266. These two, then, Felix has stored away in his keeping and lodged in his house at Christ's command, adopting them as guests forever in my company. So now I take joy in being flanked by these aides, and in one person's words I dedicate the vows of three; one breath speaks for the thoughts of three.

272.[31] Come, boys so dear, and join me in glorifying God, singing noble hymns with trained voices. As ten-stringed lutes resound to the plucking of the strings, and the discordant notes are assembled in harmonious modes, so let the holy lyre of our combined voices resound as though three tongues were singing in one mouth. For though we are three in number, we are one in mind, and with the three of us gather other souls whose names the heavenly book preserves inscribed. The leader of this chorus is Albina, with her companion Therasia;[32] joined with this pair is their sister Avita, so she is the third leader of the column of the hymning chorus.[33] These three mothers have two dear charges of the same sex, twin blossoms, the flowering Melania and Eunomia;[34] these are the dear charges of the menfolk, too, for the divided sexes are joined in affection.

288. In company with father Paulinus there is Turcius,[35] a father no less than I; age gives me the title, whereas offspring accords it to him. Our ages are different, but we share one title. We are not both old, but both of us are fathers. So this is the entire assembled retinue—three mothers, four children, two fathers.

294. The youngster who is Melania's husband[36] in the body of Christ has been lent his name by God from the pine tree. The reason is that a boy born for eternal life might take his name from the tree that is forever verdant. For the pine always thrives with blossoming top, and always loves to sprout aloft on high ridges. It does not change its appearance with time, for in heat and snow it remains unchanging with green foliage. The mother-tree is fertile with a harvest of nuts good for eating inside, and contains tender milk within its curly covering; the rich pine-torch exudes sweet-smelling resin, so that the tree is not sterile even in its wood.

306. Thus the pine is a type of the eternal body—beautiful, fruitful, living, tall, fragrant and flowering. Pinian, this blessed boy, will personify this tree for the Lord, so that the grace in him can abide. He is already planted for God, and stirring; growing in holiness, he is raising his fruitful head like a high pine. He is outstanding, the first son in my own flock. But I have an equal light in the person of Asterius.[37] His devoted parents with true affection together appointed him a child consecrated to

Christ, so that like Samuel marked from his first years[38]
he could grow by God's nourishment among holy men, as
one promised to Him. His first sounds his father dedicated
in Christ's name, and his first utterance was the name of
the Lord; and now God is his father, and he is reared for
the kingdom of heaven. He shines forth with starry name
and starry face alike.[39] Saintly grace made him both son
and brother to his father, for they have been born alike
through the holy stream.[40] Nature had separated them in
status, but God by His kindly gift will bring them into
His kingdom as brothers.

326. So let all nine of us, parents and affectionate children together, live with harmonious hearts like a single
lyre;[41] let all of us form a lyre assembled from different
strings to sing the same song. Aemilius must join us as the
tenth,[42] and then at last the mystical law will sound in us
with full complement. With this number of persons the
living strings on the harp of peace will sound forth a work
which brings salvation. For this lyre Felix will be the
plectrum; with Felix as quill, Christ will delightedly pluck
this ten-stringed lyre.[43] This harp in us will resound to
Christ's playing in full harmony, once our thoughts are
made perfect, if only our peace is at one with God to the
depths of our being, so that we are united in body, mind,
and faith. The man who by pursuing upright laws per-
sonifies this lyre, and orders his life well in all measures,
must live a life which harmonises with the sacred law in
all things, for every string will sound forth unbroken.

344.[44] Now I shall change my manner of address and
speak words of gratitude to you, revered father and perennial patron, my guardian Felix most dear to Christ. You
have conferred on me numerous services comprising

varied gifts. I recall that I owe to you all that obtains for
me possessions in this life and hope for the next, for Christ
has bestowed me from my earliest years to be your slave.
If I possessed eloquence racing like river waters, or a
thousand mouths resounding with a hundred tongues,[45]
even if I chanced to abound in the resources of their
combined streams I could not retail all the gifts of Felix
such as Christ the Lord has given to His friend, and which
the confessor has passed on to me, his servant and his
ward. Which services should I put first, which later?[46]
Many splendid kindnesses, differing in their gifts but equal
in weight, jostle each other, and I could never select one
of these in isolation to relate in preference to the rest; the
ready abundance confounds the discrimination of my
judgment. If I were to begin from the beginning[47] and
recount all the things which he has bestowed on me at
different times but with identical love, I could count the
hairs of my head before I could recount all the gifts
which, kind Felix, you have bestowed on me.

365.[48] It was you who prompted incidents to effect my
salvation, and so you inserted in me seeds of heavenly
possessions, in the hope that I could attain them. When as
a boy I journeyed here from the western regions of the
Gallic provinces,[49] the first moment I set foot with apprehensive step on your threshold, and saw the marvellous
proofs of your holy deeds aglow before your doorway,
where your body is enclosed in burial but where you range
widely in the lofty merit of deserving deeds, I drank in
with my whole heart a belief in the name of God, and
rejoicing in your light I loved Christ. Under your leader-
ship in my early years I wielded the office which embraced
the *fasces*;[50] you guided my hand and secured my welfare,

so that I remained untainted by the hazardous shedding of human blood.[51] Then, too, I shaved off my first hairs as an offering before your tomb, almost as if you plucked them out for me.[52] Already at that time I had pledged my promise to honour your abode, and had decided that I must make my home in the region of Campania. You laid the foundations of your servant's future resting-place when you implanted a commission in the silence of my heart, for you bade that a road be built and paved leading to your dwelling, and that close to your own gables a roof should rise, covering a large area, under which the poor then used to shelter.

386. Subsequently the dwelling thus built was extended with a second story, and now continues to give hospitality in its rooms. The portico beneath it serves the needs of the poor in distress, and also supports us, for we dwell in the additional accommodation of the lodging superimposed;[53] and it provides under the same roof that association with the needy which heals our wounds. So we do each other a friendly service, for the poor strengthen our foundations with their prayers, and in our building we keep warm the bodies of our destitute brothers.

395. So once I was lightened of the sixfold symbols of magistracy, and had laid down the axe which had been stained by no slaughter,[54] I was restored to my anxious mother when you called me back to the region of my former native land.[55] From there I journeyed abroad across the ridge of the Pyrenees to our neighbours the Spaniards.[56] There you allowed me to be yoked in marriage by human dispensation,[57] so that you might gain instead the lives of two of us, and through the yoke of the flesh the double salvation of our souls could compensate for the delay in

the salvation of myself alone. Though as a result of that marriage my life ran along another path, and I lived far distant in another world, where Gaul resounds as it is lashed by the waves of the Atlantic,[58] in my mind I was never torn from this place. I always clung fast to Felix's embrace, and in return I felt that Felix attended on my affairs, investing with every blessing all the business I had to transact at home and abroad. Felix alone was my property and the guardian of my property; he had won Christ's assent in constantly diverting what was hostile and bestowing what was beneficial.

413. Felix, you were ever happily[59] a father and a guardian to me, bestowing continual love on me and preventing my wretchedness. When I was troubled by the bloody slaughter of my own brother,[60] and this case of my brother's was bringing hazard to me as a blood relation, and a purchaser[61] was already laying hands on my property, you, my father, removed the sword from my throat and the treasury officials from my estate. You kept me and my possessions in trust for Christ the Lord. The reason for Christ's bringing aid on that occasion to my property and person, and for Felix's protection being so powerfully present, became clear through the significant outcome. Faith made me renounce the world, my native region and my home; the destiny and plan of my life was changed, and practised its celebrated business in another land.[62] Through the sale of all my goods I purchased the carrying of the cross.

428. Hence earthly possessions purchased the hope of the kingdom of heaven, for the hope extended by faith is stronger than the possessions of the flesh. This hope which rests on God brings immortal possessions, whereas the

property of the flesh destroys the hope of heaven. Yet this hope does not there and then deprive us of our possessions; if it prevails and faith conquers, it changes for the better and refashions our property according to God's law, making it no longer frail but eternal, removing it from earth and setting it in heaven, where Christ as trusty Guardian keeps what is lodged with Him. He does not keep for us merely the amount which he took from us here on trust, but He repays with manifold interest those who have lent Him the talents entrusted to them, and He will make Himself the property of those who believe.[63]

440. What property could be more precious than this? If the whole world were my private possession, it would surely not be preferable to Christ the Lord? And who has now made me the owner of this great property, at least in hope? Who forced me to reject the property of this world in favour of Christ, so that he could make Christ my property? It was none other than you, Felix, ever the great power in my life,[64] hostile to my sins and the friend of my salvation. Making a better provision for me, you changed my native land, giving me yourself in place of that native land. You have broken for us the bonds of the flesh.[65] You secured our deliverance from the decline of our transient stock, you arranged our departure from the region of our native land to join your family, so that with ambitious hearts we aspire to heavenly things. You have transformed our genealogy from mortal forbears to set us among the friends of the heavenly Lord, where you will cause our names to be signed in the eternal book. By this transference of our mortal origin, you will ensure that we are removed from death's purview and enrolled instead for salvation. Did I have anything when I was called

senator to match what I have here and now when I am called impoverished?

460. See how my house extends through all these basilicas[66] of the blessed martyr, their dimensions so large, their roofs so lofty, their high vaulted ceilings so splendid, their fountains playing and their porticos surrounding them! All that is here on every side, all that is cultivated, famed, and preserved in Felix's name in this entire region is my abode. There is no place abutting on or within the confines of the shrines where my estate, so to say, is not in evidence. But why should I glorify myself in the matter of this gift, seeing that I possess this property, visible in its covering of stone, as guest and native slave of my beloved Felix? How much more important to me is the fact that Felix himself by God's gift is the house in which my living self possesses a living house which no lapse of time will bring down!

474. The fact that Felix's house is also mine, since he grants me free rein with his possessions, is attested by my bold conduct, for in my capacity as host I have received my comrades into this dwelling; now all of us with equal right wield the rights of Felix, and we are cherished together in Felix's bosom as his dear ones. You know them, and you see them now sharing with me the maintenance of the lodging we have established in Felix's abode. They are oblivious of the exalted roofs of their ancient houses, and rejecting ambition they reside more securely in the narrow compass of the tiny cells which have the martyr close by.[67] For Christ attends on modest dwellings and turns away from lofty ones. He prefers to visit the tiny roof of an impoverished hut rather than the high pinnacles of proud estates.

488. So to enable me to compare the abode I now in-
habit with the pinnacles I have forsaken, and my present
possessions with what I recall once having, compare them
if you will by criteria appropriate to both. What house of
mine could ever be so fine, what land so fertile in the
transient world, as that which Christ has now bestowed in
my present poverty? For it is through Christ that Felix
is my plentiful possession, rich in inexhaustible returns.
Whereas, to recall the estates of my previous wealth,
whatever important property I had earlier was earthly, an
empty appearance of a shape without substance. Whether
they comprised gold or precious stones, those household
goods were a prize of no value in the eyes of good men,
but a poison precious in the eyes of the greedy. But now
that I am bereft of wealth—or more truly, of reprobate
burdens rather than wealth—I am freed from possessing,
and I enjoy untroubled poverty. The hostile bonds of
posterity[68] have no means of binding one who is stripped
of possessions. When a man is not choked by the love
aroused by the enticing picture of the deceiving world
with its manifold shapes, he abandons his body readily
and lightly.[69]

506. Poverty of Christ, how adorable you are to me,
more precious than the whole world! Those whom you
strip of riches, clearing the earth of its rubble, you enrich
with heavenly treasure. You destroy what is earthly within
us, and in turn build up what is heavenly.[70] By a new law
you convert earthly losses into the reward of life; you
reverse loss and gain, so that preserving our money brings
loss, and losing it brings gain. Yet squandering it in in-
auspicious fashion also involves loss, for a man only profits
from disposal of his possessions if he does it in Christ's

name and at God's command. Outlay on impious vices is truly thrown away. High living and ambition are as heavy in the scale as the sin of greed, being diseases fraught with great danger, for underlying both is an equal cause of death, which is attained equally by the stain of lust and by the evil-inducing desire for the possessions of the world. Noblest Felix, you desire that I become empty of these riches so that you may make me rich in life, and by my impoverished existence you rid me of the death which the rich in this world must suffer as expiation without cease; for their death-bringing use of gold wins for them eternal fires and the worms which accompany them.[71]

526. It is not in this house alone that you desire to have dwelling in union with you those of us whom you seek to nourish to share eternal life with you and to guide towards that form of life which you lived on earth after the pattern of Christ the Lord, once rich but subsequently poor.[72] Who remains unaware,[73] Felix, of that poverty of yours which after the disposal of your wealth you joyfully embraced as confessor for Christ's holy name, and which you maintained up to old age, always cultivating your crops in a rented garden?[74] Hence you strive to make all whom you receive under your hospitable roof to be like yourself in holy poverty, for an alien way of life could not merge with you. The paths of the rich man and of Christ are as separate as the disharmony of wolf and lamb, of light and darkness. It is the broad and open road,[75] so slippery on its downward slope as it leads to hell, which oppresses the greedy rich, who are driven on their course to hell by their own massive possessions. But Christ's path, the road which extends before holy confessors and martyrs, is a difficult way open only to the few,[76] so it does not accept those

who stuff themselves, and it debars those heavily laden. Therefore it befits the servant and follower of the blessed martyr to confine himself, to strip himself of his burdensome chains, and to become spare and light through healthy poverty, so that he can pass through the narrow gate and climb the lofty mountain of the Lord.[77]

551. But why do I, who am without the insight to judge the importance of such matters, set down these lines in return, best of fathers, for your great gifts? Yet though these gifts are great in my eyes, they are still small if I speak of the better ones. How small a part of your activities on our behalf is the value of the gift by which you have granted us land for a lodging and permission to establish a dwelling house, seeing that you, father, have granted us your own heart! For it was nothing other than the depths of your heart, dear saint, which you offered us when you deigned to expose for us the recesses of your tomb. Our purposes were awakened by your buried dust. You wished to demonstrate the unique love of your attachment to us by so great a sign that you determined to open during our lifetime the abode of your body, so silent and unmoved for many previous generations,[78] with the sudden emergence of your ashes, kindly father.

566. So in praising Felix I shall merely touch with cursory haste on that wealth of his here which I have mentioned. These are lesser gifts which he has diligently and abundantly bestowed on us whom he has taken in his charge, and he will never cease to shower us lavishly and continually with countless gifts from his rich wealth. He does not merely supply the needs of the body; he has also bestowed on us the means of gratifying praise now and of abiding fame in the future. Though he was never so housed

in those great ages of the past, he allowed his basilicas to be built by our hands, and to be extended or renewed with porticoes and residences.[79] He has also unfolded to us the holy secrets of his own tomb. I shall tell briefly of this revered gift, so that it may shine forth as an exemplar of his great devotion to us. Though we are unworthy of this great love, he has allowed our eyes to draw near to the awesome mystery, as though he were exposing his bones to friends as dear as his inner self.

583. So I shall recount to you in its entire sequence the circumstances in which he has allowed us to set eyes on the neighbourhood where his limbs lay, and to touch the very coffin that housed his body. The appearance of the place continues to be familiar to all. Above the tomb of the enclosed martyr, where a rail encloses the sides of the sepulchre,[80] there is visible a kind of marble slab on which a silver covering is superimposed.[81] This table set over the tomb has twin holes,[82] allowing perfume to be poured into the recesses below. From the holy ashes stored there comes a healing breath and a hidden fragrance, conferring a sacramental quality on the pouring vessels. For after they had poured in the liquid perfume, and at once as usual scooped it from the tomb lying below in the earth, and those who had bestowed the nard on the tomb prepared to draw it up to apply it to themselves, they found the vessels miraculously filled not with nard but with a heap of dust which burst out from below. They fearfully withdrew their hands, covered with heaps of dust, from the aperture to the tomb. This strange event affected everyone, and they were fired with eagerness to discover the reason for this sudden prodigy.

602. So we decided to appoint a fixed day to examine

the deep-set tomb by removing the marble cover. I must
confess that we were extremely exercised and apprehensive about the possible content of the dust from the holy
body which had been drawn out by hand from the tomb
through the apertures. It had been brought out caked with
associated debris, with fragments of bone and sherds
covered with rubble. The fear of those present, expressed
in their conversation, was that perhaps some creature enclosed in a hidden den below was throwing up the ashes
from the saint's body, just as strange animals in the isolation of the countryside often dig up the ground with their
sharp beaks, and pile up heaps of black earth around the
pits. This was what they feared from Saint Felix's burial
place within.

616. To make the incident still stranger, a remarkable
eruption of accumulated earth caused a delay of some days.
So on the day decreed, the operation useful for many
purposes was set in hand. The bishop[83] entrusted the matter to all us priests. As we superintended, a band of workmen bent to carry out our instructions. Their first job was
to remove the railings from their sockets, and their second
to detach the upper slab by removing the nails which held
it down. But when we saw that the coffin sustaining the
weight of the marble cover was still in place with the
structure of the tomb unbroken, our faith became untroubled, and drove from our hearts all hazard of error.
Touch and sight afforded them proof[84] that the tomb was
not damaged or split at any point, that the body of our
martyr who had served his time was enclosed by strong
defences, and did not yawn open through some wicked
deed; that his holy bones were still in possession of the
honour which their flesh merited. The Holy Spirit never

fails to attend them, and this is why living grace abides in the tombs of saints, proving that those who expired in Christ are buried but not dead, for their bodies are temporarily in tranquil sleep. So when we had rearranged Felix's tomb with due honour, we left it all carefully protected, so that his bones may rest undisturbed in their bed until that day of the Lord on which the saints will be aroused together to have the shining honour they deserve under Christ's presidency. So the same peace which awaits his holy soul in the heavens possesses also his revered body in the earth.

643. What remains for further telling? Not that I have recounted worthily the song I have sung, or mentioned fully all the gifts of my generous patron. There are many hidden from my verses, but all are implanted in my mindful heart. Though very many have been related, more remain still untold. But the law regulating composition advises that from many the greatest should be selected.

650. When all the buildings which are visible clustered together in different styles had been completed, and the colonnades formed a wide circumference round the lofty roofs of the basilicas and their forecourts, all the buildings and their depressed tenants seemed to be alike praying for the single boon of water. I myself, as I freely admit, kept rebuking my Felix with words of complaint on the grounds that he was slow to attend to these prayers[85]—he was permitting a share in the water from our confederate city[86] to be denied to us for so long. In fact our haste was ill-considered, and he was making us wait because his design was better. He was extending the delay till the appropriate time. The order of operations reasonably demanded that there should first be the completion of that work

which our diligent application was preparing with manifold endeavours around the holy basilicas of the revered
martyr. Then, when divine grace had applied the final
touches to these works, and our vows had been completed
in full order, he was to bring and channel water into the
churches now built. At last, when the whole construction
stood here fully finished, the dry thirst of our prayers was
not long kept waiting. God willed it, and then the townsfolk, earlier hard-hearted, lent ready agreement with complaisant hearts.

672. So I shall now speak of this gift of water. Felix,
successfully entreat the Lord and grant that my words
may now run with an eloquence as ready as the abundant
flow of the fountains which you have allowed to well up
in your forecourts and your dwellings. All that the kindly
Lord has granted us on your recommendation He has
adorned and increased by the gift with which He brought
water to the thirsty fields. Christ the famed Rock[87] once
more flowed forth from the fount of holy fecundity,
bringing anew that gift of ancient love. Thus He watered
all that sandy soil previously dry and unused to moisture.
He made the arid earth flow with sudden streams, and
when visiting crowds of different races had gathered in
Felix's holy churches, He made fresh water from the
flowing stream[88] pour abundantly up through wells, cis-
terns, and huge containers.

687. Highest Fount, who could grant me the favour of
Your irrigation of the desert within me, of Your bursting
through the stony rock of my heart? Who could confer
the boon of my founding my house on Your rock, and of
drinking from Your source the water which could bring
forth in my arid heart a living stream of perennially gush-

ing water? But this thin trickle of my eloquence with which I address You is certainly drawn from the same source as the welling fount of rivers, for who could tell of You even in a minor key without Your aid, O Christ, highest Power of the highest Father? It is Your Spirit which inspires our praise of You, for by that Light we see the equal Light of Father and Son, so that by the inspiration of His guidance we may confess both Christ and the Father. Yet as I poised on my lips the name of the living Fount, a distillation from the stream of the Word dripped into my mouth, and perhaps my lips will reproduce some flavour of it; so now my tongue will not be arid or my throat dry, and it will speak more copiously because it has been watered.

704. Now that I have listed all these numerous-sounding works, at this point I must make mention in a few words of devoted Abella,[89] for the town appears worthy of the distinguished fame of being praised so as to confer praise on Felix. Willingly, for the glory of Felix, she undertook toil, and she considered the heat of the sweat undertaken on precipitous cliffs as repose and reward. Abella is a town small in circumference, but its praise will be great for this pious deed. It is situated six miles from our Nola here between high mountain ridges, from which close at hand it draws its drinking water, which is gathered in a single reservoir. Pipes[90] are connected to it from which the town first claims the water for its own use, and with the remainder gives abundance to the city of Nola, and also irrigates many country estates in various places.

718. But I shall return to my thanksgiving for the work performed as a boon. The aqueduct had fallen down because it was very old, and the townsfolk lent abundance

of welcome aid to renew it both for their domestic use
and for conveying water elsewhere. The site lay between
high rocks, denying access even to mules by any path, so
that the height of the huge mountain made it difficult to
find even a paid gang of workmen. This makes even
greater the glory which enriches Abella as reward, because
the town readily lent its service to the sacred honour of
Felix, and with generous devotion provided gangs without payment. You could see conscientious bands gathered
there from the whole population, upper class and common
folk alike, with a single purpose. Aroused at dawn, they
were gladly rushing as one to the task, eagerly vying as
they sped to the top of the mountains. Their necks were
bent beneath the heavy burden of hods as they carted
quarry-stones over the bushy heights. Beneath a blazing
sun they made repeated trips over the same ground, and
for the whole of the long and lingering summer's day they
strained from dawn until the late hours of evening. Then
with minds unsleeping, with bodies barely rested in the
brief night, they rose again before dawn to seize their
tools, forgetful of their toil since God refreshed them.

741. In short, so favourably did the great task progress
that the whole job was concluded and the work discharged
like a game within a few days. By means of that crowded
column of workmen, the aqueduct from those distant
mountains, which was earlier tumbledown through long
neglect, collected the streams from the slopes on every
side, and brought back the gathered water to cities long
thirsty. Passing along the canal of the aqueduct for many
miles of journeying, with its abundant stream it joyfully[91]
poured into and filled the new cistern of our Felix. As
proof of God's gift, a greater amount of water has flowed

here in the summer months than previously used to issue after the storms of winter.

754. At this point, my Nola, I shall justly indict you before our common patron. With the anger of kindly love and without irritation, I shall impersonate the ire of your patron, and rebuke a dear daughter with the substance of an old complaint. When, Nola, I sought the share in your water supply that was our due, what fear so disturbed you that you hard-heartedly refused to dispense our share like a good host? Forgetful of God's rights, you thought that my request looked solely to human needs. Forgetful of Felix, you thought that your gift would be extended to my own person, and your sad lament was that if you granted it, your territory would soon be dry and drained of water. This was what you repeatedly shouted, even to the point of raising a riot.[92] You did not know that supplies would be available by God's help, as you have now discovered.

767. For God the Creator Himself then demonstrated that hearts that do not trust in Christ are cowardly; once peace prevailed and you devotedly shared with Felix your partner, you now obtained the use of the aqueduct, so that God could better rebuke your complaint with overflowing goodness. When the water was divided, He did not make you thirst, as you had feared. Rather, as Maker and Nourisher of created things and men alike, He who made all things by His word demonstrated to you that the possession which you refused to His friend, through distrust in the Lord of creation, was His and not, as you had inferred, your own. Certainly you realised and acknowledged under the compulsion of events the transcendent power of the eternal Father and the powerful merits of

Felix; for during that time of anxiety, after that devoted
sacrifice by which you bestowed a share on the martyr's
churches, your water was greatly reduced, but God and
Felix caused the sudden appearance of the waterway.
Once the fecund stream had been unleashed at its source,
it flowed as bidden into your town, a repayment with
abundant interest. At the very time when you who held
stores of water became inured often to forgo it, God restored with plenty what He had taken from you, and
water flowed in abundance for your drinking and washing
needs.

788. So with what gift can I, so poor in resources,
repay your great gift, Abella? I shall at any rate pay you
by proclaiming and witnessing your service and your
fame in my song. You will have as your payment the prize
of being perennially associated with the written praise of
Saint Felix, and of being labelled the ward of that great
patron whose gifts you have so extensively shared. Now
you have a task urged on you by Felix's inspiration, and
common folk and upper class alike must harmoniously
attack and perform it with great sweat; the summer season
will redouble the hard toil. There is an aqueduct built
long ago over steep and unfavourable terrain, familiar to
previous generations. But now it is not used, and the water
has ceased to flow. It lies concealed between huge ridges
under a great weight of forest which has engulfed it. Your
task is to divest it of its thick covering, restore its long
forgotten function, gather its stream now sprinkled over
that pathless countryside and absorbed deep within the
porous soil, compel the various rivulets to return to their
former courses, channel them when thus realigned into
the mouth of the parent aqueduct, make its course long

empty through the defection of the water overflow with the returning stream, and thus water the town of Nola. She has long complained at the withdrawal of her supply, and has abandoned hope of your course. Because the city no longer has her own resources, she enjoys the waters of Felix. In return for her gift of a small trickle, she has been enriched by the abundant flow sent by divine aid and gained through the zeal of Felix. So you, too, Nola, must with me cherish tiny Abella as a mother, for as you know, though she is your daughter she is the mother of your water supply. From her native mountains will flow upon you all the abundance which you had when you accorded Felix's felicitous followers[93] first arrogance, but later service bestowed with more edifying zeal.

822. So be glad, and account yourself fortunate, dear Nola. Rejoice to Christ in your extensive resources. It was He who fashioned you through his beloved friend Felix, and His lofty hand enhanced your beauty through nature, His handmaid. Look at your shining new appearance today, so that you may decide whether you made a contribution to Felix's glory or whether you are enhanced and cultivated by God's Felix. Where rough stones lay arid in bare fields, there is now the pleasant transformation of greenery on the watered turf. These are not the only fountains, Nola, that the rich grace of Christ has poured on you through the merit of Felix. He has also brought here to your city the fountains that flow from heaven. He has set them in the delighted abode of Felix, and ordered them to course out from your city in full spate to many towns.

836. I refer to Christ's servants here, the couple famed in God's eyes, the couple ennobled by Christ's name. Now

they and their mother Albina are the children of your
estate, the dear charges of all the saints and the joy of
heaven, the blessed pair Pinian and his wife Melania.[94] God
has made them the children of Felix, but also his fruitful
breasts, breasts dispensing the flowing milk of God's goodness, from which every needy person obtains plentiful
sustenance, and every rich man a salutary example. See,
these are the waters from Christ's loving river, welling up
through the earth with invisible stream and offering in
plenty the living water of compassionate love.

848. Christ, make these fountains gush out for you with
unfailing plenty in the bosom of your Felix; let them
never become a trickle at any season. You Yourself, O
Christ, flow into the hearts of those dedicated to You,
and grant Your Felix this favour on behalf of the sinners
entrusted to him. Never let Your love withdraw the
stream of this wealth from our persons. May Felix, the
fount from Your fount, water us so generously that Your
spring may gush in us, O Christ our King. So Felix may
ensure that after our wretchedness and need we may now
share his name and live in felicity.

# POEM 22[1]

## *To Jovius*

I promise myself that you are now basing your poems on the sacred books, and that inflamed with the power of Christ God you will loose your eloquent tongue to the highest Father.[2] Start to devote your heart solely to God's affairs. Raise your thoughts from earth and direct them up to God. Then before your eyes the sky will open and a new light will emerge. The Holy Spirit will enter with silent movement your hidden parts, and will rustle in your heart with His glad breath. Come now, wield your lyre, stir your fertile heart to essay a great theme; let that fluency devoted to your customary songs give place, for a greater sequence of topics is now inaugurated for you.[3] Your theme is now not the judgment of Paris or the fictitious wars of the giants. True, this was your sport of old in your childhood days, for games were appropriate to a young child. But now that you are more advanced in years, and accordingly more serious in purpose, you must spurn with adult mind the unsubstantial Muses.[4] You must take up subjects demanded by your age, for which chaste manners are now apposite, and by the venerable appearance of your countenance. You must conceive thoughts of God.

20. If you have won any glory from fictitious themes or great fame from empty ones by singing of fanciful events in classical lays or by recounting earthly deeds to praise the glory of triumphing kings, you did not deserve

to win praise out of those men whom you preferred to
adorn with the gift of your rich eloquence. How much
greater fame will accrue to you from those themes which
will not only exercise your tongue but will also inform
your scrupulous mind, and from which you will obtain not
only praise but also life! By your sagacious reading and
recording of the true wonders of the highest God, your
apprenticeship will make you closer and dearer to God
Himself. Once you believe in and admire Him, you will
begin to love Him, and by loving God you will win reciprocal love from Christ. Let the trumpet of your tongue
which has thus far blared for empty purposes now sound
forth on a higher note the works of God.

35. You seek to discover the causes of creation and the
beginnings of the universe. Do not search aimlessly for the
innumerable worlds of which Epicurus idly dreamt, which
that lunatic posits as originating from parent-atoms in the
void;[5] your heart would be fruitlessly journeying into
vacuity. Moses the lawbringer, that revered figure of
ancient fame who tells of the formation of the world from
its beginning at God's creation, will clear away for you
your empty worries. He tells of the fashioning of man
from mud and the breath of the Holy Spirit, and so he
will teach you by whose gift you are higher than all living
creatures on earth.[6] Do not count yourself as cheap as the
stones of Pyrrha or the clay of Prometheus,[7] for the supreme Hand made you[8] lofty in face and mind, and
deigned to fashion you in His own image. Then again you
will grasp the decision which bound us to death, and
realise who laid down the conditions in which we drag
out our lives; this will prevent your entrusting our free
will to the fates.[9]

51. If you can cast your mind higher than the sky, desiring to know what is above the stars or what was before time began, John teaches what lies beyond the universe and beyond time's beginning. He says:[10] *In the beginning was the Word.* God rejoiced in the Word His Pledge, and the Word was both the Word of God and God. This is *the Word without whom there is nothing,* by which all creation flourishes, which governs all things, which all things obey as subjects, before which the whole of nature, prostrate in eternal service before God, venerates the name of Son and Father. *Every tongue* throughout the nations now *confesses that the Lord Jesus reigns with the majesty of the Father.*[11] On His name our salvation is securely based and our faith depends, extending to eternity. By relying on His divine gift we mortals succeed in conquering our frail nature by pure deeds, in bursting the bonds of clamping death, and in observing in our bodies the laws of the spirit.[12] We pursue the divine footsteps of Christ God. Our minds govern both soul and body beneath the protection of sacred armour, for the mind which subjects itself to God obtains the armour of salvation,[13] and holds dominion over its soul and its flesh. Every man rightly becomes master of himself if he surrenders himself forever to the one Lord, and thus becomes ruler over his own limbs. He is unconquered by sins and hates wickedness; he is stronger than the powers that oppose him. By genuine classification he is a true man, because he has the strength of mind in which he contains the light of reason, and he governs without conflict his servant senses, and he directs his heart with gentle reins.

79. Since your noble mind burns with the fire from heaven's spark, you must mentally mount into the secret

shrines of the sky and rest your head on the Lord's bosom.
Then Christ will generously place in your open mouth
His breasts flowing with sacred milk, and will bathe your
mind in divine light; then, the mist dispelled, you will see
the awesome God's mighty laws by which Christ the all-
begetting Wisdom, whilst remaining within Himself, constantly renews the whole of creation. God the Controller
of His own works preserves or changes their appearance
at will, and extends or abbreviates their length of life. He
governs sky and sea, stars and winds with the same power
with which He made them. The huge exodus from
Egypt[14] and the returning sea which drowned the tyrant[15]
after he had experienced the considerable motions of the
elements[16] demonstrate the God whom all creation fears
and serves.[17] (For there was a time when the Jews, then
God's only chosen race, dwelt in a common land, but the
anger of God oppresses proud foes, and they have now
been separated and have sped away to dwell among intermingled races.)[18]

98. After this I am sure that you do not claim that
chance with its random storms governs the sea,[19] since you
read that the sea parted when bidden to part, that a path
drained of unyielding waves extended through the waters,
and that the sea which had thus dissolved returned to its
watery depths at the command of the holy prophet's rod.
The power of the sea registered double obedience, giving
the holy people both a path and revenge.

105. Again, what of the prophet who was fleeing to
Tharsis, who was cast into the sea when the lot dictated
by danger fell on him, and who was swallowed by the
huge gaping maw of the whale and then vomited forth
unscathed from its monstrous belly?[20] He surely teaches

us that sea and stars are moved under God's control. By vainly seeking to flee from God the Controller of all things whom none can escape, he aroused the anger of both sky and sea. Nature, which belongs to the almighty Lord, realised that he was revolting and she was afraid to play conspirator by transporting the guilty man safely through her demesne; she chained the runaway with winds and waves. That prophet was chosen by God to frighten sinning nations by his threatening advice. Once he had spoken of the calamitous outcome, had shattered the guilty and diverted God's anger, he washed away his sins by the shedding of tears. Nineve reformed itself and so escaped its final end.[21]

119. Again, that famed king[22] surely avoided his destined fate, for when death was near he prayed to the Lord. He knew that God alone could bend His laws to extend further his spent life, and he deserved to live for fifteen further years, surviving beyond his span rather than living merely his allotted years. After this, can we admire Plato's fabrication of the three Fates,[23] or Aratus' poems,[24] or the stars which Manethon describes?[25] Let them, I ask, answer this: when holy Ezechias by prayer and strength of faith diverted the paths of the stars, confounded the course of heaven, and drove back the light of the bidden sun,[26] how did they assign to human beings then born their fleeting hours of life, and which stars were in conjunction with which? Again, when that same sun by the order of its holy Commander postponed the darkness and halted the movement of daylight so that the victory of the holy race could be completed,[27] the heavens remained poised and the solar sphere moved back so that stronger light could bathe that great triumph.

135. Moreover, Christ, who is the Offspring, Strength, and Wisdom of God, is enough to remove our obsession with empty errors. By both word and action He teaches that the one God governs all; and so that we may believe that nothing exists without the purpose of God the Creator, He says that no foliage falls from a tree nor any bird from the sky without His bidding.[28] When the Almighty calms the sea with His word or by the implanting of His foot, with a word expels disease or represses devils or restores returning life into dead bodies, bids men long dead to emerge from their opened tombs and renews their crumbling, entombed bodies with reinstated life,[29] it is clear that the Maker who alone guides all nature and all life sufficiently reveals His peculiar power.

148. I beg you, devote your studies and efforts rather to reading and writing about these events. Sing of the mighty projects of the Thunderer,[30] write of the beginnings of the universe created by the Word, of the chaos before there was day and the dawn of the first light. Write of all the words and deeds of God achieved in the different ages through all the elements. You will learn of them through the holy books—the words inscribed on the tablets of the Law that Moses taught, or the teachings of the new Law of the Gospel witness, disclosing the mysteries of Christ earlier concealed.

157. Then I shall pronounce you truly a poet divinely inspired, and I shall drain your songs like a draught of sweet water when they provide for me nectar from the heavenly fount[31] as they sing of Christ the Lord of Creation and attest that your mind is potent with God. Thus I can obtain from you wealth of tongue and mind, and, already rejoicing to have you as kinsman by marriage,[32] I

will be able to felicitate you on being also akin to me in holy religion. The chains that bind us will not be loosed with our mortal bodies, and I will be able to embrace you with eternal pledges as my revered brother.

167. Read this, Jovius, and blessings in Christ Jesus our Lord.

# POEM 23[1]

The spring releases the birds' voices, but my tongue has its own spring, Felix's birthday. On this day the very winter blooms before the rejoicing folk. Though winter is in the midst of its frosts, prolonging its season further with malevolent cold, and holding the year hard-fast and the fields white, our holy joy converts this day into joyful spring. Grief, the winter of the mind, flees, and cares are driven from the heart; the storm clouds of depression vanish from our unclouded breasts. I am like the gentle swallow, and the white bird with black wings,[2] and the turtle, kin to the affectionate dove, birds which recognise the friendly days; or the finches, which make the thickets echo[3] only at spring's beginning; or the birds which hitherto were silent as they roamed beneath prickly hedges but now in diverse places take pleasure in the returning spring, their tunes as various as the colours of their dappled wings. This is how I, too, acknowledge this day which our holy festival renews each year with the appropriate honour to Saint Felix. Now is the rebirth of my peaceful spring this joyous year; now I take pleasure in freeing my voice in rhythmical lays, in discharging the songs I have vowed, in flourishing with the fresh voice of spring.

20. Christ God, pour into my heart and slake my thirst with heavenly waters. Even a drop from You sprinkled into my heart will be a stream. It is not surprising that

You can fill my minuscule soul with a tiny drop, for though born a man with small frame, You filled the world with undying seed, and saved the whole world with a drop of Your blood. Source of the Word, God the Word, assent to my prayer. Make me now tuneful and sweet-voiced like the springtide bird which lurks hidden beneath the green foliage,[4] constantly charming the pathless countryside with manifold songs, and with one voice issuing forth varied tunes and changing songs. Its feathers are uniform in colour, but its song is dappled. One time it rounds off fragile lays, at another it extends a shrill whistle with prolonged sound; now it embarks upon what seems a threnody, then it brings its lament to a sudden close and beguiles our astonished ears with broken melody.[5]

37. May Your grace, O Christ, flow continually from You into me. But I pray that like that bird I may be granted the powers to diversify my song, to utter the verses promised each year with varied style though from the same tongue; for the riches of grace constantly confer on me different subject matter through the wondrous powers of the Lord. Christ God is embodied in these in the person of His dear Felix, and He performs manifest miracles offering signs which bring salvation.

45. Those miracles we are accustomed to witness every day, when He oppresses the savage devils which form the serpent's brood, and with hidden hand scourges the enemy till they cry out. Yet we mark this strange phenomenon in this power. Though Felix harries and tortures devils all year long, bidding them evacuate human bodies, he yet prolongs the presence of some of them. This is so that punishment may oppress the evil foe for longer; or so that the people who have merited serving as vessels for evil

spirits may experience a deserved delay in gaining the remedy, and may more fully expiate the whole of their sin by this lapse of time. Or alternatively, he is keen to grant this concession to his birthday—to lend aid to only a few at other times so that he may generously offer more gifts on his own anniversary. At any rate, as the year glides by and the day approaches, his pressure is more frequent and more intense. You can see at this time more crowded gatherings of columns of the sick, of people seeking a full return to health by attending the feast.

61. At this time the devils ignite and blaze more fiercely than usual. Their howls are more tearful, and they now lament their extreme tortures when greater force represses them. But they are not permitted easy egress. First they are sorely harassed by punishments curious and various. They are raised aloft and made to hover higher than usual; they are belaboured in the empty spaces of the lower air, held fast with bonds invisible as they suffer this extended sojourn in the deserted heavens. These foes are exhausted by personal punishments, though oppressed in alien bodies. The human beings who appear to be enduring the physical pain are actually free of pain. Their inner selves are unaffected, and they witness the tortures of others enacted in their own limbs. Once the devil is trapped, the human person is freed, and the pains in his body are only apparent. He does not feel them because the torment is not the man's, but the devil's. Bitter foe, why do you assault us, what hope impels you to possess us? See now how you who wickedly made sport of others are in turn made sport of by the device of our Redeemer. Your wiles have now become your bonds; in you the captor is captured, the enchainer is in bonds. Ensnared man is become the snare,

and the brigand is hoodwinked by his own prey. He is caught whilst seeking to devour as his unlawful food the body he has seized, and his mouth has closed over the hook which spells his death.

82. I shall recount things still better, yet fully authenticated. Notable before all others is the man whose limbs were the stronghold of a long-established foe. He was ejected and dragged from the crowd of sick people to the holy threshold of the sacred martyr, and placed against the consecrated balustrade[6] before the threshold. He hung there upside down with his feet bent over it, gazing at that abode; and even stranger and more edifying to relate, his clothing did not tumble over his face, but seemed held fast or sewn to his feet, so that his private parts were chastely clothed and draped.[7] Doubtless this was to ensure that respect for God's work was maintained by the covering of men's bodies, so that demon could not exult, during the very pains which tortured him, in the betrayal of the modesty of those naked parts. That devil's torture was more oppressive when modesty remained unaffected, for though the man's body was upside down, the man's clothing remained in place. Events like this are strange and significant, as all will agree. But the more familiar they become by experience, the less remarkable the hearer finds them, however awe-inspiring they are to witness, however imposing in achievement. So I beg you hearken to some new if small-scale deeds of my patron, which Christ by His manifold power performed through him. All these acts He performs in His eagerness to strengthen within us the one faith, so that through them we may see blatant proofs that the hidden God is with us, that with fatherly care

the heavenly Lord tends our human affairs and hearts, by
means of that word with which He created everything.

106. My brother Theridius[8] must provide me with the
starting point for my tale, for what better deed of Felix
is worthier of my song, or should have preference before
the work he performed beneath the very roof where he
dwells as proprietor? From the darkness which earlier prevailed, our season has passed into the present daylight.[9]
You know our habitual custom of fasting before the feastday, how we offer the sacrament late in the evening and
then return individually to our homes.[10] So on this occasion, once the crowds had poured from the Lord's temple
and we had rested our weary bodies and taken food, we
began to sing hymns of joy to the Lord, and to prolong
the night with Psalms.

117. Meanwhile, my dear Theridius took leave of the
friendly choir to take a breath of air outside, to dispel the
sweat induced by his cell, which was smoke-filled with
wax tapers. Though his route along the snaky corridor of
our narrow dwelling was unlit and hard to discern in the
darkness, he advanced with confident step through the
familiar abode, sadly heedless of the danger which now
loomed. Close by in the middle of the house, between
ceiling and floor, hung a lamp on a swaying rope with
triple metal sections attached to the end of the cord.
Soldered on to the glass lantern is a pointed handle, and
in addition to its handle the lamp has three hooks attached
to it all around.

129. The water at the base shows white, and above it
the oil gleams yellow.[11] Fluid stands on liquid, the smooth
solution floating on the water beneath without the two

uniting or intermingling. Remarkably, the fatty liquid floats. The thick matter does not force its way down through the liquid water, but the light element supports the thick substance, the water (which is thinner than the treacly fluid) lying below the oil and acting as foundation for the liquid above it. The inner repulsion by each of the other is so clear when they associate with each other that you can see the mingled liquids separating out. Lying inside the same cup they are clearly distinct for the natural quality of each preserves each liquid's colour.

140. The triple base of lead is joined at the centre, from which the hollow top rises, filled with fuel for the oily wick. The dripping tow ignites to form a slender torch. Spreading round the surface of the still oil, the tiny wick shines in the shallows of the glass. The light flickers keenly from its trembling tip, and gently throws a shadowy light into the inner part of the house, diffusing the thick darkness with its tranquil brightness. This light, however, had vanished as the night wore on, for the servants were keeping vigil during the extended hours, and the thirsty flame had devoured the oil and gone out. One of the servants had removed the lamp-holder because the flame had failed. He had untied and let down the rope, but had neglected to draw it up again and fasten it with the usual knot. So the cord was hanging looser and swinging low, bereft of its welcome illumination and full of dark danger. For it was armed with the teeth of those menacing hooks to form a most dreadful snare, and with these it now evilly confronted our brother. One might say "evilly," or again "happily" through Christ's will, for He happily converted that dangerous accident into a cause of memorable joy for us.

160. Observe, then, Christ's hand in this. That rope in
the darkness was perversely hanging lower than usual,
below its customary height. So it was poised at the level
of Theridius' head, and its three points caught him in the
face as he jauntily advanced. One hook struck and caught
his eye. The point slipped down off the sensitive eyelid
and jerked inside where even a careful hand equipped
with healing skill is reluctant to insert the doctor's probe
with apprehensive restraint, and where even the slightest
contact makes the eye fill with tears. Theridius, reeling
under the sudden impact of so grievous a wound, cried
out, and in panic clapped his fearful hands over his affected
eye. He kept the metal fast held with his eye to keep it
in position, or, if it slipped, to catch the falling eyeball,
which preserves under a thin skin the inner part of the
eye. Behind a barrier of fluid the glassy reflexion of the
pupil hides beneath it the white retina. This is the foundation, so to say, supporting the eye with the marrow which
emerges from it, and feeding the eye with the liquid sustenance of the veins. The eyes depend for their moisture on
the twin pupils.[12] But if the skin of the fluid eye is broken
by serious illness or unhappily forced apart by a wound,
the eyeball jumps out; deserted by the sap that nourishes
it, it loses its sight and abandons its socket.[13]

184. Meanwhile, a servant was roused by the shout of
the anguished man, and sleep fled. He left his bed in haste,
holding a lighted lamp before his eyes. Theridius held his
face in his hands; his head was bent back and he gazed
upward, like a youth balancing a staff on his forehead.[14]
He sought to hold his body poised and thus to keep the
rope still, controlling his trembling limbs as the wound
dictated, and fearful of opening the wound by a prejudi-

cial movement. He was avoiding danger to the affected eye through the agency of its comrade which he could freely use. But he did not dare touch or draw out the metal lest the eyeball adhere to it and come out with the metal point. Yet he could no longer endure the continued presence of the weapon implanted within his eye. Despairing of a remedy by human aid, he prayed to Felix, who then drew near by God's aid. Theridius called on him in the affliction of his great wound, and uttered his lament in these terms:

201. "How great, alas, must be the sins compelling these pains of mine, since I, poor wretch, have deserved to sustain so grievous a wound, in spite of my having Felix as my patron and my neighbour, and on this his very birthday! Huge must be my guilt and great my crime, for punishment strikes me on the day it usually withdraws. Dear saint, I beg you, help your son. I know that you are close, that your ears are pricked in this direction from your shrine near by, that you have heard the weeping of your unhappy charge. Or if at this time you reside as confessor and friend close to the side of the great King in heaven and before His throne, you must direct God's ear beyond the clouds to these words of your poor follower. Do not spurn me; rather seek from the pitying Christ in heaven the salvation which you can mediate to me. So come, Felix, eternal guardian of my soul; hasten as my physician to deal with my physical danger. I beg you, hasten. Place your holy hands against my eye which threatens to fall from its socket. Pull out the metal which you see implanted. I do not dare to remove it with my own hand for fear that I would deprive myself of sight in seeking to rid myself of the shaft; I can feel the bolt driven

firmly in, and its point has pierced the inner recesses of
my eye. Heavenly hand which bestowed our eyes on us,
hand which conferred on us additionally your own person with its powers of healing strength, with which you
torture and restrain dark devils, with which you can remove all pain from mortal bodies through the lofty name
of Christ—for your power lies in almighty God—I beg you
only undertake my healing under His guidance.

228. "Let not my sins prevail over you. Rather let them
fall in defeat at your hands. I admit that I deserve this
wound more than the kindness of the gentle Christ. Only
recall the word and deed of the Lord Himself, who by
His coming redeemed the life of sinning man. If you wish
to pass judgment in my case according to the rights of
justice, I deserve to be deprived not merely of one eye,
but of both, for then my face would correspond with the
darkness of my heart which causes me to misuse my bodily
eyes, which makes me blind to justice and alert for
wickedness. I admit it is fitting for a sinner to lose an eye.[15]
But if it is appropriate for such a man to belong to you,
once he has begun to be yours he becomes worthy of pardon, whatever the sin that binds him. I have long ago
commenced to be one of your followers. No desire for my
ancestral land made me follow them; I traversed and
despised hazards of sea and land through the desire
prompting me, dear saint, to dedicate myself to you.[16]
Following the ideal of the good, I broke my connexions
with the land of my kin to serve you in the company of
the men with whom I count myself as yours. You must
demonstrate that this is so with your immediate help, so
that I may not lose my eye, which is pierced by so great
a wound. I pray you, confer this noteworthy gift on your

unworthy servant to enhance the Lord's praise. Bestow this signal deed, dear saint, on your birthday. In this way, that day which your proclamation of Christ's glory has established forever as your birthday into the era of eternal light may be for me the birthday of my eye, and I may hymn together Felix and the recovery of my sight obtained from Felix."

255. After this ingenuous lament, the favouring hand of the blessed Felix shortly appeared, and with his kindly breath he silently strengthened the wavering purpose and hand of the fearful Theridius, so that he did not shrink from extracting the metal with assurance and safety. Scarcely had he made the attempt when the hook slipped from his eye as though it were greased; and from the eye[17] there followed nothing more than a flood of tears, which washed out all the suppuration which it caused to discharge. Then, once the eye had been cleansed of this immense, dark danger, it shone with as bright a reflexion as it is seen to have today, all healed and shining through the kindness of the undying Christ. In fact, I believe it may shine brighter now than it did before, because the feastday that restored it lends it additional lustre.

266. So you who embrace the faith must observe and weigh this deed, which reflects a kindness as great as the danger it dispelled. A man now corpulent with advancing years and of big stature was impaled like a fish on the bent hook of the rope. Suspended like the lamp, he hung there perforce by his open eye. It was prised open by the nail which pinned and engaged the eyelid, but which caused no wound since the hand of heaven prevented it by rendering the point of the metal harmless and its weight light. Who could believe that in that organ where suppuration

is oppressive and the presence of a hair unbearable, where we cannot endure the smallest speck of dust, this heavy steel with its bent point, attached moreover to a lamp smeared with hardened grime, engaged the tender eye with its metal for so long without damaging it, and left the sight unharmed by any wound? What hand employs fingers and healing skill so dextrously that it could probe the tiny gap where eye and lid join, enter the eye without damaging it on that double journey along the frail passage between the two, and unhook the point of the steel which filled the whole eyeball in which the solid mass of substantial metal was buried? What hand could probe the eye with the scalpel's point without causing a wound? Surely none but the Hand which made all things. It was the Spirit of God that everywhere enters all the elements of creation, and is finer than any gossamer; it was He who restored to the blinded their lost sight, who bestowed new eyes even on the man blind from birth.[18] It was He who restored the facial faculties of bodies deficient by nature, working with the Creator's skill by which He perfects the whole world; it was the Son of God, the Hand and Wisdom of the Father, Christ the Source which begets and sustains all things.

298. God had set Him of old in the womb of one not fully a mother, so that subsequently the Creator Himself could become man, and append to the demonstrations of God's work the wonderful achievement of bringing to perfection eyes bereft of sight. Accordingly, He spat on the ground and made mud, and with this He gave to His believing disciple the sight denied him at birth. Thus He put the finishing touch to the half-made man by applying to his defective member the same stuff with which He had

fashioned his whole body. This was His way of proving that He who in company with God the Father had from mud and breath endowed Adam with the features that They shared, had Himself come on earth in our flesh.

309. The Craftsman Himself, God our Light, sought to adorn the birthday of His friend Felix with this mighty healing, so that He could demonstrate by this powerful gift the lofty merit of His confessor. He did not seek by this deed to increase the martyr's glory, for long ago He bestowed on Felix with honorific appellation and blessed fame that exalted palm of victory which the kindness of Christ the Lord extends forever, for the powers residing in him continue unwearying.

317. But God wished to confer on us a particular joy at this time, and by performing some such work to offer a sign to the servants who belong to Felix, their own patron. By this He meant to show that we are the particular charges of the heavenly Felix, and to teach us that our lives depend on his merit and his care; Felix is the guardian through whom Christ preserves our safety and regularly wards off the enemy, so hostile in the hazards of night,[19] from our limbs and minds alike. This is why we now rejoice in the glory of our danger; and when we see Theridius' eyes shining with their old brightness after appearing before us unsightly, one eye almost out, we are touched with joy to our hearts' depths because our brother here is safe, and in him Christ has bestowed on us a gift of such kindness. I rightly reckon him as dear as my own eyes, for in his gaze shines out the hand of Felix, my glory in Christ. O happy hazard, goodly wound, sweet danger, which brings me to realise that the martyr cares for me! So valuable to me has been the near loss of that light[20] that I have now obtained light by Felix's generosity.

# POEM 24[1]

## *To Cytherius*[2]

Meropius Paulinus greets Cytherius, his brother in Christ.

We have welcomed here Martinianus,[3] my brother in spirit and my true kinsman in the one faith. You had charged him with an eloquent letter and sent him on his way to us; but now he has scarcely survived with his life, and is stripped of the letter he has lost. Still, we have welcomed him as your spokesman who gives us full assurance of your love for us; he is a letter[4] more genuine than a written message, for your heart has put its seal on him, and since he brought you to mind with the writing of his soul, we read this letter with mind as well as ear. Now we are both joined and allied to each other in the kiss of sacred peace. We make *a sacrifice of praise to God*[5] and render thanks to Christ, who delivered him from the sea so that he survived to cross our threshold as guest. He has endured a grim experience, yet experienced a miracle in his danger.

21. He left his native soil and opted for travel on foot on the mission known to you. But when he pondered with himself the huge extent of the land journey, he changed his mind about the route, and preferred indolent seasickness on the billows to foot-weariness. He set sail from Narbo[6] over the rough sea, entrusting himself to a frail bark, and subsequently his reluctance to walk brought a change of fortune and regret that he had taken ship. He set out from the coastline and sailed into the deep sea in

thick darkness, but the sea was calm and its smile bright. The stars were the sole guides for the journey, for the moon was absent from the heavens. Then suddenly that obsolete and crumbling ship could carry its load no longer; the structure of its hull sagged and let in water through the chinks. The calm weather had induced sleep in all those aboard. Only the helmsman was awake. As the ship glided over the calm waters, he had no anxiety, but cleaved a foaming course through them, and tried to whistle up stronger breezes to advance the ship's progress.

47. Meanwhile, the hull sank deeper as it filled with water, and as the planks yawned wider the water rushed in increasingly. Those aboard had experienced no waves from the sea breaking over them, but now waves began to lap in the ship, washing beneath their bodies as they slept and arousing them with the chilly water. One by one they came to consciousness, and fear dispelled the slumbers of all, the fear awakened by apprehension of death, though they were still unaware of the causes of their fear. How could those wretched men escape the cruel ocean? They were sinking in their own ship. If the seas had been seething high under the wind, they might have found safety in a ship, but now that the sea had seeped inside the vitals of their vessel, where could they find survival? What harbour had they when the sea was in their ship, bringing them low and claiming their lives within?

67. But all the time God, the Harbour and Salvation of all, was stretching out His fatherly hand, and amidst the high ridges of mid-ocean was extending His loving arms with which He rescues those slipping into precipitous death, and sets them in the shallows of life. He had pro-

vided a skiff behind the four-banked vessel to afford this
aid; thus from the crowd aboard, those whom God had
decided to save could be rescued by the skiff, as it floated
close to the ship which yawned open to the sea.[7]

78. Novatianus, the ship's captain, was a man possessed
by death, and his thoughts were ripe for death; his heart
was shipwrecked and the faith within in tatters. When he
was first putting out to sea from shore, he refused to take
the skiff as usual as part of his tackle. He made haste to
embark speedily in his ship, and though encompassed by
extreme danger, he sought to jettison the skiff by cutting
the rope attaching it to the ship, and letting it drift over
the ocean. But he was defeated by the opposing clamour
of the great majority, and his intention remained blocked
from two quarters; for the opinion of all aboard prevailed,
and Christ inspired it to make it stronger, so that later
there would be a boat to survive the sunken ship and
provide a safe refuge.

97. The nature of the shipwreck was unusual; it was
the calm sea which brought death to the sailors. On the sea
outside was the silence of calm weather, but in the ship
there was a storm. No rocks, no tempest destroyed the
vessel; it was age, stronger than these, and the friction of
the years which had loosed the strong timbers from the
iron nails that held them. The sky was bright, the clouds
without menace, and the sea reflected the glitter of the
stars. But what help did the happy tranquillity of winds
and sea afford to those abandoned on the still ocean's
depths by the collapse of the ship that carried them? The
waves sucked in the ship, the ship drank in the waves; the
water was both swallower and swallowed. The sailors,
drunk with the draught of salt water, died from this grim

intoxication. The sea smiled kindly on other ships, and was harsh to this vessel alone.

117. Yet amidst the danger to the greater number was visible the action of the heavenly host. The danger of death remained common to all aboard the one ship, but note how they were detached by different fortunes, allotted either to life or to death. You should not imagine that good and evil were mingled indiscriminately in an allotted fate, for it is clear that no Christian perished and that the faithless died. The malevolent Jews and those guilty of arrogant disunion[8] alike perished, but all those signed with the orthodox faith of Christ were recognised by life as her own. But there were others not yet consecrated with Christ's name who were saved from the deep in addition to the Christians, because they joined with them in flight and clung fast to them.

135. No believer was drowned with the crowd of unbelieving travellers. God revealed in the persons of the few—as clear truth of the great mystery[9]—that at the end of the world there will be a division among the tribes and a separation among all mankind, when the avenging angel will leave unscathed those whose faces are marked with the banner of the cross.[10] In the same way, no person on that ship who was endowed with the truth was consigned to death. Unbelievers who stuck close to the Christians survived, for light overcame darkness. Death had no strength to plant Christians amongst the dead, because glistening on the foreheads of the Christians was the mark before which death collapses in subjection.

151. The captain himself, the commander of the lost ship, was the first to die. He was already wrecked in mind before he died in shipwreck on the sea. Twice he drowned,

for the ship submerged him in the waves, and sin in hell.
He could have forced his way from danger, but death had
a claim on his life, which his captive heart had lashed
tight with the appropriate bonds of greed, and bound to
death. He preferred death to survival so that he might not
outlive his ship and his cargo.

163. Martinianus' thread of life was now almost spun.
He was amongst the men who were drowning when the
sound of the panicking crowd aroused him, aroused him
from the sleep of death. At that time in his exhaustion he
was snoring soundly in an isolated pocket in the prow,
untroubled in his blameless life, like Jonas of old hidden
away in the belly of his ship.[11] Roused by the despairing
shouts of men dying all around him, his limbs all trampled
by the feet of the mob, he leapt from his hard bed. Many
had been drowned below in the ship's womb. The sailors,
stripped for action, were rushing about the port and star-
board sides trying the usual devices of jettisoning the sails
or hoisting them with poles. The ship, covered by the
deep, still floated on its outermost timbers. Martinianus
joined those who sought a path to safety by this route.
Under Christ's guidance, he shunned the crowd consigned
to death, and joined the survivors by leaping headlong
into the boat which lay at some distance and which was
a harbour for a large number.

187. He had almost been left behind as death's companion, doomed to drown in the sea with the ship. But
Christ snatched him—seized him, it seemed, by His own
hand—out of the pit of death. As Joseph of old fled the
lust-maddened woman with his clothes torn off him,[12] so
our friend left all behind when he escaped naked in flight
from that unfaithful ship. Again, just as that whale of old

held out his mouth as bidden and welcomed in Jonas, and as he slid down that wide and gaping throat passed him into its stomach, swallowing his body untouched by its parted teeth and refusing to eat the man it swallowed,[13] so, when Martinianus tumbled into the waves from the high deck, the boat met him and took him in. Throughout the night it bore him faithfully in its safe womb till it could take him back to harbour.

205. Now that I have made mention of the great prophet, whose person, typifying the holy mystery, foreshadowed the death which lasted three days and the salvation it restored,[14] I should like to retrace the footsteps of my poem and briefly hasten back to Jonas. Wondrous are the Lord's stratagems. Though plunged in the sea, he tossed on the waves unharmed.[15] Though devoured, he lived on, and the beast that swallowed him remained unfed by the living food. He was the booty but not the food of the whale whose belly he used as a home. What a worthy prison for God's holy runaway! He was captured on the sea by which he had sought to flee. Translated to the deep belly of the massive beast, he was imprisoned in a living gaol. Thrown from the ship to destruction, he yet sailed upon the waters, an exile from land, a guest of the brine. He walked in the cavern of the whale's body, a prisoner both captive and free. He was free upon the waves as he floated in that floating whale, both within the sea and outside it; and though physically incarcerated, the prophet emerged in spirit to fly to God. Body was constrained by body, but the bonds of earth did not constrain the flight of his mind. Though enclosed in that belly, he broke out of his prison by prayer, and reached God's ears. Free for prayer but detained from flight, he proved himself by

his faith. He had thought to escape God by sea, to hide from God in a ship, but now he believed[16] that the Lord was with him even inside that whale submerged in the sea.

239. Now I must redirect the rhythm of my pliant words to my own Jonas, taken in by the roomy boat as by the whale. Enclosing him in its womb, it transported him shivering with cold and fear, and delivered him safe on dry land. What he recounts is a miracle; how at that time, after jumping headlong from the high stern, landing in the ship's boat, and positioning himself where deep water had seeped through the boat's chinks to form a malodorous, scummy pool, God immediately warmed his frozen limbs. He fell asleep in blessed peace, though in that naked, soaked condition from which sleep usually recoils. He slept more comfortably than on a bed, and during the whole voyage back to land he was sleep's captive, awakened neither by the water that dripped from him nor by the cold induced by his nakedness. Though it was autumn, a warm period of the year, it was wintry for shipwrecked travellers suffering the harsh deprivation of lost clothing, and racked by icy shivers.

263. Dear brother, praise God and embrace your holy brother as you hear this further astonishing incident to grasp the grace which Martinianus gained by faith. When he realised from the boat's grating on the sand of the shore that the boat was gliding into harbour, sleep left him. He came to himself and finally remembered who he was. As he awoke, he touched Paul's epistles which lay next to his heart. In the panic when he left all else behind, he had unconsciously lifted this book, or else the book which is alive with the Holy Spirit had attached itself to him with-

out his knowledge. Ponder this, I beg you: who but Christ provided for His servant the protection of Paul? Martinianus bears witness that at the moment of crisis he did not think to remember to remove the tiny manuscript wrapped in his rucksack. Even if the thought had entered his fear-struck mind, there would have been no time to look for it. But the master Paul was at hand in the physical presence of his epistles. He loved this man who read him with a chaste heart, and so he rescued him from the hand of death. Once more God bestowed on Paul the deliverance of men from the depths of the sea.[17] That same power of grace which the apostle possessed when he was himself afloat had now through his letters lent support to Martinianus; and for the others who then in their flight clung fast to the Christians, he made harmless the danger which followed their danger, just as he had separated the believers amongst the shipwrecked from the godless.

299. So when the twin-banked boat put into shore and disembarked the soaked voyagers, they at the same time preserved their lives and begged for them, for they asked for help to survive in case they had landed in territory more savage than the waves, to die from cold and hunger. However, Massilia, a daughter of the Greeks set on Gallic soil, a city which is a ward of holy Church,[18] was close by and opened its kindly arms to them. The shipwrecked men made for that city, recounted their misfortunes, and asked for sustenance and shelter. The brotherhood[19] gave hospitality to Martinianus, and warmed him with shelter and food. The poor with abundant charity lent him their tiny mite.[20] Their abundant affection compensated for their small gifts. They enriched their guest with prayers,

and with their offering of peace sped him on his way, rich
with the parting-gifts of the spirit.

319. However, they did present him with cheap sandals,
to ensure that he did not stagger on his ship's legs—even
though he would have preferred to go warmly clothed
and barefoot rather than shod and frozen! Yet his shame
at his nakedness rejected a land journey, however much he
had suffered at sea. Moreover, he was anxious not to be
thought to be feigning nakedness through love of gain, if
he passed like a Teucer[21] in ragged garb through cantons,
villages, and towns, like those greedy beggars who make a
habit of wandering over sea and land, swearing that they
are monks or shipwrecked survivors, and recounting their
names and adventures at a price.[22] But this Christian of
ours, though he had been genuinely shipwrecked, was
anxious not to be thought an impostor like them—for he
remarked that he was never deceived by other such.[23]
Hence he refused to go by road for fear he would acquire
the new label of mountebank. He preferred to put his life
at hazard on the sea rather than endure the sweat of his
brow by walking.[24]

341. Thus shabbily attired in rags, but with shining
sandals, he chose to sail once more. He returned to the
harbour, preferring the sight of the sea to the safety of
the land route, so that the ship could protect him till he
reached the shore he desired. So this light-journeying
traveller could escape the shame of nakedness by sharing it
with the sailors. The divine King showed indulgence to
his faithful constancy, and furthered his bold faith; He
transformed the lot of the men who had endured grim
suffering, compensating their evil fortune with good by

preparing a ship built of stout timbers to carry them. He enjoined a respite from storms, routed the clouds, and steered their course with a breeze. He governed sky and sea with unruffled motion, but in such a way that the ship was neither becalmed nor put to hazard by the dangerous speed induced by a fierce wind.

361. In this way Martinianus through the soft-smoothing hand of Christ traversed the harsh sea and glided towards that harbour named Centumcellae that lies at some distance from Rome.[25] From there the ship had to be steered farther to enter the harbour where the lighthouse stands.[26] Martinianus could scarcely believe he had gained the shore of Italy he so greatly desired. He disembarked, bounced joyfully to earth, and hastened on foot to Rome. There he found a friendly lodging amongst Roman brothers as a guest long desired. He recovered his spirits, rested his body, and exchanged with them expressions of joy. For their part they reciprocated, taking joy like fathers,[27] and they proclaimed their thanks to God. Martinianus joyfully recounted to his brothers the tribulations he had endured, and the tears from their overflowing hearts mingled with their felicitations.

381. My Theridius,[28] Christ's gift to me, was absent from Rome at the time in my company. He is a man of peace who observes the Law and abounds in grace; he is my recreation, my delight, my own dear heart. Paulinus, his fellow host,[29] who was with devoted care keeping safe their Roman residence, stripped Martinianus of the clothes damaged in the wreck, and invested him with his own. To the gift of the tunic with which he adorned his comrade he added the present of a hood. So then the bestower of

the gift was in turn like the survivor of the shipwreck in having only one garment.

393. Then Martinianus proceeded on that route to us where the stone has made the level road to which the builder Appius gave his name.[30] He wore down that wearing road. The sailor who had travelled with worn garments now wore out his feet by walking. But even this journey was not to be wholly without the hazards to which he was inured. Not without penalty did he adopt the lazy plan of shirking the continuation of his journey to Nola on foot. From the city of Capua, which lies twenty miles from my abode, he obtained a mule without a load, unencumbered as pack animals often are when brought back home. He hired it for a trifling sum to cover the short journey, and mounted it. Then halfway along the road the beast took fright, and its rider was unseated and fell far from his mount which had withdrawn its support. He fell on his face, but without damaging it, though he sprawled among rocks and brambles. He did not bruise his face on the thorns nor his limbs on the rocks, for he was rescued by Felix's hand. Felix did not allow our brother now approaching his shrine to encounter evil and sustain hazard on his own estate. So our confessor dislodged the jealous enemy, and conducted Martinianus into his abode, now that his faithful vow had been completed. Thus Felix our patron brought his welcome guest to our abode as well.

423. When asked, he revealed to us his native region,[31] recounted his misfortunes, and told us blessed tidings about you. Then he quoted a few of your written lines, sprinkling his lips, so to say, with honey, and providing me with the sweetest taste of drops from your honeycombs.[32] This

made me feel the more the loss of your letter which he failed to deliver into my eager hands. But since he came to deliver your letter, I beheld that letter in the person of our goodly brother, written not with ink but with the pen of the mind. Previously he was unknown to us, but as soon as we came to know him he became most dear to us. Grace shone out of him through his words, which are the messenger of the mind.

439. Scripture says: Every good man brings forth good from good, and you know a tree by its fruit.[33] Thus Martinianus, so pleasant in word and pure in faith, so bright in nobility of countenance, has become dear to our hearts through the sweet stream of his kindly affection. And beyond this, his rightly boasting of your friendship has made him more loved still, for there is no harmony between darkness and light, and the wolf does not associate with the lamb.[34] Hence the prophet says: Just as birds of a feather flock together, so justice joins with the condition appropriate to it, with a good character.[35] This is how a brother's heart has entwined Martinianus with you, for he is very much your equal; the love of men like him is as a mirror of your mind and a mark of your faith.

457. God the blessed Creator and Source of saintly men does not now choose only the foolish and feeble elements of the decaying world to destroy the lofty.[36] As He Himself said, He now draws all things upward,[37] and claims the lofty things of the world also. For He made both the weak and the strongest, and unites them both in grace. Those whom the Creator fashioned by the one act He renews by the one gift. A general lack of belief circumscribed all men so that faith could heal all,[38] so that the whole world might become subject to God, and every

tongue, every power should proclaim that Jesus alone rules above every name in the glory of the Father.[39]

473. Even secular potentates are now bending the knee and surrendering their necks to this God; princes confess the kingship of Christ, and lower their sceptres before the Cross.[40] Royal robes and rags harmoniously form a single flock under God the Shepherd. Christ is the common Kingdom, the one Blood for all, both highest and lowest. He enriched you, so splendid in the vaunted possessions of worldly position, literature, and family, with humility of heart so that he could bestow on you eternal eminence, and so that by loving the poor here on earth you could share the inheritance of the rich in heaven. You are blessed now because you are poor in spirit[41] but rich in the hope in which the poor take joy; for they are deprived of the fleeting goods of this world, but will enjoy the delights of heaven.

491. Amongst these poor, high in the arms of father Abraham, the God of the living is preparing for you a place far removed from the fire engulfing the rich, a place cooled with the drops of life.[42] A clear sign of your great expectation of this already shines out in the person of the child you esteem so greatly. He has been planted for the Lord in the courts of Jerusalem,[43] the offspring of your seed. For God demanded your son of you so that He could set you with that father of faith,[44] so He enrolled your seed in the seed of Isaac, and demanded him as a second Isaac. You have rivalled the love of Abraham and have offered him as a living victim; by consigning him to God you have for your part now executed him to keep him more securely safe.

507. Now he remains a stranger to you, yet still your

own, playing no role in the secular world. As soon as he was delivered from his mother's womb, before he could recognise his own father and mother, before he could savour good or distinguish evil, the blessed boy chose the good. Now the child plays in God's house, and sings with a mouth still nourished by milk: *Thou, Christ, hast been my protector from my first day, since my emergence from my mother's womb.*[45] You have heard, too, the words addressed to the blessed: *Your seed will be powerful;*[46] and you know the saying: *I shall set in my abode him who is the fruit of your womb.*[47] Admittedly these words of David are proclaiming Christ, but they also are apposite to those living in Christ who will be set in God's abode because they form part of Christ's body. A partnership with Anna is also being prepared for you, because the consecration of her child[48] forms a precedent for you. This Samuel of yours has also been growing in God's temple. He is now a lamb, but later he will be a shepherd.

529. The hand of his diligent mother must spin for him the sacred robe[49] appropriate to his stature, and spiritual instruction in God's word must weave for him its sacred threads. He must be clad in the woven heavenly garment of the queen, with its golden fringes.[50] As a Nazarite,[51] he must deck his head, sacred to Christ, with consecrated locks, and the head of his soul, so handsome in its hair, must be endowed with efficacious faith. No razor must mount to cut or cause the loss of these locks. Like the famed Samson, whose power lay in the strength of his hair, whose locks were endowed with sacred might, he must throttle and bring low the lion by means of the strong arms of prayers, and pluck the sweet fruit of notable victory from its dead mouth.[52]

546. But this triumph must be a lesson to him not to make alliances with foreigners. That woman of another race[53] I interpret as the law of the flesh, so wily with its alluring nets. If this law proves stronger than the law of the mind, it will drag him into the dominion of sin. The evil counsel of its pleasant words weakens with its deceitful guile the male spirit. It blinds the eyes of the mind and shaves the head; it plunders and disarms faith.[54] I would not have our boy a Samson in this respect, becoming involved in a love-encounter immediately followed by captivity, enervation, and blindness, even though the strong Samson later recovered his strength when his hair grew again. For he was led by the hand from the mill to be the sport of the vaunting enemy, and though physically blind he used his mind's eye, and summoned God to take vengeance. Then, when his hair restored his strength, he brought down that house of the enemy. Once his hands, more powerful than any stone, gripped the pillars of the house in their fierce embrace, the roof collapsed upon him when its props were prised from the earth.[55] Yet even in his death God's powerful hero involved the foe in destruction, and by a glorious death avenged the disgrace of his life as a slave. He had lived a life of subservience under an exultant foe, but even as he fell he conquered the eclipsed enemy, destroying more thousands at his death than he had killed in his life.

581. I pray that our son may imitate Samson's death by his own, that while remaining in the flesh he may conquer that flesh and live for God, subduing the sins of the flesh. I would not have him devoting his heart in enslavement to the flesh's joys as to the wiles of that criminal woman, to become subsequently the property of the foe, stripped of

the strength of grace. May he play a Samuel in continuing holy and unshorn throughout his life; may he complete his holy span of life with thread unbroken, and up to his final years recollect his childhood commenced in God's service. May he kill Amalek[56] and with holy savagery offer to God the sacrifice of the sins of the flesh, the destruction of which will spell the death of the devil, who is loathed forever in God's sight. May the Saul in him fade, and the David rule. May the tiny child destroy the giant[57] that he may not be tall with the spirit of pride, nor envious with the evil of jealousy. Rather, may he mount the royal throne through possessing lofty virtues within a humble heart;[58] may he play Samson by imitating those earlier achievements, breaking new-plaited ropes like threads but without breaking his faith and so losing his hair in sloth.

609. His hair will sprout with the strength of heavenly deeds, he will break his confining bonds, he will tear forth the props, he will eclipse and lay low a thousand with his single right hand. For Christ God is our Strength and our Head, for He is the right Hand and Strength of God. We who have attained Him overcome the serpent when he attacks us with a thousand wiles. May our boy's soul be courageous in mortifying that ass of his,[59] that beast of a lazy body. May reduced drinking by its hard sobriety turn his face yellow with pallor, and his purity quench the fire of sins by a victory over his afflicted flesh.

623. For when our outer selves are wasted through the pressures of self-control, our inner persons are renewed, and gain strength through the weakness of our conquered bodies.[60] Then *a thousand will fall at our side, and ten thousand at our right hand*,[61] if our throats continue parched, if our jaws, so pliant with regular eating, win

salvation through inactivity; for the wantonness of a sap-filled body is blunted by fasting, and then unnourished bones bring forth for us a triumph and a sustaining spring. Our jaws which afforded a weapon to the aggressor now provide refreshing drink for the thirsty man, since the Holy Spirit waters the bones of the dead flesh, which are dry of nourishing moisture.

639. But what holy men earlier carried out as a fore-shadowing has been set down for us to perform[62] so that we may regularly achieve in the spirit what our fathers carried out in the flesh. *The former things have passed away, and all is made new;*[63] truth has emptied the shadow, and *the day of salvation is at hand.*[64] *The winter is past, the earth sprouts with flowers; the voice of the turtle is heard*[65] singing that the time for cutting out the old leaven is near. *So let us feast without the old leaven on the un-leavened bread of truth, for Christ our Pasch is sacrificed,*[66] and the kingdom of God is within us.[67] We are thus loosed from the old laws and no longer dwell in the shadow, for Christ the Son of God has Himself lightened us of the cloud of the Law and the yoke of the statutes as though they were a weight of hair. He has become as the Head of those who are redeemed. With Him as our Head, we advance in freedom over the noisome head of the dragon we have defeated. A load of hair, forming a shadow over their heads, was appropriate for those whose hearts were screened by a veil blotting out the holy mysteries. But we, for whom the veil of the letter has been removed,[68] behold the truth unclouded in the light of His body, the face of Him revealed by faith.[69]

669. So may our boy, ward of both Law and grace, be formed from both for spiritual glory to bring forth

things old and new. May he grow the strong hair of chaste deeds without experiencing the razor of sin, so that he may preserve his faith spotless from the sword's edge of harmful heresies. But may he also have his mind uncovered from above by the light of the Gospel so as to lay aside the burden and the covering of his hair, and be at once a slave to faith and freed by faith. May the schooling of the Law nurture him with his first milk from the breasts of the Prophets, and the sweetness of grace feed him with the bread of angels and with honey from the rock.[70] May he be drunk with sobering draughts from the spring of the Holy Spirit. May you yourself be then joined to your sons to become a flourishing palm for God.[71]

689. See how your wife who shares Christ's yoke with you is like a good and fruitful vine within your house;[72] she is your strong rib in God's eyes within the confines of your home.[73] She sustains her husband's cares, and guards her chastity as the crown of her revered spouse. She nurtures her children in purity, and they dedicate their lives to God; for I believe that this shoot sprung from your vine must be strengthened for God in such a way that the branch becomes the root of its own root, and draws with it the stock from which it springs.

701. Just as that famed boy of old was by God's providence dragged into slavery and sent to fertile fields so that he could precede both his father and his brothers, and so that subsequently, when hunger ensued throughout the world, he could feed his father and his brothers,[74] so perhaps this son of yours has preceded you into the sacred house of bread[75] that he may feed his parents and his brothers during their period of hunger in this world, where the earth is more fertile in producing thistles for us,

and is in need of the harvest of good men. He also can be
described as one sold to a eunuch,[76] because he is a slave
to chastity; he has been entrusted to the dominion and
control of Severus,[77] who is a *eunuch for God's kingdom.*[78]
Through Severus' nurturing he has been strengthened in
the faith and in manly chastity, so he will spurn with a
haughty and chaste disdain the enticing pomp of the enmeshing world as though it were a shameless woman.[79] He
will avoid it by fleeing naked from it,[80] preferring to endure the pain that leads to salvation rather than the joys
that lead to death.

725. I pray that like Joseph of old he may now endure
prison to defend his chastity,[81] so that from his youth he
may sit alone, and enclosed within a silent house he may
love his abode of noiseless solitude where he can hedge
in his ears with thorns.[82] May he prefer his house of grief
to houses filled with food, that he may sow the seeds of
joy with tears. May he freely bind himself with a hard
regimen, to loose himself from the chains of sin; may he
shackle himself with the manacle of patience, roaming
neither in lodging nor in thought. Then he will deserve to
attain high status from his lowly life, because He who
brings low the proud exalts the humble,[83] and by granting
grace to the insignificant resists the haughty. This is why
illustrious Joseph was first made lowly, to become great.
If he had not been a slave, he would not have become
mighty in the land of his slavery. He obtained royal status
and wealth where he had endured slavery and imprison-
ment; justice won its reward through enduring the bonds
of injustice.

749. May our son, too, pass the test as guardian of his
body, keeping fast the bolts of his prison. If through fear

of Christ he keeps tight hold on the sins of the flesh, he will have precedence over those who are enchained by them; as one free and his own master, he will be teacher and guardian of others[84] still enclosed in the prison of the world and shackled to this life. For he who keeps guard over himself rightly keeps watch over others—not out of a desire that free men should remain in the darkness of prison or in bonds, but to teach those whom he has recovered by his example that they are stripped of the chains of the world. Since he is freed from his own bonds, he will easily teach them to detach themselves from sin. Since he is a good helmsman of his own mind, he will be able to steer the barque of the Church. How could a man who cannot control himself have charge over his neighbours?

769. But my tongue has slipped and diverged too far, so I will return to my Joseph. May he blossom in purity with the bloom of blessed grace, like the lily of Paradise; may he chastely drink with purity of heart the draught of heavenly wisdom. As God's intimate expounder, may he provide answers to men in doubt,[85] and as the fame of his good name shines abroad, may he become known in the house of the king,[86] and when the king finds him pleasing in the spirit of wisdom, may he be adopted to guide the kingdom.[87] As chief over the royal possessions, may he act as overseer in the king's house, and wear a long linen garment and a golden chain,[88] adornments appropriate for Christ. The woven garment he must don is that of heavenly grace, and he must be clad in innocence. The garment woven with strong strands of linen is the mark of unbroken faith, for they say that linen threads are stronger even than ropes of broom. The sweet yoke of golden love must be the chain around his neck, the yoke sweet to

Christ and light in weight[89] which engages our necks
without oppressing them.

795. Amongst these adornments he must take up also
his gift, the ring which is the mark of royal power, and
thus adorned with the triple gift of the Trinity ride in the
royal chariot.[90] This royal chariot is the Church, Christ's
flesh and sacred body, and in it as driver rides the God of
Israel to the joy of thousands.[91] Follow Christ; do good
and avoid evil;[92] live the life of heaven on earth. Then the
King Himself will set you in His chariot, and make you
sharer of the kingdom. He will entrust to you the highest
powers in His kingdom, and open His treasures to you.
But first He will bestow on you worthy pledges of affection, so that you can mount the king's high throne adorned
with the royal insignia, and unbar the royal store wearing
the chain of wisdom, the long tunic of glory, and the ring
of faith.

815. Now Joseph, who became supreme throughout
Egypt, was a foreigner on Egyptian soil; and likewise our
boy must prove himself stronger than Egypt by rising
superior to the world's strength. As a foreigner in the
house of the Egyptians, he must intermingle yet remain
detached, so that the race of the holy may be distinct
from that of the impious, though their abode is together.
At present he must linger in the world as though set in
Egypt; as a dweller in the heavenly city, he must be a
foreigner to the business of the world. Though living in
the flesh, he must be exiled from the life of the flesh. The
law which he must observe is the inner law; the whole of
the royal demesne entrusted to him and traversed by him
consists of the Holy Scriptures.

831. Just as Joseph, that holy man of God, journeyed

over the lands of Memphis,[93] stacked its luxuriant and fertile resources in enlarged granaries, and with the abundance of blessings from the years of plenty provided food for the era of famine, so this son of ours must traverse God's kingdom in the consecrated books. For the breath of the Holy Spirit breathes over Scripture, which is the mother of the eternal kingdom. I pray that the Spirit with His ghostly care may make provision by erecting huge granaries within the boy's mind, so that he may store in distended heart abundant provisions for a lasting life. When he has made his land rich in life's sustenance, then you will journey as a second Israel in your old age to enjoy your son's dominion, and you will gladly enter there together with your retinue of relatives whom he has summoned.[94]

851. Your son will feed your aged frame with the bread he has obtained in the house of the King. Just so the eagle's young is said to feed and tend its parents in return when the onset of age has stripped them of their feathers and confines them to feeding in their nest. Then their bodies gain a covering of fresh feathers, and they blossom out with new wings. By a strange law of nature, the aged birds are transformed with the aid of their offspring into fledglings.[95] Then, once their youth is purged of its senility and has made new birds of them, schooled by their offspring they learn afresh to use their unpractised wings as oars.[96] They mingle with their fostering offspring and fly with smooth course through the breezes. They take pleasure in cutting serene paths through the bright heavens with lazy motion, fanning peacefully the translucent air. In line, their wings at rest, they alternately follow and lead each other, and group to form a circle.

873. These dumb birds spontaneously reveal the mysteries of the heavenly kingdom. Their bodies poised on wings form the sacred shape of the potent cross.[97] The circling course of their flight gives promise of a reward for toil.[98] May this fledgling of ours, that graceful son[99] who is the harbinger of your salvation, in spirit emulate those birds that wing their way through the lofty clouds. May he entrust himself to the arms and wings of the cross on high, and fly to a crown of glory.

885. He draws his water from his own source, so that the whole spring flows into his own course. Both of you must run swiftly down this stream of your son's, so that together you may form a running river.

889. How blessed a root is your saintly offspring, how fruitful a branch of a goodly tree! You gave your son to God to nurture, and God rears him for you in such a way that the boy in his turn nurtures his white-haired parents, so that the child is become your master in your old age. Through the wonderful mystery of love, he has become his parents' parent. So later all of you, the whole retinue of your holy family, will fly up to join the body of that Head[100] in which the saints will gather like the eagles.

901. But those whose weight of inherited wealth prevents their rising from the earth will not be able to achieve this. When the first trumpet thunders forth from the sky its signal to rouse the dead, such men will have become gross through arrogance of spirit, and distended through their empty wealth; so they will remain shackled on the ground, unable to free themselves from their bonds with which their lack of faith now binds them with their consent. When the trumpet sounds, they will be constrained from winging upwards, because the slender clouds

will be unable to bear up the rich of this transient world, who are so heavily laden and burdened with their possessions, to encounter God our King. They will be stuck in their own muddy foulness, and weighed down by the massive weight of their wealth they will be overthrown by death's sudden cascade in the noontide conflagration of the world.[101] I pray that the Lord God may not raise against His chosen ones the rod appropriate for such men, nor allow us to extend wicked hands towards the harvest of these rich men.

923. So do you, who have so heavy a claim upon my heart, lighten yourselves in preparation for Christ, and being now relieved of your burdensome luggage, free your feet of its bonds. Become naked in this world to be clothed in abundance of light, so that when *the prince of this world*[102] comes, he may find in you nothing of his own. May the clouds which transport the saints readily bear you in their unsubstantial grasp, once you are free of the mass of oppressive possessions and purified of the stain of sins. And when you are borne to the face of the royal Bridegroom, may God steep you in His brightness, that the shining glory of eternal life may draw your mortality within it. Then, restored to your heavenly form, you may attain the glorious beauty of your Master,[103] and like the immortal angels live forever with God our King.

# POEM 25[1]

Souls harmonious are being joined in chaste love, a boy who is Christ's virgin and a girl who is God's. Christ God, draw these matching doves towards Your reins, and govern their necks thrust beneath Your light yoke; for Your yoke, Christ, is indeed light[2] when assumed by an eager will and borne with the ready complaisance of love. This holy burden of the law of chastity is oppressive for the reluctant, but for persons of devotion it is a pleasant imposition to keep in subjection the role of the flesh.

9. This marriage must see nothing of the wanton conduct of the mindless mob; Juno, Cupid, Venus, those symbols of lust,[3] must keep their distance. The chaste, dear offspring of a bishop[4] is being joined in sacred alliance, so peace, modesty, and holiness must assemble as attendants. For a harmonious marriage-alliance is at once a holy love, an honourable love, and peace with God. God with His own lips consecrated the course of this alliance, and with His own hand established the pairing of human persons. He made two abide in one flesh[5] so that He might confer a love more indivisible. While Adam slept, he was deprived of the rib which was removed from him, and then he obtained a partner formed of his own bone. He felt no loss in his side, for his flesh was extended to replace it; he acknowledged the accession of a twin. Once he beheld this other self sprung from himself in the flesh they shared, he then became the prophet of his own situa-

tion, speaking with tongue renewed. *"This flesh,"* he said, *"is the flesh of my flesh. I recognise the bone of my bones.*[6] She is the rib from my side."

27. So since this pair are the ancient type of the holy alliance now being sealed between the dear children of Aaron,[7] our joy must be sober and our prayers unimpassioned. Christ's name must resound everywhere on the lips of his devoted people. There must be no mob dancing in decorated streets. None must strew the ground with leaves, or the threshold with foliage. There must be no crazed procession[8] through a city where Christ dwells.[9] I would have no secular display befoul devoted Christians. No wind must waft the scent of foreign ritual, for our entire proceedings must be redolent of the elegance of chastity. Saintly people recognise as their sole perfume that sprinkled by Christ's name, which breathes forth the chaste fragrance of God.[10]

39. There must be no trays lavishly laden with superfluous gifts, for real worth is adorned by character and not by wealth. The holy wife of a bishop's son, the spouse of a boy already consecrated,[11] must receive as dowry the light of life.[12] She must reject garments tricked with gold or purple,[13] for the shining grace of God is her golden garment. She must spurn also necklaces adorned with motley jewels, so that she herself may be a notable jewel for the Lord God,[14] for no weight of loathsome avarice must oppress a neck dedicated to bearing the yoke of Christ the Lord. Rather, her adornment designed to please must depend on an inward grooming, and her mind must be decked with the dowry that brings salvation.[15] She must not long to squander her income vainly on costly jewels or silken wraps;[16] instead, her soul must be adorned

with the virtues of chastity so that she may be a precious
asset and not a liability to her husband. When a person
seeks to attain a name by bodily display, such a fault
cheapens and devalues. The mind is sorely blinded by
lust for this debased aim; the body's gleaming spoils be-
grime the mind. The shameless individual fails to realise
the foulness of the adornment thus put on, which makes
the wearer delighting in such garments cheaper than the
clothing itself.

61. God forbid that one who has become a daughter in
the house of an apostolic family[17] should appear as the
daughter of the temple where idols are worshipped.[18] Her
skin should not be foully disguised with rouge, her eyes
with mascara, her hair with yellow tint.[19] The girl who
spurns the chaste beauty of nature is guilty of the sin of
pride, for she condemns God's creation of her. A women
adorning herself with such a range of disguises[20] will gain
no credence when she claims she is chaste.

69. Young persons who belong to Christ, flee from all
things which bring damnation as their prize, and death
if enjoyed. You must believe the words of God that such
adornments are the source of punishment for those who
desire them. Isaias threatens[21] that women now clad in en-
sembles of white silk and purple garments, who wear long
dresses bright with purple and rustling with gold, with
folds flowing down to the ankles, are to be fastened with
a rope tight-drawn; thus girt with ropes, they will wear
sackcloth forever, and will turn huge grindstones in their
prison of a mill. And those who pile their heads high with
hair long-grown will have them uncovered in shameful
baldness.[22] Avoid the adornment of such endowments,
new bride of a saintly husband, for these are the delights

of an empty mind. Do not wander abroad with perfumed clothes and hair, seeking recognition from men's nostrils wherever you pass; do not sit with your hair structured and castellated, with layers and ropes of interwoven locks.[23] Do not through your lustre be a cause of unhappy vexation to many, nor an evil cause of baneful attraction. You must not seek with foul purpose to delight even your own husband by thus adding inches to your person.

91. You, too, saintly boy so dedicated to the consecrated books,[24] must show a love which spurns all eagerness for a handsome bearing. Christ has compensated you by generously adorning your handsome soul with perennial riches, and He has enriched you both with holy wedding gifts—hope, devotion, fidelity, peace, chastity. Your silver is God's word, and your gold the Holy Spirit; your jewels are the brightness of good works glowing in your hearts. If shabby raiment is an affront to respected persons, if proud hearts take pleasure in expensive appurtenances, then the example of our saints and the holy simplicity of our first ancestors must dispel such shame.

103. Cast an eye on our parents of old in their abode in Paradise, for whom a single field comprised their whole world. Their covering consisted of sheepskins;[25] are we now ashamed that our woven garments are spun from wool? When the beautiful Rebecca came as bride to consecrated Isaac, she was covered simply, with the veil of modesty.[26] We read that she came adorned with no varied jewels, but muffled in a cloak. With this covering the maiden modestly concealed her face, for she feared to confront her bridegroom's eyes.

113. Will you prefer to these the dancing girl Hero-

dias,[27] who obtained the death of the Baptist as reward for
her performing feet? She took such wicked vengeance
for her mother's lust-inspired anger as to obtain as reward
for her wantonness a human head—that head from which
had been proclaimed to the nations the news that the
Lamb of God was at hand.[28] What other than her
seductive dress gained this wicked reward won by that
ungodly dancer, a daughter worthy of her father?[29] She
prevailed on him in this wicked purpose, and against his
will[30] forced him to commit this crime by the enticements
of her attractive body, for by her movements and clever
feet she won the applause of guests who were worthy of
that wicked king's feast. If sandals of glittering gold had
not covered her light ankles or allowed her to sport more
wantonly with heels adorned, if she had not worn a garment flowing with curling train or set her hair back to
show the jewels on her gleaming brow, she would not
have won the depraved hearts of those who watched her,
nor cleverly achieved her unspeakable success. Herod himself also waxed proud in royal garments; crazily inflated
with sacrilegious airs and puffed up by his raiment, he
forgot the honour owed to God, and he perished stinking
from a worm-infested wound.[31] His punishment was what
he deserved, for after considering himself divine in the
majesty of his robes, he died covered with unsightly sores.
But granted that such mad airs befit the hearts of kings,
what connexion have we with Pharaoh? The hollow glory
of the world is at odds with our kingdom, for saintly
light does not join with hostile darkness.[32]

141. A cleric must love a wife who glories in Christ
as her hair, whose beauty lies in her heart's radiance. A
lector[33] must learn from the divine history that she was

made as man's helpmate by God's dispensation.³⁴ In her turn the woman must strive to attain equality with her consecrated husband by welcoming Christ's presence in her spouse with humility of heart. Thus she can grow into his holy body and be interwoven with his frame, so that her husband may be her head as Christ is his.³⁵ In such a marriage as this Eve's subservience came to an end, and Sara became the free equal of her holy husband.³⁶ When Jesus' friends were married with such a compact as this, He attended as a groomsman, and changed water into wine like nectar.³⁷

153. A bridal couple like this will fittingly be visited by Mary, mother of the Lord, who gave birth to God without loss of her virginity. In this consecrated virgin God built Himself a pleasing temple with a hidden roof-aperture. Silently He glided down like the rain that falls as noiseless dew from a high cloud upon a fleece.³⁸ None was ever privy to this secret visitation by which God took the form of man from His virgin mother. How remarkable was the deception of the Lord which sought the salvation of men! Without intercourse, a woman's womb conceived new life. This bride did not submit to a mere human husband. She was a mother and bore a child without the woman's role in intercourse. The compact made her a spouse, but she was no wife in body. She became the mother of a Boy though she was untainted by a husband.

167. What a great mystery was this, by which the Church became wedded to Christ and became at once the Lord's bride and His sister! The bride with the status of spouse is a sister because she is not subject. . . .³⁹ So she continues as mother through the seed of the eternal Word, alike conceiving and bringing forth nations. She is sister

and spouse because her intercourse is not physical but mental, and her Husband is not man but God. The children of this mother comprise equally old and infants; this offspring has no age or sex. For this is the blessed progeny of God which springs from no human seed but from a heavenly race. This is why the teacher Paul says that *in Christ there is no male or female, but one body and one faith*,[40] for all of us who acknowledge Christ as Head of our body are one body, and are all Christ's limbs.[41] Because we have now put on Christ and stripped off Adam,[42] we are at once advancing towards the shape of angels. Hence for all born in baptism there is the one task; both sexes must incorporate the perfect man, and Christ as all in all[43] must be our common Head, our King who hands over His limbs to the Father in the Kingdom. Once all are endowed with immortal bodies, the frail condition of human lives forgoes marriage between men and women.[44]

191. So remember me, and live in chaste partnership forever. Your yoke must be the revered cross. As children of that mother who is both spouse and sister, you must train your hearts to be worthy of the holy names you bear. As brother and sister hasten together to meet Christ the Bridegroom, so that you may be one flesh[45] in the eternal body. You must be enmeshed with that love by which the Church holds fast to Christ, and by which Christ in turn hugs her close.

199. May your father the bishop[46] bless you, and lead the singing of holy lays in company with the hymn-chanting chorus. Kindly Memor, lead your children before the altar, and with a prayer and blessing of the hand commend them to the Lord. But what fragrance is this seeping down from the sky and gliding down to my nostrils? From

where comes this unexpected light which grips my eyes? Who is this approaching with serene steps, so remote from the life of men,[47] attended by Christ's abundant grace and surrounded by a blessed train of heaven's children resembling an angel band? I recognise him as one attended by God's fragrance, as one whose face gleams with heavenly beauty. This is the man, this is he[48] who is so rich in the countless gifts of Christ the Lord—Aemilius, a man endowed with the light of heavenly life.[49]

213. Memor, arise in deference to your father, and embrace your brother; the single person of Aemilius demands both titles from you.[50] Memor is both the younger and the elder. How remarkable are the gift and work of the great God, for here the younger is the father! The one born later is the older, because as bishop of his see he wears in his heart the gray hairs marking his seniority as successor of the apostles. Memor, his son and brother, is delighted that the father he shares with his dear ones[51] is at hand. Justice and peace embrace each other[52] when Memor meets Aemilius of like mind. As bishops they are united in heavenly distinction by their badge of office;[53] their devotion makes them partners in human love.

225. Then Memor, not unmindful[54] of his duty, follows the correct procedure and entrusts his dear ones to the hands of Aemilius, who joins both their persons in the peace of wedlock, puts his right hand over them, and consecrates them with a prayer. Christ, O Christ, hearken to your bishops' entreaty, hear the pious prayer of these consecrated suppliants.

231. Christ, instruct the newly married pair through your holy bishop. Aid the pure hearts through his chaste hands, so that they may both agree on a compact of vir-

ginity, or be the source of consecrated virgins. Of these
prayers, the first condition is preferable, that they keep
their bodies innocent of the flesh. But if they consum-
mate physical union, may the chaste offspring to come
be a priestly race.[55] May the whole house of Memor be
a house of Aaron.[56] May this house of Memor be a house
of anointed ones. Preserve the memory of Paulinus and
Therasia,[57] and Christ will preserve the memory of
Memor forever.

# POEM 26[1]

See how the year has run its course. We greet the day
which on its return again proffers a light brightened by
Felix's name. If only the troubled times allowed such expressions of delight, this would now be the moment to
publish our joy in words of happiness. Yet even amidst
battles this day will be for us one of joy and peace. Even
the most gruesome wars can rage, but the peace of
freedom must attend our minds. Since our thoughts custo-
marily turn to discharging our hearts' holy vow, and to
celebrating on this holiday innocent joy in our Lord, we
do not forget how to take sweet enjoyment in our delight.

11. So though the times are glum, banish unseasonable
sadness. On Felix's day we must embrace goodly joy,
pleasant greetings, and all that is holy and happy. This is
his birthday forever, for on this day Felix was born into
eternity. He brought to an end his days in the flesh, and
departed to heaven into eternal life. So depressing fears
must go, and joys return to our hearts refreshed. It is
right that all sadness should flee before this holy day, for
the fame of our great confessor makes it shine conspic-
uously amongst all days of the year's seasons, and adorns
it with crowds of visitors. I would gladly celebrate it even
if I were an unhappy prisoner of Gothic arms or amongst
the harsh Alans.[2] However many the chains weighting my
neck, the enemy would not bind my mind prisoner with

my captive limbs, for in my unchained heart proud devotion would tread underfoot my unhappy slavery. My love
would be free even amidst barbarian bonds, and would
sing the hymn I had vowed in words thought fitting.

29. So now, though rumour wandering over diverse
regions strikes our apprehensive ears with fearsome tidings,[3] our constant trust in Christ the Lord must strengthen
and equip us with minds intent on the direct way.[4] No
black fear must cast its cloud over the day which God
makes cloudless to give heavenly honour to Felix. In days
of old the lawgiver Moses in the land of the Egyptian
tyrant dedicated the consecrated lamb according to the
first Law; at that time, despite the fact that the wicked
enemy by brute strength forced the Jews to hasten their
flight from their homes, that holy race gained boldness
from the freedom within their dedicated hearts and did
not neglect the solemn command in the panic of fear.
Trembling and fugitive as they were, they completed the
solemnities prescribed by God, and in joyous throng
feasted on the lamb which brought salvation.[5] Then, victorious through the symbolic blood of Christ, Moses
overcame Pharaoh and triumphantly led away his happy
band. This is why the Jews (now preserving the mere
title of that earlier race) even today eat unleavened bread
in memory of their flight, because when they were expelled and fled from Egypt their loaves were made without
yeast.[6] Nowadays they observe this ancestral ritual under
the same form, gratefully reliving the traces of that ancient
fear, but on a sabbath which is superfluous. It is in vain
that they observe the empty shell of the old law; Christ
alone has fulfilled the true pasch for us when on behalf of

us all he was presented as a Victim to the Father.[7] Because He is with us as living Body, the shadow of that symbolism now vanishes.

55. So now let us be like those Jews of old, joyful in a time of turmoil, and with devotion of mind all celebrate the feast of our beloved martyr, uniting in eager and glad observance. Such devotion will doubtless bring us greater safety, if we are disposed to lay aside our anxieties to offer glad hearts to our confessor. God is delighted that Felix wins honour, because the martyr spurned his own honour in defence of the name of Christ the Lord. He made himself cheaper in his own eyes to become more precious in Christ's. This is why we must determine to rejoice in such a patron, to relinquish our cares and gladly celebrate the birthday of our martyr, now sleeping in blessed peace. He will attend on those who vow themselves to him all the more if our impulse towards joy emerges stronger than the wellspring of fear which clouds the heart and deranges the mind.

70. Be sure that what we are to fear is not the armed strength of foreign races, for they are being roused by God's angry displeasure at our sins. God is trying to rouse our sluggish hearts to take thought for life by inspiring us with fear of death. So amidst the savagery of the enemy it is God's kindness we must fear. We must not be apprehensive of the enemy, for fear of them is the deserved outcome of a failure to fear God. We neglect Him when we are relaxed in tranquil peace, so let us at any rate tremble before Him under the pressure of violence. Our humility in grief finds His favour, even though we scorn Him when he brings us happiness and that very prosperity breeds subsequent arrogance.

80. Let us contemplate the ancient examples of saintly forbears. In enduring deserved wounds when war was unleashed against them, they decided that they should not protect themselves by arms or by walls.[8] Hoping for salvation by human resource is no salvation, for mortal means will not rout death. So those who live in a time of anxiety[9] should be anxious to pray to the Lord of heaven, who dispenses sadness or gladness, and who alone by His transcendent sway can ensure that troubles are removed and happy times restored. This indeed is the practical way by which God, the Arbiter of our fate, governs and varies human affairs—He always makes clouds succeed fine weather, and then in turn the rains recede at the return of bright skies. The power of prayers and the healing efficacy of tears in the presence of God our Father is the lesson we must learn from Nineveh saved by its grief, from Amalek overcome by the devoted prayer of aged Moses, from the accursed Haman destroyed by the supplication of holy Esther.[10] Haman had mixed an evil draught for holy men, but the roles of punisher and punished were happily reversed. That wicked man alone drank it, and he himself justly hung on the cross which he had set up for the Lord's servant.[11]

99. So the faith which relies on God should strengthen panicking hearts, and its trust in God should in time of sorrow anticipate untroubled days. For fear of God ensures freedom from fear, whereas the man who does not fear God alone is right to fear everything. Those who have no confidence in Christ as Bearer of salvation must put their trust in legions and repair their walls as a defence prepared for refuge. But the sign of the unconquered cross and our proclamation of it defends us. Our hearts have

God as their armour, so we seek no armour for the body. Though we appear unarmed in body, we none the less are bearing arms with which even in time of sunny peace we grapple in spirit against the unsubstantial foe.[12] Now we need God to help us, and Him only we must fear; without Him our armour falls from us, but with Him our armour gains strength. He will be your Tower within the walls; He will be your Wall where walls there are none.

114. Let us hereafter recall the deeds of our ancestors recorded in the consecrated books. Observe who had the better protection—those enclosed in a city girt by great walls but without God, or those defended by God's strength and friendly support but without city walls. I refer to the city destroyed by the eager Joshua, whose own name was changed to delineate his power.[13] He did not subdue it in the usual military way, by conducting the regular long and weary blockade. No, through God's help his army in sacred symbolism performed a lustration,[14] brandishing its weapons without using them. It withdrew its violence, its arms were silent. For seven days they made seven repeated circuits round the walls.[15] By the strength of this powerful number[16] and by the fearful din of the priests' trumpets, which aped the flashing thunder of divine wrath, they laid hold of the enemy trapped within. Then that people which trusted in its wealth and city perished, and their graves were mingled with their houses.

132. Only the harlot Rahab escaped. Amongst that wicked people she preserved a chaste fidelity, and put her faith not in the walls of her city but in God's fatherly love. So she gained the reward of that devotion by which she afforded the hospitality of her safe house to the Lord's servants. Once they were hidden, she made holy mockery

of her wicked fellow citizens, whom she tricked by a
deception which was good, and by lying out of motives of
fidelity. Because she proved faithful to her holy guests and
faithless to her impious fellow citizens, this rejected
woman by putting God first found life and a land and a
home, and thereafter all things in the person of the kindly
Lord. If she had looked to the city for defence, she would
have fallen amidst the debris of her race, and God would
not have protected her. But the harlot had a symbolic role.
She foresaw that Christ would purchase with His blood
nations that had been corrupted, and so she designated
her house with a purple fleece, and obtained her personal
salvation in the destruction of her native land. Thus she
showed that when the world collapses, those marked by
the blood of the invincible cross will be saved. Grasp from
this the great power of Christ's blood, seeing that its representation brought such safety.

150. Having trust in Christ, consigning everything to
the God of powers, regarding God alone as all that is
highest—this has always been efficacious in achieving every
good. This is the faith that has prevailed over all weapons.
This was the strength that made that slight boy great, for
he grew stronger by spurning weapons, and brought low
the armed giant by the power of a stone.[17] We find that
arms have always needed faith, but faith has never needed
arms. The rod of faith parted the sea which submerged
the army bereft of faith together with its wicked leader.[18]
A holy faith has endowed women's character with the
strength of men, for through such faith the holy woman
destroyed the fearsome Sisora, whose temple was pierced
with a stake.[19] The wily Judith with her chaste cunning
deceived and mocked Holofernes, who had terrorised

mighty people far and wide. She remained inviolate in that lewd bed, and then fled from the barbarians' camp victorious after slaughtering their leader.[20]

166. *Faith unguarded is armed by God.* Hezekiah, through the power of faith, proved stronger with his puny force than Sennacherib, king of Babylon and rich Nineve, with his thousands.[21] Sennacherib had enlisted the forces of Assyria and the realm of the Medes. Laying waste with his huge legions all the neighbouring kingdoms, he proceeded towards the city sacred to the Lord and against it alone concentrated his whole massive war machine. But as he made preparations for this, God hindered him, for warfare delayed his unholy designs. He sent to Jerusalem a letter brusque in its arrogant threats. Hezekiah received it with grief, and bore it to the Lord before the altar. There in prostrate prayer accompanied by his people in mourning black, he read out those harsh words and bedewed the letter with abundant tears, and so he prevailed on God. By prayer alone, though absent from the scene he won a shattering victory over the Assyrians, who suffered a grievous death when God warred on them. This favour he won was so considerable that he did not even clap eyes on the enemy he conquered. Once his tears of complaint had passed above the constellations, once his lament from a humble heart had risen beyond the stars and his devoted words had assailed the ears of the highest Father, the lofty doors of heaven swung open and a winged angel glided down, breathing the fragrant air on his smooth descent. Armed with the sword of the Word, he smote that wicked army, and glorying in the silent slaughter of the sleeping foe he brought simultaneous death to one hundred and eighty thousand men.[22] A single night was the accomplice

in an engagement on that scale. Next morning the king arose still threatening, but then took flight with his depleted column, wretched because his army was thus stripped of its slaughtered soldiers. He fled from Hezekiah though the prophet was far removed in another district, and though he had only recently in his presence threatened to clap his fetters on him.

195. At that time Isaias was mediator for Hezekiah. Likewise let Felix now be our go-between to the Lord. Let us cast and transfer our cares and fears to Felix. Our weight will be for him a light burden, for giants make light of dwarfs' luggage. So God Himself bore men's sins without imbibing them, and endured death on the cross without incurring moral fault. He lost His life to restore mine on the cross. He was arraigned that I may not be arraigned. He was condemned, He died between wicked men to separate us from the wicked. My Lord died a holy death that I may live for Him, and deserve to live the life of an immortal being. This is why the martyrs have greater esteem as limbs in His revered body; they are rightly influential with God because their suffering was similar to Christ's. Amongst them Felix has outstanding efficacy and brillance as one of the holy eyes shining in the divine Head. So with hope as our companion let us hasten to Felix our patron. He will listen to our lament with tranquil affection. As we joyfully celebrate his birthday, our loving father by his lofty merit will bring our prayers to realisation. Because with inner dedication we take joy in him, he in turn will weep on our behalf.

216. The saints are not new to the task of imploring God on behalf of suffering sinners, and of outweighing our evil deserts with the power of their outstanding merit.

We read that Moses by prayer quenched the heavy wrath of the eternal Avenger against his sinning people.[23] When a rain of fire showered the region of the Five Cities,[24] Lot as he fled detached tiny Zoar from wicked Sodom, for by the efficacy of his holy prayer he delivered Zoar. Then he chose and obtained it as his home because he had dwelt in his chaste house as an uncorrupted inhabitant of a lewd land, physically among the dwellings of Sodom but a stranger to its manners.[25] Need I mention the prayers of Elias by which the skies closed and reopened, how famine lingered on the earth and how salvation reappeared at the saintly words of the sublime prophet?[26]

230. Such were the men whom those of ancient days had as their support, and likewise we have Felix for our salvation. Our confidence in such a patron must lead us to ask for all we dare, and to hope for all we desire. Holy Felix, loved by God, God's right hand, I pray you, be our impregnable tower. The God of Abraham, Isaac, and Israel is your God also. The God who divided the Red Sea, who sweetened the waters of bitterness, who dispensed manna from heaven and quails from the south, who watered the thirsty earth with a blow on the rock,[27] is your God, too. He is the same God who blazed a trail through the desert land for His people who followed, who changed the substance of the cloud He raised before you by an alternating scheme for night and day, who for forty years in the desert fed His people with the bread of angels from heaven, who refreshed their thirst when the rock exploded into a torrent.[28]

246. I beg you, ask Christ to lend our cause His benevolent support. Yours is that same God by whose power brave Joshua bade sun and moon hover motionless over

his victory.[29] Once the Lord has allowed you fair fortune for the Roman domain, bid the elements that serve you, Felix, to minister to our good. Let the daylight emerge more brightly while the stars remain motionless. Let sun and moon in harmony under your control remain poised, and keep the stars stationary in suspended course till the victory of Rome is finally accomplished.[30] In Assyrian Babylon, Daniel victoriously tamed the lions by welling prayer;[31] so now, Felix, you must tame the uncivilised barbarians, and Christ must shatter them so that they recline as captives at your feet. This was how the beasts of old lay around the prophet's feet, and with benevolent tongues licked his feet as he prayed; God changed their nature so that he could condemn bestial men of bitter purpose through the gentleness of beasts which was appropriate to men. So, too, the fire confounded the cruel tyrant as he watched the furnace defer to the wishes of the saintly children, and as he witnessed his prisoners singing while his servants were ablaze.[32] How will such wretched princes succeed in vindicating themselves for raging with such subhuman minds against men spared by beasts and flames?

269. Just as a dew-laden wind quenched the blazing fires when the boys re-echoed hymns of eternal life,[33] so now may kind Felix restrain the fires of war with a peaceful breeze wafted by God. Damping down the blaze which has blared forth in the realm of Romulus, may he bring the cool refreshment of tranquil peace to the heat of our anxieties. May he free our weary hearts and quench our cares.

276. But why do I foolishly beg you to offer help in our need by citing the example of our ancient parents, as

though I were a guest of yours who has not experienced your character or has forgotten it? You will ensure that the boon God grants you is transmitted to us. I have witnessed sufficient examples of your powers, Felix; Christ pours out His heavenly gifts no less richly on you than on those ancestors whose noble progeny you are. For, Felix, you are alike the son of patriarchs and stock of the apostles; you are an heir who has not fallen below his great ancestry. As holy confessor of the holy law and faith, you manifest signs rivalling the powers of those ancestors. Even if the appearance of your achievements is not the same, your powers are like theirs. Your charism differs, but your fame is equal, since all holy men emanate from the one source and belong to the one kingdom of God. Prophets and consecrated martyrs had tasks which differed according to their various eras, and their achievements do not manifest identical signs because their causes make them different. So they are distinguished by the gifts God bestows on them in heaven, but they are equal in merit.

294. Felix, it is true, did not achieve or endure all that Daniel did, for he did not enter a furnace nor was he surrounded by fearsome lions. But then Daniel did not suffer the grim experiences of Felix for his Master's name— scourging, fetters, the fears and darkness of a murky prison. The God who clamped shut the mouths of the beasts and made them gentle towards the prophet who adored Him, the God who at the prayer of the boys chilled the fires and made their clothing wet in the midst of the furnace, has also given to Felix the power of high dominion, a control over the baneful legions of Satan, so that it is amongst these that he quells all beasts and flames, for that mob incorporates every possible reptile and beast.

307. To end with, I shall recount just one incident from
many, so that from it you may learn that devils have the
impulses of beasts. Recently an individual was distracted by
so monstrous a demon that it did not merely devour with
ready maw the usual run of human food, or banquets laden
with abundant fare; it even snatched hens from the thresholds of people's houses, and with manic mouth tore them
to pieces and devoured them uncooked without choking
on the feathers. It even thirsted for the blood of dead
animals, and licked their bones; it chewed the abandoned
carcases of cattle, the disgusting mate of dogs at their
feasting.

318. But see him now, this man but recently possessed
by the dread devil. He works soberly on a small rented
farm some distance away. God tended him in the holy
church of Felix, and he is restored to his former self, thus
proving by this quite certain sign that Felix has power by
his merits and Christ's name to subdue monstrous beasts
and to prevail over fire. Speak out, you who are here as
witnesses of Felix's deeds. Does he not master beasts and
flames when he crushes the devils which destroy souls
through sin and bodies through disease, which inflame men
with blazing desires and devour them by their sins? When
Felix tortures and routs them, is he not crushing beasts and
flames? The fiery Felix soars and takes vengeance on the
fire-brandishing band, and quenches their injurious flame
by God's fire. The fire of darkness is vanquished by the
holy fire of light. The devil flees, and God makes His entrance. The person becomes a dwelling happily transformed, a happier abode which denies entry to any foul
tenant because God is its owner. God is a bright and healing Fire, and with this Fire my Felix waxes hot so that he

can extinguish the flaming devil, and cool the man thus released from the blazing foe.

338. Felix, wondrous power, strong rod, lofty strength, has detached from each other spirits joined by a hostile compact within a single body. He entered its hidden heart, and being of finer texture than they, he parted those unsubstantial spirits, separating soul from devil. Once the devil was expelled, the mind was free to welcome a human occupant. This achievement was as great as that achieved by the type of the cross when through the sweetness of its sacred wood it transformed the harsh and bitter liquid into drinking water for God's people.[34] Felix has similarly powerful holiness, for as the noble confessor of the exalted cross he transformed the man who resembled the harsh draught of bitter water. That person who but recently was puffed up with a bitter devil, who exuded the poisonous tang of vipers from his foaming lips, who constantly jumped up and down with much shaking of sides, hiccupping from open throat, and belching of bitter breath, has now reverted wholly and solely to the human condition. His tang is sweet, his breath controlled, his speech calm.

354. So Felix, too, is girt with a right hand of power, and so with this strength he swallows up the assorted guile of the prince of darkness, just as the rod of Moses swallowed up the serpents of the magicians.[35] We can observe how the heavenly Lord makes resources as great as those of ancient days attend on Felix's merit, how even the shape of his deeds is in accord, how all that the patriarchs performed in the flesh, as proofs of the holy God, Felix achieves not in the flesh but through his life in Christ. We observe that while the bones of his buried body lie at rest,

his soul has vigour and signal intelligence, and demonstrates by clear signs before the time of its return to earth the kind of crown that Felix will get as his deserts, once he stands restored in physical completeness.

366. All the saints will have their own brightness, different in each case, yet equal. Christ's judgment will not advance one at the expense of another's deserving merit. All will have Christ as their kingdom, light, life, and crown. Note how the teachers of the Old and New Testaments differ in their deeds but are paired in glory, for the one Wisdom issued twin Laws in the two Testaments, so equal distinction gives the same weight to differing powers. Peter did not divide the sea with a rod, but then Moses did not walk on the waters.[36] However, both have the same bright glory, for the one Creator inspired both the cleavage of the waters with a rod and the treading of the waves underfoot. The God of the saints of old is also the God of the new. Grace has sprung from that Lord who issued the Law. The God of Daniel and of the three boys[37] is also the God of Felix, and He is no less God in holy Felix, for through him He practises kindly bounty and healing assistance on land and sea.

384. Every day in dense crowds pressing on every side we witness either men restored to health discharging vows of gratitude, or the sick begging and experiencing diverse remedies. We also see many who have journeyed from foreign shores stretched out before the consecrated church of our holy martyr, recounting as they thank him the hazards they have endured. They attest that their ship was battered by heavy storms, but that they were rescued in God's mercy by the guidance of Felix's own hand. So they emerged from the sea's depths, and obtained peace

and the salvation of which they had despaired. Water and fire, they claim, yield before the deserving virtue of Felix.

395. I shall not mention the evidences of this powerful merit from the distant past. We know it by experience, and the apprehension arising from a recent panic makes our mindful hearts still patter when we recall the conflagration which we endured and which almost destroyed our dwelling.[38] The remembrance of that fire somehow extinguished is rekindled in our minds and increases our love for the great Felix. It seemed as if we observed him in person here taking physical action, confronting the flames with his hands and guarding our threshold which abuts on his. The flames were almost licking it, but then shrank back as if terrified by the appearance of the saint blocking their way. Then, driven from the rafters of our dwelling (the loss of which seemed inevitable), they burned themselves out close at hand, after levelling a neighbouring cottage.[39] Here I shall proclaim a miracle. The air remained motionless, without a breath of wind. No breeze made the foliage tremble in the woodland, and so the devouring fire could not advance farther by leaping along the interwoven beams of our joined dwellings. Deserted by the dying winds, the flame refused to spread, and it died of enervation once its food was exhausted.

413. Felix, you must deliver us from our dangers by offering similar help. Let no evils approach our house. May the grim anger of war with its blood-flecked scourge be repelled by you to resound far off. Keep the war at its distance[40] by putting on that strength by which you redirected the river. The stream was gliding threateningly down from the local mountains, having overflowed its banks

when its racing flood was swollen by sudden rains, and it repeatedly rushed down towards your threshold. With its massive waters it fiercely assailed the abodes close to your dwellings. But you changed its course, so that now a bed guides its raging progress through strange territory, and it skirts our buildings with a distant detour. In like manner now divert from our region the river of battles resounding with the din of war. May wicked violence eschew this consecrated territory, which has your grace as its rampart. May the enemy emulate the demons, and fear your church; may no bloodshed pollute this shrine from which fire and stream have fled.[41]

# POEM 27[1]

Come forth, dawn of this day. I find you always laggard in your rising, but then fleeting in your haste to set. You come round reluctantly, but you leave on the wing. I endure the long period of your delay, until the glistening wheel of the sluggish year completes its revolution, by discharging my vow with devoted mind. O, how I could wish that you shone on me every day, or that when you come at last you could atone for the delay by prolonging your light over the whole summer season! Could you not re-enact that day on which the stars were bidden to stay their course and the world grew weary with protracted light,[2] when night's postponement redoubled the toils of men? As it is, the law of the wintry season withdraws you from us, dear day, and your all too fleeting light. The winter presses on the shortened hours of day, its light so swiftly passing, its darkness so lingering.

15. Happily, however, you have a sun in Felix, who shines for you with his abiding grace and Christ's illumination. He forms his own orb to gleam on his birthday, and the brightness of his eternal glory is never hidden by any evening setting. Pass on, glide away, fleeting day, for I shall not recall you nor grumble further at your brief stay, since without your presence Felix is here to offer me the perpetual brightness of unquenchable light. Even though your birthday takes leave of us, there is the greater and abiding presence of Felix, the light of this birthday.

It is not the day which makes him a saint; no, it is his glory
which is the reason for celebrating the day.

25. But if the presence of a crowd which hastens in
thicker array than usual towards the holy threshold makes
a birthday take precedence over other days, then almost
all the time we see Felix's birthday being celebrated by a
milling attendance. For what day is there that dawns
without some vows being discharged, or without huge
crowds being normal? However, I shall admit that this
day rightly keeps its special distinction, for on it long ago
Felix completed his span, laid aside his earthly garments,
and was summoned to the stars on high to lodge in his
blessed abode. Such a procedure strengthens the faith
which marks out the yearly calendar with fixed designa-
tions, and signals the days devoted to yearly festivals. On
these days our remote ancestors of old trembled in the
presence of the Lord's miracles, which will always be a
cause of terror to the profane and of celebration to the
saintly, for they brought blessings to the saints and grim
times to evil men. Witnesses to this are the land of Egypt
and the sea which of old became land to the holy but
water to the wicked;[3] and we recall with mindful affection
the other miracles as great as these which God performed
in Egypt and many other lands.

43. Likewise, the gifts that Christ conferred are hymned
as divine. Thus the day on which God was born of a
virgin, and assumed humanity for all, is revered by all
mankind. So, too, the day on which the Wise Men were
guided by a star, brought their symbolic gifts, and prostrate beheld the Child.[4] Or again, the day on which the
apprehensive Jordan washed Christ, when John immersed
Him as He consecrated all waters to achieve the new

creation of mankind.[5] Then, too, there is the day consecrated by the sign with which He began His work, when
He transformed the water and changed it into the nectar
of outstandingly sweet wine.[6] There is also the feast of
the Pasch. Of course, the Church proclaims the Pasch in
all lands on each successive day, witnessing to the Lord's
death on the cross, and to the life gained by all from the
cross. Yet the whole world with equal devotion everywhere venerates this lofty mystery of great love towards
mankind in a particular month each year, when it celebrates the eternal King risen with body restored.[7] After
this solemn feast (we calculate seven weeks before this
holiday comes round for men) comes the day on which
the Holy Spirit was of old sent down from the heights of
heaven in parted tongues of fiery light.[8]

64. Then He, the one God, sped over diverse lands and
with one voice spoke aloud in tongues of every kind. He
gave men the power of speaking to all in languages unknown, so that each individual acknowledged his own
tongue being spoken by a foreigner, though out of his
own mouth he could not converse in a strange language.
The barbarian uttered tidings fully comprehended in a
language he did not know, for he spoke words foreign to
his own. Yet the one Spirit was praising the one God in
different languages before all men.

72. Think of a man playing a harp, plucking strings
producing different sounds by striking them with the one
quill. Or again the man who rubs his lips by blowing on
woven reeds; he plays one tune from his one mouth, but
there is more than one note, and he marshals the different
sounds with controlling skill. He governs the shrill-echoing
apertures with his breathing and his nimble fingers, clos-

ing and opening them, and thus a tuneful wind with haste
of aery movement successively passes and returns along
the hollow of the reed, so that the wind instrument becomes alive and issues forth a tune unbroken. This is how
God works. He is the Musician who controls that uni-
versal-sounding harmony which He exercises through all
the physical world. God is the Craftsman of all creation
natural and contrived. In all this creation He is the Source
and the End. He makes what is good and preserves it
once made, abiding in Himself with that interchange of
mutual love by which reigns the Father in the Word and
the Son in the Father. Without Him nothing was made.[9]
Through Him all that comes to life abides in the same Being. He renews all things under the guidance of the Word,
who mounting aloft from the gleaming cross with the
purple of His precious blood reached the heights in swift
ascent, flying on a cloud beyond the Cherubim.[10] He took
His seat on the right hand of the Father, and from there
poured forth on His followers the heavenly gift of the
Holy Spirit.

93. The Holy Spirit proceeds from the only-begotten
Son and the Father, and is Himself God coming forth
from God.[11] Though the Spirit is everywhere, His fiery
presence was actually visible gliding speedily over the
place where the harmonious gathering of young apostles
was in session.[12] Then, when a large number from Jerusalem had assembled at the unusual sound, the Spirit settled
like a flame on all those present of every race, and with
the same breath spoke differently but simultaneously to
each of them. Like a musician strumming the strings of
the lyre with fluent quill, the Spirit proclaimed the same
message in different tongues, instilling into men's ears the

varying sounds. Once such intoxication possessed these chosen souls, their hearts were drunk with God, and they belched forth from abstemious throats songs of sacred praise. Who will take pity on me and give me to drink from this stream[13] which with its intoxication brings sobriety?

107. Accordingly, just as the Lord has decked the sky with stars, the fields with blossoms, and the years with seasons, so He has marked out those seasons with feast-days. His purpose is that our minds grown sluggish with their daily obedience may at any rate distinguish these days, and after a due interval may joyfully celebrate such holy feasts by renewing their vows; by these yearly feast-days our sluggish hearts can be refurbished for the Lord. A continuous life of chaste slavery to righteousness is wearying, and it is hard for those inured to wickedness to refrain from sin. We run downhill into every valley, but we cannot reach the summit of a climb at speed. So the slippery downhill path is easier, and the road to life is harder. The first can be achieved by the many, the second is difficult and for the few.

119. So the good Lord seeks to protect us all with His fatherly wings, and has provided for the weak these holy days appropriately spaced out as a means of striving for the citadel of virtue. By such modest service men can at any rate clutch the edge of Christ's garment, and be healed even by its hem;[14] for such persons are not wholly exiled from the territory of salvation. Their lodging is within the perimeter of eternal life, and though far removed from the first group they are not greatly distant from the second. The life of that first group consists in interweaving all their days in unbroken goodness, in perpetually cele-

brating Christ's holy pasch in chaste worship. But if my
corn sprouts amongst thorns,[15] if the prickles of wordly
toil prick my uncultivated heart, I must be eager to consecrate myself to the Lord at any rate on feastdays, so that
some part of me may touch the borders of life, and my
whole body may not be dragged into partnership with
death.

135. Hence though we who dwell closest to Felix
continually cherish the glory of our holy patron (for we
glorify the saint with constant and devoted attendance
at other times besides his birthday), yet we house-slaves
on our master's feast must take a break from our chores
and sing the hymn we promised. So I shall lead my
brothers in song amidst this rejoicing. Like a standard-
bearer I shall head the column of comrades. It is true that
on this day crowds of people from different districts proclaim their holy joy with vows like mine; but it is fitting
for me to celebrate the day more copiously and vehe-
mently, because no one is bound as debtor to Felix more
closely than I, and this day brought him forth as my great
patron for ever—more especially my own than any
individual's star.[16]

148. Greetings to you, day so welcome! Greetings,
light of mine! For me you are always a festive day, but
this year the brightness of your rising has been more splendid still. For besides bringing new glory to Felix, you
bring back Nicetas[17] to me; and so I celebrate twin birthdays today out of affection for two saintly men. I commemorate the physical death of our martyr, but note how
I also in my plenty venerate the bishop on his physical
return, and welcome Christ who lodges in his humble
heart. My soul can rejoice now and utter the words which

the loving bride of old sang aloud to her loving Lord: "The rain is gone, the winter is past, the voice of the turtle aloft resounds in our land; the vines give forth fragrance, and we marvel at the lilies of heaven blossoming also on earth."[18] I ask you, how has this sudden change in season caused the year to introduce spring weather, so that flowers are visible in the frozen fields? It is because Nicetas, the anointed[19] of Christ the Lord, is here in the company of his friends. That is why the winter wears the face of spring, and the animating air breathes fragrant warmth on us. The breath of the fields thus blessed is from Nicetas' heart. His chaste life and his mind radiant with the clarity of truth make Nicetas the blossom and good odour of Christ.[20]

169. What words of heart or tongue could I utter in my poverty, foolishness, and insignificance that would be worthy of so great a blessing? Felix himself must now provide me with the boon I need for this. He must obtain from Christ resources to bestow on me so that I can thank him in worthy fashion. If only a living spring of eternal water would emanate from my belly, so that I could announce my joy not by my tongue but through Christ's gift! For it is through His gift that joy floods my tranquil heart to unprecedented depths, and my affection which invests Felix's birthday is redoubled. Today I witness Nicetas in the flesh smiling upon me, and when I behold the father for whom above all others my love prevails, I myself become a Nicetas, not in blessed name but in heart now triumphant, since my prayer has succeeded.[21]

184. When I realise that he is here on your birthday, most glorious Felix, after all this time and after travelling so far, I must surely proclaim that your hand guided him

here. Who could fail to observe this clear evidence that
your prayer has brought me a blessing which I could
scarcely pray for or even dream of attaining—namely, that
I should look on and embrace Nicetas again in the flesh
on Felix's very birthday, and that he should once more
be listening as I sing, Felix, the hymn I owe to you? But
what can I do? I am a poor guest at the rich man's table,[22]
and wretch that I am I presume to lay my hands on the
splendid fare, without thinking that I should reciprocate
similarly, and by offering words worthy of Nicetas' appreciation provide fare commensurate with what I take.
So, dear saint, grant your resourceless servant the boldness
to speak words worthy of you, my patron, and words
appropriate for your friend.[23]

200. Felix, I request the attendance of your fathers with
yourself to hear your promised offering. When I say *your*
offering, I mean mine; for it is more truly mine, whereas
your exalted distinction rejects these earthly joys. Yet
because our joy is directed to your glory, and because
you deign to claim as your own the vows of your followers, I beg the presence with you of your fathers. You
are here at Nola as well as in heaven; request them to
answer my summons and come as well.

207. I call on you who dwell in the luxuriant demesnes
of heaven's paradise and who are at rest beneath the lofty
altar of the Lord. You are a splendid gathering, apostles
and patriarchs in line. Your two troops of princes are a
race preferred; in your twin lines God has marked you out
with your twelve names[24] as fathers to summon nations
and peoples to the kingdom of heaven. Your presence, too,
I humbly demand, saintly prophets. You foretold that God
would appear in our flesh; you, too, as martyrs with muti-

lated bodies and shedding of blood bore witness to the Lamb who was slain yet lives. All of you are of one stock from a heavenly seed. Holy Abraham, consecrated Isaac, gentle Jacob sired you for God; you are their seed beyond all counting who performed deserving deeds both heavenly and transient, the first equalling the numbers of stars in the sky and the second the sand-grains of the earth.

222. I believe that you have assembled from all quarters out of love for Felix, to show your fatherly love on this day by hymning the distinction of the confessor who is your comrade. However, I do not claim such high distinction for myself as to pray that all the saints may at once direct their kindly favours on my intelligence alone, as though I were worthy of a boon so great, and so as to induce on my lips the resounding voice of the turtle which the earth joyfully heard throughout the world.[25] I make the request because heaven-inspired utterance is appropriate to Felix's glory, and because Nicetas, at once the Lord's child and His bishop, has arrived in time for this very day, though so recently sped on his way to me from a distant land; and he is a man as goodly in his tongue's teaching as he is holy in his victorious spirit or his flesh subdued.

235. If only one of the Cherubim would with shining tongs take a coal from the Lord's very altar, to bear it afar and burn the lips of this sinner,[26] unhappily rustic as they are! Then my mouth would be cleansed of the filth that has hardened in it, and I could draw off a draught worthier than my mouth, not, however, from my own mouth, but from the mouth[27] of the listening Nicetas; then, too, the rough, inarticulate tones of this doltish sinner would not ravage and scourge his chaste and learned ears. But since

my master is himself seated at my side, I shall see him established here at hand, far from his own land, and my eyes will often revere him. And perhaps through the words of this sage man I shall conceive fertile thoughts in my barren heart, even as the unproductive cattle of the shepherd Jacob became fecund. For Nicetas, too, is, like the gentle Jacob, the Lord's blessed one; like Israel he sits as shepherd of sheep and goats before a well of living water.[28] He, too, with similar mind plucked three rods from three trees,[29] and setting them in the water he summons the flock. When they gather, he impregnates them, and dyes the offspring with the three rods. Thus through the rods, striped by shaving from them rings of bark, the progeny of his holy flock can be established by their marking.

256. Laban's flock have no marks on them. The mark denotes life, for Christ will regard those unmarked as marked for death.[30] This is how grace brings fresh life to barren souls through the three Persons. The Spirit as husband impregnates the Church by the intercourse of the Word, and the offspring conceived for God is given an inward marking by the Church.[31] The Church, so fertile in her virgin's womb and the mother of salvation, with her gaze on the three rods absorbs the moist seed of the Word, and is marked with the brightness of God's immortal countenance.[32] *Hence the barren one has borne seven, whereas the fecund one was left forlorn,*[33] for God supplies plenty to the needy and deprivation to the proud. The sight of Nicetas was for me like the discovery of that fountain; parched, I ran like a thirsty sheep to the living stream, and at once felt my udders distending. I looked long and observantly at the face of the master who fed

me, and examined the several rods in his learned heart. My eyes trained on him drank in the colours I beheld there, and his dew-laden heart sprinkled me with drops from heaven.

273. Because the three rods have been mentioned, we can examine further, if you are agreeable, the symbolism of the kingdom implicit in them. The patriarch chose for himself three rods from three trees. The first was perfumed from the storax tree,[34] the second smooth from the plane tree, the third unbending from the almond tree. The plane contains the Spirit, the storax the Virgin, and the almond Christ. For the plane extends its spreading branches to provide shade; so the Holy Spirit fashioned Christ by casting His shadow over the Virgin. I believe that the rod from the storax, the tree of David, is the Virgin who in childbirth brought forth a sweet-smelling Blossom. The rod of the almond tree is Christ, for there is food within that tree, which has an outer casing consisting of bitter bark over its green skin. Here you must recognise the divine Christ clothed in our human body. In that flesh He can be broken; the food lies in the Word, the bitterness in the cross. His hard covering consists of the tidings of the cross and the food of that cross, and it encloses within the divine remedy in the flesh of Christ.

288. Yet in His cross He is also sweet, because God our life brought forth life from that tree. My Life hung on that wood so that my life might remain with God. Christ my Life, what return can I make to you for my life? My only course is to take the chalice of salvation[35] with which Your right hand can nourish me so that I may be cleansed with the sacred draught of Your precious lifeblood.

294. Yet what can I do? Even if I were to count myself so cheap as to cast my own body into fire or shed my blood, I could not pay You the debt which is Your due, for I should merely be returning my person to You on my own account. Whatever exchange of this kind I make, I shall always fail to match You, Christ, because when You endured suffering for Your wicked servants, it was my debt and not Yours that You discharged for me. What love could balance Yours? You, my Lord, put on my likeness so that I, Your servant, could put on Yours; in view of this, do men still think it notable that I should purchase my own salvation with possessions that wither? That I should exchange the transient for the eternal, that I should sell my land and buy heaven?[36] See how God purchased me at much higher cost, His death on the cross. He suffered, He donned the lowly likeness of a slave, in order to purchase cheap slaves at the price of His precious blood.

307. What, then, can I do? I rashly launch out into the hazardous heights, I dare to trust myself aloft on frail wings.[37] I was following my practice of singing the lighter theme of our glorious martyr's birthday, but I have suddenly flashed up to the heights. I fly above the stars, and have directed my impudent thoughts and utterance towards the Source of creation. How have I acquired such boldness? What breeze wafts me upwards in my arrogance? I am so inflated that I do not recognise my own inner self, for my mind is acting beyond its powers. I am conscious of Nicetas sitting by me, touching me, breathing on me close to my side. As he exhales his breath close by, his eager breath enters me, and with its power rouses in

my thoughts a novel fire, lending life to my cold vitals
with the warmth it brings.

320. However, I shall repress my swollen airs. Since I
am so diminutive, I shall not aspire to exalted speech beyond my level, or be accounted insignificant in midair. I
shall proceed with modest song, foot on the level ground.
Though I cannot proclaim Felix's lofty merits without
praising God, you, holy Nicetas, must take me in your
fatherly arms, and as I rest my head on your heart which
is so indulgent to me, and your learned breast supports
me, your salt must season my insipidness, your rich course
must water my thirsty mind with undying flow.

329. Once more will I express my joy, and renew my
question, even now scarcely believing the boon I have
gained. Tell me, please, have you come back? Is it Nicetas
himself that I embrace, to whom I have hitherto clung
night and day only in weary and wasting soul? Have you
finally returned to me after three years' absence?[38] But
thanks be to Christ for bringing you back even as late
as this, for how great was my fear that the foe would
keep you cut off in the heart of his territory, by banking
up a cloud of war against you! But our longing prevailed,
and you broke the bonds barring your way to us. Neither
the ocean, nor any hardship, nor the terrors inspired by
the Goths,[39] nor the grim cold of your long travels kept
you back. But in these great hazards, Nicetas, you were
both conquered and conqueror by reason of your kindly
love; you were at once strong and weak, but showed your
power in both. Overcome by your friendship, overcome
by love of Felix, you overcame grim hardships by your
tender affection.

345.[40] Come now, holy father, and offer me your ear and hand. Let us clasp hands to bind ourselves in comradeship to each other, and when our hands are entwined in this interchange of friendship we can converse on various matters as we stroll around. Your fatherly interest makes me eager to describe and indicate what we have achieved during the entire period of your absence. Who has a greater right to hear me recounting my achievements and renewing all that Felix's hand has done for us than he whose charge we are? He exercises twin rights as teacher and father, both to approve our good achievements and to condemn our bad, to correct our mistakes and kindly to organize our course of future action. Our bishop must aid our unfinished tasks with prayers, and consecrate what is completed; he must traverse the full extent of Felix's house as if his thoughts were full of Felix, and as if he prided himself at being in his father's abode.[41]

360. So, father, come and walk in company with me as I lead you round our buildings one by one. Here, where the outer door welcomes us, you see this portico, previously buried in darkness by a gloomy top but now spruce with paint and a new roof.[42] Next the entrance court, enclosed and roofed on its four sides but in the centre open to the sky. It was earlier a small garden with ground poorly tilled, a shabby plot which provided few vegetables and was quite unserviceable. But we meanwhile conceived a desire to erect the present structure here, for the site itself seemed to demand such adornment. By this means when the doors facing it at the front are opened, a gladder splendour can brighten the martyr's revered church from a distance. Its gleaming facade, exposed through the arches with double doors, can flood the interior with abundant

light.[43] It confronts the entrance of the prominent tomb in which our sleeping martyr is covered, now that he has cast aside his body. When the twin doors are thrown open to admit redoubled light, Felix delightedly looks upon his courtyard before the threshold of his gleaming tomb, and he rejoices that his walls cannot contain the crowds of worshippers, nor his huge churches the glad congregations; he is pleased to see thick crowds dispersing through the several doors.

382. The church in which the tomb of the holy martyr still stands has itself been cleansed of its ancient appearance, and has put on a new one. Three men have been at work on it, enhancing it with different kinds of embellishment, two of them craftsmen installing ceiling panels and marble facings, and the third an artist adding representations of God's appearance. All that you see is smiling brightness in the church, which seems to be taking on fresh life. The ceiling gives a wavy effect to the panels decorated in relief;[44] the wood on it simulates ivory, and the lamps suspended from it are secured by brass chains. The lights sway in midair on their loose ropes as a light breeze assails the bending flames. Earlier the roof rested on pillars, but now it despises the cheap stucco, which it has exchanged for the marble of the columns now supporting it.[45]

395. But let us go back to the forecourt. Notice the cells set above the long porticoes which have thus acquired a second storey;[46] they are lodgings fit for the occupancy of good men whom eagerness for prayer rather than the desire for drink[47] enticed here to offer appropriate honour to Saint Felix. These upper rooms attached to the consecrated roofs look from their windows

above on the inviolate altars, beneath which the bodies of saints have their recessed abodes. For the ashes even of apostles have been set beneath that table of heaven, and consecrated amongst other holy offerings they emit a fragrance pleasing to Christ from their living dust.

406. Here is father Andrew, the fisherman sent to Argos who there taught vain-sounding tongues to observe silence; Andrew, who broke the net of wicked error to extricate the people from it and to draw them to Christ's net, and who later by shedding his blood brought condemnation on Thessalian Patras.[48] Here, too, is John, who both preceded and baptised the Lord, who is both the holy gateway to the Gospel and the finishing point of the Law.[49] He, too, has come to the dwelling of my Felix as guest, and lends distinction to his brother's remains with a relic of his ashes.[50] Nearby lies the doubter Thomas, whose surname Didymus means "twin";[51] Christ allowed him to be hesitant and uncertain in fearful mind for our faith's sake, so that we, too, strengthened by his example, can fear our Lord and God and confess that Jesus physically lives on after death and demonstrates the living wounds in His flesh.[52] So, when the day comes on which He will come as God recognisable in the open light of day, those who took up arms against Him will tremblingly identify the One they nailed to the cross now shining in His crucified body.

424. Here lies Luke, a physician first by profession and later by preaching; so Luke was doubly a physician, for just as previously he tended the physically sick by earthly resource, so subsequently he devised medicine to give life to diseased minds through his two books.[53]

428. Joined with these apostles in devotion and faith,

power and honour, are the martyrs Agricola and Vitalis[54]
together with Proculus,[55] and Euphemia who as martyr
in the area of Chalcedon marks and consecrates that shore
with her virgin's blood.[56] Bononia[57] gives shelter to Vitalis,
Agricola, and Proculus; the faith they had sworn summoned them to fight for their devotion to God, and their
victories of equivalent merit have clothed with the palms
of salvation their glorious bodies transfixed with nails as
huge as beams.[58] Here, too, is the martyr Nazarius,[59] whom
I received in humility of heart as a gift of faith from the
noble Ambrose, so that he, too, lends distinction to Felix's
dwelling, and as a fellow resident sets his own resting-
place close by the house of that brother.

440. Although through the agency of the one God all
the saints are everywhere throughout the world, and
through Him are manifest as His own bodily limbs, at the
same time regions are apportioned to the bodies of saints.
Yet the influence of an interred saint is not confined to
the area where his whole body lies. Wherever there is part
of a saint's body, there, too, his power emerges. God takes
a hand in offering proof of his blessed merits; the great
power evinced even in a particle of the saints' ashes proclaims the power of the bodies of apostles at the prompting of the Word.

449. So all who dwell in the chastity of the cells above
will have these saints for neighbours, as will also the visitor
from afar who is moved by a feeling of righteousness to
hasten to this holy house. When they wish to draw near
to pray to Christ in solitude, or should they desire day
or night to make a solemn vow, such guests can eagerly
draw near from the neighbouring threshold.

455. You must also admire the fact that the martyr's

house has three entrances in harmony with the lofty law of the mystery,[60] for Felix proclaimed one kingdom under three names. Note, too, that the linking of the buildings and their interconnexion of structure are by their holy disposition a sign; for though the buildings have several roofs, they are a single dwelling of consecrated peace. Harmony makes one body from many members, a body constructed with Christ as its Head.[61]

463. As you view these sights, you may perhaps inquire with interest about the water supply to all the fountains in which the courtyard abounds, for Nola is a distance away and the aqueduct from the city is virtually non-existent, directing here only a thin trickle along its narrow course. My answer is that we put no confidence in our own ability, no trust in earthly resources. We have entrusted everything to the powerful God, and we expect our water from heaven. In short, we have built tanks all around the buildings so as to catch the streams which God pours from the clouds; and from these the hollow basins of marble can likewise be filled to the brim. But even if from time to time we experience a water shortage, the yard will doubtless still be worth seeing when the fountains run dry, for it is laid out and adorned with their differing shapes, embellished by both the appearance of the basins and the ornamented columns of the fountains.[62] You recall how even in the great temple of Solomon a dried-up sea was depicted in decoration, for that wise king portrayed it in solid bronze which rested on brazen bulls.[63]

480. Now examine the other side, how there is a single portico, and how this wall of columns flanked by open spaces joins by its passage the churches with separate

roofs.[64] It is time for our roaming eyes to pass to the church over here, which is open on its long side and so gets both daylight and additional space through extending into the courtyard attached to it.[65] So it joins together separate areas by means of arches inset there, and provides the congregation with an outlook on to watered turf, but turf shut in with the enclosure of a constructed wall, so that the holy house is not exposed to irreligious eyes and the courtyard open to the breezes can protect the hidden mystery.[66]

491. Do not marvel that our holy flock swells in the additional space available. The mighty glory of the eternal Christ is increasing everywhere, the honour paid to saints is redoubled. All men acknowledge the one God because the Holy Spirit is illuminating the world, the Son is ruling as heir with His coeternal Father. Hence the diffusion of truth's light allows sanctifying grace to multiply among men the seeds of eternal life. And because the good Shepherd is increasing the number of His sheep, Christ on high looks favourably on the extension of folds large enough to keep pace with the redeemed flocks.

500. Dear bishop, enter here singing songs and hymns. Commend my vow to the Lord, and join your joy to my vow in celebration of the feast of the patron we share. It will be a fit moment for you to beseech the Lord for this sinner when He rejoices at the honour paid to His confessor. With Felix as guide, your prayers will hasten easily on their path, for he will be your forerunner in reaching God's ears. If you dedicate your devoted service with offerings of Psalms, Christ will come down benevolently inclined to clothe His people and His shrine in a holy cloud, pouring a snowy mist over the hidden sanctuary.[67]

511. Now I want you to look at the paintings along the
portico, with which it is adorned in extended line. Crane
your neck a little till you take in everything with face
tilted back. The man who looks at these and acknowledges
the truth within these empty figures nurtures his believing
mind with representations by no means empty. The paintings in fact depict in the order prescribed by faith all that
aged Moses wrote in his five books. Then there are the
deeds of Joshua, who was marked out with Christ's name;[68]
under his guidance the Jordan kept its stream stationary
and its waters still as it recoiled from the countenance of
the divine Ark. A strange power divided the river. One
section came to a halt, its stream flowing back, while
another section hastened in its gliding course to the sea,
leaving the river bed exposed. Where the current surged
strongly from its source, it held back and piled high its
waves, so that a threatening mountain of water hung poised
in quivering formation and looked down to see human feet
passing across the dry, deep bed, and grimy soles hastening over the congealed mud, dry-footed in mid-river.[69]
Next pass with eager eyes to Ruth, who with one short
book separates eras—the end of the period of the Judges
and the beginning of the Kings. It seems a short account,
but it depicts the symbolism of the great conflict when
the two sisters separate to go their different ways. Ruth
follows after her holy mother-in-law, whereas Orpha
abandons her; one daughter-in-law demonstrates faithlessness, the other fidelity. The one puts God before country,
the other puts country before life.[70] Does not such disharmony continue through the universe, one part following God and the other falling headlong through the world?
If only the two groups seeking death and salvation were

equal! But the broad road seduces many, and those who glide on the easy downward course are snatched off headlong by sin which cannot be revoked.

542. You may perhaps ask what motive implanted in us this decision to adorn the holy houses with representations of living persons, an unusual custom.[71] If you listen, I shall try to explain the reasons in a few words. Everyone is aware of the crowds which Saint Felix's fame brings here. Now the greater number among the crowds here are countryfolk not without belief but unskilled in reading. For years they have been used to following profane cults in which their god was their belly, and at last they have turned as converts to Christ out of admiration for the undisputed achievements of the saints performed in Christ's name. Notice in what numbers they assemble from all the country districts, and how they roam around, their unsophisticated minds beguiled in devotion. They have left their distant homes scorning frosts and warding off the cold through the warmth of their faith. See how they now in great numbers keep vigil and prolong their joy throughout the night, dispelling sleep with joy and darkness with torchlight. I only wish they would channel this joy in sober prayer, and not introduce their winecups within the holy thresholds. Yet though the abstemious section of the congregation shows a higher devotion in its lusty rendering of holy hymns with voices undefiled, and in its sober sacrifice of sung praise to the Lord, I none the less believe that such merriment arising from modest feasting is pardonable because the minds beguiled by such guilt are uninitiated. Their naivety is unconscious of the extent of their guilt, and their sins arise from devotion, for

they wrongly believe that saints are delighted to have their tombs doused with reeking wine.

568. But how can the saints approve after death what they condemned in their teaching? Does Peter admit to his table what his doctrine rejects?[72] The Lord's cup is one and the same everywhere; so is God's food, His table, His house. Wine must retire to the taverns, for a church is a holy house of prayer. Serpent, depart from our consecrated thresholds. No perverted sport is your due in this church, but punishment. You, our enemy, are introducing jesting to your own execution. You are a person divided, howling under torture even as you sing in your cups. You fear Felix even as you foolishly despise him. You drunkenly insult him, yet convicted you beg for mercy. You wretch, you play the wanton before the very judge who takes vengeance on you with the cudgel and by fire.

580. This was why we thought it useful to enliven all the houses of Felix with paintings on sacred themes, in the hope that they would excite the interest of the rustics by their attractive appearance, for the sketches are painted in various colours. Over them are explanatory inscriptions, the written word revealing the theme outlined by the painter's hand.[73] So when all the countryfolk point out and read over to each other the subjects painted, they turn more slowly to thoughts of food, since the feast of fasting is so pleasant to the eye. In this way, as the paintings beguile their hunger, their astonishment may allow better behaviour to develop in them. Those reading the holy accounts of chastity in action are infiltrated by virtue and inspired by saintly example. As they gape, their drink is sobriety, and they forget the longing for excessive wine.

As they pass the day sightseeing over this quite large area, their cups are rarely filled. They have spent their time on the wonders of the place, and only a few hours subsequently remain for feasting.

596. To end with, these buildings and paintings can, I suggest, be the theme of your prayers on my behalf, for I am begging you to play the part of Felix and pray diligently for me. It is appropriate that as his associate in devotion of mind, you should equal him also in your love for me, and so resemble him in inward features and imitate his dispositions. I am not so depressed as to doubt that I am loved by the martyr. I am accounted worthy of a lapdog's love at any rate, for God gives me Felix as my life and home, property and friendship, fame and bread. Follow his lead in demanding that my foundations be laid on holy mountains,[74] and that this tower now begun may be completed without interruption in building.[75]

607. I beg you consult Genesis for the tenour of your prayer. Let me not continue as an earthly Adam, but be born of the virgin earth, fashioned as a new form after putting off the old man.[76] May I be led forth from my land,[77] and be untrue to my race. May I hasten to the honeyed streams of the promised land,[78] and be preserved from the fire of the Chaldaean furnace.[79] May I be like Lot, hospitable with door ever open, so that I may be delivered from Sodom.[80] May I refrain from looking back, that I may not turn into a pillar of salt[81] through lack of salt within my heart. May I be offered like the young Isaac as a living victim to God,[82] carry my own wood, and follow my kindly Father beneath the cross. May I discover wells, but I pray that the jealous Amalek, who impedes the course of living water, may not fill them in.[83]

May I be a fugitive from the world as blessed Jacob fled from his brother Edom,[84] and may I place a hallowed stone beneath my weary head[85] and find peace in Christ. May my love be pure, and may sinful love disgust me; then, like the unpolluted Joseph, I may shun the enticements of the flesh[86] and, having cast off the chains of my body, I may be free of sin and leave to the world the spoils of the flesh. It is time to put embraces at a distance.[87] The final day approaches, the Lord is now nigh; it is already time to rise from sleep, ready and awake for the Lord's knocking.[88] May I obtain a safe departure from Egypt, and journey under the guidance of the Law through the divided waters[89] of my storm-tossed heart; so I may escape the Red Sea's billows and, when Pharaoh is drowned, sing of the Lord's triumph. To Him, trembling in my joy and rejoicing in my fear, I dedicate with suppliant prayer my toils which are my devoted gifts to Him.

636. Nicetas, demand in prayer that for which I pray. All you too, assembled here together in holy devotion,[90] with dedication and gratitude address the Lord with me: "Christ God, we build these things for you from our slight and fragile store. Yet things built with hands cannot confine You, highest Creator, for the universe with its entire frame cannot confine You. For You, heaven is small and the earth is a pinpoint. But by paying devoted service to Your perennial saints, with paltry homage we revere those great men. We hope that by their intercession You will perfect our completed works, and that as Lodger You will dwell here in the edifice of our hearts."

# POEM 28[1]

As we perform our longstanding practice, a new element is introduced, for the usual festival is enhanced by the completion of a novel vow. These buildings newly risen in Felix's house provide a theme for redoubling my song, and amplify the birthday of our kindly patron. As you see, they have shot up, built high all round, and glitter with matching beauty. On this side a courtyard is open to view with extended cloisters forming a wide circle round it, an open area enclosed by the covered structure, so that the stars are open to view and the courtyard is available for strolling. On the other side are the churches, companions because their walls adjoin. Side by side they are outspread on extensive sites, yet their vying roofs are joined by interlocked beams. Their beauty is different but equal, with the adornment of marble and paintings, panelled ceilings and columns; amidst this decoration small recesses provide pleasing variation.

16. These recesses are set in the side of the cloisters where one portico covers a narrow unbroken stretch, and three entrances close to each other provide admission to them, three gates in a continuous lattice. The middle one is adorned with the holy names and portraits of martyrs who though of different sexes are crowned with equal glory. The two extending on the right and left are adorned each with a twofold inscription and depiction of faith. One is covered by the holy achievements of saintly men—

the trial of Job by ulcers, and of Tobias through his eyes.[2]
The other gate is occupied by the lesser sex in the por-
trayal of renowned Judith and also the powerful queen
Esther.

28. The inner court smiles with varied embellishment—
overhead, cheerful with roof and facade bright under the
open sky, and below, wreathed with snow-white columns.
In the open area of it a shining fountain wells up, enclosed
by a protective structure of bronze with latticework
around it. The other basins equipped with miniature fountains stand beneath the open sky. They have been installed
with pleasing variation, the workmanship being different
but the nature of the material the same. From these different mouths the same stream flows out, into basins large
enough to contain it.

37. This open courtyard adjoins all three basilicas, and
provides entry to all by different routes from the one
starting point. So, too, with its spacious central paving it
welcomes in its single embrace the separate exits from the
three churches. However, its succession of bright basins
planned and built in five rows crowds the courtyard with
an accumulation of marble, and makes it confined to walk
in though marvellous to look at. But there is plenty of
space for walking in the surrounding colonnades, and
when one is tired one can lean on the latticework between
the columns, and from there view the plashing basins, eye
the soaked turf without treading on it (thus keeping the
feet dry), and admire the fountains as in agreeable compe-
tition they spurt forth with tranquil murmur. It is not
merely in the winter season that this amenity is there to
provide pleasure, for the roof's shade is no less pleasant in

the heat than are its sunny warmth in the cold season and
its shelter when it rains.

53. On the other side is an open outer court likewise
surrounded by porticoes, less embellished but more spacious. This forecourt extends in front of the holy shrines
and is visible from afar. With its cells constructed as a
second storey, the sight of its wall presents the appearance
of a fortress, for the converging beams interconnect the
buildings. This open space is suitable for gatherings, and
there is plenty of room to walk about.[3]

60. I shall now quickly tell of the sign which our
revered Felix recently made manifest to us on this spot. In
the middle of the open space facing the threshold of our
honoured church there stood two huts, made of wood.
They were inconveniently placed, and were eyesores; they
annoyingly ruined the whole beauty of the buildings, for
their grisly appearance interposed itself and blotted out
the view. When the basilica lay open, the entrance was
darkened because one of these little huts excluded the
light, so that the door was open to no effect, being in fact
closed. When we sought to pull down the huts, the people
lodging in them mocked us, and swore to put their lives
at possible risk before they could be forced out of their
dwellings. Such threats seemed to carry little weight, but
I must confess that the situation was hateful to me, for
even victory was repugnant if it meant a brawl.

75. Then one night when people were asleep in initial
enjoyment of early repose, in a corner of one of these huts
a spark flew from the deserted hearth and suddenly ignited
the layer of hay on which it lighted.[4] Then it spread
through the hut, gaining strength from the dry fuel feed-

ing it, and from this light tinder it raised a huge flame. It glided easily on, and burst up through the rotten timbers of the old roof. It sent boisterous flames issuing in great whirling motions, filled the air with a hot cloud, and blotted out the stars with black smoke. Then, too, the angry fire made a fearful din, ringing out with a crackling all the louder because the timber was thin. The whole vicinity inhabited by the countryfolk of the village, and even farms quite a long way from it, were so afflicted by the heat, the inhabitants so dazzled by the fearful light, the roofs far and near so besprinkled by the fiery shower of flying sparks, that we were suddenly aroused by the wails of grief on every side. When we saw the buildings wreathed in monstrous light and beheld everything around us shining as brightly as if it were day, we believed that the whole complex of buildings was being harried and burnt by the flames, that the very palaces of the saints were ablaze in that great fire, and that the glow emanated from all the roofs combined. For the flames were filling even distant areas with scattered fire, and roasting[5] the countryside with excessive heat, so that each individual feared the flames as if they were all encroaching on his own house. All felt the heat around them, and the air they breathed was polluted by the foul smell.

104. In our fear at the proximity of the danger to our own buildings, we put no trust in our own powers; for where in our weakness could we obtain the strength and resource sufficient to quench that massive fire once the flames waxed hotter from the tinder feeding them, burst suddenly out of that tiny hut, and sprayed all the roofs simultaneously with threatening fire? So relying on faith and suppliant prayer alone, we ran to the threshold of my

Felix close by, and from there to the neighbouring church,⁶ making similar prayers and demanding a remedy from the power of the apostles' ashes as we pressed our lips on the altar which covered the relics. When I left to return to my lodging, I took out that piece of wood, small in itself but a huge aid to salvation, which was obtained for me from a fragment of the eternal cross.⁷ I held it in my hand, and carried it all the way to the confronting flames. I kept it as a shield before my breast, to protect myself and to ward off and drive back the enemy by a thrust of the boss.

120. You must believe and impute nothing to me, but render thanks to Christ and offer to the Almighty the praise that is His due. For our salvation resides in the cross and the name of Christ. So also in this crisis, our faith, relying on the cross, proved beneficial; the fire experienced our Salvation. No word or hand of mine deterred that fire, but the power of the cross, which compelled the flames to die down on the spot where they had flared up, as though they were walled in within set limits. So the fire went out, its roaring died, and the tempest which blew up from ashes returned to ashes. How great is the power of the cross! To make nature unnatural, the fire which devours all wood was burnt by the wood of the cross! At that time many hands had sought to conquer that fire by pouring gallons of water on it from numerous vessels. But though they exhausted the wells, and poured on it a virtual rainstorm, the fire had greater power, and defeated all the water, so that those who poured it on grew tired. But we put out the fire with wood; the flames which water could not quench were defeated by a tiny splinter.

138. Later on, when our fears had vanished, and the toilsome day had brought back the light for which we longed, we went out to inspect what had happened in the night and to survey the traces of the fire with eyes untroubled, though smoke from it still billowed over a wide area. We assumed that we would see extensive damage to the buildings when we recalled the great fire and the panic it had caused, but once we had seen the actuality our premonitions quickly vanished. We saw that nothing was burnt except what had deserved to be consumed, for the only casualty of the fire was one of the two cottages which we would have demolished in any case, even if the fire had not. In fact, Felix in his kindness was thinking of us and doing us a favour. He made this fire usefully anticipate our toil, and he shortened our building-operations in a further way. The flames had left there the cottage which was the mate of the burnt one, but his intention was not to allow even this to remain as a similar barrier blocking the double doors of the church. The fire was intended to punish the rustic owner in a second way, by preserving one dwelling for him to demolish personally subsequently. Only days previously he had put more value on his huts than on the sacred dwellings, but first he was punished when the fire deprived him of one, and then he began to lay waste the other mean dwelling with his own hand. With swift destructive rage he made his loss complete as he wept for his beloved dwellings which he loved superfluously. When he saw the burnt and the demolished houses side by side, he gazed in wonder at the parallel mounds surviving from dissimilar modes of destruction, rubble and ashes side by side manifesting the twin colours of their fallen remains. And thus realising that we had

gained the victory without a dispute, the wretched man had only himself to blame for losing the lasting goodwill of deferring to us, and for gaining the lasting shame of his punishment.

167. So now the obstacle is removed, and the view of the facade is open, and we can happily stroll in the precincts in both mind and speech. We can hasten into the holy churches and admire the sacred representations which recall the men of old. In the three areas inside the courtyard[8] we can read the two Testaments, and understand in the proper light the arrangement by which the new Law is painted on the old building, and the old Law on the new one.[9] The new theme in an old setting and the ancient theme in a new setting are decorations equally useful to us, for thus we can have both new life and the wisdom of age. Old in our seriousness yet babes in our simplicity, we can derive balance of mind from the two ages, and unite these different stages of life in our characters.

180. Somewhat farther within the larger church a room has been built into the outer wall, almost as a kind of offspring. Its star-spangled dome makes it beautiful, and it winds in and out with three parallel recesses.[10] The source of devotion at its centre lends it brilliance, and in a remarkable way it both transforms the whole and is itself transformed. Today a twin renovation embellishes it, for the bishop there wields two gifts of Christ. He consecrates that revered shrine for a double purpose, associating the holy sacrament of the Eucharist with the font that purifies. In this way the Victim transforms the shrine and grace renews the font; the font renewed renews mankind[11] and bestows the gift it receives, or rather it begins to pass on to men by God's use the new life which it loses by

use. When once the font has been used for causing new life, it ceases to be new, but since it will be used perennially to bestow this gift, it will never cease to bring new life to the old man.

196. Observe here, in the twin basilicas of Felix with their walls renewed,[12] this gift of the Lord, this manifestation by which through Christ's gift the old man dies and the new man is born in the same person. The old is now seen to emerge as new. Previously it had stood on unsightly pillars in a crude line, but now it is transformed and rests on the columns which have been erected. These give it more space and light, so that it has cast off its grime and become young again. In fact, these buildings afford to the eyes bright pleasure which is redoubled because the restored building vies with the new one in matching brilliance. The ages of the structures differ, but their appearance merges, for the workmanship of past and present craftsmen is in harmony. The same embellishment adorns the similar facades of both buildings, so that the ancient foundation accords with the new. The eyes detect no difference, for old and new sites gleam with identical elegance.[13] The grimy blackness is covered over, and the paintings have restored the gleam of youth to the ancient building by the application of various colours. This is how the different ages of the buildings merge. A new look gleams on the outside of the walls while the antiquity is hidden, enclosed within. The old age is concealed and daubed with the face of youth, so that advanced years have blossomed afresh with youthful appearance. They are simultaneously old and new—neither equally new nor equally old. They are the same yet not the same as they depict the shape of future and present blessings. For it is

salutary for us even now to wipe off the filth of our former life, and to become renewed in devotion of mind, to follow Christ, and to prepare ourselves for the kingdom.

223. So will it be on the day when men are permitted to rise again with life renewed. Amongst those who rise, precedence will be given to the group whose flesh is covered with a shining garment. They will change their slaves' appearance for the likeness of the Lord; soon to reign with God, through similarity to Christ but by His gift they will obtain a distinction resembling His.

229. The renewed appearance of the church also warns us to shed our former appearance and to wear a new one, to erase our past deeds and to direct our changed hearts to the future which lies with God; to draw an apposite oblivion over our former preoccupations and to introduce into our minds zeal for the kingdom of heaven;[14] to be dead towards human things and the ways of the world in spirit before the death of the flesh, and not to be freed from the chains of the body before being loosed from those of sin. Therefore, let us renew ourselves in mind, and hasten to prise away from our bodies the filthy activities of our earthly forms, so that, having sloughed off our external apparel, having shaken off this grime, we may shine and may cleanse the clothing which is our body and soul.

241. Let us avoid not merely committing sin but even thinking of it, as we would hold our noses to avoid the infectious emanation and the foul stench from a rotting corpse. Solomon warns us that sin is to be feared and loathed like the appearance of a snake, and says it is armed with lion's teeth.[15] He speaks the truth, for sins with bestial maw savagely devour the soul conquered by the

sick pleasure of the body and appropriated after defeat by
the serpent for his meal. That serpent devours "the peoples
of the Ethiopians,"[16] not those roasted by the sun, but
those whom sin has darkened and guilt has made black as
night. Such are the Ethiopians that the serpent devours,
and amongst them the condemned Satan finds food to eat.
God used the single word "earth" to describe both the
sinner and serpent's food, and so the man who devours
sins[17] is devoured by the dragon.

255. It is time to change our ways, to rise from sleep
and at last to remain awake for God,[18] and, on the other
hand, to remain asleep to those activities in which the
mind dead to Christ remains awake. If God's teaching does
not give us understanding from the light of the Word, let
us at least obtain a model for life from these buildings. Let
the stone and timber teach us dullards, so that by faith we
may achieve the kind of building we have completed here
with our hands. The mental achievement and the manual
labour are not identical, but from these different sources
a like pattern of work is derived. Observe my demonstration that these dissimilar types of activity are in harmony
by their similar form.

266. The sites of the new buildings can be recalled by
many, for it is not long since that all now standing were
begun. The works we sweated over for two years have
been completed in the third, through the prayers of the
saints and Christ's aid.[19] Part of the building area was a
small garden, part a heap of rubble,[20] which was removed
by the combined efforts of our diligent people, who also
dug out the paltry vegetable herbs and the thorns to leave
the cleared site bare, its surface spick and span. Now its
extensive paving gleams, its area adorned with marble

blocks, and it has forgotten its former appearance. How splendidly it has changed its face! The adornment of marble has followed the application of manure. The ground bears Parian marble basins after cheap cabbages, its waters shining out where previously filth shone.

279. How, then, can this structure furnish for me a pattern by which I can cultivate, build, and renew myself inwardly, and make myself a lodging for Christ? It is clear how we are to explain my earth, the rubble within me, and the source of the thorns sprouting in my land. My earth is my heart, the rubble the sins of that debased heart. Slothful pleasure, polluted love, stained lust are the rubble of the soul; so, too, troubled care for the body, devouring envy, greedy hunger, oppressive anger, unsubstantial hope, aspirations spendthrift with personal possessions and thirsty for those of others—all these are thorns for the soul because they are ever pricking ambivalent souls with their pointless goads, and making them smart continually with the fear of wretched failure and the wretched zeal for possessions. In this fashion they are poor amidst their wealth, thirsting like the fabled Tantalus amidst water. They do not possess what they seem to possess, for they are afraid to enjoy the wealth they have gained, and they bequeath all they have saved; and so they waste the days of their lives in laying up resources for their sustenance.

296. So we must dig out these thorns, this rubble from our overgrown minds. We must tear out from our hearts this initial root of all our sins from which a barren tree shoots forth. That tree must be excised at the roots by the Lord's axe, and must fall so that it may never bud in our fields. Once this root has withered after all that nourished

it has been cut away from us, all the wickedness will fall away, all the sin will die, all evils will fall with the fall of the mother-tree, for when the tree dies its fruit will perish with it.

305. Then, when the garden is well cleared, the house will be built, and the materials of God's structure, founded on living soil, will rise gloriously to heaven. Christ Himself will set up columns in us, and dismantle the old pillars which impeded the path within our souls. So the King will clear an area within our minds for strolling in, just as Wisdom used to stroll with healing presence and holy words in the five colonnades of Solomon, healing bodies by His touch and hearts by His teaching.[21]

314. Therefore, let us not continue old amidst new buildings, so that Christ who dwells in men's hearts may return to find our hearts renewed. For when old and new are forced together, the rent becomes worse, and it is good to put new wine in new bottles.[22] Let our earlier lives die so that our future lives may not die. Let us leave the world of our own accord, because if we do not flee it voluntarily, we will have to forgo it under compulsion. Let us die so that we may not die. Let us supplant death-bringing life with life-bringing death. Let our earthly form die and our heavenly form replace it. Let Adam be transformed into Christ. Let us change ourselves here so that we may be changed also in heaven. He who persists in remaining inwardly unchanged now, will likewise experience no change forever.[23]

# POEM 29[1]

Usher in spring with verses, let the words flow free, given shape by unassuming measures. Draw near, Felix, rich fount of my eloquence, and glide into my heart with silent breath. Your spirit will speed forth from my mouth. Be the source of all I speak; I shall be the pipe for your streams, which you will provide for me from the river of God's word. So arise, and enter my heart with your kindly inspiration, Felix my father, lord and patron, Felix my home, my healing and my wisdom. Lend an edge to my mind now blunted with extended leisure, and with your flaming light bring life to my heart. . . .

12. But my words must not be poured forth on this plain. I must not run through the deserving deeds or miracles of saints, nor try to describe in verses God's provision and activity through all His saints from the beginning of creation, for all this the human mind cannot entertain, nor the human tongue proclaim. It is not surprising that the sheets of a whole book cannot embrace it all, for the whole world cannot contain it. The Creator of the world is greater than the world. God Himself is the King who fills earth and heaven. But though this world cannot contain Him, the saints can; not because their bodies are huge, but because they are humble in devotion and spacious in the purity of their hearts. . . .

23. So in recounting the godlike benefactions of my patron Felix (the material advantages he has conferred on

me, the unceasing gifts which almost every day he bestows
with fatherly generosity on many from his heavenly store,
offering his devoted services by manifold signs), the
hierarchy of merit demands that Christ now be praised. I
shall be seen to praise no man, but rather Him who is the
source of Felix's strength, of the revered names he wins,
of the healing aid he bestows when he returns to sick
bodies or delivers imprisoned minds from the power of
the black devil, who is vanquished by God. Yet it is not
only in this aid that the generous Felix acts out Christ's
gifts and with the utmost strength triumphs over the
enemy serpent. . . .[2]

# POEM 30[1]

Fresh light and extended space now open the shrine of Felix to men's eyes, though it has long been revered and venerated. When you recall his tiny tomb, you must rejoice to see how it now glitters in praise of our patron.

\* \* \*

2. This place was earlier confined and small for celebrating the sacred ritual. It did not allow those at prayer room to raise wide their arms. But now it affords the congregation a shrine with plenty of room for their sacred duties, embraced by the martyr at the centre.[2] All things renewed are pleasing to God; Christ is ever renewing all things, and ennobling them to enhance His light. So He has honoured the tomb of His beloved Felix by improving both its brightness and its access.[3]

# POEM 31[1]

Celsus was previously a boy on earth, with famous parents and ancestral glory, but now he rightly dwells *in excelsis,*[2] for Christ the Lord adorned him with such a great blessing that he departed young in years and renewed by baptismal water. A double grace transported him to God, for he was doubly a child, both in span of age and through the water of the font.

7. But how should I proceed? I am caught in the toils of hesitant love. Shall I show joy or sorrow? The boy is worthy of both. My love for him urges tears, yet also joy, for faith bids me be glad and affection bids me weep. I mourn that so little reward from so sweet a treasure was granted to his parents for so short a time. On the other hand, when I think of the eternal blessings of everlasting life which God prepares for the innocent in heaven, I rejoice that he has completed his span in so short a time. So he came soon to enjoy the riches of heaven, and did not long carry in the frail lodging of his body the infection of the world caught through association with the wicked. Rather he was unstained by any sin in this world, and he advanced to the eternal Lord in a worthier state.

21. So the boy was owed to God rather than to us, yet it was for our sakes that he was acceptable to God. The tiny boy had begun to live his eighth year and was enjoying his early life as it raced swiftly by. He was now bearing on his young neck the yoke of boyhood, subject to the

harsh dominion of the schoolmaster. All that the boy was taught he notably absorbed with a brain eager to learn, while the master stood and marvelled. This caused his parents pleasure, but their hearts were anxious, presaging and fearing that such great gifts were begrudged. And it was not long before Christ God from heaven summoned this soul that pleased Him, and drew it to Him with honour well-deserved. He snatched it headlong from the earth, because it was worthier to dwell in company with the assemblies of the saints.

35. The cause of death was moisture welling in his throat, which caused a severe swelling to distend his milk-white neck. It was defeated there and left his throat, but in its flight slipped into the inner part of the body and drove the life from his vitals.[3] The earth took its portion in the flesh that was entombed, but the spirit departed, transported in the arms of an angel. And while the bereaved parents escorted the lifeless corpse, Celsus was dwelling in joy in the grove of heaven.

43. Dutiful parents, I would not have you sin through copious weeping. Let not your love turn to blame.[4] For it is a wicked love which laments a soul in blessedness, and a baneful affection which bewails one who takes joy in God. Surely it is clear how much sinning is involved in love like that. We are convicted of maintaining our faith by deception, or of rejecting God's laws by rebellious sinning unless we accept what the Lord has decreed. It would be more righteous to grieve this darkness of mankind, which we cause through the corruption of our souls, when we forget that divine likeness of our earliest beginning which our pitying Father is summoning back to His kingdom. Out of love for that likeness, His son took on

my limbs, was conceived and born of a virgin, bearing all
the attributes of men, and though He is the Lord of all
He became a servant to undertake in one body the burdens of all.[5] He who dwelt on high took the likeness of a
slave,[6] though He was reigning as God with the likeness of
God, in company with His regal Father. He took on the
likeness of a slave, and destroyed that guilt by which man
of old was a slave to punishment and death. Bearing the
form of a slave, the Lord became our flesh and restored
His servant to freedom, so that through Christ's plundering of the earthly Adam on the cross, my heavenly form
might return to me. So my glorious Creator endured to
the end my flesh and my death, and by His death redeemed that costly deed of old.[7]

69. He had earlier given me both numerous promises
and comands for salvation by which to be guided on the
right path. But I did not apply the remedy of the law to
heal the ancient wounds of my first parent. I did not
trustingly await God's gifts announced by heavenly
prophets sent forth from the mouth of God. So despair
in our salvation had plunged the human race into scattered
darkness without the light of faith. At the one time sin
governed our bodies, death governed sin,[8] and the devil
governed death. Melancholy fear and wretched error
caused captive man to fall more steeply into death.

81. Meanwhile, the Father Himself in the high heavens
took pity on the mortal lapses of erring men.[9] He did not
allow the serpent to have dominion over those who were
falling in grim death, but sent His Son to accomplish every
good. The Son gladly obeyed, since He is God and in
harmony with the Father in all things, and takes thought
for the common good with equal devotion. He came and

became man; and being perfect in both natures, He showed that God who combines both dwells in the frailty of the flesh. He performed the duties of a man, but He exercised the marks of the God within by His healing commands. His voice was human but His teaching divine, yet in the flesh He performed all mortal acts except for sin.[10] For since He sought to restore for Himself merely the substance of His creation, He came to assume nature, not sin.

95. In fact, the good God made man good by nature for good ends. It was man who polluted himself by falling from his purpose. So the Creator of men entered a mortal body, but did not become man by mortal sinning. He would not have destroyed sins if He had not been free of them, nor could He have freed the guilty if He, too, had been guilty. Death would never have yielded to a sinner, since it would rightly have held the sinner bound by the bonds of sin. So it was right that it yielded to Christ when He burst open hell, for in Him it had nothing to fetter. Death was condemned for an unjust judgment, and in turn rightly became subject to a Man who was criminally slain. The serpent grew pale with envy when he saw his law overturned, the bolts of hell unfastened by the Man who had returned from there, death in its turn bound, mortal man loosed from death's bonds, and his body uncovered and sent rising from its earth. Moreover, when he saw it revived and mounting to heaven, he was consumed with hatred and vainly gnashed his grim teeth. Now he fades away; the waster himself wastes away, as the column of the faithful ever swells through Christ.

115. So Christ has healed the vices of my soul, and taken on Himself the sicknesses of my body,[11] Man by His mother, God by His Father. He bore the weaknesses of

the flesh that are appointed by nature,[12] and evinced the feelings of the human body. He ate and drank, and closed his eyes in sleep,[13] and grew weary with journeying in accord with His human sensibilities. He shed tears over the death of a friend like a man, but then as God raised him from the tomb.[14] As a man He sailed on a ship, and as God He governed the winds; by His strength as God the Man walked over the sea.[15] With His human mind He feared the hour of imminent death, but with His divine mind He knew that the moment of execution was at hand. As man He was nailed to the cross, and as God He terrified the world from the cross.[16] The Man endured death, but death itself endured the true God. The Man hung on the cross, but as God He forgave sins from the cross, and by dying destroyed the life of sin. He who was counted among the guilty,[17] and was assessed as worse than the thief whom the Jews ranked before their devoted Lord,[18] gave the kingdom of heaven to the thief who believed,[19] and while still confined to earth opened the gates of Paradise.

135. Hence it is right for us to strengthen our spirits, raise our minds, and thrust cowardly fears from our hearts, since, as you see, the Son of God laid down His life for us and took it up again[20] whilst remaining God in every way. God victoriously celebrated a triumph over our death and conveyed our human body with Him to the stars. He considered it insufficient to have drained the entire cup of mortal life for us, so as to remove our wounds by means of His own; He also rose again with the body in which He fell, so that the troubled anxiety of a hesitant mind should not keep me in uncertainty. He appeared after His death just as He was before it, and thus the evidence was

made crystal-clear to men's eyes; for He showed Himself of His own accord to His doubting disciples to be inspected by their eyes and hands.[21]

149. It was not without divine purpose that the apostle of old doubted; it was so that none might be dubious of life after death. By his doubting, he strengthened faith. When the doubting Thomas was refuted face-to-face, all mankind was given instruction. Because Thomas was bidden to see and feel in person, I learn to believe unswervingly and with steady faith that human faith was overcome by the death of Christ crucified, and that the hope of resurrection resides in our bodies because Christ rose again victorious in the flesh which I bear and in which I die.

159. It was to teach me and on my behalf that He presented His limbs before the doubters, proving that the flesh was solid over the framework of the bones, and then pointed to the wounds in His side and hands, and bade the doubting one place his fingers in them. He said: "Come now, behold My side, My hands, My feet; see the nails of the cross, and the course of the spear. See how clearly the structure of My whole body is alive with sinews and bones, in complexion and skin. So preserve belief in what you see and also touch, cast all doubt from your hearts, be witnesses of this great salvation to all, and loose the hearts of all men from fear. Let the fear of death perish in all, and equally let this hope of resurrection fire all peoples. But such salvation is for those who believe, for those who will receive with believing hearts what you see with your eyes. See how in Me the death of all men without distinction is overcome and departs, and salvation abidingly revives. I have given life out of death, and subdued death by dying, and restored by My blood the human

race. In the flesh I have overcome the sins of the flesh, destroyed the substance of guilt, and given birth to righteousness. Death has perished in the body, and life has risen in it. Man has regained life in that flesh in which he previously died. See, now I bear in My body and boast an Adam restored to life, victor over death and the serpent."[22]

185. What consolations, pray, will ever be enough, what rest will now cure our weary hearts if even this great remedy cannot heal this sick, with its teaching that after death lives are restored? Grief, make way! Fear, depart! Sin, you must flee! Death is fallen, life has revived, and Christ calls us to the stars. I have died my death, I am dead to and victorious over myself, so that for me the death of sin means life in God. For example, He saved the thief and led him from the cross along the broad path where Paradise lies, and by this kindness He gave proof of the expiation of sin and of the mastering by faith of the barriers to the glade which had been forbidden.

197. With such examples as this, with so great a Guarantor of our salvation, we should be uplifted with gladness, and expel sorrow. We should drive from our ungrateful hearts plaintive grief and let the clear light return to our dried eyes. Let us trust Christ, because through Him we have seen that we rise with the same bodies in which we die, and that then we are changed into the appearance of angels clothed in the garment of God's glory. But if a thick darkness obscures your clouded hearts, and your thoughts are sluggish and dull through the crassness of your body, so that divine truths are hidden from your bodily eyes, and you say that the Scriptures have no reliability, then Paul must teach you that things visible are transient, and things eternal hidden from men's eyes.[23]

Foolish one, visualise the world with your eyes but God
with your mind. This is how you win the faith of great
price. Just as grace is no longer grace when attached to
deserving deeds, so there is no faith save that which believes in the unseen, and pursues eternal possessions with
hope as guide.

217. Wretched mankind, whose nature is to grumble,
soften your hearts and finally shrug off your wicked ten-
dencies. To what purpose, pray, do you so sadly and continually seek falsehoods with burdened hearts, and vainly
love slippery pursuits?[24] Amend your ways, burst asunder
the chains of death,[25] and offer your necks freely to the
sweetest of yokes.[26] As your freedom, take on the divine
bonds which loose from sin and bind with devotion. The
one among you who courts darkness goes astray in the
clear light; the one who sees by night is blind by day. So
let us open the eyes and ears of the mind to Christ, so
that our minds may remain closed to sin and open to God.
For God is now exposing His promises to bodily eyes and
showing His secrets to clear sight.

231. All the seeds of the earth and the stars of heaven
give thought to this phenomenon of resurrection of the
entire body. Night and day, rising and setting, succeed
each other. I die at night and rise again with the day. I
sleep and become unconscious with the appearance of
bodily death, and am roused from slumber as though from
death. Again, the plants and leaves of the glades, and the
seasons, all surely die and return according to these laws.
When spring rises again, all creation has a new appearance
restored to it, and is revived and enlivened after the death
of winter. Man who has dominion over the creatures of
the world is to do on one occasion what all creation be-

neath the sky regularly performs. But men ask with what body every dead man will be restored, or how he will become a man from ashes. If the indications given by the holy prophets are not enough, mute creation cries out its guarantee, so you must believe what is manifest. Observe that no seeds come forth from their soil unless they first perish and dissolve in crumbling decay. You sow them in their nakedness, you reap them in their garments. You scatter the dried seeds, and reap them many times over in the harvest.[27]

251. What perverted faith and lack of trust are ours when we show confidence in the earth and doubt towards God! In truth, the earth dared not and could not promise me anything. On the contrary, the soil has often played deceiver, scarcely returning the plants entrusted to it, yet I have no hesitation in entrusting to it the prospect of the harvest, though I have been deceived, nor do I weary of devoting regular sweat and labour to a dubious harvest and entrusting the naked seed to the naked soil. Now if the earth can reproduce the decayed seed, even if only by the eternal Lord's law, does anyone believe that it will be a hard task for the Almighty to restore us from something, when we were made from nothing? I was nothing, and God fashioned my birth that I might exist; and presently I shall again exist from the seed that is my own. Even though my bones are reduced to thin ashes, the dust contains the seeds of my whole body, and though the earth empties tombs and absorbs even the ashes which mingle with the kindred sod, even then the Almighty keeps them intact, though to men's eyes they seem to have faded away.

271. On the great day we shall see the bodies we now believe consumed rise in their entirety to God. None of

His natural creation dies, for everything everywhere is enclosed in the Creator's arms. Those whom water has devoured with its rivers, seas, and fish, those whom birds and beasts have torn asunder, all are owed to God by the earth.[28] When people are drowned off the shore, or are given a last resting-place in the levelled earth on some farm, the earth that covers the bones of the mangled corpse scattered in sundry places is the same, though it receives them in a plurality of graves. Again, bodies that are devoured and the creatures that devour them fall in the same bosom of the earth at death's behest. If a corpse has been devoured, the animals after digesting their food restore the limbs to earth wherever they purge themselves. In such cases, there is the transfusion of the human body from one not its own, but without loss of the potentiality of its own species. Even though bodies have been transferred to the earth from the bodies of beasts, they remain unaffectedly human with the seed alive in them. When a beast dies after chancing to feast on a human corpse, the reason remains apart from it; man is a rational animal, and accordingly in his very body he is superior to and king over other bodies. So, though he can be given as booty to dumb animals, he refuses to share their lot. So only that flesh which was the vessel of the rational soul will experience the power of resurrection, so that when the soul returns to earth the flesh may renew its physique and receive it in an imperishable garment. Just as on this earth mind and flesh are associated in every activity, so they are to be allied in eternity, to obtain the rewards of their deeds in the harvest they share, as partners which have merited the region of light or the region of fire.

303. Accordingly, though we share with other breath-

ing creatures the same substance of flesh, we are not at death's dissolution restored to nothingness as souls excluded because of the death of the flesh. No, when the trumpet sounds[29] every region of earth will restore our bodies from their hidden seeds; our body, mind, soul will be joined in their compact with each other, and we shall be haled before the Lord God in our wholeness.

311. If you are sceptical that ashes can be reassembled into bodies, and souls restored to their vessels, Ezechiel will be your witness,[30] for long ago the whole process of resurrection was revealed to him by the Lord. In his pages you will behold the dusty remains of men of old come to life over the entire region, bones scattered far and wide over the broad plain spontaneously hastening to fuse together when bidden, sprouting sinews from the innermost marrow, and then drawing the skin over the flesh which had grown on them. Then the limbs are perfectly ordered more quickly than words can tell, and from the ancient dust stand forth men made new.

323. But in case you perhaps consider the clear vision of the sacred prophet to be the empty dreaming of a man asleep, listen to a greater witness speaking the full truth on this matter, for the Lord of prophets Himself speaks: "I am the Life. He who believes in me shall not be destroyed by death, but shall live in blessedness with me in the company of light."[31] Then He proved by His power what He had said in words, for He called back His own human person from the abyss. Yet at that time when He died in victory on the cross, Christ did not confine the signs He gave to His own body. For when He shook the earth, laid open hell, and loosed the chained Adam from his prison below, buried men arose, splitting rocks in two, and

a new church flowered in the holy city.[32] Many saw the
bodies of devoted men of old restored and given life by
God's descent. At that time, too, the world was blinded by
the flight of light, and it feared it was atoning for its sin
in everlasting darkness. The temple, too, was exposed by
the veil's being rent asunder, and forfeited the awe given
to a sacred shrine, to indicate that the temple would be
stripped of deity, and the holy things profaned by an
enemy's hand; and the subsequent massive destruction
under a Roman leader, in which temple, citizens, city,
and sacred objects were annihilated, taught this lesson.

347. Indeed it was right that the Jewish race, who
rejected the sacrificed Christ as their own and through
whom He was a Victim, should be stripped of their abode
and of the site of their ancient ritual, and should lose all
their religious life since they had denied their faith. For
the end of the law is Christ. He was foretold by the law
of faith, and by coming became the Law for the law,
enjoining an end to the old law and establishing the law
of faith, the law of the prophet for the Gentiles. This is
why Paul the master said: "The old passed away when
the time was run, and now all things new replace it everywhere.[33] And now God's face is uncovered, and we see
Him openly in Christ, in the glory of His own light."[34]

359. I believe that the mystery of the rending of the
temple veil denoted also what grace bestows on us. Just
as by the tearing of the veil the sacred objects were exposed, so faith unbars for us the secrets of the law. So we
recognise Moses under the ancient veil,[35] though he is
still hidden from the Jews by a mental fog which Christ
in whom I believe removes from my mind's eye. He dis-
perses the shadowy figures, and teaches me that He Him-

self was veiled in the ancient shadow of the Law, and that
He is now revealed in His physical form as the prophets
sent before Him prophesied He would be, and as He
manifested Himself in person to the apostles' eyes. The
Jews gazed but did not see Him in this way, since their
minds were blunted by their lack of devotion; but we see
Him thus with the inner light of belief, though we have
not seen Him in the flesh. What our truthful masters teach
us that they have seen and felt, I touch and see by faith.
It is open to all to know by faith the Christ who blinds
the wicked hearts of those who betray Him, and who
pours His light over the hearts of the faithful so that He
may dwell in and make glorious the souls that please Him.

381. So, dear brethren so close to my heart, bring gladness to your grieving hearts with this faith. Dispel your
sadness readily by faithful devotion. Trust in God and
wear the garb of gladness. Unhappy grief and crazed sorrow befit those without remaining hope and without
faith, those whose entire good is life only in this world,
with no hope in God and with belief only in the physical.
Inner numbness must circumscribe the inconsolable hearts
of those whose feelings are forsaken by the truth, whose
faithless minds alienate them from God, and whose fate
which has no part in Christ is to tumble into the darkness
below. But Paul the apostle must attend to console us
through the mouth of God, and the loving Christ must
teach us through the Gospel. The example of the patriarchs, the preaching of the prophets, and the book of the
history of the apostles must strengthen us.

397. In that book[36] we see the bodily Christ returning
to heaven, borne to the stars on the bosom of a cloud, and
we are bidden to expect His return from heaven just as

we saw Him going to heaven to the Father. All creation now waits in suspense for His arrival; faith and hope train their gaze totally on this King. The world, which must be transformed anew, is already pregnant with the end to come on the final day. Oracles of truth[37] warn all men to believe in the books I have mentioned, and to prepare themselves for God.

407. Make haste, I beg you, whilst the chance is available here, to lay in a store of blessings and to take precautions against evils. Be converted, and have done with debased preoccupations. Faith instructs us to weep tears that profit us. It is helpful to lament our sinning, and to wash away with copious tears the wounds caused by sins—tears such as those which the great David in his heavy grief shed on his bed night after night, a man whose strength lay in humility of heart.[38] If David beloved by God ate ashes for bread and mingled tears with his cups,[39] what are the appropriate steps for me to take in my wretchedness? How shall I win atonement or make satisfaction, or by what resources shall I be saved? My heart of stone has no tears to summon, the ashes cleave[40] to my throat, and delicacies are my pleasure while my soul goes hungry. Who could furnish me with a spring for streams of tears, so that I might lament my deeds and days?[41] For I need a river to lament the heavy strokes which I deserve for a life spent in sin. Break the stone that is my heart, saving Jesus, so that the inner man may be softened and a stream of devotion pour forth.

427. I beseech you, Christ my Spring, to make Your source in my heart, so that the living stream of Your water may gush out from me. You are the Spring from which life flows and grace wells forth, from which light pours

out on people of all nations. Those who drink of You, Christ, will be restored by the sweet flowing water, and will thirst no more;[42] or rather they will still thirst, for those sated by the abundance of God's word are made to thirst the more by the sweetness they imbibe.

435. So many souls always hunger and thirst for You, Lord God, the Bread and Spring of salvation. No fasting hunger, no parched thirst will ever destroy a man's life if his mind eats and drinks of You. Your constant flow is drunk without cease, yet when You are drunk dry You pour forth more abundantly to outlast the crowd of imbibers and their thirst. For You, Christ God, are all sweetness and love, and with these You can replenish rather than satiate. Always thirsting for You with greedy longing, we snatch You as You flow into us,[43] yet our love is not satiated; so complete is our devotion that we love You unceasingly, the Christ who will give eternal life to Your own.

447. O God, allow me now to mourn, and by the weeping which brings salvation to sow in good time the seeds of eternal joy. May mourning await me in this life, I pray, in which every attendant circumstance has only a short journey. Be far from me, you men that are happy; I prefer the company of them that weep, so that by short-lived tears I may reap lasting joys. Provided that my sackcloth, heavy with its hairy covering, both covers and pricks me with its goats' bristles,[44] the Father will be appeased, the ring of deserved glory will be conferred on me, and the robe of gladness will clothe me. Then the Father will rightly kill the fatted calf for me,[45] if only in fasting I hunger for justice. I prefer to endure fasting from bread than from the holy word. I desire no wine-house,

but thirst for the water of light. Cruel hunger can torture me in this life; humiliating poverty can emaciate me and enclose me in wretched rags. The rich man can pass me by in front of his house, refusing to fill me even with the crumbs from his table.[46] I have no wish for garments of silk dyed with Tyrian scarlet to flame about me (a source of envy towards my body, itself doomed to flame), for fear that enduring fire may succeed that crimson garb around me, and the price I pay for that clothing be exacted by fire.

469. I would rather lie wretched here on a foul dung-heap, and let dogs lick my sores,[47] so that after a grim life I may be delivered by peaceful death; then an angel may be kind to my coming, and bear me off to set me triumphant in the arms of the patriarchs, far from the hell that rages in yawning anarchy. I speak not here of the lies of poets which frighten children—the dog barking at the threshold with triple mouths, Charon frightening the shades with his repugnant foulness, the Furies savage with their snaky tresses, Tityus eternally the food for the grisly vulture, Tantalus dry with thirst among the waters, the one who endlessly turns the wheel and the rock that rolls back, or the frustrating jars of the sweating daughters of Danaus.[48] These are the tales which poets without the resource of truth have composed in empty words, poets who have not laid hold of Christ the Source of truth. But God has taught us the truth, and the Creator Himself has related to us the whole truth of His works.[49]

487. Learn from the Gospel the abode of the poor man and that of the rich. The poor man reclines in Abraham's arms, the rich man in hellfire. Justice reverses the roles, and he who had wept in this life rejoices in the next.

While the poor man is filled, the rich man is in need. The
poor man enjoys blessed repose while the rich man groans
in the flames, for the rich obtains the punishment for
wealth, and the poor man the wealth. The rich man begs a
tiny drop of water from the poor man whose supplication
he had spurned in this world above. And for this reason
not even a tiny drop of refreshing water dripped from the
end of the poor man's finger upon him as he burned, because not even a crumb had fallen from the abundant
table of the man with plenty into the mouth of the poor
man in need.[50]

499. We should be warned by this, and learn to live a
life of holy righteousness for Christ, dispensing a share to
the poor. If the poor man is repulsive to you, if you
shudder at the sight of one in need, if you regard an encounter with a suppliant man of God as ill-omened, even
as you admire your own gleaming appearance in costly
garments you do not realise that your inner garb is repulsive. All that makes you shudder in a poor man's body
you yourself possess inwardly, for with your riches you
are more repulsive than his rags and sores. When you
spurn the blind and avoid touching the leper, greedy man
of wealth, you love your own leprosy. The leper is
wretched and feeble in men's eyes, but you are cheap
through feebleness of soul in the eyes of God. Wicked
creature, you despise the poor man, though he shares your
natural status, and through your greed you disinherit him;
for all that you have in excess and do not need, unjust
man, all that you thrust away in a hole in the ground, is
the portion of the poor.

515. Why do you keep the property of others? What
hope induces you to cling to what you should surrender,

without restoring it to its owners, even though you ought not to possess it? If a poor man is repulsive in your eyes, if your title to wealth makes you insane enough to raise affronted eyes and tremulous brow, if you do not deign even to address as men those whom you see unsubmerged in the same luxury as yourself, then observe the form in which the Son of God came. Though He was rich, He was poor in this world; and when He who was God came, He chose not the exalted but the lowly things of the world, so that He might destroy strength by weakness.[51]

525. The rich man must not now rejoice in his wealth, or the strong man in his strength, or the wise man in his massive intellect. No man must trust in his own resources, or be self-satisfied, because all his attributes have been implanted or bestowed by God their Source. Christ has become the Refuge and Representative of the poor, a source of shame to the rich and of glory to the poor. We must eagerly hasten to His fragrant perfume, so that the smell of death may flee far from us. If only someone would allow me to pour the costly nard from the jar of alabaster, and to wash the sacred feet of the Lord with my tears![52]

535. As I devote myself to you, so, I beg you, devote yourselves to acts of devotion, and offer yourselves to the boundless God with mind wedded to Him. The time is near, the Lord now at hand, so hasten to prepare yourselves to meet the King while one short hour remains.[53] Employ your riches with kindly devotion, and thus root out evil from your hearts. All that has value in your lives you must concentrate in the persons of the poor, and so anoint your heads with devoted giving. Both of you must lick the holy feet of Christ the Lord, wipe them with your hair,[54] and wash them with your tears.

545. If you long to enjoy Celsus forever, you must ensure that the heavenly court lies open to you also. A holy faith, a life that knew no sin, and piety of heart kept him chaste in body, so our confidence is assured that he has reached the land of heavenly dwellers where the flaming altar of God gives protection to the saints. So I would not have you, dear brethren, as distressed over our dear one as men without substance. If you believe unshake-ably that Christ Jesus died[55] and now lives in God's cita-del, the Father will likewise draw to Himself together with the returning Christ all who rest in the peace of a living faith.

557. For this is what is taught in the Lord's word by the great master, by whose guidance we strive to tread the path to heaven: "Those who have spent their lives in Christ will have eternal life with Him."[56] When the pre-siding angel sounds with a trumpet the coming of the Lord from the lofty throne of the Father, those who died in Christ will be the first to rise, for they will be reckoned worthy to confront God on the clouds of heaven.[57] All will have a new life in the flesh in which they lived, but not everyone will experience a transformation into light. We shall all rise, but not all of us will change;[58] this will be the cleavage among the nations before God's face. The bodies of the ungodly will also rise from their tombs un-corrupted, but to become the food of long punishment. Their life will be unending death, and their death a life of punishment, for their flesh will survive to nourish their tortures. The sinner will himself bring forth his execu-tioners from his own body, and he will be food for the worms within him. But those whom a life of devotion in saintly behaviour has borne upwards will wear garlands

in common with God their King, and they will live forever in the image of Christ the Lord, their bodies clothed
in divine light.

579. Because of this, you must take consolation from
my words, and with hope in the truth revive your spirits.
Believe that Celsus, whom you jointly love, is enjoying
the milk and honey of the living in the light of heaven.
Kindly Abraham has him in his arms and nurtures him, and
Lazarus benignly feeds him with water from his finger,[59]
or he is in Paradise with the children of Bethlehem whom
the wicked Herod struck down out of jealousy,[60] and he
is playing in a scented glade, weaving garlands as rewards
for the martyrs' glory.[61] He will mingle with such as these,
and accompany the Lamb who is King, a child newly
joined to the bands of virgins.

591. Celsus, you are now a youthful dweller in the
chaste land of the blest. Celsus, you are your parents' grief
but likewise their glory. Celsus, you are the love, the longing, and the light of your family. Celsus, our pleasure in
you was short, but your own is long; yet the pleasure you
bring can be long-lived for us, too, if you remember us
before the Lord. For your age was young, but your merits
great, your life short in years but powerful in its godliness.
It is certain that the kingdom of heaven belongs to children
such as you were in age, purpose, and faith, like our own
boy who bore your blessed name and who was summoned
the moment he was bestowed. He was a child long desired
but not awarded to us, since we were unworthy to rejoice
in the devotion of a progeny.[62]

605. We believe that he shares your joyful life, sporting
with you in eternal glades. In the city of Complutum[63] we
buried him, alongside the martyrs with whom he shares

the compact of the tomb, so that with the blood of the saints close by he may sprinkle our souls when they are in the fire after death.[64] Indeed, perhaps this tiny drop of our blood will some day be a source of light even for us sinners. Celsus, assist your brother, working together with allied deeds of devotion, so that we may find a room in your resting-place.

615. Brothers, live as comrades forever, dwell in the regions blest which you both deserve, and as children well-matched in the innocence of your deserving lives, prevail over your parents' sins with your chaste prayers. Your tally of years, Celsus, at the time your life was taken from you was matched in days by that earlier Celsus.[65] He was younger then, but he is older as your predecessor. He was younger in his shorter span of life, but by dying earlier he is now older than you in heaven. Celsus, at your brother's side lend support to your family, with whom we range ourselves, for we are your blood on your father's side.[66] Count Paulinus and Therasia as your own, as well as your father Pneumatius and your mother Fidelis, so that by your prayers and by Christ's pity we, too, may have a common support in you, Celsus. But it remains for us, too, to ensure that we can follow you with like ingenuousness. Then we shall be able to live as comrades of our Celsus, and be the parents of our own sweet loved one forever.

# POEM 32[1]

Antonius,[2] I claim to have examined the beliefs of all the schools. I have sought out very many and run through each and all of them, but have found nothing better than belief in Christ. This search I have decided to describe in agreeable verses. Do not be offended at my composing a work of this nature, for David himself prayed to God in words set to music. I shall follow his example, and sing my song; mine will be slight by comparison with his, but the content and inspiration of the whole are praiseworthy. I shall tell what we must avoid, and what we must pursue and cultivate.

10. Not even the wondrous grace of God stirred the Jewish people in their early days. They were rescued from the unjust Pharaoh, they crossed the sea on foot with a pillar to light their way.[3] They beheld the enemy horsemen drowned with their leader, and in the desolate countryside they wanted for nothing at any time.[4] Manna poured down on them from heaven, and water from the rock.[5] But then they denied the God who bestowed these great gifts on them. With crazed hearts they sought another God, and lost their gold which they cast into the fire they kindled.[6]

19. The heathen is like the Jew.[7] He adores stones which he hews out, and thus creates for himself an object of necessary fear. Then he venerates the statues which he fashions from bronze in such a way that he can break

330

them up for dispatch to the mint when he so desires, or as often happens, change them into still more shameful shapes. In the interest of such deities he slaughters wretched cattle, and examines their steaming entrails to ascertain the intention of the gods he believes are angry,[8] and so he prays to save the life of a human being by the death of a farm beast. How can a man seek pardon by demanding mercy through bloodshed? How stupid and blameworthy is such conduct! Man dares to fashion a god, though almighty God fashioned man long ago; to ensure that he sins, man even sells that god of his, and the purchaser buys for himself a lord.[9]

32. Can I believe that philosophers possess any reason when they are without reason and their wisdom is empty? There are the Cynics who are like dogs, as they reveal by their name.[10] There are those who follow the tenets of the vacillating Plato, who are deranged by their long search for the substance of the soul; they are always discussing it, but they cannot define it. This is why they love to transcribe Plato's book on the soul, which has in it nothing definite beyond the title.[11] There are also the Physici, whose name derives from the word for nature, and who delight in the old, rough, uncivilised life. One of them used to carry a stick and an earthenware vessel, which in his view were the only useful and necessary possessions, the first to support him and the second for drinking. But when he observed a farmer standing and drinking water from cupped hands to slake his thirst, he broke the earthenware cup and threw it far away, saying that all non-necessities should be cast off. The farmer taught him that he could reject even the cup! These philosophers of nature drink no wine, and reject the nourishment of bread; they

have no beds to lie on, or clothes with which to ward off the cold. Thus they reject what God has afforded them, and show Him no gratitude.[12]

52. What of the various rites and temples established for gods and goddesses? I shall first describe those of the Capitol, in which there is a god and the god's wife whom they posit also to be his sister; Virgil who tells of them describes her as both sister and spouse.[13] There is further detail of Jupiter, that he debauched his daughter and gave her to his brother, and that he changed his shape to seduce other girls, becoming now a snake, now a bull, now a swan and a tree. By thus changing himself he revealed his own nature; he preferred the forms of other creatures to his own. Then more basely still he pretended to be an eagle, and sought the impious embraces of a boy.[14] What do the crowd of his worshippers say about this? They must either say that it was not Jupiter or acknowledge this shameful deed. At any rate Jupiter enjoys a fame which is not approved by reason. His devotees sacrifice to him and call him "Jupiter the best"; they pray to him, but they put father Janus in first place.

68. This Janus was a king who gave his name to the Janiculum. He was a wise man who had the ability both to foresee many future events [and to visualise the past with wisdom],[15] so the old inhabitants of Latium portrayed him with a double form, and called him the twin Janus. Because he reached the shore of Italy by ship, in his honour coins were first minted in such a way that one side had his head in relief, and the other side a ship; it is in remembrance of this that people talk of "heads and ships" of coins no matter what is stamped on them.[16]

78. What expectation can they have of Jupiter, when

he comes second after a king, a mere appendage in the
mouths of those who pray at sacrifices? Jupiter also has a
mother who was seized with love for a shepherd—yes,
there was a shepherd before there was Jupiter or Jove himself; in fact, the shepherd behaved better, because he
wished to keep his chastity unpolluted, and so he repulsed
the goddess. In her savagery she cut off his private parts,
so that the man who refused her approaches might never
attain marriage with another.[17] Was this the effect of the
gods' just decree, that the man who avoided adultery
should not obtain a wife? Even nowadays there are
eunuchs who make lament in her foul mysteries, and men
are found to devote themselves to this unclean practice.
They adore some hidden, inner object as a greater power,
and call it holy. If a chaste person seeks to draw near it,
he will be accounted profane. And the priest himself is
more austere than the devotees in avoiding intercourse
with women and enduring it with men.[18]

94. How blind are men's minds! Stage performances are
forever awaking laughter about their religious practices,
yet they do not abandon such error.[19] They say that Saturn
is the father of Jupiter, and that previously he devoured his
children, later vomiting forth his impious meal from his
stomach; but then through his wife's guile he gulped down
into his belly a stone which had been planted in place of
Jupiter—and if the wife had not done what she did, Jupiter
would have been devoured! This Saturn they call Cronos,
and mendaciously Chronos, because he wastes the time he
creates and promises it back once wasted. Yet why do they
falsely and indirectly represent time by his name?[20] They
also say of him that he often feared for his safety at the
hands of his offspring, and that after he was cast out of

heaven by Jupiter, he lay latent in the fields of Italy, and so it got the name Latium.[21] Two great gods indeed, one of them hidden on the earth and the other unable to detect his earthly hiding-place! This story explains why Roman citizens of old established the wicked festival of Jupiter Latiaris, so that the slaughter of a human being could appease an empty name.[22]

111. How dark is the human mind, how unforseeing men's hearts! The object of their worship does not exist, yet bloody sacrifices are conducted. For example, they keep the Unconquered One down in a dark cavern, and dare to call him the sun though they hide him in darkness.[23] Who would think of worshipping light in darkness, of hiding the star of heaven in hell, except the initiator of wickedness? Then, too, there are the mysteries of Isis, the rattle and the dog's head which they do not seek to conceal, but put on public display. At any rate, they search for something or other, rejoice when they have found it, and lose it again so that they can find it again![24] What man of sense could endure on the one hand the followers of Mithras burying, so to say, the sun, and on the other hand the followers of Isis flaunting the barbaric symbols of their deities in the light of day? How did Serapis deserve to be beaten as he is by those devotees in sundry foul places? In fact, he is always becoming a beast or a dog or the rotting carcass of an ass; now he is a man clad in rags, or one wasting with a sick body.[25] When they act in this way, they are admitting that Serapis has no feelings.

128. Is there need to mention Vesta when her very priest admits that he does not know what she is? Still, she is conceived to be fire preserved perpetually unquenched within the recess of the shrine. Why is she a goddess, not

a god? Why is fire said to be female? According to the approving account of Hyginus,[26] in days long past she was the first to weave a vestment, which got its name from hers, on the newly invented loom; she gave it to Vulcan, who at that time had shown her how to tend the concealed hearth. Vulcan, delighted by the gift, in turn bestowed the garment on the sun, by whose aid he had previously detected Mars committing adultery. This is why today the whole of that gullible throng hang up their clothing to the sun during the festival of Vulcan. At that time also a statue of Adonis is carried in procession to bring discredit to Venus; they throw dung at it, and deride Adonis as dung.[27] The more one investigates all these practices, the more laughable they appear. There is a further detail. I am told that the so-called Vestal Virgins every five years provide a feast for a snake, which either does not exist, or if it does, is the devil himself, who of old gave an enemy's advice to the human race.[28] The Virgins, then, worship a snake who is now trembling and in suspense at Christ's name, and who admits to all his deeds. How strange are the minds of men, preferring false utterances to the truth, worshipping what they should abandon and abandoning what they should worship!

151. This will now suffice for our catalogue of empty fears, all of which I entertained before attaining the clear light. Then after my long uncertainty and the tossing of so many storms, holy Church received me into the harbour which brings salvation. She set me in an abode of peace after my wandering over the waves, so that now the cloud of evils is dispersed, and I can hope for cloudless light at the promised time. Now that earlier salvation, which Adam at the persuasion of an evil breeze heedlessly

lost, will emerge to abide forever, rescued from the rocks by Christ our Oarsman. For our Ruler so controls the whole of reality everywhere that He who recently removed error from my mind opens the gates of Paradise to which we proceed by the better road.

164. How happy is the faith we have, devoted as it is to the one and certain God! For there is only one God, there is only one Son of the one substance; in each is the one strength, the one power. For Christ, God's Word, flashed forth from His Father's heart, yet always existed. He was not, as it were, born, but emerged from God's mouth and dispelled the confusion of the void. He removed the shapeless chasm of cohering darkness, and apportioned to their places the sea, land, air, and sky; dissolving the blackness, He gave them twofold light.[29] But when the whole of creation was stunned at the rising of the new sun, He enriched the four elements with their varying properties. Human persons have been set on earth, stars in the sky; birds hover in the air and fish swim in the clear sea.

177. Thus He adorned each of the elements with its proper forms. Though they were disparate, He interlocked them, uniting their distinct substances yet in their unity delimiting them, so that they are now divided yet united. The ocean marks off the land, and the land the sea. The pole of heaven encloses the air that lies between. Even the sky which we see on high lies below six other heavens which rise at equal intervals.[30] Beyond the seven planetary seats and the seven heavenly kingdoms, the rest of outer space projects beyond all creation, transcending it, and everywhere extending to the heights. It is open and unbounded, and no mind comprehends it. It is the house of unapproachable light, the sacred abode of the powerful

God; from there He beholds from afar His creation stretched below, all of it remaining in place while the Spirit encloses it.

191. So, too, this region granted to our use, which the lowest heaven embraces with its great sphere, is preserved in a single peace though its parts are separated; indeed it has one name, for the whole of it is the world. The earlier Greeks called it also the *cosmos*, and subsequently the two languages make a distinction, calling the ordered world *cosmos* by reason of its adornment, and *mundus* because of its light.[31] For the whole area over which the sun now shines was previously shabby and shadowy, and whenever night makes everything unsightly, the lesson is continued, teaching us what a grace has been granted to us by light.

201. He who has achieved all these blessings and worked in this way in all places is the Lord from the heart of God, the Breath from His mouth, the Word of the holy Father, the Skill which created these mighty things. The pagan should not praise himself for ignoring idols, or think it sufficient to believe in one godhead. How can he worship God when he does not worship His Word, when he does not with like honour revere His Strength? Then the man who proclaims that God cannot be seen or grasped will upon consideration discover that Christ is precisely like this, for none can grasp or behold the Word, and only His works are visible. For the Son has achieved all things in the Father, and the Father all things in the Son; and all that He grants through His power He maintains by His loving care.

214. Thus He who endured my false beliefs and made the truth plain, He who restored the dying world to His appeased Father, was, is, and will be the true Saviour for-

ever. It is not surprising that all things are governed by Him who created all, who bestowed all things upon nothing, Who repelled darkness from light and ordered day to supplant night, and who because He lived in the flesh absolves the sins of the flesh. He realises that man is a frail creature who falls easily, and though He rebukes us He will grant the same pardon to all. This is a new concept which I shall declare, yet I shall not repent having said it[32] —His fatherly love will be greater than His justice. Indeed, if He insists on His justice, none of us will be innocent and escape punishment, since in His justice He condemns wickedness, but in His love He bestows all things. He does this to ratify the gift of life to come, and in His mercy to restore what sin snatched away. If this mercy is not granted to His imploring people, there will be virtually none who is free from every sin, so who will be able by his deserts to obtain the promised light?

232. Then in our joy we shall be able to attain the kingdom of heaven, then death itself will be enabled to die, for life will be eternal and enduring. In that blessed abode there will then be no opportunity for sinning, for there there is no evil desire. This is the great glory which remains in keeping for God's faithful people. He has bestowed a greater boon, He has granted a larger gift; He does not assign to the ranks of the sinning throng the sinner who repents of his earlier fall, for the man who grieves over his own transgression is punished enough. Fear is its own punishment. He who confesses that he has deserved punishment for his guilt is in a sense suffering it.

243. What could be superior to or better ordered than this? He who conquers all but is not conquered by anger itself judges, investigates, rebukes, spares, and glorifies. We

can see from the evidence of the present that this will be. Often God threateningly gathers bristling stormclouds, instils terror induced by love when He makes the red lightning blindingly flash, and thunders amidst daunting rain and dark clouds, so that the whole human race fears destruction. But then that living power subsides, and makes sunny both skies and human hearts. By this means also He bids men hope, for He shows that He is able to destroy the whole world but refuses to wish to do so. In this way we are shown that salvation will again be enacted for us in the age to come, and the devoted love of the eternal Father will remain forever.[33]

# POEM 33[1]

How blessed is the man who has abandoned wickedness, who is not accountable for sluggish delay in believing, and on whom faith without works has bestowed life![2] Note this man well, depicted with remarkable authenticity in the portrait beneath the high gilt dome;[3] it is Baebianus,[4] famous for the proud name of the Verii and for the blood of consuls that flows in him, Baebianus the personification of the abundant grace of the powerful Christ. Previously he was a prisoner enchained by the transient world; poor in God's eyes amidst his worldly riches, forgetting that he was mortal, he hastened through a life agreeable with the wealth he had accumulated. But when he recognised that he was mortal and that death was the victor, he turned his weary eyes in search of the kindly God, and was at once enlightened and found Christ. He craved pardon, and fell in self-accusation and suppliant veneration at the feet of priests. By denying that he was worthy of grace, he made himself worthy of it. He vowed his entire life if he survived, and expressed joy at the prospect of death if he met it after fresh birth.

21.[5] The bishop gave credence to his prayer, donned his robes, and sprinkled with pure water the man who thirsted for the stream of life.[6] After the bishop then completed the holy ritual in due sequence, Baebianus tasted God's sacrament and smelled sweetly with the chrism,[7] and expressed his wonder at the marvellous majesty of the rite. But what was the fragrance, he asked, which he felt slipping into his heart, healing with sweet nectar his inner parts? Then his attentive wife informed him that the ointment breathed forth life springing from Christ's name; and the bishop urged him to pray for a long life, and guaranteed that he would get it. Baebianus, now wholly God's, replied: "The gift I now have is enough for me; death is now my gain, and Christ is life.[8] See how grace has been bestowed on me on earth through Christ eternal." So Baebianus is the happy thief who at life's close confessed Christ, and though he was guilty gained heaven by his faith.[9] Baebianus is the man who was hired late at the eleventh hour, and departed with the gift of a whole day's pay.[10] So when he was reborn and glistening with the sanctifying water, he rested his heavy limbs on soft pillows, and with heart renewed addressed his loving wife.

41.[11] "My life has been in course of adding a further year to my age of forty-five. It has been happy because of my loving marriage, sweet because of my dear children, and glorious in its distinctions. Now it is cleansed of the stains which destroy it, and is journeying in holy death to the loving God." At these words his dutiful wife with devoted tears begged him to pray for extended life. Then he said: "Woman, you know not what you are asking. Can you now be sure that I can live the holy life which will keep me in full possession of this great gift? What use is life if in the course of it salvation dies?" Valiantly he spoke these words, his eyes flashing forth a frown, and looking awe-struck up to heaven he said: "I see a flaming orb of light, a circle into which no woman enters. How fortunate I am to have been granted while still in the flesh a vision of the eternal world, in which there is no need for marriage since sex plays no part in immortal bodies!"[12]

61.[13] As he uttered these words, he appeared to lose consciousness in sudden death, and pallid stiffness spread through his prostrate limbs. His wife, agitated and terrified by this sight, turned as pale as death and stretched out her trembling hands to his mouth now mute. Training her eyes on the limbs of her prostrate husband, she bent over his lifeless body, and was herself paler than he. The period of time elapsing prompted the belief that he was dead, for two days in their course saw the sun set, and twice the evening shut off their light while the appearance of death deceived men's eyes. But Baebianus had been borne away through the clouds by the hands of angels, and had left the lodging of his body to which he was soon to return. At that time he was gazing at the sequestered regions, the blessed abodes of the ethereal heaven. God was pointing out the sights, and while there was mourning on earth his holy mind, found worthy of Christ, was taking joy in heaven. The only grief he felt was the continuing fear of returning here. Then his soul returned, dispatched from its journey above[14] to relate what he had seen and to strengthen the faith of those who doubt that the dead live on. When on his return he saw his wife's face pressed close to his limbs, he promised that he would tell a wondrous tale, but postponed the account to the following day.

81. So when the morrow's light gleamed on its first rising, at dawn the priest[15] offered the sacrifice, for he happened to be present. When with devoted adoration he performed the ritual, Baebianus looked up to heaven, extended his hands, and then hugged his arms tightly to him as though grasping in greedy embrace some gift dispensed

from the sky. "Is all this mine?" he asked. All were astounded at his words, and asked what he saw which was shrouded from men's sight. Repeatedly mentioning the patriarch Isaac, he replied in Greek: "How beautiful it all is! It is the godhead, the godhead sweet to behold!" Then in fear and adoration he recounted how an angel carried him off through the void, how he saw many thousands mingled amidst the troops of angels and lambs, and Christ God reigning over all in company with the Father. He also told of the eternal city with its jewelled gates, and of the heavenly grove of Paradise on high. As he recounted this, he pressed his wife's right hand on his enclosed bosom and said: "We two are one and the same flesh."[16] As he repeated these words he met his end peacefully in a holy and ordered way, for he gave up the ghost as he uttered the Gospel phrase.

101.[17] Now Baebianus is taking joy in God, and promotes the welfare of his blessed wife to whom he is bound in eternal love. But the father was unable to bear the loss of all his children, so he has borne off one son to console him. But once you, mother so renowned for the dear offspring you bore, have at the appropriate age ended your days, you will be met by that boy of yours in company with his father, and on his head will be the crown he has gained, all blossoming with light. In his company your husband will joyfully draw near you from the skies, will stretch out his hand and fondly say: "The time is come, so detach yourself now from your cares and your limbs. You have lived for your children; you must now return to me. Our marriage is no longer that mortal one which a short and grudging span of life earlier bestowed on our feeble bodies. Fleeting age with its unsubstantial harvest deprived us of that, after we had scarcely aggregated ten years and three. Your life had advanced to twenty-five years when mine preceded it on the last journey. My life had seen twenty years more than yours ebb away,[18] yet our united love made us equal in age. But now we are secure under a better yoke, and hymned by devoted believers we shall live a life of splendour in the kingship of God. Rise, and come after your husband and your son. See how the gate of sunny heaven lies open to your merits. . . .[19] . . .the angel who flies before Him. God Himself is extending His holy hand from the cloud, and with His beckoning arm summons you to heaven. Blessed Apra, you have been permitted both on earth and in heaven to preserve abiding happiness with a husband who lay with no other. Hence on earth you will have glorious fame, and by the same token lasting glory in heaven."[20]

# APPENDIX

*[This epitaph, found on the site of Cimitile, should be included in the works of Paulinus]*[1]

Cynegius[2] has ended his life while in the bloom of manhood, and he rests in the holy abode of tranquil peace.[3] The holy house of Felix now contains him; Felix has received him and possesses him through the long span of years, Felix our patron[4] now takes joy in his silent guest. Young Cynegius will show similar joy before Christ the Judge, when the dread trumpet shakes the earth with its din,[5] and men's souls return to their vessels. He will deservedly be joined to Felix before the throne; meanwhile he lies in peace in Abraham's bosom.[6]

# NOTES

# LIST OF ABBREVIATIONS

| | |
|---|---|
| ACW | Ancient Christian Writers (Westminster, Md.-London-New York-Paramus, N.J. 1946– ) |
| Blaise | A. Blaise, *Dictionnaire latin-français des auteurs chrétiens* (Strasbourg 1954) |
| CJ | Classical Journal (Athens, Ohio 1906– ) |
| CSEL | Corpus scriptorum ecclesiasticorum latinorum (Vienna 1866– ) |
| DACL | Dictionnaire d'archéologie chrétienne et de liturgie (Paris 1907–53) |
| DHGE | Dictionnaire d'histoire et de géographie ecclésiastiques (Paris 1912– ) |
| Diehl | E. Diehl, *Inscriptiones latinae christianae veteres* (Berlin 1925–31) |
| DTC | Dictionnaire de théologie catholique (Paris 1903–50) |
| Fabre *Chron.* | P. Fabre, *Essai sur la chronologie de l'oeuvre de saint Paulin de Nole* (Paris 1948) |
| Fabre *Paulin* | P. Fabre, *Saint Paulin de Nole et l'amitié chrétienne* (Paris 1949) |
| Goldschmidt | R. C. Goldschmidt, *Paulinus' Churches at Nola* (Amsterdam 1940) |
| Green | R. P. H. Green, *The Poetry of Paulinus of Nola* (Brussels 1971) |
| HSCP | Harvard Studies in Classical Philology (Cambridge, Mass. 1890– ) |
| Jones, LRE | A. H. M. Jones, *The Later Roman Empire.* 3 vols. (Oxford 1964) |
| JRS | Journal of Roman Studies (London 1911– ) |
| JTS | Journal of Theological Studies (London-Oxford 1900– ) |
| Lagrange | F. Lagrange, *Histoire de s. Paulin.* 2 vols. (2nd ed. Paris 1884) |

| | |
|---|---|
| Latte | K Latte, *Römische Religionsgeschichte* (2nd ed. München 1967) |
| MG | Patrologia graeca, ed. J. P. Migne (Paris 1857–66) |
| MGH | Monumenta Germaniae historica |
| ML | Patrologia latina, ed. J. P. Migne (Paris 1844–55) |
| ODCC | The Oxford Dictionary of the Christian Church (London 1957) |
| Prete | S. Prete, *Paolino di Nola e l'umanesimo cristiano* (Bologna 1964) |
| RE | A. Pauly-G. Wissowa-W. Kroll, *Realencyclopädie der klassischen Altertumswissenschaft* (Stuttgart 1893– ) |
| REL | Revue des études latines (Paris 1923– ) |
| SC | Sources chrétiennes (Paris 1940– ) |
| SIFC | Studi italiani di filologia classica (Florence 1920– ) |
| TAPA | Transactions and Proceedings of the American Philological Association (Cleveland, Ohio 1869– ) |
| VC | Vigiliae christianae (Amsterdam 1947– ) |

# INTRODUCTION

[1] ACW 35 and 36, translated and annotated by P. G. Walsh.

[2] See A. Momigliano (ed.), *Paganism and Christianity in the Fourth Century* (Oxford 1963); for Paulinus' importance in this movement, W. H. C. Frend, "Paulinus of Nola and the last century of the Western Empire," JRS 59 (1969) 1 ff.

[3] See P. G. Walsh, "Paulinus of Nola and the Conflict of Ideologies in the Fourth Century," *KYRIAKON: Festschrift Johannes Quasten* (Münster 1970) 565 ff.

[4] CSEL 30, ed. G. de Hartel (Vienna 1894).

[5] On the spurious poems, see below, p. 27.

[6] See P. Courcelle, "Un nouveau poème de Paulin de Pelle," VC 1 (1947) 101 ff.; S. Prete, *Paolino di Nola e l'umanesimo cristiano* (Bologna 1964) 83 ff.

[7] See the initial notes to these poems.

[8] Diehl 3482. See R. P. H. Green, *The Poetry of Paulinus of Nola* (Brussels 1971) 132.

[9] On the secular career of Paulinus and the degree of importance he attached to it, see now J. F. Matthews, "Gallic Supporters of Theodosius," *Latomus* 30 (1971) 1073 ff.: "They (sc. Ausonius and Paulinus) are better seen as preeminently Gauls by origin and allegiance, who briefly and for their own purpose (prestige and titles to enhance local position) chose to assume office."

[10] See Fabre *Paulin* 26 ff., drawing especially on the evidence of Poem 21.398 ff.

[11] See Fabre *Chron.* 111 ff., with earlier bibliography.

[12] An eyewitness account of his death in 431 by the priest Uranius (text in ML 53.859 ff.) has survived. Letter 51 to Eucher and Galla was written in the middle 420s; see Fabre *Chron.* 87.

[13] Cf. Augustine, *De civ. Dei* 1.10, with the information that Paulinus was taken prisoner.

[14] Cf. Letters 7.3, 22.3, 38.6 (= ACW 35.75 and 199; 36.190).— Jerome's account of his dream is in his *Ep.* 22.30 (= ACW 33.165 f., where see the note of T. C. Lawler at 243 f. n. 283).

[15] See my comments in ACW 35.16 ff.

[16] See Green's useful study (n. 8 above) ch. 3. There are interesting statistics of Paulinus' adhesion to the various patterns of the Virgilian hexameter in G. E. Duckworth, *Virgil and Classical Hexameter Poetry* (Ann Arbor 1969) 132 f.

[17] So C. Mohrmann, *Études sur le latin des chrétiens* I[2] (Rome 1961) 151 ff.

[18] So C. Witke, *Numen litterarum* (Leiden 1971) 63 f.

[19] Witke, *op. cit.*, has a useful final chapter on this new Christian genre.

[20] If Poem 32 were included, this would make a fifth, but the arguments against Paulinus' authorship are conclusive. See my final note on that poem.

[21] See in general Fabre *Paulin* ch. 4; Green 29 ff. The Latin word is used by Paulinus himself at Letter 28.6 (= ACW 36.99) to describe these commemorative poems written for the anniversaries of saints' deaths. See also Ambrose, *Ep.* 57.1.

[22] On the dating of the poems, see below n. 1 on Poem 12, and above all Fabre *Chron.* 113 ff. On the problems of Poem 29, see n. 1 on that poem.

[23] See RE s.v. *Genethlios Hemera;* F. J. Cairns, "Propertius 3.10 and Roman Birthdays," *Hermes* 99 (1971) 149 ff.; Cesareo, *Il carme natalizio nella poesia latina* (Palermo 1928).

[24] Cf. Seneca, *Ep.* 102.26.

[25] See Letter 1.10 (= ACW 35.37).

[26] On this, see Green 26 ff.

[27] See Fabre *Paulin* 340: "on peut dire que les Natalicia élèvent, pierre par pierre, année par année, un monument à la gloire de Felix."

[28] Augustine refers to him both in his correspondence (*Ep.* 78.3) and in his *De cura pro mortuis gerenda* 16 (ML 40.606). Bede, a close student of Paulinus' poetry, wrote a biography, the *Vita Felicis* (in ML 94.789).

[29] See my comments in ACW 35.10 f. on the unhistorical nature of his narrative of such important matters as the career and achievements of Victricius of Rouen. Compare in the poems the statement at Poem 19.329 ff., and my nn. 61 and 62 on that poem.

[30] See below, nn. 29 and 33 on Poem 15.

[31] See ML 61.799 ff.

[32] Note especially Poem 18.169 ff., the description of the burial mound of Felix, *ut seris antiqua minoribus aetas / tradidit;* Poem 21.563, *per tot retro saecula,* and cf. 21.575; Poem 19.300, *a veteri tumulis absconditus aevo.*

[33] On the persecution by Decius, see Eusebius, *Hist. eccl.* 6 f.; the view that Felix suffered under this has been most recently proposed by C. H. Coster, CJ 54 (1959) 146 ff. For the more popular view that Felix suffered under Valerian, see now D. Gorce, DHGE 16.906; S. Prete in *Bibliotheca sanctorum* 5.349. There is a good summary of the historical setting in W. H. C. Frend, *The Early Church* (London 1965) ch. 9.

[34] See Eusebius, *Hist. eccl.* 7.13. A minor inconsistency is involved in this suggestion. At Poem 18.154 ff. we read that there was persecution after Felix's death which prevented the citizens of Nola from raising a more elaborate tomb. But on the other hand, Poem 18.258 f. accords best with A.D. 261. Paulinus may be passing inferences from the state of the old burial mound rather than recording documentary evidence that persecution was still continuing after Felix's death.

[35] See Poem 21.365–459.

[36] Mentioned also in Poem 13.8 f.

[37] Cf. Poems 18.154 ff., 27.345 ff., 28.1 ff., and in general the useful monograph of R. C. Goldschmidt, *Paulinus' Churches at Nola* (Amsterdam 1940).

[38] See Poem 27.511 ff.

[39] See Poems 14.82 ff., 19.378 ff.

[40] Poem 21.643 ff.

[41] Poem 21.48 ff. There is an appendix on the community by Muratori in ML 61.567 ff.

[42] See n. 17 on Poem 27.

[43] See the initial notes on Poems 26 and 21.

[44] See especially Poem 27.395 ff.

[45] See Poem 15.257 ff. and n. 33 thereon.

[46] For the healing of Theridius' eye, see Poem 23.106 ff.; for the animal stories, Poem 20.388 ff. J. Fontaine in his edition of Sulpicius Severus, *Vita s. Martini* (SC 133.198 ff.) distinguishes four kinds of phenomena amongst these alleged miracles: (1) "les miracles objectifs"; (2) "le miracle coincidence," where the author's "providential" interpretation envisages as a miracle something within the natural order; (3) "les miracles folk-

loriques," in which some curious occurrence has been developed by credulous oral tradition or literary stylisation; and (4) "le miracle littéraire," where the author himself deliberately invents a story. It would be easy to illustrate the first three types from the *Natalicia*, but more difficult to find an example of the fourth, though Poems 18.448 ff. and 23.82 ff. are possible candidates.

[47] Cf. Poems 18.62 ff. and 19.385 ff., and the indications in other poems listed by Fabre *Paulin* 342.

[48] Cf. Poem 27.542 ff. for a description of the unlettered crowds.

[49] Cf. Letter 28.6 (= ACW 36.99) to Sulpicius Severus; and note the description of Poem 15 as a *liber* at Poem 16.17 f.

[50] See the good comments of Fabre *Paulin* 372.

[51] For the biographical detail, see below, n. 1, on Poem 25.

[52] See the passages collected by W. G. Holmes, *The Age of Justinian and Theodora* (London 1912) 117 n. 4.

[53] These poems in honour of Honorius and Maria, and of Palladius and Celerina, can be consulted in the Loeb Claudian, 1.230 ff., 2.204 ff.; see further A. Cameron, *Claudian* (Oxford 1970) 193 f.

[54] Paulinus did not keep up his Greek sufficiently (see my comment in ACW 35.20 f.) to know Theocritus 18, but those of Catullus (61–62) and Statius (*Silvae* 1.2; cf. Vollmer's edition, *ad loc.*) were obviously familiar to him.

[55] For further discussion of this *epithalamion*, see J. Bouma's commentary (Amsterdam 1968); C. Morelli, SIFC 18 (1910) 318 ff.; Green 35 ff.

[56] See Ch. Favez, REL 13 (1935) 266 ff. and *La consolation latine chrétienne* (Paris 1937); Fabre *Paulin* 212 ff.; Green 37 f.; P. Maas, RE s.v. Threnos, VIA 1, 96. Poem 33 has perhaps some claim to be a *consolatio;* see my final note on that poem.

[57] See Favez, REL 13 (1935) 267; Green 38.

[58] See Poem 31.601 ff. and the note thereon.

[59] Cf. Ausonius 8.1 ff. for the conventional treatment, and in general Vollmer's edition of Statius, *Silvae,* 316 ff.

[60] See below, n. 1 on Poem 17.

[61] See above all Statius, *Silvae* 3.2; also Horace, *Carm.* 1.3; Propertius 1.8a; Ovid, *Amores* 2.11; Tibullus 1.3.

[62] See F. Jäger, *Das antike Propemptikon und das 17. Gedicht des Paulinus von Nola* (diss. Rosenheim 1913) 16 ff.

[63] On the *propemptikon,* see also Green 34 f.; Fabre *Paulin* 221 ff.

[64] See ACW 35.24 for references to this concept in the Letters.

[65] Commodian is conventionally regarded as a third-century African, but he is relegated to the fifth century by H. Brewer and others.

[66] Edited by J. Huemer in CSEL 24 (Vienna 1891). See further P. de Labriolle, *Histoire de la littérature latine chrétienne*[3] (Paris 1947) 470 ff.; Witke, *op. cit.* in n. 18 above, 199 ff.

[67] So, for example, *Intende qui regis Israel* (Walpole, *Early Latin Hymns* [Cambridge 1922] no. 6) is a Christian meditation on Psalm 79.

[68] See below, n. 1 on Poem 3.

[69] See below, n. 29 on Poem 6. Green 21 regards the poem as complete and as a panegyric; Prete 140 regards it as a *vita.*

[70] See L. B. Struthers, HSCP 30 (1919) 83 ff.

[71] See Cameron, *op. cit.* in n. 53 above, 254; H. L. Levy, TAPA 77 (1946) 57 ff.

[72] See Hartel's Index in CSEL 30.380 f. for verbal echoes.

[73] Note especially lines 84 and 132.

[74] See my article cited in n. 3 above, 568.

[75] The closing lines of the poem, indicating that Horace intends us to interpret it ironically, do not prevent Paulinus from adapting it to his own purpose.

[76] See below, n. 10 on Poem 7.

[77] For the poems of Ausonius, see especially A. Pastorino's fine edition (Turin 1971), unfortunately adopting a different numeration for the *epistulae* from Peiper's. See also Fabre *Paulin* 156 ff. and *Chron.* 100 ff.; C. Witke, *Numen litterarum* ch. 1.

[78] *Ep.* 23–26 Peiper.

[79] I cite the order proposed by Schenkl (MGH *Auct. antiquiss.* 5.xi-xiii) as refined and dated by Fabre *Chron.* 106, a solution which has won wide acceptance.

[80] So S. Dill, *Roman Society in the Last Century of the Western Empire* (2nd ed. London 1899) 6.

[81] There is an excellent discussion of this question in Pastorino (see n. 77 above) 34 ff.

[82] *Ephem.* 2.11 ff.: *nec tus cremandum postulo / nec liba crusti mellei / foculumque vivi caespitis / vanis relinquo altaribus. /*

*Deus precandus est mihi / ac filius summi Dei, / maiestas unius modi / sociata sacro Spiritu. . . .*

[83] *Ephem.* 3, alluding to John 1 at length, and with several quotations from Paul's Epistles and Old Testament passages. This is Poem 5 in our present collection; it was at one time wrongly attributed to Paulinus.

[84] *Ephem.* 3.59 f. and 71 ff.: *nil metuam cupiamque nihil, satis hoc rear esse / quod satis est. . . . pace fruar, securus agam, miracula terrae / nulla putem, suprema dii cum venerit hora / nec timeat mortem bene conscia vita nec optet. . . .* These are the commonplaces of Horatian and Juvenalian satire.

[85] *Ephem.* 4: *satis precum datum Deo / quamvis satis nunquam reis / fiat precatu numinis. / habitum forensem da, puer, / dicendum amicis est have / valeque, quod fit mutuum. . . ,* adding that he must have a word with his cook about the menu for luncheon.

[86] See ACW 35.2–4 on his friendship with Delphinus and Amandus.

[87] Letter 1.5 and 7 (= ACW 35.32–4).

[88] Poem 10.316 ff.

[89] Poem 11.49 ff. The change of metre signals that Paulinus wishes this section to be read as a self-enclosed unity.

[90] There is a further example contained in Letter 8 (= ACW 35.78 ff.) in which Paulinus exhorts the youthful Licentius not to be blinded by the lure of the secular world.

[91] See the final note on that poem.

[92] See ACW 35.151 ff. The evidence of relationship is at the end of Poem 22.

[93] See below, nn. 5 and 7 on Poem 22; also nn. 7 ff. on Letter 16 (= ACW 35.245 ff.).

[94] Line 11; Virgil, *Aen.* 7.44.

[95] Line 149.

[96] Poem 24.481 f.

[97] See Poem 24.715. For an apparent allusion to the monastic school, see Letter 27.3 and n. 13 thereon (= ACW 36.91 and 320).

[98] So Fabre *Paulin* 196.

[99] See ACW 36.138–151.

[100] They also appear in a manuscript (Paris Bibl. Nat. Nouv. Acq. Lat. 1443, 9th century).

[101] See the edition of A. Ferrua (Rome 1942). For a useful

survey, see G. Bernt, *Das lateinische Epigramm im Übergang von der Spätantike zum frühen Mittelalter* (München 1968) 55 ff.

[102] Some are published in Diehl, nos. 1800 f., 1841. See Bernt, *op. cit.*, 63 ff.

[103] For Paulinus at Rome, see Letters 17.1, 18.1, 20.2, 45.1 (= ACW 35.163, 167, 186; 36.244).

[104] For the relationship with Ambrose, see Letter 3.4 (= ACW 35.46); for the relics, Poem 27.436.

[105] CSEL 30.344 ff.

[106] See ML 61.771; also Green 131.

[107] See especially lines 16–30 of the poem.

[108] See lines 97 (*non metuo exsilium*) and 105 f.

[109] It was published by C. Barth, but Hartel was unable to trace it. See Hartel's comment in CSEL 30.xxxv.

[110] ML 61.774.

[111] Green 132. See also Witke, *Numen litterarum* ch. 2.

[112] Note *malagma* (line 16) and *pharmacum* (line 34).

[113] See CSEL 30.xxviii f., xxxv.

[114] See lines 224 (*homo*), 61 (*penetrat*), 163 (*dies*), 76 (*extra, intra*), 147 (*conscientia*), 165 (*tua*); 117, 223 (arsis lengthening); 84, 144, 160, 240 (lengthening of diaeresis in pentameter).

[115] Note lines 6 (lengthening of *-at* in *generat*), 7 (lengthening of *-us* in *captivus*), 24 (*-em* of *finem* not elided before *his*), etc.

[116] See n. 4 above.

[117] See the Loeb Ausonius 1–2 (Cambridge, Mass. 1919).

[118] See n. 77 above.

[119] Diss. Washington, D.C. 1956.

[120] Diss. Washington, D. C. 1959.

[121] Diss. Washington, D.C. 1956.

[122] Diss. Washington, D.C. 1963.

[123] *Het Epithalamium van Paulinus van Nola* (Amsterdam 1968; translation in Dutch).

[124] *Op. cit.* in n. 37 above.

[125] Notably Ch. Pietri, *S. Paulin de Nole: Poèmes, lettres et sermon* (Namur 1964); D. Gorce, *S. Paulin de Nole* (Paris 1959).

[126] *Meropio Ponzio Paolino, Antologia di Carmi* 1 (Introduzione, Testo, Traduzione) a cura di Salvatore Constanza (Messina 1971).

## TEXT

### POEM 1

[1] This verse letter and the next, preserved only in the oldest ms., the 9th-century Vossianus, must be ascribed to the years before Paulinus' departure from Aquitania to Spain in 389, for there is no hint of the religious preoccupations which dominate all his subsequent writings. They are "des témoins précieux de la vie qui menait alors la haute société gallo-romaine, et qui fut pendant plusieurs années celle de Paulin" (Fabre *Chron.* 100). There is an English translation of the poem in the Loeb Ausonius 2 (trans. H. G. E. White) *Ep.* 33.

[2] No information outside this letter documents this earliest-known friend of Paulinus. The deferential address and content establish him as a landed proprietor whose estates abut on the Atlantic; cf. Fabre *Paulin* 155.

[3] The verses commence at this point.

### POEM 2

[1] See above, n. 1 on Poem 1. Though there is no name prefixed to this letter, the content suggests that like the previous one it was sent to Gestidius before 389. There is an English translation in the Loeb Ausonius 2, *Ep.* 34.

### POEM 3

[1] This fragment of Paulinus is preserved by Ausonius, who reveals (*Ep.* 23) that it is part of a rendering in verses of Suetonius' *De regibus*, a lost work in three books. It had been sent by Paulinus to Ausonius with an enclosing letter, presumably before 389 (see Fabre *Chron.* 107). There is a translation in the Loeb Ausonius, 2.83.

[2] Sallust, *Jugurtha* 27.3, not in fact consigning Africa to Europe, but leaving open the question of whether it is a third continent.

[3] Illibanus and Avelis are unknown. Vonones of Parthia is known from Tacitus, *Annals* 2.1 ff., a description of his deposi-

tion from the throne in A.D. 16. Caranus was the first king of Macedon (so Livy 45.9.3). For Nechepsos, see Julius Firmicus Maternus, *Math.* 8.5; for Sesostris, Herodotus 2.104 ff.

[4] Hartel puts these two lines of verse after the rest because they come later in Ausonius. But Ausonius indicates that Paulinus is using these mythological exemplars to illustrate his own rashness and Ausonius' prudence as versifiers, so that the lines clearly belong to the exordium of Paulinus' poem. For the story of the flight of Icarus and Daedalus from Crete, the imprudence of Icarus and his drowning in the Aegean north of Lebinthos and Calymna (the "sea of Icarus"), and Daedalus' arrival in Italy at Cumae, the colony of the Chalcidians, see Ovid, *Met.* 8.220 ff. The second line echoes Virgil, *Aen.* 6.16 f.

## POEM 4

[1] The attribution to Paulinus of this poem in the mss. V (Vossianus, 9th cent.) and N (Colbertinus, 9th cent.) has been challenged by P. Courcelle, VC 1 (1947) 100 ff., who on the basis of similarities of phraseology in the *Eucharisticon* attributes it to Paulinus of Pella. Fabre *Chron.* 107 and Green 130 concur; but the arguments against composition by Paulinus in early life are not conclusive. There is a translation in the Loeb Ausonius, 2.149.

[2] Cf. Virgil, *Aen.* 10.100.

[3] Cf. Virgil, *Aen.* 4.5; Prudentius, *Cathem.* 6.121 ff.

[4] Cf. Poem 5.64 ff., with which this poem is in general closely related.

[5] So also Martial 2.90.9: *sit mihi verna satur. . . .*

[6] A common classical motif. Cf. Virgil, *Georg.* 4.133; Horace, *Epod.* 2.48.

[7] This and the final line reflect the influence of Juvencus 1.18, 4.812. If the poem is by Paulinus, the joy of children must be anticipated; see below, n. 18 on Poem 5.

## POEM 5

[1] The mss. ascribe this poem to Ausonius, and editors support the ascription on arguments of style; see Fabre *Chron.* 108 ff., stressing additionally that lines 68 ff. cannot apply to Paulinus'

situation before A.D. 383. There is a translation in White's Loeb edition of Ausonius, 1.17.

² Cf. John 1.1.

³ Cf. John 1.3.

⁴ Cf. Matt. 5.34.

⁵ Cf. Rom. 9.24.

⁶ Cf. Rom. 11.17 ff.

⁷ John 12.45, 14.9.

⁸ Cf. Gen. 3.6–13; 1 Tim. 2.14.

⁹ Cf. 4 Kings 2.11.

¹⁰ Cf. Gen. 5.22; Heb. 11.5.

¹¹ The poet thinks especially of the famous statue of Jupiter on the Capitol by which men swore. Cf. Cicero, *Fam.* 7.12.2: *Iovem lapidem orare.*

¹² Christian apologists make great play with the difference between the pagan notion of bloody sacrifice and the Christian ideal of sacrifice by excision of sin and by dedication of a spotless life. See the remarkable passage in Paulinus' Letter 11.7 (= ACW 35.96 f.).

¹³ Cf. Gen. 1.2: *et spiritus Dei ferebatur super aquas.* The phrase "intermingling with both" (*mixtumque duobus*) lays emphasis on the orthodox teaching in the *Filioque* issue. Cf. Paulinus, Poems 6.3, 27.9; Paulinus' words in his Letter 21.3 (= ACW 35.193) are more ambiguous.

¹⁴ This phrase is an evocation of Virgil, *Aen.* 6.743: *quisque suos patimur Manes,* on which Servius comments: *Manes, id est supplicia.*

¹⁵ Cf. Juvenal 10.357 and 360; Horace, *Epist.* 1.16.65.

¹⁶ Cf. Matt. 7.12.

¹⁷ Cf. above, n. 4 on Poem 4.

¹⁸ As Fabre *Chron.* 110 f. remarks, this prayer suggests that the author has children but no longer a wife. Ausonius' wife had died in the 340s, and two of their three children survived. Paulinus' only child Celsus died in infancy, and his wife Therasia (whom he married by 383) was still alive in 408 (see Paulinus' Letter 45; cf. ACW 36.352 n. 1). This is accordingly weighty evidence for ascribing the poem to Ausonius in support of the mss.

¹⁹ Heinsius' *suetis* ("their customary functions") for *quietis* may well be right.

[20] Cf. n. 15 above.

[21] Here and throughout echoes of the Nicene Creed should be noted.

## POEM 6

[1] Fabre *Chron.* 111 ff. persuasively argues that Poems 6–9, devoted to scriptural themes, were all written about the same time, and he echoes the judgment of Lebrun (ML 61.755) that a date about 389/90 is probable—the period in which Paulinus departs from Aquitania to Spain in search of a life of greater Christian commitment. The poems reflect the preoccupations of an author making his first steps in the spiritual life, but the content of the compositions makes precision of dating impossible.

[2] See Intro. pp. 17 f. This account of St. John the Baptist is essentially versification of Scripture, a technique already exploited by writers like Juvencus earlier in the century. Poem 3 shows how Paulinus is here adapting a technique earlier exploited for secular themes. Prete 138 ff. regards the composition as a *vita;* Green 21 ff., as a panegyric.

[3] Cf. above, n. 13 on Poem 5.

[4] Cf. Isa. 40.3.

[5] Cf. Matt. 3.1 ff., 14.1 ff.; Luke 1.5 ff.; Acts 19.3 ff.

[6] Cf. Luke 1.5. The theme of Elizabeth's equal nobility with that of Zachary is resumed by Paulinus in his Letter 29.7 (= ACW 36.106 f.).

[7] Cf. Luke 1.25.

[8] Cf. Luke 1.8–10.

[9] The two speeches of Gabriel in Luke are here fused into one. See Green 21 f.

[10] Cf. Luke 1.13.

[11] Cf. Luke 1.13.

[12] Cf. Luke 1.17.

[13] Cf. Luke 1.22.

[14] Cf. Luke 1.26–30.

[15] Cf. Luke 1.30–35.

[16] Punning on the meaning of the name John, "beloved of God."

[17] Cf. Luke 1.41 ff.

[18] Cf. Luke 1.57–61.

[19] Cf. Luke 1.62 f.

[20] Cf. Luke 1.65 f.

[21] Cf. Ps. 1.2; Poem 7.

[22] Cf. Matt. 3.4.

[23] Cf. Mark 1.6; Matt. 3.4.

[24] This passage is an interesting example of how Paulinus adapts the cliché of the decline from the Golden Age, so pervasive in the Augustan poets, to the theology of the Fall (see Ovid, *Met.* 1.130 f.; Tibullus 1.10; Virgil, *Ecl.* 4, *Georg.* 2.460; etc.).

[25] Cf. Matt. 11.30.

[26] Cf. Matt. 3.17.

[27] Cf. Isa. 40.3 f.

[28] Cf. Matt. 11.11.

[29] The poem has survived in only one ms., which breaks off at this point. It may have continued with the account of John's death, developing the account of Matt. 14.1 f.; and perhaps in conclusion pointed to his posthumous influence, demonstrated by Acts 19.3 ff.

## POEM 7

[1] For the dating, see above, n. 1 on Poem 6. This work is essentially the exploitation of Ps. 1 for a meditation on the Judgment, but I have argued elsewhere (*art. cit.* in n. 3 to the Intro.) that there is also a sustained evocation of Horace, *Epod.* 2: *Beatus ille qui procul negotiis,* an ambivalent glorification of retirement to the country. Paulinus claims for Christian retirement a deeper conception than for the classical, but orientates educated Roman readers by introducing them to Christian retirement by way of a poem they know; see Intro. pp. 18 f.

[2] The image of the "living wood" is not in Ps. 1.3; we think at once of the cross as *lignum vitale* (cf. Poem 19.676).

[3] Cf. 1 Cor. 15.25 ff.

[4] I translate *index* for the *iudex* of the mss. and Hartel.

[5] Cf. Rom. 2.12.

[6] Cf. 1 Cor. 3.13 ff.

[7] Cf. Poem 31.557 ff.

[8] Cf. Matt. 7.13.

[9] Cf. Matt. 7.14, 19.24.

[10] Cf. Ps. 1.6. Paulinus thus returns to this Psalm at the end of

his poem, but lines 13 ff. are essentially a Christian elaboration of Ps. 1.5: *non resurgent impii in iudicio*. Since this poem is written shortly before Paulinus' espousal of monastic life, it is important to realise how prominent a part such meditation on the Final Judgment played in his conversion to the full Christian life.

## POEM 8

[1] For the date of this developed versification of Ps. 2, see n. 1 on Poem 6. For Paulinus' exploitation of the theme for Christian apologetic, see Intro. pp. 18 f. It is notable that Augustine exploits the Psalms for a similar purpose in the 390s. See his *Enarr. in Ps.* 6.13, 62.1, 149.7, and R. A. Markus, *Saeculum* (Cambridge 1970) 30 f.

[2] Cf. Matt. 3.12; Luke 3.17.

[3] In these last lines Paulinus again incorporates the motif of the Last Judgment, but this poem is more faithful to the original than is Poem 7.

## POEM 9

[1] This versified elaboration of Ps. 136 is probably to be dated to the same period as Poems 6–8. See above, n. 1 on Poem 6. For the fourth-century relevance, see Intro. pp. 19 f.

[2] At the time of composition of Ps. 136, the Edomites were again showing their traditional hostility to Israel (cf. Ezech. 35.5 ff.). They had assisted Babylon in the overthrow of Jerusalem (cf. Abd. 10 ff.) and the psalmist regards them as the foes of Yahweh and doomed to be overthrown (cf. Jer. 49.7 ff.).

[3] This is the final verse of the Psalm, paraphrased. The remaining lines of Paulinus' poem here form a Christian interpretation of the Psalm.

[4] The Hebrew *balal* means "to confuse." The Genesis narrative plays on *Babil* (= Babylon) and *balal*.

## POEM 10

[1] This and Poem 11 are the two surviving verse letters from Paulinus' side of the famous correspondence with Ausonius, seven of whose letters to Paulinus are extant. The first four of

these letters of Ausonius, *Epp.* 23–26 Peiper (the Loeb edition follows this numeration; in Pastorino's [Turin 1971] they are Nos. 19–22) date to the period of intimacy before 389, the year Paulinus finally quitted Aquitania. The order of the other three (27, 28, 29 Peiper = 25, 23, 24 Pastorino) is controverted; see Intro. pp. 20 f. and the summary discussion in Fabre *Chron.* 100 ff. The present poem is probably to be dated to the summer of 393, and is written from Spain. There is an English translation by H. G. E. White in the Loeb Ausonius 2, *Ep.* 31; and one in Italian in Pastorino's edition, 841 ff.

² Evoking Virgil, *Georg.* 3.442.

³ The sheaf of letters from Ausonius referred to here include *Epp.* 28 and 29 Peiper (= 23 and 24 Pastorino), and a further letter now lost. They reached Paulinus in 393, the fourth year after his departure from Aquitania to Spain.

⁴ These hexameters begin at line 103 of the present poem.

⁵ On the significance of this rejection of the pagan symbols of inspiration by a pioneer in Christian poetry, see C. Witke, *Numen litterarum* (Leiden 1971) ch. 2; Green 16.

⁶ An adaptation of Terence, *Andria* 189.

⁷ For a similar attack on secular learning in Paulinus' Letters, see Letter 38.6 (= ACW 36.190).

⁸ The political careers and literary activities of Ausonius and Paulinus were closely interrelated. Ausonius could not have instructed the mature Paulinus in any systematic sense, for his employment at Trier as tutor of Gratian began c. 364/5 when Paulinus was scarcely ten. Family acquaintance is attested (see Ausonius, *Ep.* 25.9) before that date, and a continuing relationship which prompted Ausonius to promote Paulinus' interests at court. Paulinus became suffect consul at Rome in 378, a year before Ausonius, and subsequently governor of Campania, a high career post.

⁹ At this point Paulinus changes from iambics to heroic hexameters.

¹⁰ An evocation of Catullus 64.59.

¹¹ Cf. Virgil, *Aen.* 4.210 (the African Iarbas praying to Jupiter and asking if his thunder is vain).

¹² Cf. 1 Cor. 3.19.

¹³ Paulinus is himself this "first fruit" of Ausonius.

¹⁴ Ausonius had used Bellerophon as a classical exemplar of

the deranged hermit at *Ep.* 29.70 ff. After slaying the Chimaera with the help of the winged Pegasus, Bellerophon returned to Lycia, where he later incurred the hatred of the gods, and wandered in solitary melancholy.

[15] See Ausonius, *Ep.* 29.51 ff. Peiper.

[16] See n. 14 above.

[17] Tanaquil, wife of Tarquinius Priscus, appeared to Ausonius an apposite parallel because she encouraged her husband to desert his native Tarquinii for Rome (Livy, 1.34) and symbolized the ambitious, dominating wife (Juvenal 6.566). Ausonius made the allusion in his *Ep.* 28.31. Paulinus' riposte draws the standard comparison with the model of the ideal wife, whose rape by Sextus Tarquinius and subsequent suicide led to the expulsion of the Tarquins (Livy 1.58 ff.).

[18] There is a play here on *patrium caelum* in the two senses of native land on earth and native land in heaven.

[19] "religious law" here = *legum*. I take *legum* here as referring to the "old law" and "new law" of the Old and New Testaments.

[20] Vasconia was in the region of Navarra in the Tarragona area.

[21] Cf. Horace, *Carm.* 1.22.1.

[22] The modern Calahorra and Calatayua, these towns were famed as birthplaces of Quintilian and Martial respectively.

[23] Lerida.

[24] Gibraltar.

[25] Saragossa, Barcelona, Tarragona.

[26] The Guadalquivir.

[27] At *Ep.* 27.88, in a passage which echoes this section, Ausonius likewise calls Tarragona "Tyrrhenian" or "Tuscan" because it looks over towards Italy and the Tyrrhenian Sea.

[28] Burdigala is Bordeaux; the Boii (according to Caesar, *B.G.* 1.28.5) lived between the rivers Loire and Allier, but are here set in the Bordeaux area.

[29] The location is uncertain; perhaps Mareuil, between Angoulême and Périgueux.

[30] I.e., the region of Bigorre, in the Hautes Pyrénées.

[31] They lived at Bazas, southeast of Bordeaux.

[32] The modern Röm.

[33] I.e., Rome, Quirinus being Romulus.

[34] Paulinus calls it Lucanian (*Lucanus fundus*) here, but Ausonius regularly calls it *Lucaniacus*. There is dispute about its

site, traditionally placed near Libourne. There is a comprehensive discussion in Pastorino, p. 24 n. 36.

[35] A port at the confluence of the Dordogne and the Isle near Libourne (see Ausonius, *Ep.* 5.32); it has now disappeared.

[36] A phrase appropriately adapted from the Roman satirist Persius, 5.86.

[37] An evocation of Horace, *Carm.* 4.7.16.

[38] This striking synthesis of the Pauline vision (cf. 1 Thess. 4.16 ff.) with the Neoplatonist notion of God resident in the upper air is notable; cf. Poem 19.162 ff. for further Neoplatonist ideas.

[39] The clouds in Origen's explication of Paul (cf. MG 14.1302c) are the prophets. Cf. C. W. Macleod, JTS 22 (1971) 370.

[40] Reading here Rosweyde's *commissisque deo ventura in saecula rebus.*


POEM 11


[1] Poem 10, which is dated to the summer of 393 (see n. 1 on Poem 10), was answered by Ausonius with *Ep.* 27 in 394, and the present poem, also written in 394, is a reply to that (see following note). This order, proposed by Schenkl in the MGH Ausonius, is generally accepted by scholars. There is a translation by White in the Loeb Ausonius 2, *Ep.* 30.

[2] The language echoes Ausonius' *Ep.* 27.1.

[3] Cf. Theocritus, *Idyll* 5.

[4] Cf. Virgil, *Ecl.* 1.25.

[5] Cicero and Virgil.

[6] There is a play here on different meanings of *orbis*, "world" and "face."

[7] Another Neoplatonist concept; cf. n. 38 on Poem 10.

[8] I have noted elsewhere (*art. cit.* in n. 3 to the Intro.) that in this moving poem of twenty iambic lines (49–68) Paulinus tries to demonstrate to Ausonius that the Christian concept of friendship goes deeper than the *amicitia* by which the Romans laid such store. Christian friendship does not depend on personal confrontation, but transcends both place and time. In later writings of Paulinus, this notion of the unity of separated hearts and minds is developed with the framework of the mystical body of Christ. See my comments in ACW 35.24.

## POEM 12

[1] This is the first of the *Natalicia,* birthday poems addressed to St. Felix on the day of his entry into eternal life, January 14. On the nature of these poems, see Intro. pp. 6 f. Paulinus composed at least 15 of them, according to the Irishman Dungal (see below, n. 1 on Poem 29). The 13 which have survived in full can be dated with certainty to 395–407 on the basis of the content of the 8th (Poem 26, A.D. 402) and the 13th (Poem 21, A.D. 407). Hence this poem is to be ascribed to January 395, and was written in Spain shortly before Paulinus' departure to Nola. See further Fabre *Chron.* 113 ff.; Goldschmidt 11 ff.; ACW 35.211 n. 1. The poem has been translated by M. McHugh (diss. Washington, D.C. 1956).

[2] With a play on the meaning of Felix, as also in Poems 13.1 ff., 14.104, etc.

[3] Paulinus lays great emphasis on the status of bloodless martyr in Poems 14 and 15. Felix is normally called confessor, but because he endured torture, Paulinus, Gregory of Tours, and others call him martyr. See H. Delehaye, *Sanctus* (Brussels 1927) 109 ff. The schematic discussion in St. Thomas, *Summa theologiae* 2a2ae 124.4, concludes that perfect martyrdom requires death but shows that the term had still a wider connotation (cf. the distinction made in the Celtic Church between "white" and "red" martyrdom).

[4] These lines make it clear that the poem was written in Spain.

[5] Cf. Matt. 11.30.

[6] As Green 26 ff. notes, this and the following *natalicium* are in the form of a prayer.

## POEM 13

[1] This is the second of the *Natalicia,* dateable to January 396. It will be noted from line 6 that this is the first January to be celebrated at Nola, whereas the preceding poem depicted Paulinus on the point of departure from Spain to Italy. The poem has been translated by M. McHugh (diss. Washington, D.C. 1956).

[2] *lustra.* The *lustrum* was the purification ceremony performed by the Roman censors every five years, so that the word became synonymous with quinquennium. This suggests that Paulinus had

been away from Nola for fifteen years, and accordingly we may date his departure from Campania back to Aquitania to about 381-3. Earlier he had been active in the secular world as governor of Campania. For his career, cf. Poem 21.365 ff.; Fabre *Paulin* 26.

[3] There is a more detailed account of such crowds of pilgrims at Nola in Poem 14.44 ff.

[4] Paulinus in his letters lays emphasis on the presence at Rome of the tombs of Saints Peter and Paul, which he visited annually from Nola for a considerable period. See Letters 17.1 (= ACW 35.163, with comment at 247 n. 2) and 45.1 (= ACW 36.244).

## POEM 14

[1] This is the third in the series of birthday poems, and is accordingly dateable to January 397. See Intro. pp. 6 f. The poem has been translated by M. McHugh (diss. Washington, D.C. 1956).

[2] Cf. above, n. 3 on Poem 12.

[3] On Christ at His nativity as the *sol novus*, see H. Rahner, *Greek Myths and Christian Mystery* (London 1962) ch. 4, with further bibliography.

[4] In the catalogue of Italian peoples and cities which now follows, Paulinus makes extensive use of the famous "gathering of the clans" passage in Virgil, *Aen.* 7, intermingling also cities mentioned in Virgil's *Georgics*. See Fabre *Paulin* 361; Green 42 f. The evocation is intended to be recognized; the gathering is now of Christian clans, and for worship, not war. Virgil's poem is, so to say, being baptized.

[5] I.e., the Tyrrhenian and Adriatic seas, with "Latium" loosely envisaged as extending over to the east coast between Picenum and Apulia. At Poem 19.153, "Latium" seems to mean "Italy."

[6] Sixty is occasionally used in Latin of a large number. Nola is in Campania, so the feast was "Campania's own."

[7] Gaurus is the modern Monte Barbaro, a region famed for wine. Monte Massico, also in Campania and likewise famed for its wine, is mentioned at *Aen.* 7.726. So also are the rivers Ufens and Sarnus (7.802, 738; for the formula here, cf. 715), the Ufens being in Latium, the Sarnus (Sarno) in Campania.

[8] The Tanager (Tangro) and Galaesus (Galaeso), in Lucania

and Calabria respectively, are mentioned by Virgil at *Georg.* 3.151, 4.126.

[9] Cf. Virgil, *Aen.* 7.630, 762: *Atina potens . . . mater Aricia.* Both are famed towns of Latium.

[10] The exit taken by those journeying on the Via Appia to Naples.

[11] The inland highway from Rome to Capua.

[12] Praeneste (Palestrina) and Ardea are both in the catalogue in the *Aeneid* (7.682, 631).

[13] Virgil, *Aen.* 7.727 f., groups together Cales (Calvi in Campania) and the Aurunci. Apulian Teanum is the modern Civitate.

[14] Venafrum (Venafro) in Samnite territory was famous for its oil; cf. Juvenal 5.86.

[15] Hartel brackets lines 86–89 ("and you have won second . . . of the apostles") since they are found in only two of the six mss., and occur virtually verbatim at Poem 13.28 ff. also. But Paulinus is guilty of such duplication on other occasions, as at Poems 12.10 and 13.5.

[16] Cf. Poem 18.30 f. and other texts at ML 61.907 for this practice.

[17] Cf. Poem 23.119.

[18] Cf. Ps. 112.1.

[19] I.e., when their bodies are laid out before burial in the basilica of St. Felix at Nola.

[20] Cf. Matt. 6.12.

[21] Cf. Apoc. 14.4.

[22] Cf. Matt. 25.32 f. Letter 32.17 (= ACW 36.150) describes a mural in the new basilica built by Paulinus at Fundi with this theme of the Judgment.

## POEM 15

[1] The date of composition of this, the fourth *Natalicium*, is January 398; see Intro. pp. 6 f. In this poem Paulinus takes up the theme of the life of Felix, and it has been reasonably inferred that the *Vita s. Martini* of Sulpicius Severus, published in 397 or earlier, inspired Paulinus to sacred biography (see Fabre *Paulin* 364). This poem has been translated by M. McHugh (diss. Washington, D.C. 1956).

[2] Cf. Luke 8.11.

[3] Cf. Matt. 11.30.

[4] Cf. Rom. 6.1 ff.

[5] The Castalian spring on Mt. Parnassus (in Phocis, close to Delphi) was sacred to Phoebus and the Muses; the Aonian rock refers to Helicon in Boeotia, where the Muses were said to dwell. The rejection of such pagan inspiration is characteristic of fourth-century Christian poets. See C. Mohrmann, REL (1948) 280 ff.; C. Witke, *Numen litterarum* (Leiden 1971) ch. 2.

[6] Cf. Num. 22.28.

[7] Cf. Ps. 8.1 f.

[8] Cf. Exod. 17.1 ff.; Num. 20.7 ff.

[9] Cf. 1 Cor. 10.4.

[10] Cf. 1 Cor. 1.27.

[11] Cf. Eph. 2.2.

[12] On the history of Felix, see Intro. pp. 8 f.

[13] Cf. Rom. 10.18.

[14] Cf. Gen. 12.1 ff.

[15] In this sense, Felix is a second Abraham, a father of faith.

[16] Cf. Rom. 8.17.

[17] Cf. Gen. 25.22.

[18] I.e., Esau; cf. Gen. 25.29 f.

[19] Esau; cf. Gen. 36.43: *ipse est Esau pater Idumaeorum*. But the word *Idumaeus* connoted "Jewish" to a Roman audience (see Virgil, *Georg.* 3.12; Juvenal 8.160; etc.), and there is a double sense intended here.

[20] Hermias clearly served in the Roman army; eastern Christians integrated themselves with the secular world more completely than the smaller number of western Christians.

[21] I.e., Jacob. Cf. Gen. 32.28.

[22] On the rank of exorcist, see J. Forget in DTC 5.1762 ff.

[23] It is striking that Paulinus should use *infula*, the fillet of the pagan priesthood, as the symbol of the Christian priest. This is an element of that Roman traditionalism which is a feature of his diction in the poems.

[24] This is usually hazarded to be the persecution of Decius in 250, a period in which Pope Fabian, Bishop Cyriacus of Ostia, and others were executed, or that of Valerian a decade later; see Intro. pp. 9 f.

[25] Cf. *Martyrologium Romanum*, Jan. 15; *Acta Sanctorum*, Feb. 19–22; Leclercq in DACL 12.2.1425.

[26] A reminiscence of Virgil, *Aen.* 5.439.

[27] Cf. Apoc. 12.9, 20.2.

[28] Cf. John 10.11.

[29] The correspondence here with Paulinus' description of the sufferings of Victricius in prison in Letter 18.7 (= ACW 35.173 f.) should be noted; that letter is to be dated to 397/8, precisely the time of composition of this poem. Since Paulinus in Letter 18 is recounting Victricius' sufferings to the sufferer himself, we can assume that they have influenced the narrative on Felix rather than vice versa.

[30] Cf. 3 Kings 17.6; Deut. 34.6.

[31] Cf. 1 Pet. 2.19, 3.14.

[32] Cf. Virgil, *Aen.* 2.494, 255.

[33] Cf. Acts 12.7 ff. This is a statement of the greatest interest, justifying the reenactment of biblical miracles in the lives of later saints by this thesis of the harmony of grace.

[34] Cf. John 13.23.

[35] Cf. Matt. 11.30.

[36] With G. Wiman, *Eranos* 32 (1934) 104, I retain the *turba* of the mss. against Hartel's *orba*, and construe: *anus una maneret turba domus et summa census.*

[37] When a person received property in trust, it was customary for him to have the transaction witnessed to ensure that it could be reclaimed. See Pliny, *Ep.* 10.96.7 with Sherwin-White's note. So this is a play on Roman legal procedure.

[38] *Felicemque suum revocans.* As McHugh suggests, there is a play here on *revocare* in the sense of "echo," for Maximus repeats the language of Felix. Cf. *cape / cape* (lines 345, 351) and *depositum / deposito* (lines 345, 354).

[39] Cf. Gen. 27.28.

## POEM 16

[1] This is the fifth *Natalicium,* written for Felix's feastday on January 14, 399; see Intro. pp. 6 f. There is a translation by R. Kalkman (diss. Washington, D.C. 1959).

[2] Cf. Horace, *Carm.* 2.18.15: *truditur dies die / novaeque pergunt interire lunae,* suggesting that "the wheel" here is the monthly course of the moon.

[3] Cf. 2 Cor. 5.17.

[4] I.e., the yearly poem.

[5] *prior . . . liber.* At Letter 28.6 (= ACW 36.99) written in 403/4 (see ACW 36.321 n. 1), he is sending a book of these verses to Sulpicius Severus, and the present passage indicates that Poem 15 has been published separately. This evidence of a reading audience does not preclude the possibility of a listening audience also, at Nola; see Poem 18.62 ff. and Fabre *Paulin* 341 ff.

[6] Cf. Virgil, *Aen.* 8.114.

[7] I.e., the rank of priest. Cf. Poem 15.112.

[8] Cf. Virgil, *Aen.* 2.525.

[9] I.e., Maximus, who had come to regard Felix as a son; see Poem 15.122 and 352.

[10] Cf. Virgil, *Aen.* 3.518. The sense here is metaphorical, as immediately below ("fearful at the recent storm"). If a date of 250 for this persecution is correct, the respite might have come with the death of Decius in 251.

[11] Cf. Virgil, *Aen.* 12.288.

[12] Cf. Ps. 2.1 ff.

[13] Cf. Eph. 6.14 ff.

[14] Cf. 1 Cor. 1.27.

[15] These biblical *exempla* are later developed, showing that by "giants" Paulinus is thinking of Goliath (see 1 Kings 17.1 ff.); by "Egyptian kings," the Pharaoh from whom the Jews escaped (see Exod. 14); and by "Jericho," the fall of that city (see Jos. 6.1 ff.).

[16] Pharaoh was not personally present at the Israelites' crossing of the Red Sea; Paulinus here succumbs to the temptation to evoke Virgil's description of Priam's corpse in *Aen.* 2.557.

[17] Cf. Ps. 22.4.

[18] Cf. 3 Kings 17.6, the ravens who fed Elias.

[19] Cf. Dan. 14.32 ff.

[20] Cf. Dan. 6.22, the artistic conflation of a separate incident.

[21] Cf. Judges 6.37. This theme of Gideon's fleece as providing refreshment appears also at Letter 44.7 (= ACW 36.242).

[22] Cf. Letter 32.5 (= ACW 36.139), where Paulinus' lines written for the baptistry at Primuliacum conclude with a similar phrase.

[23] This theme of the abrogation of position and wealth is of course important in the evolution of Paulinus' own Christian vocation. See ACW 35.15.

[24] Cf. 1 Cor. 6.12. The restitution of ecclesiastical property makes a date of 261 probable here; see Intro. p. 10.

[25] Perhaps with a play on the meaning of her name in Greek.

[26] There is unfortunately nothing surviving of the sources used by Paulinus for this verse life of Felix in the preceding poem and in this. It seems probable, from the wealth of circumstantial detail and from the structure, that Paulinus was able to draw upon a life similar in scale to Jerome's *Vita s. Pauli;* see Intro. p. 9.

## POEM 17

[1] Fabre *Chron.* 115 reasonably assigns this poem to the year 400, since it is addressed to Nicetas on his departure from Nola. Nicetas was at Nola twice within three years, for Poem 27.333 mentions his return "in the fourth year," which is 403 (see n. 1 on Poem 27). Poem 17 makes no allusion to an earlier visit, so this poem of farewell can be assigned to the year of his first stay. It is clear from Paulinus' Letter 29.14 that this is the same year as that in which Letter 29 was written, and this will be 400. On Nicetas, see ACW 36.326 n. 61.

This poem, written in the sapphic metre, is a *propemptikon*, a song of farewell to a departing friend, familiar to Paulinus from such Latin compositions as Tibullus 1.3; Propertius 1.8; Ovid, *Amores* 2.11; Horace, *Carm.* 1.3; and above all Statius, *Silvae* 3.2. The conventions of the genre, and Paulinus' adaptation of them for Christian purposes, are well set out in F. Jäger, *Das antike Propemptikon und das 17 Gedicht des Paulinus von Nola* (diss. Rosenheim 1913); see Intro. p. 15. There is a translation of this poem by Fantazzi (diss. Washington, D.C. 1956).

[2] Epirus, on the other side of the Adriatic from Italy, had been divided by Diocletian into two provinces, Vetus and Nova; cf. Th. Mommsen, *Provinces of the Roman Empire* 1.194 ff.

[3] This is a preliminary description in summary of the main areas on Nicetas' path. The correct topographical sequence would be Epirus, Thessalonica, Dacia.

[4] The phrase is reminiscent of Horace, *Carm.* 3.5.28, *Epist.* 1.10.27. Canusia (now Canosa) in Apulia was famous for its wool.

[5] The reading *merra* is supported by the Itala version of Exod. 15.23, a transliteration of the Hebrew.

[6] The tree with which Moses sweetened the waters of Mara is interpreted by the Fathers as a type of the Cross. Cf. Tertullian, *Adv. Jud.* 13; Paulinus, Letter 37.1 (= ACW 36.177).

[7] Cf. Exod. 10.22 ff.

[8] Cf. Isa. 40.3.

[9] Both are Calabrian towns, today Otranto and Lecce.

[10] Cf. Ps. 54.7.

[11] Sailyard and mast together form the cross. The image is a popular one in the Fathers; see Letter 23.29 and note thereon (= ACW 36.33 and 308 n. 182).

[12] As Fantazzi (diss. Washington, D.C. 1956) notes, the word *celeuma* can connote both the chant of oarsmen and a hymn of Christians. Paulinus exploits the ambivalence.

[13] I.e., Nicetas and his companions will sing the Psalms.

[14] Cf. Jonas 2.1 ff. Paulinus elsewhere, in Letter 49.10 (= ACW 36.268), depicts the incident as a type of the Resurrection.

[15] Cf. Eph. 6.17; also Letter 23.1 and 11 (= ACW 36.1 f. and 13).

[16] Cf. Tob. 5.5.

[17] Cf. Gen. 28.12 f.

[18] Cf. Gen. 32.28. For the mistaken interpretation of Israel as "seeing God," see Letter 5.7 and note thereon (= ACW 35.58 and 220 n. 21). Nicetas is the Greek for victor.

[19] Cf. John 8.12 and 9.39; Matt. 5.14.

[20] Paulinus employs the image similarly at Letter 23.30 (= ACW 36.33; see *ibid.* 308 n. 182).

[21] Paulinus envisages Nicetas as crossing the Adriatic to Dyrrhachium (Durazzo), going overland across Macedonia to Philippi, across Thrace and up the Euxine coast to Tomi, and back westward to Scupi (Skoplje). *Dardanus hospes* suggests a visit to Troy before proceeding to Tomi. But the names are hardly more than vague pointers; they have historical and literary associations for Paulinus' readers (Tomi was the place of Ovid's exile) rather than topographical precision.

[22] The Rhiphaei are a range of Russian mountains north of the Caucasus. Paulinus derives the epithet from Virgil, *Georg.* 4.518, and Lucan 4.118 to describe the northern wastes.

[23] Northern Thracians who lived around Mt. Haemus.

[24] Gold-mining was an established source of wealth in Dacia;

see F. Millar, ed., *The Roman Empire and its Neighbours* (London 1967) 227; Jones, LRE 1.838.

[25] Cf. Matt. 11.12; also Paulinus, Letter 25.5 (= ACW 36.75 f.).

[26] Abel is the type of Christ at Letter 12.2 (= ACW 35.106) and Letter 38.3 (= ACW 36.187).

[27] Cf. Matt. 25.21.

[28] Cf. 1 Pet. 2.5; also the comments of J. C. Plumpe, "Vivum saxum vivi lapides," *Traditio* 2 (1943) 1 ff.

[29] Dacia had never become urbanized, even before the evacuation by Rome in 271. See F. Millar, ed., *The Roman Empire and its Neighbours*, ch. 12; Jones, LRE 1.716.

[30] Cf. Matt. 25.21.

[31] On this concept of *caritas Christiana,* central to Paulinus' thought, see ACW 35.24; also above, Intro. p. 24.

[32] Throughout this section there are echoes of Poem 11.49 ff.

[33] Cf. Isa. 38.11, 32.14.

[34] Cf. Luke 16.24. For the importance of the Lazarus parable in Paulinus' Christianity, see ACW 35.240 n. 69.

[35] Cf. 2 Cor. 5.1.

[36] Cf. 2 Tim. 4.7.

## POEM 18

[1] This is the sixth *Natalicium,* written for January 14, 400; see Intro. pp. 6 f. After recounting Felix's life in the two preceding *Natalicia,* the sequence is here continued by demonstrating the saint's *Nachleben,* the veneration of his grave and the miracles attending it. There is a translation by R. Kalkman (diss. Washington, D.C. 1959).

[2] The address suggests that this poem was recited at Nola; see above, n. 5 on Poem 16.

[3] The whiteness of snow is a "holy sign," as symbolising the regeneration of baptism and the garments of the saints in heaven.

[4] Reading here *teneris* with the majority of the mss. against the *cineris* of Hartel. See S. Blomgren, *Eranos* 38 (1940) 63 f.

[5] For this as evidence that the poem was written as well as declaimed in January, see Fabre *Paulin* 359.

[6] See Poem 21.59 ff. for the custom of pouring oil on the tomb

of a saint and then scooping it out for use as a healing unguent.

[7] Cf. Luke 21.1 f.

[8] I retain the reading *concessus* from the best mss. against the conjecture of Hartel, *concessa est*. The *hic . . . istic* ("for my part . . . for your part") requires a second noun to balance *dignatio*.

[9] See Poems 15 and 16, the *Natalicia* for 398 and 399.

[10] Cf. 2 Macc. 12.44.

[11] There should be a stop in the text after *respicio hanc aliquando diem* (Hartel has a comma), and an exclamation mark after *casto . . . ab ore*. The thought involved in the last phrase is comparable with such phrases as *animam exspirare*, the notion of life passing away through the mouth.

[12] Cf. Virgil, *Aen.* 6.487.

[13] This is the district of Cimitile (about a mile from Nola) where the centre of devotion to Felix was established; see Goldschmidt ch. 4.

[14] Representing the seven choirs of angels.

[15] For the arrangement of buildings round the tomb of Felix, see Paulinus' Letter 32.10 (= ACW 36.144); also Poems 27 and 28.

[16] This and other narratives of miracles in Paulinus' poems are discussed by R. Argenio, *San Paolino da Nola, Cantore di miracoli* (Rome 1970).

[17] Cf. Virgil, *Aen.* 2.490.

[18] Cf. John 13.23.

[19] Retaining here *cui* ("for what purpose") of the mss. against Hartel's emendation *cute*. See Wiman, *Eranos* 32 (1934) 106, comparing Virgil, *Aen.* 4.323; Sulpicius Severus, *Vita s. Martini* 3.10—"This opening [of the prayer] with its Virgilian echoes . . . could not be in a more elevated style; Paulinus is for once showing some humour" (Green 28). Perhaps; but more probably this shows Paulinus once more writing for his sophisticated audience with the classical texture to which he knows they will respond.

[20] Reading here with several of the mss. *quos etiam manus una tenet* in preference to Hartel's *quos licet et manus una tenet*.

[21] With the return to the theme of the beginning of the poem (lines 25 ff.) Paulinus identifies himself with the rustic in the gift of praise.

## POEM 19

[1] This is the eleventh *Natalicium,* composed in January 405 and devoted to the theme of the power inherent in Felix's relics; see Intro. pp. 6 f. The translation of A. Kern (diss. Washington, D.C. 1963) is especially useful for its annotation on the ornamental cross. For further bibliography on this, see n. 77 below.

[2] On the theme of Christ as physician in patristic texts, cf. H. Arbesmann, "The Concept of *Christus medicus* in St. Augustine," *Traditio* 12 (1954) 1 ff.

[3] Cf. Matt. 11.30.

[4] With this statement should be compared the interesting remark of Paulinus in his Letter 29.13 (= ACW 36.116) written in the year 400: "For even Rome herself in the greater number of her population is the daughter of Sion rather than of Babylon." Elsewhere, in Letter 13.15 (= ACW 35.131 f.) written in 396, he seems less inclined to regard Rome as a Christian city, though in that passage he is criticising the senatorial class rather than the population at large. However, this period about 400 is an era of rapid Christianisation in the capital. See A. Cameron, *Claudian* (Oxford 1970) 365 f.; P. R. L. Brown, JRS 51 (1961) 1 ff.

[5] Numa as the legendary founder of Roman religion symbolised the pagan Roman beliefs. The books of the Sibyl (allegedly brought from Cumae to Rome in the reign of Tarquinius Superbus) were destroyed by fire in 83 B.C., but were replaced by a collection of oracular utterances gathered from overseas shrines. For a contemporary discussion of them, see Augustine, *De civ. Dei* 10.27 f.

[6] The Hebrew word expressing assent to a prayer would identify a Christian congregation. Paulinus doubtless thinks of the close of the doxology at the end of the Canon of the Mass; see Justin, *Apol.* 67.

[7] The Capitol at Rome was regarded as the symbol of her indestructibility. Cf. Virgil, *Aen.* 9.448; Horace, *Carm.* 3.30.8.

[8] Cf. Jerome, *In Gal.* II praef. (ML 61.512), from where Paulinus may have adapted the motif.

[9] This whole passage (lines 72–75) is Virgilian pastiche; cf. *Aen.* 9.341, 9.64, etc.

[10] Origen testifies that Andrew preached in Scythia; the apocryphal *Acts of St. Andrew* (3rd century?) depicted his imprison-

ment and martyrdom at Patras in Greece. The legend of this activity in Greece became popular in Italy (cf. *Ep.* 148 in the collection of Jerome's correspondence) when relics were sent there from Constantinople, where the putative remains had been transferred from Patras in 357. Cf. Paulinus, Poem 27.436, Letter 32.17 (= ACW 36.150 f.); Augustine, *De civ. Dei* 22.8; DACL 1.2.2031 ff.

[11] On the growth of this tradition, as old as Tertullian, that John was at Ephesus, see the texts at ML 61.513, including Eusebius, *Hist. eccl.* 3.35; and in general ODCC s.v. "John, St., Apostle," with bibliography.

[12] Matthew's burial place is claimed by many communities; the Hieronymian Martyrology and other authorities cite Parthia/ Persia (texts in ML 61.514).

[13] For this tradition, see the entry "Thomas, St., Apostle" in ODCC, with bibliography.

[14] Thaddaeus (or Jude the apostle) is called Lebbaeus in the Latin, as in some mss. of Matt. 10.3, Mark 3.18; cf. Isidore, *Etym.* 7.9.19. The popular tradition is that he was killed in Syria or in Persia (texts in ML 61.514), and it seems likely that Paulinus is following a popular etymology that connects Lebbaeus with Libya.

[15] The burial place is commonly given as Hieropolis in Phrygia; see ML 61.514.

[16] For the tradition that Titus was the first bishop of Crete, cf. Eusebius, *Hist. eccl.* 3.4.

[17] His relics were translated to Constantinople with those of Andrew in 357; see n. 10 above and ML 61.515.

[18] The tradition connecting Mark with Alexandria is found in Eusebius, *Hist. eccl.* 2.16, as well as in Jerome and the martyrologies.

[19] In the Egyptian religion the divinity Apis was worshipped in the form of an ox, and in Africa Hammon, venerated in the form of a ram, was equated with Jupiter; hence Mark expels both Apis and Jupiter Hammon.

[20] Jupiter was said to have been born in Crete (cf. Cicero, *De nat. deorum* 3.53, etc.), and his tomb was a tourist attraction (cf. Lucian, *De sacrif.*).

[21] Mount Ida in Phrygia (the scene of the worship of Cybele; cf. above all Catullus 63) was traditionally famed for its pines which made seaworthy ships. Here Paulinus evokes in particular

Virgil, *Aen.* 10.230: *nos sumus Idaeae sacro de vertice pinus*, where the spokeswoman is a nymph; she and her comrades have been transformed from Aeneas' boats of Idaean pine. Thus the point of Paulinus' phrase "virgin pines" is that the new nymphs now begotten by Mount Ida are Christian virgins. As so often, Paulinus writes for an audience of educated people orientated towards the Latin classics, and not merely for rustic listeners at Nola.

[22] Greece no longer consults Delphi, the example par excellence of the pagan oracular shrine; she treads underfoot Mount Olympus because it is the home of her pagan deities; and the journey upward to Mount Sion represents the ascent to Christianity. As Kern well comments, the "soft yoke" (cf. Matt. 11.30) on Mount Sion is the cross of Calvary.

[23] Diana, or Artemis, had a celebrated temple at Ephesus. She was the sister of Apollo, who had slain the snake Python near Delphi (cf. Ovid, *Met.* 1.434 ff.) and thus became the "Pythian" god. For Paul's expulsion of the "Python," cf. Acts 16.16 ff., where he drives out the evil spirit from a girl *habentem spiritum pythonem*.

[24] The identification of Joseph with Serapis is based on a fanciful etymology deriving Serapis from Σάρρας παῖς ("son of Sara"), an etymology put forward by, amongst others, Tertullian, *Ad Nat.* 2.8; Rufinus, *Hist. eccl.* 2.23; Firmicus Maternus, *De err. prof. relig.* 8 (= ACW 37.71). See the comments of C. A. Forbes in ACW 37.182 n. 265.

[25] Serapis is regularly represented (as in the famous bust in the Vatican) with a corn measure as crown. This symbolises his dominion in the lower world, for Serapis is the manifestation of Osiris in the world below. Since Rufinus mentions this also in the passage cited in the preceding note, he may well have influenced Paulinus' account here; cf. ACW 36.253 ff., 322.

[26] Cf. Gen. 41.25 ff.

[27] According to the Egyptian myth, Typhon, the principle of evil, tore Osiris to pieces, and Isis sought her husband to bury him. This journey was commemorated yearly in the Isiac ritual, conducted by priests whose heads were shaven. Pelusium, an Egyptian city at the mouth of the Nile, was a well-known centre of Isiac worship. The topic is also discussed at Poem 32.111 ff.; see the note on that passage.

[28] As Muratori (ML 61.520) observes, Paulinus in this state-

ment of the traditional Christian argument is very close to Firmicus Maternus, *De err. prof. relig.* 8 (= ACW 37.62 ff.), written over half a century before this poem.

[29] Osiris was the brother and husband of Isis, not her son as is here suggested. The confusion with Horus is already in Minucius Felix, *Octavius* 22.1 (Budé notation) (= ACW 39.88).

[30] *nomina.* For *nomina* meaning "persons," cf. Blaise 556, quoting also Paulinus' Letters 32.5 and 37.5.

[31] In this passage Paulinus' definition of the Trinity in relation to the *Filioque* issue is explicitly orthodox (*ex ipso* [i.e., *filio*] *simul unus cum patre verbi / spiritus*), as is also his passage at Poem 27.93 (*spiritum ab unigena sanctum < et > patre procedentem);* whereas in an earlier letter, 21.3 (dateable to 400 or 401; cf. ACW 35.253 n. 1), he is ambiguous on the *Filioque* issue, speaking there only of the Spirit's procession from the Father (cf. ACW 35.193 and 254 n. 11).—In the final sentence of the present passage (*nihil hic habet ulla / commune aut simile in rebus natura creatis*) I read *huic* for the *hic* of the mss. and Hartel.

[32] Though Paulinus may well have read the third-century martyr-bishop's treatises, especially *De catholicae ecclesiae unitate*, Cyprian's role as martyr may have been familiar through Jerome, *De vir. ill.* 67, and Prudentius, *Peristeph.* 13 (this last written five years before this poem).

[33] For the phrase, cf. Lucan 1.368.

[34] This is a reference to the martyrs of Utica. Augustine, *Enarr. in Ps.* 49.9, states that more than 153 martyrs were slaughtered there. Prudentius' *Peristeph.* 13.76 ff. (assigning the martyrdoms to the same year, 258, as Cyprian's death) is apparently the earliest extant work misinterpreting *Massa Candida* ("White Farm") as "white heap," and explaining that the heap was the martyrs' bones bleached by quicklime. Hence it is tempting to suggest that Prudentius has inspired this passage.

[35] Augustine is clearly in Paulinus' mind; perhaps also Optatus and Alypius.

[36] *Latium* here clearly means Italy (cf. Poem 14.57), for Ambrose had been born at Trier, and his ecclesiastical presence was wholly at Milan. He had died in 397, eight years before this poem was written.

[37] For the protomartyr of Spain, said to have suffered under Diocletian, cf. Augustine, *Serm.* 274 ff., and Prudentius, *Peri-*

*steph.* 5, which Paulinus may well have read. But in any case Paulinus' sojourn in Spain will have made St. Vincent a familiar figure to him.

[38] Martin, like Ambrose, died in 397. He was one of the formative influences on Paulinus. Cf. the edition by J. Fontaine of Sulpicius Severus, *Vita s. Martini* (SC 133–5, Paris 1967–9).

[39] Delphinus, bishop of Bordeaux, exercised great personal influence on Paulinus. He died about 400–404. Cf. ACW 35.4 and 36.357.

[40] Cf. Apoc. 20.2.

[41] I emend the *qui* of the mss. to *cui* and restore the reading *quibus* in line 161, where Hartel improbably proposes *quatit*. For discussion of the text here, see G. Wiman, "Till Paulinus Nolanus' Carmina," *Eranos* 32 (1934) 100.

[42] On this Euhemerist doctrine of the origin of divinities, see Fabre *Paulin* 85.

[43] The highly Neoplatonist flavour of this account of Satan's dominion should be noted. Compare for example Augustine's discussion at *De civ. Dei* 9.8, taken over from the Platonist Apuleius.

[44] Reading *ima* with Wiman, *Eranos* 32 (1934) 100.

[45] Reading *et* (with Muratori) for the *at* of the mss. and Hartel's *ut.*

[46] I.e., the *magna mater* Cybele; see n. 21 above, and n. 18 on Poem 32.

[47] Cf. Gal. 6.14.

[48] Cf. Phil. 3.19.

[49] The imminence of the Parousia, or Second Coming of Christ, is a frequent theme in early Christian literature; see, e.g., J. Chaine in DTC 11.2043 ff.

[50] Cf. 1 Pet. 5.8; John 21.17.

[51] Cf. 2 Cor. 6.2.

[52] As the legendary founder and principal deity of Babylon, Bel (a dialect version of Baal, likewise signifying "lord") is the polar antithesis of Christ.

[53] Referring to the imperial legislation of Christian emperors like Gratian and Theodosius forbidding pagan ritual.

[54] I.e., buried martyrs like Felix.

[55] The Greek cry of exultation was raised at Bacchic festivals; cf., e.g., Catullus 64.255 and Virgil, *Aen.* 7.389.

[56] *Sacerdos,* here translated as "presiding priest," could mean either priest or bishop. Paulinus makes it clear at Poem 16.229 ff. that Felix refused the popular request that he become bishop of Nola, because Quintus was his senior, but that Felix acted in many respects as bishop in all but name.–Paulinus refers to Felix as *sacerdos* also elsewhere; see Poems 14.90, 15.112, and also 21.158–164, where within a few lines Paulinus uses in succession *antistes (coronam antistitis), sacerdos (in sacerdotis stola),* and *presbyter (presbyter Felix dei).*

[57] I.e., relics.

[58] On Helena's discovery of the buried cross at Jerusalem, and its diffusion in relics, see Paulinus' dramatic account in Letter 31.3 ff. (= ACW 36.127 ff.). On the vexed question of dating, see G. E. Gingras, ACW 38.238 n. 382 and 255 n. 488.

[59] This refers to the discovery by Ambrose of the bones of Gervasius and Protasius, protomartyrs of Milan. In 386, following a "sixth sense," he dug in the church of Felix and Nabor and found two headless skeletons from which miraculous cures were claimed. They were translated to Ambrose's new basilica. Cf. Ambrose, *Ep.* 22; H. Leclercq, DACL 6.1232 ff.

[60] This was Justina, mother of Valentinian II; she had embraced Arianism. On this incident and its repercussions on Justina, see F. Homes-Dudden, *The Life and Times of St. Ambrose* 1 (Oxford 1935) 298 ff.

[61] When Constantine formally inaugurated the city of Constantinople in 330, he certainly attempted to create a Christian city in which pagan ritual was discouraged and copies of Scripture were distributed; see A. H. M. Jones, *Constantine and the Conversion of Europe* (London 1948) 236 ff. But Constantine died in 337, before the translation of the relics. See n. 62 below.

[62] For the translation of the remains of St. Andrew in 357, see nn. 10 and 17 above; for those of Timothy, see Jerome, *Ad Euseb. chron. anno 19 Constantii.* According to Eusebius, Timothy was the first bishop of Ephesus, from where his relics were translated to Constantinople in 356.

[63] Cf. Luke 16.24.

[64] Perhaps an echo of Propertius 2.13.58.

[65] For Paulinus' relics at Nola and Fundi, see Poem 27.400 ff., and Letters 31.1 and 32.11, 17 (= ACW 36.125, 145, 150).

[66] Not the new basilica at Fundi (cf. Letter 32.17 [= ACW

36.149 ff.]) but the fifth basilica at Nola, "an addition to the four basilicas" which contained "relics of apostles and martyrs" (Letter 32.10 [= ACW 36.144 f.]). It lay slightly north of the other four; see Goldschmidt's map of the excavations.

[67] The basilica was dedicated to Felix, but the relics make the apostles its guardians; hence its title of "The Apostles' Church."

[68] Reading *derigere* with the manuscript E and Wiman, *Eranos* 32 (1934) 109.

[69] This passage suggests that Paulinus is declaiming this poem to an audience at Nola; see also Intro. pp. 12 f. and n. 47 thereon.

[70] Cf. Poems 14.100, 18.35, 23.111; Leclercq, DACL 3.1.211, rendering *candelabra* as "girandoles."

[71] This is interesting evidence of the practical help lent by Paulinus to those seeking to renounce allegiance to the imperial army. Letters 25 and 35, which exhort a young friend to do likewise, are important documents in this area of the relationship between secular and Christian claims.

[72] Reading *vimine*, with Wiman, for the *limine/lumine* of the mss. and the *limite* of Hartel.

[73] Cf. Poem 28.15 with Goldschmidt's note; these were small chapels built over the graves. Cf. Leclercq in DACL s.v. *cella*.

[74] I.e., Rome.

[75] Muratori (ML 61.541) suggests that this Nuceria is in Picenum; it seems likelier that the Campanian Nuceria is meant.

[76] This will be Paul, Paulinus' predecessor in the see of Nola; see Letter 32.15 (= ACW 36.148) and ML 61.891.

[77] For what follows, cf. Muratori in ML 61.829 ff.; Hartel, "Zu den Gedichten des heiligen Paulinus von Nola," *Sitzungsb. der Akad. in Wien* (1895) 71 ff.; Wiman, *Eranos* 32 (1934) 112 ff.

[78] I.e., the *crux commissa* (T); see Muratori in ML 61.543 ff. and DACL 3.2.3061.

[79] I.e., the chi-rho symbol.

[80] This is the Greek letter tau (T). Note that at Letter 24.23 (= ACW 36.72) Paulinus likewise compares the cross to both the tau and a sailing vessel, there the ark.

[81] With Muratori I accept the reading of manuscript E: *tau idem stylus ipse brevi retro acumine ductus*.

[82] Cf. Phil. 2.9.

⁸³ That is to say, the Greek letters which spell Christ in Greek can all be traced in the chi-rho symbol.

⁸⁴ For the history of the monogram and its various forms, see Leclercq in DACL 3.1.1481 ff. s.v. "chrisme," with bibliography.

⁸⁵ For the thought, cf. Cyril of Jerusalem, *Catechesis* 13.28 (= MG 33.805); also, Firmicus Maternus, *De err. prof. relig.* 27.3 (= ACW 37.104 f.).

⁸⁶ Cf. Col. 3.11.

⁸⁷ Cf. Apoc. 22.13.

⁸⁸ After general descriptions of the two kinds of conventional representations of the cross, Paulinus here turns to the Nola cross which incorporates both. It seems clear from what follows that Wiman's reconstruction, depicted in *Eranos* 32 (1934) 118 fig. 2, is the correct one.

⁸⁹ Reading, with Kern, *examine* for the *stamine* of the mss. and Hartel.

⁹⁰ Cf. Venantius Fortunatus 2.1.1 (*crux benedicta nitet. . .* ).

⁹¹ In line 706, I read *specie*, with manuscript E, against the *speciem* of A and D and Hartel.

⁹² I retain *fidem* against Hartel's *fide*.

## POEM 20

¹ This is the twelfth of the annual *Natalicia*, and can therefore be dated to January 406; see Intro. pp. 6 f.

² This distinction between truthful history and fictitious poetry is pervasive throughout the classical period; see R. Reitzenstein, *Hellenistische Wundererzählungen*² (Darmstadt 1963) ch. 1. The declaration of truth in regard to the miraculous story should be noted.

³ On the symbolism of the body as a lyre on which God's praises are played, see Witke, *Numen litterarum* 90 f., citing the use of the metaphor in other authors (Montanus, Epiphanius, etc.). See also Green 89.

⁴ It is clear, therefore, that the theme was not planned long before, as was the case with the earlier *Natalicia;* see Intro. pp. 8 f.

⁵ At Poem 21.705 ff. Paulinus describes Abella, putting it at six miles from Nola. It lay to the northeast in the mountains.

⁶ These are the participants of the alms-feast promised as fulfil-

ment of the vow; the feast takes place in the basilica, and it is worth comparing a similar scene in St. Peter's at Rome, described by Paulinus at Letter 13.11 (= ACW 35.126). See in general for this custom F. Homes-Dudden, *The Life and Times of St. Ambrose* 1 (Oxford 1935) 51.

7 For such practices in Christian shrines, see John Chrysostom, *Hom. 30 in 2 Cor.* (MG 61.605); Prudentius, *Peristeph.* 2.519 ff.

8 Cf. Acts 3.1 ff.

9 Cf. Acts 3.2.

10 One thinks of the quip of St. Jerome: *Ubi medici, ibi frequenter interitus.* For other such criticisms, see Muratori's note at ML 61.560.

11 Modern Benevento. Paulinus envisages the farm as beyond the town from the vantage point of Nola, i.e., east of Beneventum.

12 Paulinus advances epic explanations for the miracle, suggesting that the pig was wrapped in a cloud like Venus, or borne on the wind like Mercury. It is difficult to believe that he is wholly serious here; his fancy leads him to such hyperbole as he develops the curious story.

13 I read *subito*, with Muratori, for the *subita* of the mss. and Hartel.

14 I.e., as far away as the farm east of Beneventum in the previous anecdote.

15 Cf. 1 Cor. 9.9.

16 There is an enlightening discussion of this miracle-narrative by J. Doignon, "Un récit de miracle dans les *Carmina* de Paulin de Nole; poétique virgilienne et leçon apologétique," *Rev. d'hist. de la spiritualité* 48 (1972) 129 ff. Doignon well demonstrates how Paulinus follows a tradition of animal-miracles, citing the taming of the infuriated camel in Jerome's *Vita Hilarionis* (ML 23.40) and the repentant wolf which returned to apologise for stealing the hermit's food in Sulpicius Severus' *Dialogues* 1.14 (CSEL 1.166 f.). But the language in Paulinus is Virgilian and elevated; Doignon's conception of Paulinus' purpose closely accords with my (independent) comments in the Intro. pp. 12 f.


POEM 21

1 This is *Natalicium* 13, composed for Felix's feast in January 407; the initial allusion to the great battle of the preceding year

establishes the date (see next note). This poem is of particular importance and interest for its account of Paulinus' early career at lines 365 ff., and for the information it provides on the members of the community at Nola at lines 60 ff.

² In August 406 the general Stilicho won a great victory over the Ostrogoths at Faesulae (Fiesole). See Jones, LRE 1.184.

³ Evoking Virgil, *Georg.* 1.413.

⁴ Radagaesus was captured and subsequently killed. Cf. Orosius 7.37; Augustine, *De civ. Dei* 5.23.

⁵ Paulinus refers here to the western Augustus Honorius, who was emperor from 395 to 423, and was at this time in his middle twenties. He had married Stilicho's daughter Maria, a wedding commemorated by Claudian's tenth poem.

⁶ Paulinus uses dactylic hexameters in lines 1-104, iambic trimeters in 105-271, elegiac couplets in 272-343, and dactylic hexameters in 344-858. The other *Natalicia* confine themselves to hexameters only.

⁷ Turcius (or Tureius) Apronianus, husband of Avita and father of Eunomia (see line 210 below and Palladius, *Hist. Laus.* 41 [= ACW 34.119]), was still a pagan in 399 but became a Christian under the influence of the elder Melania and Rufinus. See *Hist. Laus.* 54 (= ACW 34.135).

⁸ "Sverius" is Pinian, on whom see n. 27 below. Severus, the *cognomen* of Pinian, will not fit into the metre here, and Sverius seems to be an adaptation of the Greek form Sevēros.

⁹ Cf. Philem. 1.2. Philemon's sister is in fact called Appia in the Latin Vulgate, and Apphia in the Greek.

¹⁰ See n. 7 above.

¹¹ Evoking Virgil, *Aen.* 7.484.

¹² In fact a second cousin, the younger Melania being the daughter of Caeonia Albina and Valerius Publicola son of the elder Melania. The elder Melania and Eunomia's mother Avita were sisters. See ACW 36.324 nn. 35 and 36; F. X. Murphy, "Melania, a biographical note," *Traditio* 5 (1947) 59 ff.

¹³ The fleece visited by the rain (Ps. 71.6; cf. Judges 6.36 ff.) is the type of the Virgin infused by the Holy Spirit (cf. Letter 19.3 [= ACW 35.181]) and hence symbolises virginity.

¹⁴ The phrase is often employed by Paulinus to describe the monastery at Nola.

¹⁵ The iambic trimeters commence here.

[16] Cf. Tob. 3.1.

[17] Cf. Eccli. 11.30.

[18] I.e., the wheel of Fortune, as at Cicero *Pis.* 22, Tibullus 1.5.70, etc.

[19] Cf. Ps. 25.11 f., 26.11.

[20] Cf. 2 Tim. 4.7 f.

[21] See Intro. p. 10.

[22] See above, n. 3 on Poem 12.

[23] *sed addens et coronam antistitis.* The *antistitis* could be translated "of bishop," but Felix did not become bishop. See Poem 16.229 ff., and also n. 56 on Poem 19.

[24] Cf. Job. 3.3 ff.

[25] Indicating that this poem was recited at Nola.

[26] See n. 7 above.

[27] The basic sources for the career of Pinian are the *Vita s. Melaniae* (see D. Gorce's excellent edition in SC 90, Paris 1962) and Palladius' *Historia Lausiaca* (trans. and annot. by R. T. Meyer in ACW 34). Valerius Pinianus was the son of Valerius Severus, *praefectus urbis* in 382, or of Valerius Pinianus Severus, prefect in 386 (cf. *Hist. Laus.* 61 [= ACW 34.142]). He married the younger Melania in 397 or 398 when he was 17 and she 14, and they had two children who died in infancy. About 403 they embraced religious life. Pinian owned estates in Campania (cf. *Vita S. Melaniae* 11), a fact which attracted him to Nola. They sold their property in Italy and Spain, and in or about 408 sailed to Sicily en route to Palestine.

[28] P. Valerius Publicola; cf. Livy 2.2.11 ff.

[29] As often in Paulinus, "mystical" (*mysticus*) here bears the sense of "typological." The qualities of the first Valerius are a model or type of those of his successors.

[30] Pinian possessed properties in Spain, Italy, Sicily, Africa and Britain (cf. *Vita s. Melaniae* 11; Palladius, *Hist. Laus.* 61 [= ACW 34.143]), so that he would have dependants in these countries.

[31] The elegiacs begin here.

[32] Albina was the mother of the younger Melania (see n. 12 above); her husband Valerius Publicola had recently died. Cf. Letter 45.2 f. and nn. 10 and 11 thereon (= ACW 36.245 ff. and 353). Therasia, Paulinus' wife, was still alive in 408. Cf. Letter 45.1 (= ACW 36.244).

[33] On Avita, wife of Apronianus, mother of Eunomia and sister of the elder Melania, see n. 7 above.

[34] See nn. 7 and 12 above.

[35] See n. 7 above.

[36] I.e., Pinian.

[37] Asterius was the son of Apronianus and Avita, and brother of Eunomia. There is a play on the name Asterius, which literally means "starry."

[38] Cf. 1 Kings 2.21 ff.

[39] See n. 37.

[40] I.e., baptism.

[41] See above, n. 3 on Poem 20.

[42] Aemilius was probably bishop of the neighbouring Beneventum. The local bishops had given Paulinus support from his arrival (cf. Letter 5.14 [= ACW 35.63]). Aemilius appears prominently in Poem 25; see n. 49 on that poem.

[43] Cf. Ps. 32.2.

[44] The hexameters are resumed here.

[45] Cf. Virgil, *Georg.* 2.43, *Aen.* 6.625; Ovid, *Met.* 8.553.

[46] Cf. Virgil, *Aen.* 4.357.

[47] Cf. Virgil, *Georg.* 4.286.

[48] This section (lines 365–487) is the primary source for the detail of Paulinus' career; cf. Fabre *Paulin* 9 ff.

[49] See above, n. 2 on Poem 13, for the evidence that Paulinus' first sojourn in Campania ended in 381–3, when he was in his twenties; he probably left Aquitania for Rome in 378. See Intro. p. 2.

[50] Here Paulinus refers not to his consulship but to his appointment as governor of Campania by Gratian. On the office, see Jones, LRE 1.161; on Paulinus' tenure of it, Fabre *Paulin* 23.

[51] I.e., "hazardous" for his soul.

[52] This is interesting evidence of the Christianising of the solemn Roman ceremony of *depositio barbae*, mentioned by Juvenal 3.186, Suetonius, *Nero* 12, and others; see Fabre *Paulin* 15 n. 2; ML 61.587.

[53] Paulinus here indicates that about 380 he had built a hospice for the poor, and that after 395 he built a second story on it for the community and for guests, the ground floor continuing as a hospice. Cf. Letter 29.13 (= ACW 36.115), where the translation should read: "We have a cottage raised off the ground. The

upper story of it is supported by a portico with guest-rooms, and extends quite a distance." See Goldschmidt 175.

⁵⁴ As governor of Campania he was attended by six lictors each bearing the fasces, the bundle of rods and axe symbolising the higher magistrate's power to scourge and execute.

⁵⁵ Though the date cannot be established with certainty, it was during 381–3 (see above, n. 2 on Poem 13) that Paulinus left Campania, and Anicius Auchenius Bassus probably succeeded him as governor. See Fabre *Paulin* 26.

⁵⁶ Presumably in 383.

⁵⁷ Perhaps at Complutum (Alcala de Henares in New Castille); see Poem 31.605 ff. and n. 62 thereon.

⁵⁸ After his marriage to Therasia in Spain, the couple returned to Aquitania and lived on Paulinus' estates till 389. See above, n. 3 on Poem 10.

⁵⁹ Punning, as elsewhere, on the meaning of Felix's name.

⁶⁰ We have no other evidence for the murder except a cryptic reference at Letter 5.4, which suggests that Paulinus himself was accused. I have outlined the various theories in ACW 35.220, suggesting there that Paulinus was being accused by the new regime of Maximus to provide a pretext for the seizure of his property.

⁶¹ The word used here, *sector*, means a purchaser of goods confiscated by the state; see n. 60 above.

⁶² On the obscurity of the Latin here, see Fabre *Paulin* 35. *Prodita commercia* I take to refer to Paulinus' spiritual "business," famed throughout the western empire; cf. Ambrose *Ep.* 58.

⁶³ For this pervasive theme in the Letters, see ACW 35.24 f. with references there.

⁶⁴ Cf. Virgil *Aen.* 1.664.

⁶⁵ Referring to Paulinus' and Therasia's decision to live as brother and sister; cf. ML 61.589.

⁶⁶ On the five basilicas at Nola, see Letter 32.10 (= ACW 36.144 ff.); Goldschmidt 94 ff.

⁶⁷ The primary sense of "residing more securely" is clearly with reference to eternal salvation, as the following sentence shows, but there may also be a hint of the increasing hazards from the barbarians; see n. 2 above.

⁶⁸ I read *sequentum* with the mss. (Hartel adopts the reading

*segmentum* of Gitlbauer), and interpret it with reference to the need to provide for one's descendants.

[69] So Jerome, in his *Ep.* 58.2, had written to Paulinus that freed from his possessions, *levior scandis scalam Jacob.*

[70] Cf. 1 Cor. 15.49.

[71] Cf. Isa. 66.24; Mark 9.47 f.

[72] Cf. Poem 15.76 ff. and 102 ff.

[73] Reading *latet* (Zechmeister).

[74] Cf. Poem 16.284 ff.

[75] Cf. Matt. 7.13.

[76] Cf. Matt. 7.14.

[77] Cf. Exod. 19.20 ff.

[78] For the importance of this phrase *per tot saecula* in establishing the era of Felix, see Intro. pp. 9 f.

[79] See Poems 27 and 28; also Intro. p. 11.

[80] For this custom of enclosing with railings the tombs of the saints, see the texts collected at ML 61.593.

[81] The tombs were frequently lined on top in this way with gold or silver; see ML 61.593.

[82] These *fenestellae* were also a regular feature, allowing the faithful to touch the saint's coffin, or, as here, to pour oil on the coffin and to withdraw it after it had made contact with the saint so that it could be applied to sick persons or injured limbs. See Poem 18.38 f. and ML 61.594.

[83] This was Paul, the predecessor of Paulinus in the see of Nola; see Letter 32.15 and n. 23 thereon (= ACW 36.148 and 330).

[84] Cf. John 20.27.

[85] For Paulinus' preoccupation with the problems in 403, see Poem 27.463 ff.

[86] Nola.

[87] Cf. 1 Cor. 10.4.

[88] A poetic description of the aqueduct, an account of which follows in the ensuing lines.

[89] See Poem 20.68 and n. 5 thereon.

[90] For *calices* = pipes, cf. Frontinus, *Aquaed.* 34; but at line 750 below it may mean "cistern."

[91] Reading *laeta* with the mss. for Hartel's *tecta.*

[92] One imagines that a public meeting, called to discuss the proposal to share the city's water with the settlement at Cimitile,

broke up in disorder and with a rejection. Later this decision was reversed.

⁹³ I take *felicibus* to have this punning sense here.

⁹⁴ See n. 27 above.

## POEM 22

¹ This poem is addressed to Jovius, Paulinus' intellectual friend in Gaul to whom he addressed Letter 16 (= ACW 35.151 ff.); see Fabre *Paulin* 171 ff. There are several echoes of the letter in the poem (see nn. 2, 5, 9, 19, 23 below), which suggests that the poem was written about the same time. Letter 16 was written a few years after Paulinus went to Nola, and Fabre's guess of an approximate date of A.D. 400 will not be far off the mark. This poem is a *protreptikon*, a work of exhortation or instruction like Paulinus' Letter 8 to Licentius (= ACW 35.76 ff.). See Green 38 f.

² In Letter 16, Paulinus attempts to draw Jovius away from his enthusiasm for Greek and Roman philosophy and literature towards the study of the Scriptures; see especially Letter 16.6 (= ACW 35.157 f.). Such a change of direction would affect Jovius' writing as well as his reading.

³ The phraseology, with its incorporation of well-known Virgilian quotations (*Aen.* 7.338, 7.44), is designedly classical to appeal to the classicist.

⁴ See above, n. 5 on Poem 15.

⁵ Compare the criticism of Epicureanism in Letter 16.2 and nn. 7 and 8 thereon (= ACW 35.153 and 245).

⁶ Cf. Gen. 1.1 ff.

⁷ These are the classical myths explaining the provenance of mankind. For Deucalion and Pyrrha, who after the deluge threw behind them stones which were animated into human beings, see Ovid, *Met.* 1.395 ff.; for Prometheus' forming of men from clay in the Golden Age, see Ovid, *Met.* 1.82 ff., Hyginus, *Fab.* 54, etc.

⁸ I read *quem* at line 46 for the *quam* of the mss. and Hartel.

⁹ See Letter 16.2 ff. for Jovius' inclination towards assent to Stoic fate rather than to the doctrine of original sin described here.

¹⁰ Cf. John 1.1 ff.

[11] Cf. Phil. 2.11.

[12] Cf. Gal. 5.16 ff.

[13] Cf. Eph. 6.13–17.

[14] Cf. Exod. 13.17 ff.

[15] Cf. Exod. 14.28. But Pharaoh was not drowned there; see above, n. 16 on Poem 16.

[16] Cf. Exod. 14.19 ff.

[17] I punctuate with a stop after *regens* in line 90, and without Hartel's marks of parenthesis in lines 90 and 93.

[18] I punctuate in lines 96 f.: *et tamen illa (dei gravis hostibus ira superbis)* / *permixtos.* . . .

[19] At Letter 16.2 Paulinus indicates that Jovius had in fact expressed this opinion.

[20] Cf. Jon. 1.7 ff. Paulinus at Letter 49.10 (= ACW 36.268, where see also 360 n. 57) interprets the event as prefiguring the Resurrection.

[21] Cf. Jon. 3.1 ff.

[22] Ezechias; cf. Isa. 38.1 ff.

[23] Plato's account of the myth of Er (*Rep.* 617b) is criticised also in Letter 16.4 (= ACW 35.155, where see also 245 f. nn. 15 and 16).

[24] Aratus of Soli in Cilicia (flor. c. 270 B.C.) wrote a treatise in verse on the stars (*Phaenomena*) with a supplement on weather-signs (*Diosemeiai*) which was popular in classical Rome. Cicero and Ovid translated it, and Virgil used it for his *Georgics*.

[25] The Egyptian Manethon, high priest at Heliopolis in the third century B.C., was famed chiefly for his history of Egypt. The Greek poem called *Apotelesmatika*, an account of the influence of the stars on human destiny which is in Paulinus' mind here, is a much later work wrongly attributed to him.

[26] Cf. Isa, 38.8. I read *iussi* in line 130 with ms. N against Hartel's *iussis*.

[27] Cf. Jos. 10.12 f.

[28] Cf. Matt. 10.29.

[29] Cf. Luke 8.24; Matt. 14.25, 4.24; Luke 7.15; John 11.39 and 44.

[30] *Tonans*, commonly found as epithet of Jupiter in classical poetry, is used by Prudentius for the Christian God (see, e.g., *Cathem.* 6.81, *Apoth.* 171), but only here by Paulinus. This sug-

gests a deliberate use of the word for the recipient who is a poet in the classical tradition.

[31] Cf. Virgil, *Ecl.* 5.45. The evocation is again aimed at Jovius.

[32] This is the sole indication we possess that Jovius was a relative of Paulinus.

## POEM 23

[1] This is *Natalicium* 7, written for the feast of Felix on January 14, 401. See Intro. pp. 6 f.

[2] Paulinus distinguishes this bird from the swallow, so it is perhaps the swift.

[3] Evoking Virgil, *Georg.* 3.338.

[4] Hartel's *fronte* in line 29 is a misprint for *fronde* as at ML 61.608.

[5] The nightingale. See the texts in D'Arcy Thompson, *A Glossary of Greek Birds* (London 1936) 16 ff., including Pliny's account of the nightingale's varying song (*N.H.* 10.29.43).

[6] For the meaning of *cancelli*, see Goldschmidt 169. For this custom of bringing a possessed man into contact with the martyr's tomb, cf. Prudentius, *Peristeph.* 1.100 ff.

[7] In his *Dialogues* (usually dated 403/4; see Fontaine, *Vie de s. Martin* 1 [SC 133] 38 n. 1), Sulpicius Severus tells us that Martin often exorcised devils from victims who were turned upside down, *nec defluerent tamen vestes super faciem, ne verecundiam faceret nudata pars corporum* (*Dial.* 3.6.4 [CSEL 1.204]). This poem predates that work.

[8] We know from Letters 16.1 and 27.1 (= ACW 35.151 and 36.89) that Theridius was a native of Gaul who acted as courier for Paulinus to Jovius and Sulpicius Severus.

[9] This line is cryptic until the nature of Felix's healing is explained.

[10] This account of the celebration of the liturgy is addressed to the congregation, and so describes the participation not only of the community but also of the crowds visiting the shrine. The incident now recorded took place on Felix's feast (see lines 203 f.), and the vigil of the feast is here described.

[11] This disquisition on the chemical phenomenon of ignited oil floating on water is a long-winded irrelevance unfortunately inserted at the dramatic moment of the story.

[12] This line (179) appears in only one of the mss.; the curious content makes its authenticity dubious.

[13] Of the ancient accounts of the components of the eye, see especially Pliny, *N.H.* 11.37.139 ff. Like the earlier disquisition on the lamp, the description of the components of the eye strikes an unfortunately academic note and detracts from the drama of the story.

[14] Compare Martial 5.13.1 for this form of sport favoured by Roman youths.

[15] I punctuate with a stop after *esse* in line 238, and a comma after *tuum* in line 239.

[16] See n. 8 above. This passage demonstrates that Theridius had travelled from Gaul to be with Paulinus at Nola.

[17] I punctuate in 260: *ex oculo cadit; absque oculo tantum. . . .*

[18] Cf. John 9.1.

[19] Cf. Ps. 90.6.

[20] I.e., Theridius' sight; but there is a play on *lumen . . . lumen* which I attempt to reproduce in this way.

## POEM 24

[1] This long verse epistle of 942 iambics (trimeters alternating with dimeters) divides into two parts, the narrative of the sea adventure of Martinianus, and an instruction to Cytherius and his wife on the proper formation of their son, an aspirant to the priesthood; on the theme which unites the two parts, see Intro. pp. 25 f. Though it is impossible to establish a definite date for this poem, Fabre rightly notes that the disquisition on Samson (lines 535 ff.) is very close in treatment and phraseology to that in Letter 23 (see the tabulated comparison in Fabre *Chron.* 120; I draw attention to these correspondences in the following notes). Clearly one account has inspired the other. Letter 23 was probably written in 400 (see ACW 36.301 n. 1), and this poem must have been composed about that time.

[2] This poem gives us the sole information we possess about Cytherius. He is an Aquitanian of noble family, distinguished as public figure and litterateur (see lines 481 f.), who has entrusted his son to Sulpicius Severus' monastic regime at Primuliacum (see line 715).

[3] This messenger is known to us only from this poem.

[4] Cf. 2 Cor. 3.2.

[5] Ps. 49.14.

[6] Narbonne in southern France.

[7] Merchantships towed small boats astern in anticipation of an emergency like that described; see C. Torr, *Ancient Ships* (Cambridge 1895), and ACW 36.358 n. 7.

[8] *schisma* is here used in a general sense to embrace heresy also; the phrase "malevolent Jews and those guilty of arrogant disunion" is an inclusive one. At Letter 21.4 (= ACW 35.193 f.), like this poem dateable to 400–401, Paulinus lists a catalogue of more notable Christological heresies.

[9] I punctuate with a semicolon after line 136, and a comma after line 137.

[10] Cf. Apoc. 7.2 ff.

[11] Cf. Jon. 1.5.

[12] Cf. Gen. 39.12.

[13] Cf. Jon. 1.17. There is a similar description at Letter 49.10 (= ACW 36.268).

[14] Cf. Matt. 12.40, and Letter 49.10 (= ACW 36.268, where see also 360 n. 57, in which I quote Jerome's *In Ionam prol.* as a parallel description of Jonas in the whale as symbol of Christ's three days in the tomb).

[15] Cf. Jon. 2.3.

[16] Reading *credit* with Zechmeister.

[17] Cf. Acts 27.13 ff.

[18] Marseilles, which was a colony founded from Phocaea in Greece, must naturally as the main port of southern Gaul and a Greek-speaking area have been an early centre of Christian belief. Shortly after this time at which Paulinus writes, John Cassian set up two monasteries there (c. 415); and about the same time another monastic centre was rising at Lérins, along the coast off Cannes (see Letter 51 [= ACW 36.293 ff.]).

[19] The word here, *fraternitas*, implies a monastic community; see ML 61.918.

[20] Cf. Luke 21.2.

[21] Teucer on his return to the Greek island of Salamis after the Trojan war was exiled, and wandered to Cyprus where he founded a new Salamis.

[22] Benedict in his Rule describes such men as *Gyrovagi, qui tota vita sua per diversorum cellas hospitantur semper vagi et*

*nunquam stabiles.* Helen Waddell's *The Wandering Scholars,* ch. 8, is an amusing survey of such behaviour.

[23] I read in line 336 *aliisque* with one of the two mss., O (B has *aliique*); Hartel's *aliosque se falli* I cannot translate.

[24] There is a lot of gentle humour in this poem, much of it achieved by wordplay lost in the translation. Here, for example, *iactum,* which I render "hazard," suggests both the throwing of dice and tossing on the sea; and *aestum* suggests both the heat of sweating and the swell of the sea.

[25] Centumcellae, the modern Civita Vecchia, was 35 miles from Rome along the Via Aurelia, and had an artificial harbour constructed by the emperor Trajan (cf. Pliny. *Ep.* 6.31.15–17).

[26] This is the port at Ostia, where the emperor Claudius had built an island and set a lighthouse on it modelled on the Pharos at Alexandria. See Suetonius, *Claud.* 20.3; Dio Cassius, 60.11.4; R. Meiggs, *Roman Ostia* (Oxford 1960) 154 ff.

[27] I read in line 375: *patriam fruentes in vicem* (Hartel: *invicem*).

[28] On Theridius, see Poem 23.106 and n. 7 thereon. This comment shows that he had a residence in Rome which he had left to join the community at Nola.

[29] We have no further knowledge of this Paulinus.

[30] The Via Appia was first laid in 312 B.C. by the censor Appius Claudius to link Rome with Capua; later it was extended to Brundisium.

[31] This paragraph makes it clear that Martinianus had not previously been known to Paulinus.

[32] Cf. Ps. 118.103, 18.10.

[33] Cf. Matt. 12.33.

[34] Cf. Eccli. 13.21.

[35] Cf. Eccli. 27.10.

[36] Cf. 1 Cor. 1.27.

[37] Cf. John 12.32.

[38] Cf. Rom. 11.32. I read in line 468 *medeatur* for the *mediatur* of O and Hartel.

[39] Cf. Phil. 2.9.

[40] In Letter 25.3 (written like this poem about 400; cf. ACW 36.316 n. 1) Paulinus again signals the Christianity of the western emperor Honorius and his predecessor Theodosius who had died in 395: "Caesar himself is now keen to be Christ's servant. . . ."

[41] Cf. Matt. 5.3.

[42] Cf. Luke 16.22 ff.

[43] Cf. Ps. 91.14, 134.2, etc.

[44] I.e., Abraham; cf. Gen. 22. Paulinus treats the Abraham-Isaac theme in Letter 29.9, probably written in 400 like this poem (cf. ACW 36.323 n. 1).

[45] Ps. 70.6.

[46] Ps. 111.2.

[47] Ps. 131.11.

[48] Cf. 1 Kings 11.

[49] The *ephod* connotes not only the High Priest's robe as described at Exod. 28.6 ff., but also the plain linen garment of priests; Anna made one each year for Samuel (cf. 1 Kings 2.19).

[50] Cf. Ps. 44.10 and 14. The theme of the Psalm, a royal wedding, is usually interpreted allegorically as the marriage between Christ and the Church. By wearing "the queen's garment," the boy commits himself to Christ.

[51] I.e., "a person apart"; cf. Num. 6.5.

[52] Cf. Judges 16.17 ff., 14.5 ff. There is an extended discussion of the symbolism of the passage in Letter 23.10 f. (= ACW 36.12 f.).

[53] Delilah; cf. Judges 16.4 ff.

[54] Cf. Letter 23.11.

[55] Cf. Letter 23.11, 14, 17 f.

[56] Amalek was the grandson of Esau and putative founder of the Amalekites, who were the continuing enemy of the Israelites (cf. Exod. 17.8 ff., Deut. 25.17 ff., Judges 6.3) and later kept in subjection by them (cf. 2 Kings 8.12). Paulinus here uses Amalek as the symbol of a spiritual enemy.

[57] Cf. 1 Kings 17.50.

[58] Compare the discussion at Letter 12.7 (= ACW 35.111 f.).

[59] The ass was regarded by the ancients as the least intelligent and most lusting of animals; see, e.g., Plutarch, *De Iside* 371C. Apuleius' *The Golden Ass* is a fable of the man who by putting off his ass-shape is able to attain true spiritual stature as a human being. Jerome in his life of St. Hilary depicts the saint likewise addressing his body as *asellus*.

[60] Cf. 2 Cor. 4.16, 12.10.

[61] Ps. 90.7.

[62] Cf. 1 Cor. 10.11.

[63] Apoc. 21.4 f.

[64] 2 Cor. 6.2.

[65] Cant. 2.11 f.

[66] 1 Cor. 5.7 f.

[67] Cf. Luke 17.21.

[68] Cf. Matt. 27.51; 2 Cor. 3.6.

[69] Cf. 2 Cor. 3.15 f.

[70] Cf. Ps. 80.17.

[71] Cf. Ps. 91.13.

[72] Cf. Ps. 127.3.

[73] Cf. Gen. 2.22.

[74] The reference is to Joseph; cf. Gen. 41.46 ff., 42.3 ff.

[75] Bethlehem means "house of bread"; it was at Bethlehem that David was anointed by Samuel (1 Kings 16.4 ff.).

[76] The reference is to Potiphar, *eunuchus Pharaonis* (Gen. 39.1); as often in the Old Testament, the reference is to the function of chamberlain rather than to physionomy as Paulinus suggests.

[77] This is Sulpicius Severus, the former intimate of Paulinus who had founded a monastery at Primuliacum and was the author of the *Vita Martini*. For further detail, see the Introduction to J. Fontaine's fine edition (SC 133, Paris 1967), and ACW 35.3 f.

[78] Matt. 19.12.

[79] Cf. Gen. 39.7 ff.

[80] Cf. Gen. 39.12.

[81] Cf. Gen. 39.20.

[82] Cf. Hos. 2.6.

[83] Cf. James 4.6.

[84] Cf. Gen. 39.22.

[85] Cf. Gen. 40.8.

[86] Cf. Gen. 41.12.

[87] Cf. Gen. 41.40.

[88] Cf. Gen. 41.42.

[89] Cf. Matt. 11.30.

[90] Cf. Gen. 41.42 f.

[91] Cf. Ps. 67.17.

[92] Cf. Ps. 36.27.

[93] The city of Noph or Memphis, a little south of Cairo, was

familiar to Paulinus from both classical and biblical sources, though it does not appear in the account of Joseph in Genesis.

[94] Cf. Gen. 42.1 ff.

[95] This description of how the eagle after moulting regains its plumage and strength echoes Ps. 102.5 and Isa. 40.31. It is a favourite theme of Ambrose; see nn. 96 and 97 below.

[96] Cf. *Aen.* 1.301; Ambrose, *Ep.* 29.17: *renovatis alarum remigiis.*

[97] The symbolism is a commonplace in the Fathers; cf. e.g., Ambrose *De virg.* 18.115. See ML 61.920 and H. Rahner, *Greek Myths and Christian Mystery* (London 1962) 55 f.

[98] I suspect that the clue to this obscure symbolism is in Poem 19.604 ff., where the description of the cross is followed by a long account of the chi-rho monogram which was enclosed in a circular frame; see nn. 84 and 88 on Poem 19.

[99] *pullus gratiarum* is a reminiscence of Prov. 5.19, a literal translation of the Greek πῶλος σῶν χαρίτων, which is rendered in the Latin Vulgate as *gratissimus hinnulus.* Paulinus has adapted the phrase to his bird-imagery, though in the Scriptures it refers to the young of a quadruped.

[100] For Christ as *vertex,* cf. Poem 17.140.

[101] Cf. Ps. 90.6.

[102] John 12.31.

[103] Cf. Rom. 8.29.

## POEM 25

[1] This poem is an *epithalamion* or marriage song (for the genre, see Intro. p. 13) written to celebrate the wedding of Julian of Eclanum and Titia. This is the Julian who about 416 became bishop at Eclanum, and was in 417 banished from his see for refusing to subscribe to Pope Zosimus' condemnation of Pelagianism. On these later events, see now Peter Brown, *Augustine of Hippo* (London 1967) ch. 32. For Julian's earlier career, see A. Brückner, *Julian von Eclanum, sein Leben und seine Lehre* (Leipzig 1897); J. Bouma, *Het Epithalamium van Paulinus van Nola* (Amsterdam 1968), who provides a Dutch translation of this poem, has a summary account in his Introduction.

The date of the marriage (and the poem) cannot be precisely established, but Julian's subsequent clerical career limits the possible range of dates. At the time of his marriage he was *lector* (line 144). By 408 or 409 he was deacon. (Augustine's *Ep.* 101.4 to Memor calls Julian *filius tuus et condiaconus*, the context suggesting this to be a recent development. That letter came to Italy in 408/9; see Fabre *Chron.* 122 and 70.) Deacons could not marry (cf. Siricius, *Ep.* 10.25 [ML 13.1184]) though married men could be deacons; hence he was married earlier. The subdiaconate will have interposed between the marriage and 408, and Aemilius (see n. 49 below) could not have attended a wedding in late 405 or 406 for he was in Constantinople. A date for the poem between 400 and 405, or shortly after Aemilius' return in 406 (see n. 47 below), is indicated.

² Cf. Matt. 11.30.

³ Juno is added to the regular love-deities probably because Paulinus recalls Virgil, *Aen.* 4.166 f.

⁴ I.e., of Memor; see lines 199 ff.

⁵ Cf. Gen. 2.24.

⁶ Cf. Gen. 2.23.

⁷ Cf. line 238 for Aaron's priesthood as symbol of that of Memor, father of Julian.

⁸ For these pagan customs of marriage, cf. Catullus 64.293; Statius, *Silvae* 1.2.230 f.; Claudian 10.284 ff.; Sidonius Apollinaris 1.5.11, etc.

⁹ For this changed face of Beneventum, see Brown, *Augustine of Hippo*, 381 f.

¹⁰ Cf. 2 Cor. 2.15.

¹¹ He is *clericus* and *lector* (lines 141 and 144).

¹² Cf. John 8.12; Rom. 13.12.

¹³ Cf. Virgil, *Georg.* 2.464, *Aen.* 9.614; and line 75 below.

¹⁴ Cf. Isa. 61.10.

¹⁵ Cf. 1 Pet. 3.3 f.

¹⁶ With Bouma, I restore *pretio neque vellere* to the text in line 51 where Hartel has *pretium neque vellera*. Chinese garments were traditionally of silk, and *vellere Serum* must here be used in the vague sense of "silken wrap."

¹⁷ The phrase *gentis apostolicae filia facta domo* indicates that Titia is marrying into a bishop's family; for *apostolicus* in this sense, see Blaise s.v. *apostolicus*.

¹⁸ Cf. 1 Cor. 8.1.

¹⁹ There are striking parallels to this passage in Tertullian,

*De cult. fem.*, and in Cyprian, *De hab. virg.* Tertullian mentions *medicamenta ex fuco, quibus genae colorantur*, then *nigrum pulverem* (1.2.1), which is Paulinus' phrase, and later (2.6.1) yellow dye for the hair. Cyprian has *cutem falso medicamine polluisti, crinem mutasti* (17), and *oculos circumducto nigrore fucare* (14). See also the next two notes for evidence of the use by Paulinus of Cyprian's treatise.

[20] The word *adulteriis* with its sexual overtones is likewise found in Tertullian, *De cult. fem.* 1.8.2, and in Cyprian, *De hab. virg.* 16.

[21] Cf. Isa. 3.24. As Bouma points out, Paulinus reflects the version of the Vetus Latina found in Cyprian, *De hab. virg.* 13: *pro cingulo reste cingeris*. Cyprian is probably Paulinus' inspiration here.

[22] Cf. Isa. 3.24.

[23] Cf. Juvenal 6.502 f.; Jerome, *Ep.* 130.7: *alienis capillis turritum verticem struere*.

[24] I.e., as *lector* (see n. 11 above).

[25] Cf. Gen. 2.8, 3.21.

[26] Cf. Gen. 24.65.

[27] At Matt. 14.6 and Mark 6.22, the dancer (Salome, whose name, however, is not given in the Gospels) is the daughter of Herodias. Some variants in the Greek New Testament manuscripts call the girl herself Herodias, and it is accordingly possible that this had found its way into the Latin text used by Paulinus.

[28] Cf. Matt. 3.3; Mark 1.3; Luke 3.4; John 1.23 and 36.

[29] Herod Antipas (4 B.C.–A.D. 39), son of Herod the Great, had put away his first wife to take Herodias, the wife of his brother Philip. Salome was thus his daughter by marriage. It was because John condemned this liaison that Herodias induced her daughter to ask for his head—hence "lust-inspired anger."

[30] Cf. Matt. 14.9; Mark 6.26.

[31] Cf. Acts 12.21 ff.

[32] Cf. 2 Cor. 6.14 ff.

[33] See above, n. 1.

[34] Cf. Gen. 2.18.

[35] Cf. 1 Cor. 11.3; Eph. 5.23; and also Paulinus' Letters 23.23 and 44.4 (= ACW 36.27 and 239).

[36] Cf. Gen. 11.29; Gal. 4.22.

[37] Cf. John 2.1–10.

[38] Cf. Judges 6.37 ff.; Ps. 71.6. Gideon's fleece is regularly represented in the Fathers as a type of Mary impregnated by the Holy Spirit. See Bouma, *op. cit.* 89; Paulinus, Letter 19.3 (= ACW 35.181, where see also 251 n. 25).

[39] A line has been lost from the text here.

[40] Cf. Gal. 3.28; Eph. 4.4 f.

[41] Cf. Col. 1.18; 1 Cor. 11.3, 12.27.

[42] Cf. Eph. 4.22 f.; Rom. 13.14.

[43] Cf. Eph. 4.13; Col. 3.11.

[44] Cf. Matt. 22.30.

[45] Cf. Matt. 19.6.

[46] As becomes clear from the next sentence, the reference here is to Memor, father of Julian. Augustine addressed his *Ep.* 101 to Memor; cf. also Marius Mercator 4.2 (= ML 48.128A). Memor's see may have been Capua; see Bouma, *op. cit.* 14.

[47] One wonders if this effusive reference to Aemilius is prompted by his return from Constantinople; if this were the case, it would date the poem to 406/7.

[48] At line 205 (*quis procul ille hominum . . .* ) and here (*hic vir hic est*) there are evocations of Virgil, *Aen.* 6.808 f. and 791, a reference to Augustus emerging to mark the climax of future Roman greatness.

[49] Aemilius is regarded as virtually a member of Paulinus' Nola community at Poem 21.330. Simeon the Metaphrast, the tenth-century Byzantine hagiographer, states that he was bishop of Beneventum. Palladius, *De vita s. Ioann. Chrys.* 4, cites bishop Aemilius as one of the legates sent to Constantinople to participate in the discussions involving John Chrysostom; see n. 47 above.

[50] The clear meaning of these and the following lines is that Aemilius is younger than Memor but his senior as bishop; they are brothers in the episcopate (see Lagrange 2.78).

[51] The phrase has led some to infer that Aemilius was the father of Titia, but spiritual paternity is more probably meant. See a summary of the discussion in Fabre *Chron.* 123.

[52] Cf. Ps. 84.11.

[53] For the adaptation of the *infula* from pagan ritual for a Christian meaning, cf. Letters 29.7 and 18.10, and Poem 15.112 with n. 23 on that poem.

[54] The play on Memor and *immemor* recalls other puns by

Paulinus on Clarus (Letter 32.6), Sanctus (Letter 41.1), and
Felix (Poems 12.1, 13.1, etc.).

[55] Cf. 1 Pet. 2.9.

[56] Cf. Luke 1.5.

[57] Thus Therasia, wife of Paulinus, is still alive at this date.
Paulinus' correspondence with Augustine (cf. Letters 45 and 50;
see ACW 36.352 n. 1 and 362 n. 1) suggests she died between
408 and 415.

## POEM 26

[1] This is the eighth in the series of *Natalicia* addressed to Felix
and is dateable to January 402 (see Intro. pp. 6 f.). The opening
lines referring to the anxieties of the barbarian invasion were
thought by Buse to indicate a date of composition after the battle
of Pollentia (Easter 402), i.e., in January 403. But Alaric's invasion
began in 401, and it is much more probable that these anxious
comments describe the situation before Pollentia, a Roman victory
which was greeted with such relief by other contemporaries.
See Claudian, *De bello Getico* 635; Prudentius, *Contra Sym-
machum* 2.715 ff.

[2] "Gothic" here = *Geticis*. "Getic," properly referring to the
Thracian Getae, is often used by fourth-century writers in
reference to the Goths. Alaric was king of the Visigoths or
Western Goths; at the time of the invasion of the Visigoths in
401 the Alans were Roman allies, but were tending towards
alliance with the Visigoths. See A. Cameron, *Claudian* (Oxford
1970) 375 ff.; this evidence of Paulinus reinforces his thesis.

[3] For the events of the invasion of 401 we are largely dependent
on Claudian's *De gello Getico*, which describes Alaric's crossing
of the Alps and his victory at the Timavus (562 f.) in late 401.
See also Jerome, *Contra Rufinum* 3.21.

[4] Cf. Ps. 25.12.

[5] Cf. Exod. 12.3 ff.

[6] Cf. Exod. 12.39.

[7] Cf. 1 Cor. 5.7.

[8] Nineveh (cf. Jon. 3) is in Paulinus' mind here.

[9] I read in line 85 *ergo quia est curae* (Rosweyde) for Hartel's
*ergo quibus curae*, and the *ergo quia curae* of the mss.

[10] Cf. Jon. 3; Exod. 17.11; Esth. 7.

[11] Mordecai; cf. Esth. 7.10.

[12] Cf. Eph. 6.11 ff.

[13] Paulinus refers to the use of the Greek form Jesus in the New Testament (Acts 7.45, Heb. 4.8) in place of the Hebrew form Josue used in the Old Testament, and suggests that his miraculous destruction of the walls of Jericho (cf. Jos. 6) prefigures the power of Christ.

[14] Paulinus naturally thinks of Joshua's marches round Jericho in terms of the Roman ritual of the *lustrum*, a purificatory ceremony in which the censor made a triple circuit of the Roman people drawn up in military formation.

[15] A lapse of memory on Paulinus' part; at Jos. 6.3 f. they are to march round once a day for six days, but seven times on the seventh.

[16] *Numerus* does not mean "host" here (as a note in the ML suggests), but refers to the mystical power of the number seven, so prominent not merely throughout the Jericho episode but in all Scripture, from the seven days of creation in Genesis to the seven seals and seven plagues of the Apocalypse.

[17] Referring to David's felling of Goliath; cf. 1 Kings 17.49.

[18] Cf. Exod. 14; on the mistaken belief that Pharaoh was drowned in the Red Sea, cf. above, n. 16 on Poem 16.

[19] The "holy woman" is Deborah; cf. Judges 4.14.

[20] Cf. Judith 13.3 ff.

[21] Cf. 4 Kings 18.13 ff.

[22] Cf. 4 Kings 19.35 (185,000 dead); for the language, cf. Virgil, *Aen.* 5.807.

[23] Cf. Exod. 32.10 ff.

[24] Cf. Wisd. 10.6.

[25] Cf. Gen. 19.1 ff. Paulinus discusses the Lot theme at greater length in his Letter 13.21 (= ACW 35.137).

[26] Cf. 3 Kings 17.1.

[27] Cf. Exod. 14.21, 15.25, 16.13, 16.14, 17.5 f.

[28] Cf. Exod. 13.18, 13.21, 16.35, 17.5.

[29] Cf. Jos. 10.13.

[30] It is notable here that though Paulinus elsewhere demands withdrawal from the secular world by those who aspire to salvation, he is far from indifferent to the fate of the Roman state. See also Poem 21.1–24.

[31] Cf. Dan. 14.

[32] Cf. Dan. 3.22, 3.51 ff. (not in the Hebrew versions).

[33] Cf. Dan. 3.50 f.

[34] Cf. Exod. 15.25. On the use of *merra*, cf. Poem 17.32 and n. 5 thereon.

[35] Cf. Exod. 7.12.

[36] Cf. Exod. 14.21; Matt. 14.29.

[37] See n. 32 above.

[38] Paulinus reverts to the subject of this fire two years later in Poem 28.

[39] The *tugurium* mentioned here cannot be the actual monastic building which the word is used to describe at Letter 29.13, but a cottage in the vicinity. See Goldschmidt 9 and 15 f.

[40] See n. 1 above.

[41] In terms of artistic structure, this is one of Paulinus' most successful poems. Beginning with a proclamation of joy in the circumstances of threatening war, he skilfully interlocks as his central theme the efficacious faith and sanctity of scriptural heroes with the equally efficacious merit of Felix. Then, in the final section of the poem, he returns to the initial theme of the contemporary anxieties of the Visigoth invasion, and begs Felix to extend his saving protection in the present crisis.

## POEM 27

[1] The ascriptions in the various manuscripts make this poem the ninth in the series of *Natalicia*, which indicates January 403 as the date of composition; this date is proposed by both Fabre *Chron.* 35 ff. and Goldschmidt 14 ff. See Intro. pp. 6 f.

[2] Cf. Jos. 10.13.

[3] Cf. Exod. 14.22 and 27.

[4] Cf. Matt. 2.11.

[5] Cf. Matt. 3.16.

[6] Cf. John 2.9 ff.

[7] Cf. Matt. 28.6.

[8] Cf. Acts 2.2 ff.

[9] Cf. John 1.3.

[10] Cf. Mark 16.19.

[11] With this explicitly Nicene formulation of the *Filioque* dogma one may compare the more ambivalent description at Letter 21.3 (= ACW 35.192 f.) and the orthodox formulation in Poem 19. See above, n. 31 on Poem 19.

[12] Cf. Acts 2.2 ff.

[13] Cf. Isa. 49.10.

[14] Cf. Matt. 9.20.

[15] Cf. Matt. 13.7.

[16] Paulinus comments acidly on such astrological superstition at Letter 16.4 (= ACW 35.154).

[17] On Nicetas (or Niceta), bishop of Remesiana and missionary in this area of modern Yugoslavia, see the bibliographical note in ACW 36.326. His earlier visit to Nola in 400 is commemorated in Poem 17 and in Letter 29.14 (= ACW 36.117).

[18] Cf. Cant. 2.11 ff.

[19] In line 163, I read *unctus* with the mss. A, D, and E, rather than the *iunctus* of other mss. and Hartel.

[20] Cf. 2 Cor. 2.15.

[21] Playing on the meaning of the name in Greek, which is "victorious."

[22] Cf. Prov. 23.1.

[23] I.e., Nicetas.

[24] The twelve sons of Jacob and the twelve apostles. It is important to note that Paulinus summons them in the role which the Muses enjoy in classical poetry. See above, n. 5 on Poem 10.

[25] Cf. Cant. 2.12.

[26] Cf. Isa. 6.6. Paulinus is guilty of a lapse of memory; it is the Seraphim and not the Cherubim who are so invoked in that passage.

[27] Paulinus uses *ore* four times here, three times at the end of successive lines, as if to stress the biblical motif of oral impurity.

[28] Cf. Gen. 29.2, 30.38. For Nicetas, the baptistry re-enacts Jacob's pool.

[29] For the symbolic sense of the three rods, see lines 273 ff.

[30] Cf. 1 Cor. 15.25 ff.

[31] Rosweyde (ML 61.923) suggests that this refers to the sacrament of confirmation which followed baptism. See the texts cited in ML 61.923 and in E. Yarnold, *The Awe-Inspiring Rites of Initiation* (Slough 1971) esp. 81 (Cyril), 124 (Ambrose), 167 (John Chrysostom), and 207 (Theodore of Mopsuestia).

[32] Cf. Ps. 4.7.

[33] Cf. 1 Kings 2.5; the Vulgate has "many" instead of the "seven" which is in the Septuagint, and which is interpreted as the seven ancient churches of Apoc. 1–3.

[34] In the Vulgate the first tree is the poplar (Gen. 30.37), but the Septuagint has *sturax*, the incense-bearing shrub, as here.

[35] Cf. Ps. 115.4 f.

[36] On the stir aroused when Paulinus decided to sell his properties and espouse monastic life, see above all the letter of Ambrose, *Ep.* 58.

[37] The evocation of Virgil, *Aen.* 6.15, shows that Paulinus has the flight of Icarus in mind.

[38] On Nicetas' earlier visit to Nola in the year 400, see n. 17 above.

[39] Paulinus thinks of the dislocation caused by the invasion of northern Italy by the Visigoths in 401–2, which must have made Nicetas' journey from Dacia hazardous; see above, nn. 1–3 on Poem 26.

[40] The remainder of this poem is translated in Goldschmidt 53 ff.; this version owes much to Goldschmidt's.

[41] Cf. Virgil, *Aen.* 1.140.

[42] See the map of the excavations at Cimitile in *Riv. Arch. Crist.* 16 (1939) fig. 5, reproduced in Goldschmidt. The portico connects the new Apostles' Church at the north with the original Church of St. Felix.

[43] "He means that the facade of the Apostles' church is visible from Felix's tomb" (Goldschmidt 134). The tomb is in the Church of St. Felix, the interior of which is referred to here.

[44] Goldschmidt 136 quotes interesting parallels to this type of sea-wave decoration, notably Prudentius, *Peristeph.* 12.42, describing St. Peter's: *credas moveri fluctibus lacunar.*

[45] For *caementa* = "stucco" and *metallum* = "ivory," see Goldschmidt 137 f.

[46] See Poem 21.384 ff. with n. 53 thereon.

[47] Perhaps Paulinus is playing on the contrast between the monastic *cella* and the profane sense of a brothel-apartment (cf. Juvenal 6.122; Petronius 8.4; etc.). But the Christian festivals at such shrines as Nola could be occasions for heavy drinking; see Paulinus' own comments in lines 559 ff. on this poem, and also the learned note in Goldschmidt 138.

[48] For the relic of St. Andrew at Nola, and the tradition of his mission and execution in Greece, see Letter 32.17 (= ACW 36.150, where see also 330 n. 28) and n. 10 on Poem 19. The reference to "Thessalian" Patras (the town in fact lies south of

the Corinthian Gulf) indicates that Paulinus had never visited Greece.

[49] Cf. Luke 16.16.

[50] Paulinus had a special veneration for John the Baptist as the precursor not only of Christ but also of monastic life; cf. Letters 29.1 and 49.12, and Poem 6. His supposed tomb at Sebaste in Samaria was desecrated by Julian the Apostate in 362, and relics from it were widely diffused.

[51] It is of course a translation of the name into Greek.

[52] Cf. John 20.24–8. Thomas is discussed in similar vein at Letter 13.25 (= ACW 35.141), and especially in Poem 31.149 ff.

[53] I.e., Luke's Gospel and Acts. The installation of a relic of St. Luke in Paulinus' new church at Fundi is mentioned at Letter 32.17 (= ACW 36.151), which is dated to 403/4 and is accordingly contemporaneous with this poem.

[54] The bones of these martyrs were discovered in 393 at Bologna by Ambrose and the local bishop Eusebius. The cult of Vitalis then spread rapidly, being particularly prominent at Ravenna and at Rome.

[55] Proculus is also associated with Bologna; see *Bibliotheca hagiographica latina* 2.1012.

[56] Chalcedon, facing Byzantium across the Bosporus and the site of the Fourth Ecumenical Council, was the centre of devotion to Euphemia, whose death is tentatively connected with the persecution of Diocletian in 307; see DACL 5.745 ff.

[57] Bologna.

[58] *trabalibus . . . clavis*. The expression *clavus trabalis* is proverbial; cf. Cicero, *Verr.* 2.5.53; Horace, *Carm.* 1.35.18; etc.

[59] His relic is also mentioned at Letter 32.17 (see n. 53 above). The body of Nazarius was discovered by Ambrose in a garden near Milan. See Paulinus of Milan, *Vita s. Ambrosii* 32 f.; Leclercq in DACL 11.1057 ff.

[60] I.e., the mystery of the Trinity. The symbolism of the three doors is mentioned also at Letter 32.13 (= ACW 36.147).

[61] Cf. 1 Cor. 11.3; Eph. 5.23 and 30.

[62] In Poem 21.650 ff., written four years later in 407, a more reliable water supply has been laid on by means of the aqueduct from Abella.

[63] Cf. 1 Par. 18.8; 2 Par 4.4. The "dry sea" was in fact the draining-channel of the altar; see ML 61.925.

[64] I.e., the Apostles' Church and the Church of St. Felix.

[65] This is the Church of St. Felix, joined on the north side to the courtyard mentioned at line 365.

[66] With Goldschmidt, I cannot accept Hartel's emendation in line 490 to *defendant,* and I translate the mss. reading *defendat.*

[67] Cf. Apoc. 14.14.

[68] See Poem 26.119 and n. 13 thereon.

[69] Cf. Jos. 3.14–17.

[70] Cf. Ruth 1.14.

[71] Before the time of Constantine such biblical themes had been restricted chiefly to funerary art. From this period onward such paintings in churches grew rapidly in popularity. On this large question, see P. du Bourguet, *Early Christian Painting* (London 1965) 8 f.; M. Gough, *The Early Christians* (London 1961) esp. ch. 7.

[72] Cf. 1 Pet. 4.3.

[73] Letter 32.3 ff. (= ACW 36.136 ff.) gives examples of the verse inscriptions accompanying such pictures.

[74] Cf. Ps. 86.1. The "holy mountains" Paulinus elsewhere (Letter 23.43 [= ACW 36.46]) interprets as the saints.

[75] Cf. Gen. 11.4 ff.; Letter 32.22 (= ACW 36.154 ff.) is an extended meditation on this and other scriptural references to building.

[76] Cf. Gen. 1.26; 1 Cor. 15.49.

[77] Cf. Gen. 12.1.

[78] Cf. Exod. 3.8.

[79] Cf. Dan. 3.19 ff.

[80] Cf. Gen. 19.1 ff.

[81] Cf. Gen. 19.26.

[82] Cf. Gen. 22.2 ff.

[83] In this symbolism of the devil, Paulinus confuses Amalek, grandson of Esau (cf. Gen. 36.12 ff.; see above, n. 55 on Poem 24), with Abimalek, who filled in the wells of Abraham (cf. Gen. 26.15).

[84] Edom is Esau (cf. Gen. 25.30); on Jacob's flight, cf. Gen. 27.43 ff.

[85] Cf. Gen. 28.11.

[86] Cf. Gen. 39.7 ff.

[87] Cf. Eccle. 3.5.

[88] Cf. Matt. 25.2 ff.

[89] Cf. Exod. 14.21.

[90] This is a further indication that the *Natalicia* were recited on the feastday to the crowds assembled at the shrine; see Intro. pp. 12 f.

## POEM 28

[1] This is traditionally the tenth in the series of *Natalicia*, dateable to January 404. The attempt by P. Reinelt, *Studien über die Briefe des heiligen Paulinus von Nola* (diss. Breslau 1904) 21 ff., and others to place this poem before Poem 27 is examined and rejected by Fabre, *Revue des études anciennes* (1934) 188 ff., and Goldschmidt 15 ff. See n. 19 below for one powerful argument in favour of the traditional dating. This poem is translated in full in Goldschmidt 73 ff.

[2] Cf. Job. 2.7; Tob. 2.11.

[3] This is the atrium previously described at Poem 27.395 ff.

[4] For an earlier account of this fire, see Poem 26.395 ff.

[5] *terrebant* ("terrified") is the reading of all the mss., but the scribe of T corrects to *torrebant*, incorporated by Hartel in his text, and rendered here.

[6] The Church of the Apostles, as the mention of the relics shows.

[7] This relic is mentioned as being at Nola in Letter 32.11 (= ACW 36.145), having been brought to Nola by Melania as described at Letter 31.1 (= ACW 36.125).

[8] I follow Goldschmidt 182 in assuming that these paintings are in the *atrium* rather than in the nave; the monastery at Monte Cassino afforded a striking parallel.

[9] See Goldschmidt's brave explanation of this obscure formulation. He compares Poem 27.511 ff., where only Old Testament paintings are mentioned, and assumes that the New Testament scenes had been added in the year elapsing since Poem 27 was composed.

[10] The various possible explanations are discussed by Goldschmidt 185; I subscribe to his tentative identification of this as a baptismal chapel within the church.

[11] Cf. Tit. 3.5—In the preceding sentence, "holy sacrament of the Eucharist" = *pia sacramenta*.

[12] We know from Poem 27.383 ff. that only one church was restored, but both churches have been embellished with paintings.

[13] I follow Goldschmidt in rejecting the reading *vetustas* adopted by Hartel, in favour of *venustas*.

[14] Cf. Eph. 4.24; Phil. 3.13.

[15] Cf. Eccli. 21.2 f.

[16] Cf. Ps. 73.14, where, however, the dragon becomes "meat for the people of the Ethiopians." Cyril of Alexandria anticipates Paulinus' reversal of the sense; see ML 61.929. Goldschmidt 191 quotes Jerome, *In Sophon.* 2.12, and Augustine, *Enarr. in Ps.* 73.16, for similar sentiments.

[17] Cf. Prov. 19.28.

[18] Cf. Rom. 13.11.

[19] Cf. Poem 27.356 ff., where the buildings are only partly completed. If the date of January 404 is accepted for Poem 28, the operations described here were commenced in 401 and completed late in 403.

[20] I.e., the remains of the demolished huts.

[21] Cf. John 5.2: *Bethsaida, quinque porticus habens.* This pool in Jerusalem is wrongly identified here with Solomon's pool, on which see Josephus, *Bell. Iud.* 5.4.2. See Goldschmidt 195.

[22] Cf. Matt. 9.16 f.

[23] Paulinus here adapts the imagery of building and of agriculture to his sermon on the need for moral and spiritual perfection. These two types of image are often developed in the Letters also; see my remarks in ACW 35.17.

## POEM 29

[1] All that survives of this poem (or poems; see Green 29) comprises three brief fragments found in a ninth-century manuscript (Ambrosianus B 102) which contains two works of the Irish monk Dungal. Dungal cites these fragments and other poems of Paulinus in defence of the practice of veneration of saints' images. This group of fragments is called in the manuscript *liber XV*, i.e., the fifteenth in the series of *Natalicia*. If this numeration is correct, we may date the fragments to January 409, and assume that *Natalicium* 14 is lost. But other *Natalicia* cited in this manuscript are inaccurately numbered (see Hartel, xxxii f.), so that the date and number are not wholly certain.

² It will be clear from the content and sequence of these fragments that they could all belong to the same poem. Lines 1–11 represent the exordium; the second fragment summarises the intervening discussion of God's creative provision mediated through all His saints; and the third part details Felix's specific role in this cosmic economy.

## POEM 30

¹ Under this single heading are combined two inscriptions recovered from the Church of St. Felix at Cimitile. See G. B. De Rossi, *Inscriptiones christianae urbis Romae septimo saeculo antiquiores* 2.1 (Rome 1888) 189; Hartel's edition *ad loc.* Paulinus' Letter 32 to Severus reproduces a number of similar verses inscribed in the churches at Cimitile and Fundi; see ACW 36.144 ff. Since the inscriptions labelled here as Poem 30 are not included in Letter 32, it is possible that they had not been composed at that date and were added later; but their content is reminiscent of Poems 27 and 28, which like Letter 32 date to the period 403/4. For a useful survey of the history of Christian verse-inscriptions from Pope Damasus onwards, see G. Bernt, *Das lateinische Epigramm im Übergang von der Spätantike zum frühen Mittelalter* (München 1968), discussing the compositions of Paulinus at 76 ff. See also Green 39.

² The tomb of Felix lay within the church.

³ Compare the description of the renovation at Poem 27.360 ff.

## POEM 31

¹ This Christianised *consolatio* or *epikēdeion* (see Intro. p. 14) addressed to Pneumatius and his wife Fidelis on the death of their child Celsus contains no detail which permits close dating. There are allusions to the death of Paulinus' own child Celsus, which took place in or after 393; on the other hand, Therasia is still alive (see line 626), which extends the limits of dating to at least 408, when she is last addressed by Augustine in his *Ep.* 95. See Fabre *Chron.* 124, 105 f. Between these dates no further precision is possible. There is a translation by Fantazzi (diss. Washington, D.C. 1956).

For the literary form in its guise of *consolatio Christiana*, see

Ch. Favez, *La consolation latine chrétienne* (Paris 1937), and "Notes sur la composition du carmen 31 de Paulin de Nole," REL 13 (1935) 266 ff.; Walsh, "Paulinus of Nola and the Conflict of Ideologies in the Fourth Century," *KYRIAKON: Festschrift Johannes Quasten* 565 ff.

[2] The Latin here is *celsus*, the pun hard to reproduce in English.

[3] Favez, *La consolation . . .* 33, cites expert medical authority to infer that this is a description of diphtheria or quinsy.

[4] Cf. Jerome, *Ep.* 39.6: *grandis in suos pietas impietas in Deum est.*

[5] Cf. Gal. 4.1 ff.

[6] Cf. Phil. 2.7.

[7] Cf. 1 Cor. 15.22.

[8] Cf. Rom. 5.13 ff.

[9] Cf. Virgil, *Aen.* 5.27.

[10] Cf. Heb. 4.15.

[11] Cf. Isa. 53.4.

[12] Cf. Heb. 5.2.

[13] Cf. Virgil, *Aen.* 4.185.

[14] Cf. John 11.35 and 44.

[15] Cf. Matt. 14.24 ff.

[16] Cf. Matt. 27.51.

[17] Cf. Mark 15.28.

[18] Cf. Matt. 27.21.

[19] Cf. Luke 23.43.

[20] Cf. John 10.17.

[21] Cf. John 20.20 and 27.

[22] A poetic meditation on Luke 24.38 ff.

[23] Cf. Rom. 1.20.

[24] Cf. Ps. 4.3.

[25] Cf. Ps. 115.16.

[26] Cf. Matt. 11.30.

[27] This line of argument was familiar in Christian apologetics, for it had been used against the Valentinians; see Tertullian, *De resurr. carnis* 52 (ML 2.918), and more particularly Ambrose, *De excessu fratris Satyri* 2.54. As occasionally in the Letters, Paulinus draws directly on Ambrose throughout this poem.

[28] On what follows, compare Ambrose, *De excessu fratris Satyri* 2.58.

[29] Cf. Soph. 1.16; 1 Cor. 15.52.

[30] Cf. Ezech. 37; Ambrose, *De excessu fratris Satyri* 2.69.

[31] Cf. John 11.25 f.

[32] *et novus in sancta floruit urbe tholus.* Fantazzi interprets *tholus* ("dome," "cupola") as the rotunda of the church built by St. Helena in Jerusalem. See Letter 31.4 (= ACW 36.129, where see also 328 n. 18).

[33] Cf. 2 Cor. 5.17; Eph. 4.24.

[34] Cf. 2 Cor. 3.18.

[35] Cf. Exod. 34.33; 2 Cor. 3.13 f.

[36] Cf. Acts 1.9.

[37] Paulinus thinks of such utterances as the "Sibyllic" prophecy mentioned by Augustine (cf. *De civ. Dei* 18.23) which foretold the Final Judgment, and which has been immortalised in the *Dies Irae* (*teste David cum Sibylla*).

[38] Cf. Ps. 6.7; also Letter 40.4 (= ACW 36.205).

[39] Cf. Ps. 101.10.

[40] I read in line 419 *haeret* for the *horret* of the mss. and Hartel.

[41] Cf. Jer. 9.1.

[42] Cf. John 4.13.

[43] Reading *influus* with A. Hudson-Williams, *Eranos* (1950) 70 f.

[44] Cf. Letters 22.2 (= ACW 35.197, where see also 256 n. 4) and 49.12 (= ACW 36.270).

[45] Cf. Luke 15.21 ff.

[46] Cf. Luke 16.19 ff.

[47] Cf. Job 2.7 f.

[48] Paulinus draws primarily from Virgil, *Aen.* 6, for this depiction of the horrors of the pagan Hades; for Charon, cf. lines 299 f.; the Furies, 281; Tityus, 596; the punishments of the wheel and the rock, 616 f. Horace's *Carm.* 2.14.18 and 3.11.23 were perhaps in his mind as he added the Danaids to the list.

[49] For the contrast between the "falsehoods" of the classical writers and Christian truths, cf. Letter 38.6 and ACW 35.15.

[50] The Dives-Lazarus parable (Luke 16.19 ff.) clearly played an important part in Paulinus' decision to renounce his wealth, and it is discussed in numerous letters and poems; cf. Letters 13.17, 25*.2, 32.21, 34.6, and 35.1, and Poem 17.310.

[51] Cf. 2 Cor. 8.9; 1 Cor. 1.27.

[52] Cf. Luke 7.38.

[53] Cf. Rom. 13.11.

[54] Cf. John 12.3.

[55] Cf. 1 Thess. 4.13 ff.

[56] Cf. 1 Thess. 4.16.

[57] Cf. Ambrose, *De excessu fratris Satyri* 2.117, a developed meditation on 1 Thess. 4.15 ff.

[58] Cf. 1 Cor. 15.51; Poem 7.24 ff.

[59] Cf. Luke 16.23 f.

[60] Cf. Matt. 2.16.

[61] The Holy Innocents are celebrated in the contemporary poem of Prudentius (*Cath.* 12), where they are described as "sporting before the altar with palm and crowns" (lines 129 ff.).

[62] It is clear from what follows that this child of Paulinus and Therasia, also named Celsus, was born in Spain; the date must have been about 392. See Fabre *Paulin* 35, 27 n. 3.

[63] Alcala de Henares in New Castille.

[64] The martyrs Justus and Pastor were venerated at Complutum; see Prudentius, *Peristeph.* 4.41–4. Augustine's *De cura pro mortuis gerenda* is a reply to Paulinus' query on the efficaciousness of this practice of burying the dead close to saints.

[65] Hence Paulinus' son died when a week old; see lines 21 ff.

[66] This is the only indication we possess of the identity of Celsus' father Pneumatius. If we are justified in assuming a relationship between Pneumatius and Paulinus (and not Therasia), it would appear that the bereaved parents were from Aquitania, and this consolation may have been sent to them there. Cf. Lagrange 2.92; but also the doubts of Fabre *Paulin* 212 n. 8.

## POEM 32

[1] This poem, preserved in two mss. (Ambrosianus C 74 and Monacensis 6412, the first containing pieces by various authors, the other containing poems of Paulinus only), is ascribed to some other writer than Paulinus by C. Morelli, *Didaskaleion* 1 (1912) 481 ff.; Fabre *Chron.* 424 ff.; F. Sirna, *Aevum* 36 (1961) 87 ff. (who ascribes the poem to Jovius, addressee of Paulinus' Letter 16 [= ACW 35.151 ff.]); Green 130 f. Those who defend Paulinus' authorship regard it as an early composition, C. Bursian dating it to about 390, and Lagrange 1.328 to about 395 (drawing attention to Augustine, *Ep.* 31: *adversus paganos te scribere didici ex fratribus*, a letter dated to 397; cf. Fabre *Chron.*

14). I revert to the problem of authorship in n. 33 below. The poem is a *protreptikon;* see above, n. 1 on Poem 22. There is a commentary by Bursian in *Sitzungsber. der k.b. Akad. der Wiss. zu München* 1 (1880) 3 ff.

2 This Antonius cannot be identified.

3 Cf. Exod. 12.29 ff., 14.19 ff.

4 Cf. Exod. 14.27 ff., 15.27.

5 Cf. Exod. 16.13 ff., 17.6 f.

6 Cf. Exod. 32.1 ff.

7 The charges that follow are staple attacks on the pagan Roman ritual practices as they appear in writers from Tertullian onwards. See ML 61.691 for the texts.

8 In reference to the procedure of Roman *haruspices.*

9 Cf. Firmicus Maternus, *De err. prof. relig.* 15.2 (= ACW 37.74): *vendebatur deus ut prodesset emptori, et emptor suppliciter adorabat.*

10 In fact they obtained their name because they first established themselves in the gymnasium near Athens called Cynosarges; but the similarity with the Greek for dogs (κύνες) caused the sect to be often associated with canine manners and canine wit; see, e.g., Augustine, *De civ. Dei* 14.20. Paulinus does not directly advert to the Cynics in his Letter 16 when reviewing the main schools of philosophers, but there may be an indirect reference there at 16.8; see ACW 35.246 n. 24.

11 There is no reference to the *Phaedo* elsewhere in Paulinus, but at Letter 16.4 (= ACW 35.155) the myth of Er in *Republic* 10 is criticised.

12 Some confusion is evident here. The poet has begun this section with brief mention of the Cynics before passing on to the Platonists, yet it is clear from the anecdote (which reproduces a story commonly told about Diogenes the Cynic; cf. Seneca, *Ep.* 90.14) that the *Physici* described here are in fact the Cynics. The term *Physici* was used by the ancients to describe different types of philosophers. Aristotle uses it of the pre-Socratic physicists like Thales who are concerned with the nature of the world. But Antisthenes the Cynic wrote a work called *Physicus* (cf. Cicero, *De nat. deorum* 1.32) to describe the ethical ideal of "living in accord with nature," and so the label is later attached to the Cynics.

13 Cf. *Aen.* 1.47.

[14] On Jupiter's debauching of his daughter Proserpine, cf. Ovid, *Met.* 6.114; she later passed to his brother Pluto in Hades. The other forms adopted by Jupiter are mentioned in Ovid, *Met.* 6.103 ff., and his love of Ganymede in Ovid, *Met.* 10.155 ff. The stories were keenly adopted by the Christian apologists; see the quotations at ML 61.695 ff.

[15] A line with this general sense has been lost from the text; see Bursian *ad loc.*

[16] Janus is traditionally accorded first place before Jupiter in ritual formulae; cf. Livy 8.9.6, Martial 10.9.28, etc. Virgil, *Aen.* 8.358, makes the connection with the Janiculum. For the cult of Janus Geminus, see Livy 1.19 with Ogilvie's note. For the minting of coins with his head and a ship, cf. Ovid, *Fasti* 1.229 ff.; *capita et navia* was an ancient game for children, like the British "heads or tails." See in general K. Latte, *Römische Religionsgeschichte* 132 ff.

[17] For Jupiter's mother Cybele castrating the unwilling shepherd Atys (Attis), cf. Ovid, *Fasti* 4.223 ff.; Minucius Felix, *Octavius* 22.4 (= ACW 39.88 f.); Augustine, *De civ. Dei* 6.7; etc.

[18] Homosexual conduct was a charge frequently levelled against Asian religious practices, not only the cult of Cybele but also that of the Syrian Atargatis (cf. Apuleius, *Met.* 8). For Cybeleworship, see Latte 258 ff. The extent of its inroads into Italian religious life can be seen at Ostia; see R. Meiggs, *Roman Ostia* (Oxford 1960) 355 ff.

[19] Cf. Tertullian, *Apol.* 15; Firmicus Maternus, *De err. prof. relig.* 12.9 (= ACW 37.70); Augustine, *De civ. Dei* 7.26; etc.

[20] The Italian Saturn was by syncretism identified with the Greek Cronos, who is said by Hesiod and others to have devoured his children at birth to ensure the absence of rivals for his throne, but to have been deceived in the case of Zeus (= Jupiter), who subsequently expelled him from heaven. He was later confused with the god of time Chronos, and accordingly was depicted as an old man with sickle. Cf. Latte 254 ff.

[21] The play on *latuisse* and *Latium* is taken over from Virgil, *Aen.* 8.332 f. by the Christian apologists; cf. Minucius Felix, *Octavius* 23.11 (= ACW 39.91).

[22] A reference to the festival of Jupiter Latiaris, at which, according to the Christian apologists, human beings were sacri-

ficed; cf. Tertullian, *Apol.* 9 with Mayor's note; and Latte 145 n. 6.

[23] The reference is to Mithraism, which originated in Persia and reached Rome in the first century B.C. to become an Imperial cult under the Antonines. The material is collected in F. Cumont, *Textes et monuments figurés relatifs aux mystères de Mithra* (Brussels 1896-9); for the title *Sol Invictus* referred to in this passage, cf. Latte 350 ff.

[24] Isis-worship was the most powerful rival of Christianity in Africa at the time when the Christian apologists Tertullian and Minucius Felix were writing, and such apologists have inspired the present passage. The rattle and the dog's head (which is the symbol of the Egyptian deity Anubis) were the externals which struck Roman observers (cf. Ovid, *Met.* 9.630 ff.; Lucan 8.831 ff.) when paraded, e.g., at the festival of the *navigium Isidis*. Each year Isis lost and found again Osiris her husband and Horus her son. Paulinus at Poem 19.118 ff. waxes satirical about this, as does Minucius Felix, *Octavius* 22.1 (= ACW 39.88), in much the same language as we find here.

[25] Serapis, identified with Osiris, is frequently found in representations with a dog, lion, or wolf. The identification with an ass's carcass may be through confusion with Typhon, the principle of evil in the Isiac dualist religion (cf. Plutarch, *De Iside et Osiride* 371C); one wonders if Apuleius' *Golden Ass* has not inspired this section indirectly.

[26] This is the Augustan author of the *Fabulae*, but there is no trace of the story there; if our poet is to be trusted, it must come from one of Hyginus' lost treatises.

[27] The festival of the Vulcanalia took place in late August. See Warde-Fowler, *Roman Festivals* (London 1899) 209 ff.; Latte 129 ff.; Daremberg-Saglio 5.1002 ff.

[28] Cf. Gen. 3.1 ff.

[29] I.e., the sun and the moon.

[30] This describes the Roman conception of a geocentric cosmos, its seven concentric spheres marked by the seven known planets. With the notable exception of Lucretius, there were few who challenged this basic assumption.

[31] *Cosmos* in Greek means "adornment" as well as "world"; a secondary meaning of *mundus* in Latin is "the sun," as in Manilius, 1.36, 3.591.

[32] *remque novam dicam nec me dixisse pigebit.* This line (223)

is considered spurious by Ebert, and the strange Latin certainly suggests that it may be an interpolation.

[33] Fabre *Chron.* 124 ff. well summarises the arguments against Paulinus' authorship as follows:

*a.* The supposed reference to St. Felix at line 163 is clearly a misapprehension, for the word is an adjective there.

*b.* Antonius the addressee is not mentioned elsewhere.

*c.* The argument from content. The author claims to have become a convert to Christianity after holding other beliefs; Paulinus was a Christian from boyhood. His discussion of secular philosophies in Letter 16 shows significant differences of emphasis and outlook.

*d.* Moreover, the criticism of the austere life of the Physici in the poem is not typical of Paulinus.

*e.* The arguments from tone and style. There is "un netteté, une vigeur un peu rude" quite uncharacteristic of Paulinus. The words *diabolus* (line 145) and *paganus* in the sense of pagan (lines 19 and 204) are avoided by Paulinus.

These arguments are convincing. In general the author of the poem is less sophisticated and less learned than Paulinus. The arguments follow closely those of the Christian apologists, and it is probable that the author is familiar with the poems of Paulinus, for they appear to be echoed at several points (cf. line 6 and Poem 6.23; 11 and Poem 22.90 ff.; 111 and Poem 19.117; 119 f. and Poem 19.118 ff.; 247 ff. and Poem 26.29 ff.; etc.).

Two further points are worth making, one in reference to content and one in reference to style. The novel feature of the Christian apologia here is the insistence that God's mercy outweighs His justice (see lines 214 ff.). Poems 7–9 indicate how much the prospect of the Judgment haunted Paulinus, who has a less sunny view of the prospects of salvation for the greater number. To the arguments from style we may add the technique of citation of pagan authors by name at lines 55 and 132; Paulinus does not cite authorities in this way, but assumes that his readers will recognise his knowledge of Roman writers when he evokes them.

# POEM 33

[1] This poem has survived in a single manuscript, a Carolingian *florilegium* containing other poems of Paulinus as well as works

by other writers; the manuscript ascribes the poem to Paulinus. The theme is the life and death of a certain Baebianus; it is composed in six sections, in various metres. Fabre *Chron.* 130 ff. rejects the ascription to Paulinus; Green 131 supports W. Brandes, *Wiener Studien* (1890) 281 ff., in the opposite view. See n. 20 below.

[2] For the exordium, cf. Poem 7, also in this metre of iambic senarii.

[3] It looks as if Baebianus' portrait was painted on the inner wall of a church. In Paulinus' Letter 32.2 (= ACW 36.135 ff.) we read that Sulpicius Severus had St. Martin and Paulinus depicted in his new baptistry.

[4] This Baebianus is not known outside this poem, but his son is mentioned in Symmachus, *Ep.* 3.41.

[5] The metre now changes to dactylic hexameters.

[6] Cf. John 7.38.

[7] He was baptised, and received the Eucharist and the sacrament of confirmation; see the texts in E. Yarnold, *The Awe-Inspiring Rites of Initiation* (Slough 1971).

[8] Cf. Phil. 1.21.

[9] Cf. Luke 23.40 ff.

[10] Cf. Matt. 20.6 ff.

[11] The metre changes here to Lesser Asclepiads.

[12] Cf. Matt. 22.30.

[13] The metre here changes to hexameters.

[14] I translate the ms. reading, *ex cursu demissa*, in preference to Hartel's *demissa excessu*.

[15] Or perhaps "bishop" (*sacerdos*); cf. lines 21 f., where, however, the word is clearly "bishop" (*episcopus*).

[16] Cf. Matt. 19.5.

[17] The metre changes here to elegiac couplets.

[18] Baebianus died in his forty-sixth year; cf. line 41.

[19] There is a lacuna in the text here.

[20] It will be clear that though the poem purports to be an account of the death-bed conversion and heavenly vision of Baebianus, the poet's chief focus of interest is the notion of the continuation of marriage in heaven. He approaches the subject in this way because his poem is a kind of *consolatio* for the surviving widow Apra (whom Brandes suggested to be the sister of Aper, the addressee of Paulinus' Letters 38, 39, and 44). It need

not be stressed that such a theme would be of particular interest to Paulinus, whose marriage to Therasia is repeatedly recalled in the superscriptions to his letters (Nos. 39, 40, 44, 45); this marriage with its purely spiritual dimension anticipates the heavenly state described in Matt. 22.30.

The style does not offer clinching indications of authorship. The polymetric scheme is favoured elsewhere by Paulinus (notably in Poem 21; cf. also Poems 10 and 11), and suggests an Aquitanian provenance. Green 131 examines in detail and refutes Fabre's list of alleged non-Paulinian usages. Two main difficulties remain. The first is the poet's apparent familiarity with Greek. I have noted elsewhere (ACW 35.20) the evidence of the letters that Paulinus was not an accomplished Greek scholar; though the elegance of the Greek in the poem may owe something to Hartel and Brandes (see Hartel's apparatus), the poet seems less inhibited in his use of the language than we should expect of Paulinus. Secondly, the style is simpler and less convoluted than Paulinus usually is. On the question of authorship, it seems best to enter a judgment of *non liquet*. Paulinus should not be excluded from consideration, but a confident attribution of the poem to him would be injudicious.

## APPENDIX

[1] *Corpus inscriptionum latinarum* 10.1370; Diehl 3482. See P. Courcelle, *Les Confessions de s. Augustin* (Paris 1963) 596 n. 1; Green 132.

[2] This young disciple of Paulinus is not mentioned in the extant letters and poems, but Augustine must have heard of him from Paulinus, for in his *De cura pro mortuis gerenda* 1.1 he mentions his interment in St. Felix's basilica at Nola.

[3] Unfortunately the inscription is not complete, the beginning of each line having been broken off. I translate here: *et paci]s sancta* (Diehl: *et laetu]s sancta*).

[4] Translating *patronus t]acito.*

[5] Cf. Matt. 24.31.

[6] For echoes of Paulinus in this epigram, see Diehl's commentary.

# INDEXES

# 1. OLD AND NEW TESTAMENT

# 2. AUTHORS

# 3. GENERAL INDEX

Aaron, type of Memor, 246, 400

Abel, 111, 375

Abella, 384; perjured man of, 159 ff.; water from, 196 ff., 408

Abimalek, *see* Amalek

Abraham, 324, 328, 345; type of Felix, 84, 262; of Cytherius, 233, 397; sire of patriarchs, prophets, apostles, 278

Adam, destroyed by devil, 36; loses salvation, 225; put off by Christians, 251, 292; Eve from his rib, 245; and Eve, types of Julian and Titia, 246, 248

Adonis, 335

Adriatic, smooth for Nicetas, 108

Aemilius, bishop of Beneventum, 14, 388; at Nola, 183; at marriage of Julian and Titia, 252, 400, 402; at Constantinople, 400

Africa, 33

Agricola, martyr, relic of, at Nola, 286

agriculture, imagery of, 411

Alans, 254, 403

Alaric, 403

Albina, Caeonia, mother of younger Melania, 181, 206, 386 f.

Alexandria, home of Mark, 134

Alfia, variant form of Apphia, 175, 386

allegory, scriptural, 273, 280, 320, 406 f.

Allier, 365

almond tree, 280

alms-feast at Nola, 161, 384 f.

Altar of Victory, 19

Alypius, 380

Amalek, 236, 257, 397; confused with Abimalek, 292, 409

Amandus, 356

Ambrose, St., 1, 136, 380; relations with Paulinus, 357; translates martyrs' bodies, 142, 382; sends relics to Nola, 286, 408; develops epitaph-form, 27; Psalm-singing, 17; as source for Paulinus' poems, 413

Ambrosian hymn, 4

*amicitia*, pagan and Christian, 24, 366

Andrew St., at Argos, 285; at Patras, 133, 285, 372 f., 407 f.; remains at Constantinople, 142, 378, 382; relic at Nola, 285, 407

Angoulême, 365

animals with divine and human wisdom, 83, 127 ff., 157 f., 160 f., 169, 172

Anna, mother of Samuel, 234, 397

Antonius, 330, 416

Aonian rock, 83, 370

Apis, worship of, abandoned in Egypt, 134, 378

Apollo, 370; rejected by Paulinus, 58, 379

apostles summoned to Nola, 277 ff.

Apostles' Church, *see* buildings at Cimitile

Appian Way, 79, 231, 396

Appius Claudius, 231, 396

Apra, wife of Baebianus, 344, 420

Apronianus, *see* Turcius

Apulia, 79, 83, 167; traversed by Nicetas, 106

aqueduct, repair of, 196, 390

Aquinum, 79

Aquitania, *see* Paulinus, St.

Archelais, widow of Nola, 104

Ardea, 79, 369

433

# ANCIENT CHRISTIAN WRITERS

### THE WORKS OF THE FATHERS IN TRANSLATION
*Founded by* J. QUASTEN *and* J. C. PLUMPE

*Now edited by*
J. QUASTEN • W. J. BURGHARDT • T. C. LAWLER